LIFETIME
GUARANTEES
Toward Ambitious Literacy Teaching

SHELLEY HARWAYNE

HEINEMANN
Portsmouth, NH

Heinemann
A division of Reed Elsevier Inc.
361 Hanover Street
Portsmouth, NH 03801-3912
www.heinemann.com

Offices and agents throughout the world

The author and publisher wish to thank those who have generously given permission to
reprint borrowed material:

Excerpt from *Gutenberg's Gift: A Booklover's Pop-Up Book,* copyright © 1995 by Nancy Willard, reprinted
by permission of Harcourt, Inc.

Excerpts by Shelley Harwayne that originally appeared in *The New Advocate* are used by permission of
Christopher-Gordon Publishers, Inc.

Excerpt from *Only the Moon and Me* written by Richard J. Margolis and illustrated by Marcia Kay Keegan,
copyright © 1969 by Richard J. Margolis. Used by permission of HarperCollins Publishers.

"Lemon Tree" by Jennifer Clement. Reprinted by permission of Jennifer Clement, author of the poetry
books *The Next Stranger, Newton's Sailor,* and the novel *Widow Basquiat.*

Excerpt from *The World is Full of Babies!: How All Sorts of Babies Grow and Develop* by Mick Manning and
Brita Granstrom. Published by The Watts Publishing Group. Reprinted by permission of the publisher.

Credits continue on p. I-12.

Library of Congress Cataloging-in-Publication Data
Harwayne, Shelley.
      Lifetime guarantees : toward ambitious literacy teaching / Shelley Harwayne.
          p.   cm.
      Includes bibliographical references and index.
      ISBN 0-325-00241-X
      1. Language Arts—United States.   2. Literacy—United States.   3. Activity programs in
      education—United States.   4. Manhattan New School (New York, N.Y.)   I. Title.
      LB1575.H38 2000
      372.6'044—dc21
                                                                                        99-462253

Editor: Lois Bridges
Production service: Patricia Adams
Production coordination: Abigail M. Heim
Cover design: Catherine Hawkes, Cat and Mouse
Front cover: Steeledan Cortes, Shariyf Ali
Back cover: Aishe Skepi, Emily Dewell, Zakiya Salik
Author photograph: Tahj Berrien with Shelley Harwayne/Photograph by Donnelly Marks
Manufacturing: Louise Richardson

Printed in the United States of America on acid-free paper
04   03   02   01   00   RRD   1   2   3   4   5

With great love for my family
Neil, Michael, J. J., and David

CONTENTS

ACKNOWLEDGMENTS

Imagine a young child winning a shopping spree at the illustrious FAO Schwarz toy store in New York City, a serious baseball fan acquiring box seats to the World Series at Yankee Stadium, or a grandmother delightfully surprised when all of her loved ones show up at a family reunion. These kinds of deliriously happy images come to my mind when I think of the work that I have been privileged to do for the last eight years. Each and every day there are twenty-two different writing workshops and twenty-two different reading workshops taking place at the Manhattan New School. In my work as principal of this public elementary school, I have been free to enter any or all of these workshops—no appointments needed, no invitations necessary. I am that child seeing beautiful and intriguing things in every direction. I am that committed fan watching a winning team. I am that grandmother honored to be in the presence of people she really cares about. As someone who has made a career out of talking to people about the teaching of reading and writing, I can't stop counting my blessings.

I am grateful to those 550 young students who so eagerly share their reading and writing with me, and to the 295 graduates who have passed through our copper swinging doors. Their words, drawings, and stories add truth, humanity, and humor to these pages. I am grateful as well to all those family members who have confidence in and enthusiasm for the ways we teach reading and writing at the Manhattan New School. I am thankful for my brilliant colleagues, who so willingly share their students as well as their insights, inquiries, struggles, and successes, not to mention their incredible libraries, with me. It is no surprise that their names, words, and actions bring life to every chapter. Some days, I catch myself looking at a child and recalling that child's history in our school. In my mind's eye, I run through the names of all the teachers that child has studied with, and think how incredibly fortunate that child has been. In fact, I recently toyed with the idea of creating photographic teacher-timelines for each graduate. Imagine how wonderful it would be if *all* the teachers each child has studied with could pose together for a keepsake parting gift. That would be a photograph for the children to frame and treasure the rest of their lives.

I am especially grateful to those colleagues who enter my office with calendar in hand, pinning me down to specific times to work with their students. Likewise, I remain in awe of those who take small suggestions and turn them into powerful projects, those who continually push the literacy envelope by conducting important inquiries of their own, and those who have found the time to publish their own important professional stories. Their groundbreaking work enriches the lives of children and the lives of their colleagues.

I am indebted to all the authors whose books have made a difference in my life, both professionally and personally. First, there are those accomplished researchers who have paved the way for the literacy work we do. Their names are studded throughout this book. It was their contributions to the field that gave us the inspiration, vision, and expertise to begin the Manhattan New School. Then too, there are the wonderful novelists, journalists, and poets whose works remind the grown-ups on staff why we so desperately want our children to value reading and writing as two of life's pleasures. I must acknowledge as well all the brilliant writers for children who make our literacy work so much easier and remind us how fortunate we are to be teaching reading and writing at a time so abundantly rich with exquisite children's literature.

I'd also like to thank our district administrators, who never expect principals to get good at paperwork but demand that we get good at instruction. I am grateful as well to all our old friends who drop by, the student teachers who work alongside us, and all the educators who visit. They continually see more in us than we see in ourselves. Their comments and compliments have encouraged us to work even harder to find the right supports for all students so that each finds a way to make reading and writing a significant part of their lives. I must also pay public tribute to all the hardworking people at Heinemann for so appreciating all that the Manhattan New School stands for and for making it possible for me to tell my stories. I promise never to write another long book.

And finally, I am ever grateful to my family—to my husband, Neil, my son, Michael, my daughter, J.J., and her husband, David. They treat my own reading and writing as members of the family, viewing my favorite pastimes with admiration, pride, and respect. Their love and support enable me to have the time, desire, and peace of mind to spend long hours doing the work I love to do.

INTRODUCTION

Many people have asked me how I was able to write this book so soon after publishing *Going Public: Priorities and Practice at the Manhattan New School*. I suggest that they imagine the difficult situation of giving birth to a child and one week later finding themselves pregnant again, with twins.

That's the best way I can describe the circumstance I found myself in when my editor and publisher advised me that the book I had written about my experiences at the Manhattan New School was too long. "Divide it into two books," was their initial advice. So one week after mailing off the manuscript for *Going Public*, I sat with the remaining chapters, those devoted exclusively to literacy, and attempted to shape them into a book that would stand on its own. I was working full-time as I began to rethink and reshape the remaining chapters. Each day I was surrounded by hundreds of children and over two dozen teachers who were devoting their energies to the pursuit of literacy. It was no surprise that those fairly manageable chapters on literacy took on a life of their own. Each day I continued to learn more and more about the literacy work in our school. Each day I worked with small groups of students who were struggling to grow as readers. Each day I met with students throughout the grades to respond to their writing. Each day I was on call to cover classes for one reason or another, and each time, I suggested to the classroom teacher, "I'll do writing." Each day I spoke with exquisite teachers of reading and writing about the work they were doing. And so those fairly manageable chapters on literacy grew and grew and grew. And I realized that the remaining chapters were overflowing and would need to be shaped not into one additional book, but two.

I spread all my hitherto unpublished thinking about literacy around my long dining room table (with all the leaves added). I circled the table many times skimming each chapter as if checking place settings, before a formal dinner party, for water marks on wine goblets or tarnish on silver. I read and reread, rethought, and reordered the contents. Finally two shapes I could live with emerged. One book would be devoted to literacy in general, and another would zoom in on the teaching of writing, the curriculum area I choose to spend the most time with.

It wasn't until I thought of titles that I could make a serious commitment to sitting at the computer screen and revising these literacy lessons into two separate books, the first of which you now hold in your hands. Although *Lifetime Guarantees* does stand on its own, I clearly see it as a companion volume to my earlier publication, *Going Public*, and to the follow-up text, *Writing Through Childhood*. (The work of shaping these three related volumes has been like a photographer's journey, using a wide-angle lens in the first volume on school culture, narrowing my focus in this volume to the literacy lessons

I have been learning, and then zooming in, in the third book, on the close study of class-room writing practices.)

The title of this book feels most appropriate because we do offer lifetime guaran-tees to graduates of our school. I tell the parents of those graduates, upon their very first visit to our school, "Your children will not just learn how to read and write, they will *choose* to read and write. Now and forever."

In June of 1998 our fifth-grade teachers invited me to write a page for the gradu-ating seniors' yearbook. I contributed the following letter.

> *Dear graduates,*
>
> *Sometimes your families buy products that come with lifetime guarantees. Perhaps there are ice-cube trays, hamburger patty presses, or pruning shears in your kitchen drawers that came with certificates guaranteeing that they would last for a lifetime. That's how sure the manu-facturers were that they were releasing quality goods. For me, at this important moment of your elementary school graduation, I can also offer lifetime guarantees because I know that we are releasing to the world of middle school some incredibly high-quality goods.*
>
> *In fact, I shared that lifetime guarantee with your families on their very first tour of our school. I promised that each of you would not only learn to read and write, but perhaps more importantly, I promised that we would teach in such ways that you would joyfully choose to read and write, now and forever. I expect that each of you will help me to keep my promise. Below, you will find a few ways that you can continue to make the Manhattan New School proud to be called your very first alma mater.*
>
> *You will keep a writer's notebook even if you are not asked to do so by your new teachers. Those notebooks were really for you, much more than they were for your teachers. And even when your student days are over, I hope that you will never leave home without a journal, diary, steno pad, or writer's notebook. Please continue to fill those blank pages with your thoughts, observations, sketches, questions, dreams, poems, and so on. You will be more attentive, compassionate, and involved if you continue to make writing a regular part of your lives. You will be better students, workers, neighbors, and citizens if you continue to make writing a regular part of your lives.*
>
> *You will continue to read great books and get together with friends to talk about those books, even if your new teachers don't ask you to. Twenty years from now I expect you to still be the kind of readers who hang out in bookstores and libraries, read book reviews, and join book clubs. Imagine if you had never heard of Lois Lowry's* The Giver. *So too, when you are older there will be many "must-reads." Please stay part of the literary in-crowd.*
>
> *You will think of daily newspaper reading as a nonnegotiable. It's essential to stay informed about what is happening locally, nationally, and globally. How else will you continue to be the well-informed, outspoken, and caring community members that we will hand diplomas to on June 23? We wanted each of you to learn to read, write, and solve problems well, in order that you can always be counted on to improve the quality of life in this city, country, and world.*
>
> *You will always stay involved in the arts. Music, drama, dance, and all the visual arts are ways to help you see the richness of the world and ways to help you to respond to the world.*

You will sing on graduation day; keep singing. You will make music on graduation day; keep making music. You will perform your words on graduation day; keep performing your words. You will act on graduation day; keep acting. You will dance on graduation day; keep dancing. You will show off your art on graduation day; please keep your hands at the easel, in the sketch pad, or at the kiln.

Then too, I trust that you will keep on appreciating the talents of others. I hope to bump into all of you someday in a Broadway theater, in a Fifth Avenue museum, at a jazz club in the Village, at a poetry recital at the 92nd Street Y. You live in a culturally alive city. Please continue to take advantage of all that New York has to offer.

And finally, our lifetime guarantee includes taking care of the people who care about you. If we are to continue being proud of each of you in the future, you must keep in touch. We expect each of you to do as the graduates before you continue to do.

I include this letter in this introduction to *Lifetime Guarantees* for obvious reasons. My purpose in writing this book is to describe the kind of literacy work we do which enables us to make such an ambitious promise. "Your children will not just learn how to read and write. They will choose to read and write. Now and forever."

Each chapter begins with a Reader's Guide and concludes with a Related Readings page, suggesting related sections in *Going Public* and *Writing Through Childhood,* the companion volumes. Appendix pages were added to facilitate educators' sharing of the literacy lessons we have been learning.

Readers may wonder why the principal of an elementary school knows enough about the teaching of reading and writing to write a book. First, as noted in the acknowledgments and expanded upon in *Going Public,* I work in a school district that expects principals to be instructional leaders and become totally involved in all aspects of professional development. In fact, my former superintendent, the visionary Tony Alvarado, published an article about the administrator's role, in the magazine *American Educator.* It was entitled "Professional Development *Is* the Job." In addition to working in a school district that understands that principals belong in classrooms, courses, and at conferences, I bring to my role many years' experience as a literacy teacher and teacher of teachers. In *Going Public* I suggest that administrators must stay close to teaching and remember the subject area that made them passionate about the field of education. For me it was the teaching of reading and writing. I go on to explain,

There is a city billboard that reads, "Literacy. Pass it on." Administrators need to be part of that passing it on.

I'm lucky. I came to this job with a strong background in literacy. Administrators who want to help children learn to read and write and who don't have the expertise, need to take courses, read professional literature, attend conferences, and most of all hang out in the classrooms of teachers who do. When children are sent to the principal's office at the Manhattan New School, I'd prefer they were coming because they were stuck on a piece of writing or they want help with their reading. Public school teachers are responsible for too many children at once. Everyone needs to pitch in.

As noted above, I wrote this book in order to share the ways we teach reading and writing which allow us to offer guarantees that students will take care of their literacy long after their graduation days. So too, this book addresses the ways the culture of the school can support teachers' efforts to do exquisite literacy work. *Lifetime Guarantees,* therefore, is intended for classroom teachers *and* their principals. Many principals may not choose to work directly with students learning to read and write, but all must accept the responsibility of creating a supportive setting for young readers and writers and teachers of reading and writing.

Lifetime Guarantees also represents a turning point in my professional career. I spent seven years as the codirector of the Teachers College Writing Project before accepting the job of principal of the Manhattan New School. I have recently completed my eighth year as head of this school. Writing this book has allowed me to reflect on all that I initially believed about literacy learning prior to becoming responsible for the life of a school. More importantly, writing this book has enabled me to crystallize new thoughts and ideas about literacy learning. Elementary schools can be as scholarly as university settings. In fact, they must be.

CHAPTER 1

DESIGNING THE LITERARY LANDSCAPE

Key Literacy Lessons

1. Books—an abundance of books—not only make a school look more beautiful, they also enable staff members to accomplish many goals.
2. When members of a community are devoted to their literacy, you can expect tributes to language and literature to be a part of the environmental aesthetics. These include alphabet art, homages to the local environment, celebrations of school life, tributes to words, art that enriches content studies, and recognition of other languages and countries.
3. Books in a school can be organized to meet the needs of the school community.
4. Special collections of books can include such helpful categories as books well-suited for a one-on-one read-aloud, books that raise questions for students to answer, books for students beginning to learn English, and books that encourage language play.
5. Schoolwide literacy events, rituals, and traditions help children feel like they belong to a school, not just a class.
6. When wonderful literature is the centerpiece of all reading/writing instruction, educators must find ways to keep up with children's literature.
7. We work hard to create an enriched literary landscape in order to provide the setting in which children will make a lifelong commitment to literacy.

Zane Howard, a graduate of our school, returned to speak to seniors on alumni night. On his way out he remarked that the building looked like a "literary mansion." I loved his way of describing our school. A visiting educator from a suburban private school sat down halfway through her tour. "I just want to look over the 'literary landscape,'" she remarked. I loved her expression as well. One morning Tammy DiPaolo, then a visitor from Mondo Publishing (soon to become a teacher on staff), was scheduled to visit our school. I entered her name in our logbook in my barely legible handwriting. When first-grade teacher Lorraine arrived for work, I overheard her commenting on the day's announcements. "Oh," she remarked, rather nonchalantly, "Tomie de Paola is coming today. That's great." I realized we had really gotten used to having literary visitors. Lorraine was not stunned to see what she thought was the wonderful children's writer's name in our book. She didn't wonder why we weren't making elaborate plans. It was just another day at the Manhattan New School. "We've become a real 'literary hangout'," I thought to myself. *Literary mansion. Literary landscape. Literary hangout.* All these expressions suit us well. We love books and all the trappings connected to books.

I clipped and posted an ad for a bookstore from the local paper. It read, "Where great readers meet great writers." "Perfect for us," I thought. Our school is a place for great readers to meet great writers. (The slogan now scrolls across my computer as a screen saver). We really believe in the poster that announces, "Reading is like eating a bagel. You are never too young to start." In Lynne Sharon Schwartz's *Ruined by Reading: A Life in Books,* she describes her lifelong passion for reading. She writes, "I burned with the zeal of a born-again reader; my bumper sticker would have proclaimed, Lit Saves." There are lots of people in our school who would proudly drive around with that bumper sticker on their cars. Literacy and literature are in the conversations we have, in the murals we paint, in the reminders we post, in the purchase orders we type, in the poetry we perform, in the articles we share, in the books we swap, and in the songs we sing. Writing about our literary landscape is a bit like writing about the air we breathe.

An Abundance of Books

In a "Style" column in *The New York Times Magazine,* Julie Iovine suggested that books play a role in the "emotional decor" of settings. She notes, "On tables and chairs they make a strange new place seem more familiar. Books are inanimate objects with a soul. More than any piece of furniture, they breathe life into an empty space."

When we opened this school, we spent days carrying in carton after carton of books from our homes, books collected through many years of teaching children and teaching teachers. And then we added more. We searched through every dusty shelf of this former elementary school, finding long-forgotten treasures. We called publisher friends to request donations. We contacted children's literature professors who graciously gave us review copies they no longer needed. We stopped at flea markets and garage sales, hunting for children's outgrown collections. We rushed to public libraries, gathering discarded volumes. We even valued bookstore remainders, unsold paperbacks with their front covers removed. Then parents joined in on the fun. They sought library donations from well-endowed private schools, held book fairs, and began donating books in honor of any happy occasion. And we spent whatever limited funds we had to add more books to our brand-new school.

Julie Iovine was right. Books did make a strange new place seem more familiar. We not only placed them on tables and chairs, but on shelves, windowsills, and atop file cabinets. We filled bookcases, magazine racks, and baskets with all sorts of books, journals, newspapers, and reference materials.

Each year we add more and more books to our collections. We continue to work hard at donations. We continue to spend textbook and library allocations on quality literature. We continue to hire teachers who bring trunks filled with books to their new school. (Of course, our recent three-year role as book reviewers for *The New Advocate,* a quarterly journal "for those involved with young people and their literature," added review copies to our collections, but even without this very unique position, we still had libraries to be proud of.)

We now have so many books, we have the delightful problem of having to invent ways to store and display them. Our makeshift "bookcases" include wooden asparagus crates from the greengrocer, a discarded greeting card display unit from a stationery store, and classroom walls lined with rain gutters. They make a perfect ledge on which to place books face forward. (When a repairman from the Board of Education visited to check on our leaky roof, he spotted the rain gutters around the perimeters of Kevin Tallat-Kelpsa's classroom on the fifth floor. "You must really have a bad roof," he remarked, "I've never seen rain gutters hanging *indoors!*" I never explained their purpose, hoping our situation would be perceived as dire enough to put our school on the top of the list for repairs.) Bill, our parent with a moving van, has also brought us an eclectic array of homey bookcases, everything from funky art deco units to grandmotherly mahogany ones with ornate carvings. Adrian Ingham, a visitor from England, in her report to colleagues after her study visit to New York schools, included the following description: "There were books on shelves, books on carpets, books in boxes, books in corridors, books on walls, in halls, books teeming, gleaming, refusing to be ignored by even the least inclined of young readers—a type I failed to observe, I hasten to add. Shelley's mantric belief in a print-rich environment seduced and persuaded."

All these books and cases do add texture and beauty to our literary landscape, but of course, they do so much more. In *Lasting Impressions: Weaving Literature into the Writing Workshop,* I present a timeline of how the use of literature changes over the course of a school year. I finished writing that book in the same autumn months in which we opened our school, and I crossed my fingers, hoping that my thoughts about literature would hold true in our very own school. Thanks to a knowledgeable and talented staff, literature was indeed used to improve the quality of the students' reading and writing as well as the quality of their lives.

Literature became a trustworthy companion early in the year as teachers and children built classroom camaraderie, discovered topics for their own writing, learned to value keeping a writer's notebook, and shared their own literacy histories. Later in the year, carefully chosen literature enabled teachers and children to develop mentor relationships, engage in powerful book talks, and closely study literary techniques. Books made our classrooms look beautiful, but more importantly, those books in the hands of thoughtful teachers and children helped create a rigorous and scholarly school life. Now, several years later, I've discovered many more ways in which literature breathes life into a schoolhouse.

Of course, no amount of books can help solve all the problems associated with big-city public school life. But literature did prove to be a trustworthy companion. Carefully selected books really did lighten our load as we faced new challenges in teaching, learning, and creating a public school from scratch. The bulk of this chapter deals with the different ways we put our trust in literature. I begin with some suggestions for creating that "literary mansion" feel through literacy-related art projects. The walls tell a very good story in our school.

(Many other literacy-related decorating suggestions appear in the "Interior Decorator" section of Chapter 2, "Rethinking the Role of Principal," in *Going Public: Priorities and Practice at the Manhattan New School*).

Language and Literature Aesthetics

Although we could never compete with the newly restored main reading room of the New York City public library, with all those painted ceiling panels, burnished brass, and ornamental woodwork, we do fancy ourselves to be a beautiful setting for reading and writing. Last year, a segment of the television show *20/20* was taped in our school. The crew asked for a beautiful wall of books to use as a backdrop for an interview with Jacques d'Amboise upon his reunion with former dancer Arthur Bell, a man who was rediscovered by a caring social worker after he had lived through some dire decades. "Every wall of books should be beautiful enough for a backdrop," I thought. That's how high our standards are.

Frequently when we ask visitors to meet us in our fourth-floor ballroom, they take an unusually long time to get up there. They claim that the delay is not due to being out of shape and taking the steps slowly, but to the distraction presented by all the incredible hallway and stairwell displays along the way. You can read the walls in our school, as well as the doors, radiators, bulletin boards, and tiles. The following are a few of the many literacy-related art projects that slow our visitors down.

Alphabet Art
In Nancy Willard's intricate pop-up book, titled *Gutenberg's Gift,* she presents a fictional account of the invention of the printing press. In describing Johannes Gutenberg, she

writes, "He loved all letters, loved the hook and dip of J, the peak of A. He loved the forward-stepping k, the knees of m, the comb of E, the hidden valley carved by V, and the deep serving bowl of U." I have never read a more poetic tribute to the letters of the alphabet. Her words serve to remind me how much we want our students to love letters, words, and books. In addition to an annual display of alphabet books, we have done several art projects which announce that we love the alphabet as much as Johannes Gutenberg did.

I suggested to kindergarten and first-grade teacher Pam Mayer that she invite her students and their parents to carve three-dimensional letters out of cereal boxes. The shape of each letter is cut into the front of a box, while the remaining-intact backs of the boxes enables each letter to stand upright. Boxes were painted in alternating aquas and purples and stretched along the top of a built-in wall of cabinets and cubbies. This durable display has lasted for several years.

Before accepting the role of Spanish teacher in our school, Carmen Colon taught kindergarten. One year, working with a student teacher, Carmen launched an ambitious alphabet photography project. Both teachers escorted the students into the neighborhood to identify appropriate scenes for each letter of the alphabet. These were turned into eight-by-ten-inch black-and-white glossy photographs that were framed and hung in a zigzag fashion going up the staircase in our main entranceway. A key was hung to explain the students' choices. It's hard to pass by our local pizzeria, quick-copy store, or Restaurante Italiano without thinking of the *P, Q,* and *R* on this unusual neighborhood alphabet. Fifth-grade teacher Judy Davis asked her seniors to parallel each photograph with an original pen-and-ink one. Their finished sketches line the opposite staircase wall. The minute you enter our building, you know that we have twenty-six very close friends.

In our friend Anna Switzer's wonderful school, P.S. 234, a talented parent-photographer invited students to create the alphabet with their bodies and then took black-and-white aerial views of the students spread out on the playground floor. It took four children, toe-to-toe, for example, to form an *X.* Five children arranged themselves to form an *E.* Anna sent us a copy of this poster-size collection. It hangs, complete with bright red frame, in our main hallway.

When our school first opened, I gathered all the alphabet blocks from my children's old toychests and began using them to compose signs around the building. They sit on shelves and beautifully spell out such messages as, "Just Poetry Books" or "Welcome Spring." They also sit in front of a collection of staff members' family photographs, this time spelling out, "From Our Family to Yours." Students can be asked to bring in their outgrown alphabet blocks and create appropriate signs to display throughout the school.

In *Going Public* I describe several schoolwide tasks that become part of our students' cumulative portfolios. One of these tasks falls into the category of alphabet art. Quite simply, we ask students to present the alphabet in the most beautiful way possible. The results can be slipped into their portfolios, but deserve for a while to adorn the hallways.

Joanne Hindley Salch's third-graders created an eight-foot-long New York City alphabet that now hangs in our main office. Joanne divided this wide expanse of black felt into twenty-six squares. Using lots of bright patches of felt fabric, the children chose and created a very New York artifact for each letter. On it you'll find such New York "happenings" as Broadway, dog walkers, knishes, the 42nd Street Library, and Yankee Stadium. Again, this is one of our projects that will last for many years.

Homages to the Local Environment

Many of our hallways offer works of art that pay tribute to our city. Skyscrapers, the Statue of Liberty, and congested street scenes appear in children's paintings on our staircase overhangs, radiator covers, and on our windowpanes. Torn pages from *The New York Times* have been turned into cityscape collages. Books standing on end have become the buildings in skyline murals. Each year our city plays host to a celebration of book publishing entitled "New York Is Book Country." Posters from these yearly events sit atop bookcases in our nonfiction reading room. Sharon Taberski's first- and second-grade students create self-portraits using New York City subway maps as the background for their faces. They also prepare works of art in response to all their field trips around New York and hang these captioned paintings in a timeline around the room. In addition, students collect, illustrate, and display New York City poems. Then too, children combine their artistic abilities with their map-reading abilities and create bold representations of New Amsterdam, Central Park, and our local neighborhood. Sharon's students have also been known to stop hallway traffic with their New York City questions carefully printed and hung low enough on their door for even the youngest reader to see. "Did you know?" the signs ask and then reveal a surprising fact, such as "There are 6,400 miles of streets in New York City." None of this surprises me because the big umbrella that covers our curriculum goals remains constant. We want our students to see the richness of their lives. No matter where our school was located, we would be inviting students to create works of art that show they are paying attention to and appreciating their world. (Also under that big umbrella of curriculum is the notion that children can use their literacies to improve the quality of their worlds. More thoughts on this issue are found in Chapter 3, "Discovering Real-World Reasons to Write.")

Our third graders collected *New Yorker* magazine covers, studied them, talked about their meaning, and then attempted to create their own, using brightly colored felt patches. They even attempted to write the title of the *New Yorker* in its distinctive style across the top of their works of art. When complete, they were hung on a huge span of black felt fabric, a child's rendition alternating with an actual cover to form a dramatic quilt. I have a plan to do likewise with Broadway *Playbill* covers, inviting students to select books they've read that deserve to be turned into Broadway shows.

In the staff restroom near my office, I began one day writing on the tiles. I started with the familiar New York City slogan, "I love N.Y.," with the word *love* represented by a big red heart. I left a basket of permanent markers in the restroom and by the end of a month over one hundred tiles were covered. They contained everything from Billy Joel lines to advertising slogans to the words to Broadway show tunes.

We have several larger-than-life murals, filled with useful information painted in large letters. One gives children a sense of place by listing from bottom to top, "Street—East 82nd, Neighborhood—Yorkville, Borough—Manhattan, City—New York City, State—New York State, Country—The United States, Continent—North America, Planet—Earth. Alongside this hangs another that invites children to become familiar with leaders at different levels of government. If we encourage students to become activists, they need to know who to send their letters to. In this mural, large bold words painted across a collage background made of maps divide politicians into their city, state, and national roles. Our students need to know the names of their borough president, mayor, governor, senators, members of the House of Representatives, vice president, and president.

Celebrations of School Life

One year, I created a Manhattan New School dictionary with our students. For each letter of the alphabet, the children selected items that truly represented our school. For the letter *L,* the children defined and illustrated the words *lunch boxes, laptops,* and *literature.* For the letter *P* they included *portfolio, playground,* and *publishing.* For the letter *S* appeared the words *surveys, snacks,* and *student teachers.* The twenty-six laminated oak tag pages covered one long wall on our top floor, the penthouse.

On another occasion I posted a chart with our school initials, MNS, inviting members of the community to think of alternate words to match these initials, ones that would appropriately define our community. Some of my favorites included "Many Novel Students," "More Nifty Scholars," and "Multiple New Stories." A marker dangled nearby for people to record their creations.

At the beginning of one school year, to help children get to know one another, I invited a class of fifth graders to create collages depicting themselves as they peeked out from behind the covers of an open book. The title of the book had to be one that they thought they could write because of their own background or expertise. Noel's book was entitled "How to Build with All the Legos in the World"; Jesse's was "How to Beat All the Video Games in the World"; and Anna's read, "How to Take Care of Animals."

My sister Barbara created two life-sized "stuffed" children, a boy and a girl, that are propped up on the bench in our main reception area. One wears a "Book-woman" T-shirt, the other wears a shirt that reads, "My head is full of children," both painted by the same artist, Kiki. They also sport jeans and baseball caps. In cold weather some kind soul usually throws a school sweatshirt over their shoulders. At first glance, standing at the right distance, onlookers think there are real children sitting in the hall. I once heard a child passing by call out, "Oh, are you two benched again?" My favorite touch is the books that are placed in their laps. The message is clear. What else would children sitting on benches do? Every once in a while we turn their pages. Or give them a new book to read (see photo, p. 2).

The door to my office even explores the role of principal in a literary way. I've hung book jackets with titles that offer comments on the work I do. They include John Winch's *The Old Woman Who Loved to Read,* Phyllis Krasilovsky's *The Woman Who Saved Things,* David Getz's *Frozen Girl* (because I'm teased for shutting the heat and keeping my windows wide open), and Jan Alford's *I Can't Believe I Have to Do This* (which is my usual response to administrative tasks). For obvious reasons I have also hung Barbara Hirsch Lember's *"The Shell Book."* Imagine if every teacher and his/her class and every administrator in a school were asked to hang telling titles on their doors. Visitors would learn a lot about the school by simply reading the book jackets that line the corridors.

Tributes to Words

Our school environment announces that we are as *wordstruck* as Robert MacNeil describes in his memoir of that title. For example, several classes have created walls announcing, "Read the Words We Wear." The children recorded all the slogans on the T-shirts their classmates wore over a period of several weeks, and then reproduced them on T-shirt shapes cut from oak tag. These shirts hung from classroom clotheslines, and the words easily became sight words for our young readers. Everyone could recognize, "I Love New York," "Yankees," and "My Grandparents Went to Puerto Rico and All I Got Was This T-shirt!"

One year, several children complained to me that they needed an elevator to take them up to the fifth floor. The walk up can really be exhausting, especially with an armload of books on a hot day. Our building was built at the turn of the century. Even in those days, New York City real estate costs prevented schools from spreading out in width, and of course, elevators were unheard of. Early one evening after the children had left, I jokingly tried to honor their request. I painted an elevator operator on a pillar in the middle of the fifth floor and filled the walls with expressions containing words such as "height," "roof," and "ceiling." The children were surprised to find the fifth floor plastered with "You've gone through the roof," "The sky's the limit," "You're at the peak of your career," et cetera. In the next few days, people added at least twenty more appropriate idioms to the board, and the children had a chance to delight in the English language. Of course, they would have preferred an elevator.

We also ask children to play with individual words. Children still love the tried-and-true challenge of creating a font or layout that supports the meaning of a word. So *lightning* is written in zigzag lines and *wide* is stretched out across the page. When we fill a wall with these student creations, I still enjoy the look on the face of the very young reader who says, "I get it!"

We've also asked children to cut out a silhouette of an item that is important to them and fill the shape by repeating the name of the item across the entire contour. For example, you can picture the shape of a clock with the word *clock* scrolled over and over again across the entire surface. But then we ask the student to surprise readers by substituting one clever word instead of the expected. So the clock may be filled with dozens of black-inked words reading *clock* and somewhere we are treated to a red-inked *Wake up*.

Children are also expected to get out their paints and brushes and markers and crayons whenever a sign is needed. We buy no commercial signs; instead we ask children to take on sign-making responsibilities. We learned years ago that to run a really effective writing workshop, our job was to put ourselves out of a job. If we wanted to have significant amounts of time to confer with students, then students needed to know how to refill the staplers, help one another with spelling, and respond honestly and kindly to one another's drafts. So too, if we are to have all the time it takes to run an effective school or classroom, we must be willing to give away some traditionally adult tasks to our students. (More on this in Chapter 3, "Discovering Real-World Reasons to Write.") Children created signs and posters to advertise their after-school ice-cream sales. I love the one that read, "Buy an Ice Cream for the Walk Home." They create attractive signs for the inside of our front doors, warning folks to "Open doors slowly," so as not to knock into any stoop-sitters. They paint large signs reminding school members, "Last one in, Close Back Doors!" to prevent intruders from entering.

Art That Enriches Content Studies

Literacy-related art projects frequently extend into the content areas. When Lorraine Shapiro's first graders were studying what our school must have been like when it first opened, they did a rubbing of the iron plaque that honors the first principal of our old building. (I gave my mother a similar rubbing of her own name taken from the wall of immigrants at Ellis Island.) I could easily imagine inviting all of our students to find interesting plaques around the city, create rubbings, and design a beautiful collection of framed rubbings for our hallways.

Judy Davis stretched a timeline from the 1600s to the present along an entire wall of the third floor. When students discovered a significant historical event in their reading, they tacked it up on the timeline in words and pictures. The upper-grade students began to develop a sense for when important inventions or significant discoveries were made, as well as a sense of all the wars that have been so much a part of American history. I even noticed their teachers' birthdays added as significant moments.

Lorraine's six-year-olds also share their science learnings through carefully designed artwork. They take lessons from the way information is displayed in museums. One year, for example, they created a huge seascape scene. Next to each creature, there was a number. A narrow strip of paper bordered the top of the mural, and the precise name of the creature corresponded to the identifying number. I adore bulletin board displays that reflect the way people outside of schools share their learnings. They really teach.

Regina Chiou and her second graders hung a beautiful map of the United States outside their classroom door and challenged us with the words, "Help Us Read Across America!" The children were searching for books that would take them to every state in the U.S.A. Each time one was found, the title was posted right atop the state. I adore bulletin boards that involve passersby.

Paula Rogovin uses murals to enhance all her young students' content studies. Visitors to her classroom as well as to the fourth-floor corridor outside her room have learned about coal miners, baseball players, shoemakers, and hundreds of other occupations by studying the large labeled murals outside her door. (Read about them in her book, *Classroom Interviews: A World of Learning.*)

Recognition of Other Languages and Countries

We not only honor English words in out literary art projects, but those of our children's first languages as well. For example, we could easily add an interesting collection to our wall of alphabets by asking families to prepare an alphabet chart from each of their first languages. Then everyone in the community would learn to recognize texts written in such languages as Arabic, Macedonian, Russian, Japanese, and Hebrew.

For years, I've been teasing Joanne that her students' eight-foot-long multilingual welcome banner belongs in our main entrance hall. (I always long to have beautiful artwork out in the corridors for all to see.) Her students painted the big, bold word *Welcome* in all their different languages. We've all learned the meaning of *Siije, Vallkomma, Hosgeldin,* and *Halina Kayo.*

We've even painted the words *Bano, Toillete, Bagno, W.C., Loo,* et cetera on our restroom doors. I could also imagine organizing a group of students to discover what other signs in the building should be painted in many languages. We would all learn to say *Office, Library,* and *Cafeteria* in many languages.

We hang a collage of multilingual artifacts to add life to our language board. (See description of this listing of languages spoken in the introduction to *Going Public*). These include poems about second-language learning, "Do Not Disturb" signs in several languages gathered from hotels around the world, newspaper clippings about students' home countries, ads and greeting cards in different languages, as well as maps highlighting the location of our students' home countries.

Cindy Michael's fifth graders honored our students' first languages by creating six panels, each for a helpful everyday expression. We learned how to say *excuse me, thank you, please, God bless you* (or whatever the custom is when someone sneezes), *I love you,* and *I have to go to the bathroom,* in all the first languages in Cindy's room. Students need to know that their language is as important as ours, and that we appreciate how much work it is to learn a second language. The panels also remind us how fascinating the study of languages is.

Carmen, our teacher of Spanish as a second language, also invites children to create language murals. These are usually connected to topics being studied in the school, and they are often interactive. Children can pass by a large painting of a chessboard and lift little flaps, to see the names of the chess pieces in Spanish. They can do likewise with items in a neighborhood street scene.

We not only honor the children's first languages but their countries as well. A wall of painted clocks, much like you would see at an airport or hotel lobby, enables all the students to look up and see the time it would be in their home country when it is twelve o'clock in New York.

Artistic Responses to the Reading Experience

Trompe l'oeil artwork is also popular in our school. One year Joanne Hindley Salch's children made paintings of bookcases, complete with titles down the spines of the books, and hung them on the doors on both ends of our hallways. If you looked to the left or to the right it appeared that you were surrounded by books. The painted bookcases, done on mural paper cut to fit the door sizes exactly, were complete with the obligatory bookshelf frames, vases, statues, plants, and clocks sitting on the shelves. We've gotten bolder now and have painted these directly onto our swinging staircase doors.

Books are the centerpieces of many of our literary art projects. I even keep a folder labeled "literary logos" and tuck in sketches, clippings, and ads of books and readers whenever I come across them. These often inspire young artists to create their own. (Not all our trompe l'oeil ideas are book related. I'd love to ask students to paint old tabletops with exact replicas of the most popular game boards. What fun to see Candyland, Monopoly, Scrabble, and Chutes and Ladders as a backdrop to the work we do.)

Joanne's third graders brainstormed all the different places people read and then divided themselves into small clusters to prepare murals of these literary scenes. If you look up on the back wall of her classroom, under a banner that reads, "Reading, Reading, Everywhere," you'll see people reading on the subway, in the classroom, at the library, in the park, at a coffee shop, in their beds, et cetera. The message is clear in Joanne's room: "You can read almost everywhere."

On the walls bordering the entrance to our nonfiction reading room, Judy Davis's students created three-dimensional nonfiction readers, complete with a selection of realistic reading materials. They cut the book jackets from dozens of nonfiction books, so just a bit of the three-dimensional spine is jutting out, and attached them to cardboard bookshelves. They completed their display by drawing several large faces peeking out from behind opened newspapers and magazines. Judy laminated pages from *The New York Times* as well as covers from *Newsweek, Time,* and *National Geographic* magazines and attached them in front of the faces so that the people appeared to be reading these texts. The display served as a warm welcome to our nonfiction reading room and reminded students that not all worthwhile reading material is contained in books.

Recently, I worked with Judy and several fifth graders to create a four-panel literary tribute to the seasons of the year. Each collage, created with paint, wallpaper, and fabric swatches, boasts scenes of people reading. The summer scene shows two folks reading under a beach umbrella. All the books stacked on the blanket have to do with the summer season. One person is reading Betsy Byars's *The Summer of the Swans,* another Bette Greene's *Summer of My German Soldier.* In the autumn collage, a young person is reading Lois Lowry's *Autumn Street* while comfortably nesting in a deep pile of leaves. The winter scene, my personal indoor favorite, depicts a child sprawled in front of a cozy fireplace, browsing an anthology of winter poems. The background bookcase is filled with such titles as Joanne Ryder's *Winter White* and Tony Johnston's *The Last Snow of Winter.* The spring scene offers readers on a park bench and even one high on a playground swing, all the while reading such titles as Tilde Michels's *Rabbit Spring* and Jean Craighead George's *Spring Comes to the Ocean.* As soon as the works of art were completed, I put out a call for writing. It read, "Do stop by the third floor to see the literary tribute to the four seasons of the year, created by our fifth graders. Let these scenes inspire you to write about your own favorite season and setting for reading." Short essays, vignettes, or poetic responses by staff members, students, and parents were displayed and eventually organized into a new school anthology.

Sofia prefers summer reading:

Reading on the Water

I sit on a wooden bridge
Over a stream,
Reading,
Going through thrilling adventures,
Spine-tingling mysteries,
And poems as beautiful as
A waterfall tumbling over a cliff
Plunging to the rocks below
That's what reading in the summer
is all about.

Maris wrote:

Winter is my favorite time to read because I like to cuddle up in my parents' bed on their white silk bedspread. I read and read. I watch the marshmallows float in my hot cocoa, careful not to spill it on their white silk bedspread. I sip my hot cocoa as I read enchanting books. The dark snowy night goes on. The snow is still falling outside the window. I feel taken away as the book goes on. I am dreaming in dreamland, in a land of love and books.

Renay's students created a wall of homemade book jackets. Instead of putting the title of a popular book on the front cover and the lead inside, they reversed this usual order. Now passersby had to guess the title of the book by reading the lead printed on the cover. For example, on the outside cover of one of the jackets appeared the words, "When Mrs. Frederick C. Little's second son arrived, everybody noticed that he was not much bigger than a mouse." Inside the students wrote, "E. B White's *Stuart Little.*" Students hung books intended for the youngest readers low on the wall, to make sure the words were at eye level. Again, when taken down, this collection, kept in a three-ring binder, makes a great permanent book to add to a classroom library; children can be encouraged to continue adding to it.

There are several reading-related art projects that remain on my to-do list. I'd love to ask students to make a sketch of books propped between a set of unusual yet appropriate objects. Can you picture sneaker "bookends" holding up sports books, palettes holding up art books, White House replicas holding up history books, and calculators surrounding mathematics books?

I once received a clever handout, put together by Koen book distributors, entitled, "All We Really Need to Know . . . We Learned from Children's Books." The sheet was filled with some of life's little lessons followed by the children's book it was gleaned from. For example, underneath "Don't cross the street without your mother" was listed *Make Way for Ducklings*. I've always wanted to challenge our students to create their own such listing. I can envision an interactive bulletin board with lessons on the outside of bright pieces of folded construction paper and their respective book titles on the inside.

Barnes and Noble booksellers has a clever advertisement that looks like a wall of buzzers in the vestibule of an apartment building. Each resident is, not surprisingly, a best-selling author. I've long wanted to ask a class to create a similar display directly on their classroom door. After all, you can find their favorite authors inside.

I'd love to ask fourth graders to use their woodworking talents to prepare graduation gifts for our seniors. I envision handmade sets of Manhattan New School bookends, created using materials donated by our local cabinet-making shop. No doubt, they would have our school logo on the side.

I have also had the urge to periodically create miniliteracy museum displays in the glass cabinet built into the wall of our main lobby. Then I would put out a call to all members of the community. Imagine a cabinet filled with sets of bookends from all over the world. Children could prepare placards explaining each item, complete with, "On loan from the collection of _____." What a beautiful way to let the world know how much we value reading and our diverse family backgrounds. I could imagine similar displays of bookmarks, old school readers, and writing utensils, as well as old-fashioned inkwells and slate boards. You never know who has what until you ask.

Just recently I had the privilege to visit the home of an incredible art collector. On his walls were hung works by such artists as Jasper Johns, Frank Stella, and Robert Rauschenberg. Going down in the elevator of this Park Avenue home, I jotted down the name Tim Rollins, to remind me to invite our students to do what this celebrated artist has done with pages taken from real books. Working with his organization K.O.S. (Kids of Survival), Rollins places actual pages from books into intricate collages. Of course, we would never destroy a book to create such collages, but what a wonderful use for those inevitable pages from well-worn books that have come undone.

Artistic Responses to Literature

Many Manhattan New School walls are adorned with responses to literature. Early-childhood teachers and their students frequently use their artistic talents to pay tribute to their favorite writers and texts. Isabel Beaton's students made Tomie de Paola's *Big Anthony* come alive across a second-floor wall. Layne Hudes's children created all the characters from *Winnie the Pooh* out of overstuffed paper bags and tempera paints. Eve Mutchnick's students make wall displays of their favorite Mem Fox books. Paula Rogovin's first graders painted murals in response to John Steptoe's *Mufaro's Beautiful Daughters*. Pam Mayer's room glows with the words from Bill Martin's *Chicka Chicka Boom Boom*. Flashlight, the dog from John Reynolds Gardiner's *Stone Fox* and the main stars of Roald Dahl's *James and the Giant Peach* have all been portrayed in larger-than-life art forms. Artistic responses to literature form an ever expanding timeline of the books Joanne Hindly Salch has read aloud to her students during any one school year.

Newspaper-Inspired Displays

Whenever I find an engaging and creative newspaper article about writers, I wonder if we can challenge our young writers in the same way that the journalist has challenged professional writers. For example, I once shared with Joanne a *New York Times Book Review* article entitled "Just What They've Always Wanted." It was a compilation of gifts authors would like to give other writers, living or dead. For example, Anne Tyler said she'd give the poet Richard Wilbur an original Picasso because he has played such an inspirational role in her writing life. Maxine Hong Kingston said she would give Wallace Stegner two carefully selected rocks because he taught his readers to love the earth. Joanne invited her students to do likewise. Each student selected an author and announced what gift they would choose and why. Roald Dahl of course received chocolate kisses in honor of that famous factory, and Marjorie Weinman Sharmat, author of the *Nate the Great* detective series received a giant magnifying glass. We posted the newspaper clipping as the source of this project and surrounded it with the children's responses and illustrations.

Similarly, I can easily imagine posting a *New York Times* article entitled "A Writer's Fantasy: Who I Wish I'd Been" and surrounding it with students' attempts at the same. In the article, accomplished writers were asked to reveal what book besides their own they would most like to have written and to explain their choices. Mark Childress, author of *Crazy in Alabama*, chose Harper Lee's *To Kill a Mockingbird*, and E. L. Doctorow chose Cervantes' *Don Quixote*. It would be very telling for fourth and fifth graders to share the books they admire so much, that they wish they had written them.

I once passed a newspaper clipping containing an interesting format for movie reviews onto Kathy Park, a fifth-grade teacher. The *New York Times* reviewer summarized responses to several movies by creating a chart with the following headings across the top: "The Gist," "The Genre," "The Setting," "What People Said," "Selling Point," "It's For . . . ,"

"Don't Watch With . . . ," and a "Rating Legend." Kathy used this format for the children's book reviews. The fifth graders substituted the word *read* for *watch* and filled a large bulletin board with astute comments. Next to Lois Lowry's *Number the Stars,* they wrote, "The Gist: Young girl hides Jewish friend during World War II. The Genre: Historical fiction. The Setting: Denmark during World War II. What People Said: 'A terrific book with deep historical impact,' Ibric and Skepi. [The last names of two students]. Selling Point: Winner of the Newbery Award. It's For . . . people who want the personal side of what happened during Hitler's reign. Don't Read With . . . Nazi sympathizers. Rating: P.N.A. (Parents Not Allowed). Next to Katherine Paterson's *Jacob Have I Loved,* they wrote, "The Gist: Twin sister Louise can't seem to get out from under her sister's shadow. Louise tries hard to get noticed and become independent. The Genre: Realistic fiction. The Setting: Takes place in early 1900s. What People Said: 'Top of the heap. Can't put it down,' Henschel and Agrawal. Selling Point: Winner of the Newbery Award. It's For . . . young people who don't know where they fit in. Don't Read With . . . adults who play favorites. Rating: P.R.E (Parents, Get Ready to Explain).

Photography Displays

Field trips turn into artistic literary displays when photographs are mounted and children carefully craft captions or passages to accompany them. Members of the community who didn't make the trip to Central Park for rock climbing, to the construction site to watch a luxury high-rise go up, or to a New Jersey farm for apple picking can really get a sense of these adventures. Paula Rogovin's children have even labeled snapshots of patterns they discovered on a walking trip in the community. We will never look at architectural trims, hubcaps, or window displays in exactly the same way.

Judy's fifth graders are asked to compose photographic essays about New York City (see pp. 117 and 166). Renay's third graders snap neighborhood photos and write poems to accompany them (see p. 187). Both these photography projects result in student work that hangs in our hallways for long periods of time. We really do love New York.

Student Writing, Aesthetically Displayed

Copies of students' best efforts are beautifully displayed on the walls of our school in order for more members of the community to appreciate our young writers' thinking and for parents to best understand our work in the teaching of writing. (Parents really are comforted to know that children do learn standard spelling and have legible handwriting as they move up in the grades.) Students should not, however, be writing for bulletin boards alone. In other words, we are determined that students' writing be treated in the ways writing is treated in the world outside of school. Letters get sent. Editorials appear in newspapers. Picture books are read aloud to young children. Plays get performed. Songs get sung, and so on.

(See Chapter 3, "Discovering Real-World Reasons to Write," and Chapter 5, "Paying Tribute to Poetry," for ideas on ways to use student writing to enhance a school environment, as well as *Writing Through Childhood.)*

Books, Aesthetically Displayed

Our students feel that they are immersed in books not simply because we pay so much attention to the above decorative displays, but also because our actual collections of books are conveniently located and invitingly arranged. We keep bookcases in out-of-the-way alcoves. We place books on marble shelves over hallway fountains. We keep baskets of magazines in appropriate waiting areas.

Organizing Books for the Needs of the School

When we first moved into our school, we shared the building with a middle school and a program for pregnant teenagers. We had just enough space for the small number of classrooms we needed, none extra. That meant no formal library. At the time, we didn't have enough books to create a separate lending library, nor a librarian to oversee the collections. (Since the severe budget cuts of the 1970s, New York City, unfortunately, no longer requires librarians in every elementary school. All the more reason for teachers to keep up with children's literature. For more on this topic, see p. 35.) In those early cramped-quarters days, out of necessity, we gave top priority to building classroom libraries. We then turned the few empty offices that were located in our living space into small reading rooms. Even when the other programs moved out of our building and we had room to grow, we never carved out a separate library. We had gotten used to a decentralized library. We enjoyed having a poetry reading room, a fiction reading room, and a nonfiction reading room. We still had no one on staff to parent a formal library. We continued to give top priority to classroom collections.

Every classroom of our school has a rich library feel. When new books arrive, if we think a child might choose to read them during reading workshop time, they go into classrooms. We want teachers and children to have the books they need at their fingertips. The nonfiction reading room is filled with more reference-type material. The poetry room is filled mostly with duplicate anthologies, as well as a considerable adult collection. The fiction reading room is filled with extras, picture books and novels that no one really longs to have in their classrooms. Teachers occasionally browse the reading rooms looking for passed-over treasures. There are no restrictions on removing them and adding them to classroom libraries. Our library system has always been based on trust.

We are presently bar-coding all of our books to facilitate locating them. When a child is studying dinosaurs, he or she will just need to type *dinosaurs* into a centrally located computer to receive a listing of the location of all the dinosaur books in the building, along with a summary of the books. A wonderful parent, Susan Geller-Ettenheim, not only worked to have this incredible library software donated by Follett, she has also trained many parents to enter the books into the database. The parents move from room to room, slowly and meticulously recording all the nonfiction books and poetry collections.

I recently read Roxie Munro's *The Inside Outside Book of Libraries*. I was thoroughly engaged and awed by the story of these diverse libraries from around our city and country. I longed to visit each one, and I wondered if our students would feel the same way. Would they be delighted to visit a bilingual Chinese/English library, a library for the blind and physically handicapped, or a library for explorers? Would they be thrilled to find out that the lions in front of our historic Forty-Second Street research library are named Patience and Fortitude? Would they appreciate that all these resources are in New York City? We want our students to love libraries, the same way they love parks, playgrounds, zoos, and the Museum of Natural History.

Every classroom library has its own unique feel. Some teachers and students develop their own personal ways of categorizing books. Some have pots filled with books on every table. Some insist on book covers facing forward, others prefer the more traditional view of the spine. Some libraries are condensed into a cozy bordered corner of the room, others are more spread out, with nonfiction books set up in different curriculum areas of the room. Most rooms have separate cabinets for multiple copies of titles, and separate sections for books on tape. Frequently, teachers keep books associated with a current unit of study in big baskets in the meeting areas, for easy referral. Many classes have systems for recommending books and for recording books read. However different the classroom libraries look and operate, all teachers demonstrate that books are revered and must be treated with respect.

Creating Special Collections of Books

I find it comforting to have well-stocked bookcases towering over my desk and lining the walls of my cave-like office. Between the bookends in my cluttered office, in addition to a wall of professional reading, you will find books in the broad categories described below. Note that I am always willing to lend these to teachers, parents, student teachers, and volunteers. They are not only for the principal's use.

Books Well-Suited for a One-on-One Read-Aloud
Children always benefit from being read to aloud by someone, one-on-one. Any engaging text, on any topic in any genre, will make these moments worthwhile. I keep a separate stack of books especially suited for the read aloud. These often contain design and layout techniques that are more difficult to appreciate when the book is read to a large group. The child benefits when he sits close to a text that has finely detailed illustrations, an extra story woven into the borders, a subtext in italics, or captions and bubble language scattered throughout. This category also includes books that are fragile, those that have pop-up pieces, unusual foldout sections, or intriguing overlays. Such books rarely survive thirty sets of hands.

Books That Raise Questions for Students to Answer

The books in this collection inspire classroom interactions. These titles ask young readers or listeners to respond to situations posed in the text. Some require children to voice an opinion, make a guess, or solve a problem. For very young children, titles include nonfiction books like Anni Axworthy's Peephole series, *"Guess What I Am," "Guess What I'll Be,"* and *"Guess Where I Live."* I can always engage kindergartners by dramatically revealing answers or having them call out the expected letters in the words before I turn the page to reveal the printed answer. Maggie Silver's lift-the-flap, *Who Lives Here?* is similarly successful with our seven-year-olds. Not all books in this category are nonfiction. Others like those told by George Shannon in his *Stories to Solve* series or the brainteasers in *True Lies: 18 Tales for You to Judge,* require older students to analyze complex situations or explain mysterious events. I also keep many "what if . . . ?" and "would you rather . . . ?" books on this shelf.

Special-Interest Books on Significant Emotional Issues

It's very helpful to have at your fingertips just the right book to share when a child loses a pet, learns of his parents' divorce, or is living with an infirm relative. Children also appreciate reading books that ease their experiences with a new baby in the family, an alcoholic family member, parent remarriages, or the loss of grandparents. These include such books as Joanna Cole's *The New Baby at Your House,* Richard C. Langsen's *When Someone in the Family Drinks Too Much,* Anna Grossnickle Hines's *When We Married Gary* and Susan Varley's *Badger's Parting Gifts.*

Books for Students Beginning to Learn English

I also have a crate in my office earmarked for young English-language learners. These books are especially worth passing on to our English as a second language teacher as well as to student teachers and school volunteers. This collection includes books with parallel texts in several languages, picture dictionaries, simple concept books, books about learning a new language, nonfiction books containing clearly labeled pictures, and books that deal with topics of conversational interest to our children. It's very appealing to our language learners to find clearly illustrated texts dealing with classroom and playground life, as well as scenes of traveling, marketing, and dining. (See Chapter 10, "On Loving and Learning Language.")

Activity Books for Indoor Recess

We ask our students to provide their own entertainment for recesses in inclement weather. Each student is asked to bring in a shoebox filled with appropriate indoor activities. On snowy or rainy days the children and their assorted card games, paper dolls, lanyards, and such, spill out over the wide expanse of our ballroom floor. It's helpful as well to add assorted word-play books, activity books, and such pass-the-time series books as those starring Waldo or those beginning with the words *I spy*. . . . These books become particularly valuable when cabin fever sets in due to long spells of winter weather. We much prefer these paper-and-pencil pastimes to showing videos.

Cultural Background Materials

Sharon Taberski recently studied the Reggio Emilia approach in Italy. (This Italian educator is the subject of Carolyn Edwards, Lella Gandini, and George Forman's *The Hundred Languages of Children: The Reggio Emilia Approach to Early Childhood Education*). Sharon returned to New York incredibly proud of her Italian heritage. Our students come from over forty different countries. We want them to be equally proud of their heritage. All our third graders make formal presentations about their countries and their cultures, but our invitation to explore and share cultural backgrounds needn't end there. Children remain proud of their backgrounds and continue to learn about their home countries when we share literature from and about their countries, when we clip and discuss news events from their homelands, and when we invite them to teach us their language.

One year, Cindy Michael's students took a class trip to a travel bookstore. (One real advantage to living in New York is the availability of highly specialized bookstores.) With a little bit of school funds, they went on a shopping spree, purchasing reference materials about all the countries they represented. These texts are now part of our growing nonfiction reference library.

On my office shelves, I also keep materials that remind children of their home countries. Naomi Nye's *This Same Sky: A Collection of Poems from Around the World* allows me to share with students poetry from Turkey, Brazil, India, Korea, Bangladesh, Yugoslavia, and many more of their home countries. Our Eastern European children have also appreciated Zlata Filipovic's *Zlata's Diary: A Child's Life in Sarajevo,* Vedat Dalokay's *Sister Shako* and *Kolo the Goat: Memories of My Childhood in Turkey,* the UNICEF Foundation's publication *I Dream of Peace: Images of War by Children of the Former Yugoslavia,* and Marybeth Lorbiecki's *My Palace of Leaves in Sarajevo*. Children have borrowed these books for independent reading as well as to share with their friends or discuss with me in a small response group.

Our students also see themselves in such books as *Tio Armando,* a Mexican American family story by Florence Parry Heide and Roxanne Heide Pierce, *Somewhere in Africa,* the story of young Ashraf, who loves to read about Africa, by Ingrid Mennen and Niki Daly, *The Boy in the Attic,* a ghost story by Paul Yee, and *The Beautiful Warrior: The Legend of the Nun's Kung Fu* by Emily Arnold McCully.

Our interest in literature and news from students' homelands reminds them how much we care about each of them. It also quickly places our students in the role of teacher, able to instruct even the grown-ups on topics they know so well. Luca knows the plants that grow in Belize. It is his turf. He delights in teaching his teachers and his classmates.

Last year, I began a bulletin board devoted to newspaper clippings about our students' homelands. The children as well as their families are pleased to see that we attend to their countries, sharing joyful as well as sorrowful news. We learned that the Macedonian president had been seriously injured in a car bomb. We learned that a Bulgarian woman known as Vanga is revered for her mystic powers. We learned that the bloody feuds continue in the former Yugoslavia.

How does the immigrant Turkish mother feel when her son tells her, "The principal asked me if we celebrate the Festival of Rumi, a poet from long ago. Do we?" I've only read a few of Rumi's poems but I do read *The New York Times* every day. If we really care about our students, we must care about their home countries. These places represent the stories they tell, feed their responses to the literature we share, and serve as grist for the writing mill we demand.

Then too, we are always on the lookout for books that demonstrate a celebration of cultures living side by side. It's no wonder that books like Sylvia Rosa-Casanova's *Mama Provi and the Pot of Rice* become so well worn. The same reading and rereading occurs with Natasha Wing's *Jalapeno Bagels,* Ina R. Friedman's *How My Parents Learned to Eat,* Erika Tamar's *The Garden of Happiness,* and Norah Dooley's *Everybody Cooks Rice.*

Books in Different Languages

I collect books that contain multilingual texts, like Jane Feder's *Table, Chair, Bear: A Book in Many Languages* and Lydia Dabcovich's *The Keys to My Kingdom: A Poem in Three Languages.* (Carmen's classroom has become home to our extensive collection of bilingual Spanish/English books.) In addition, I am always on the lookout for books that highlight the advantages of being bilingual and books written in the first languages of our students.

Songs in Book Format

Before we were able to hire a full-time music teacher, I kept a collection of very special books and materials atop the old piano in our poetry room. In addition to nonfiction books about the history of music and musical instruments, I also gathered songs that had been published in picture book format. These popular songs were used as predictable texts for beginning readers and as choice material for community building get-togethers. They include Bob Dylan's *Man Gave Names to All the Animals,* illustrated by Scott Menchin, *Hush Little Baby: A Folk Song with Pictures* by Marla Frazee, and *All the Pretty Little Horses: A Traditional Lullaby* illustrated by Linda Saport. I also have thick binders filled with song sheets. These make wonderful reading material for struggling readers. (More on this in Chapter 9, "Providing Safety Nets for Struggling Students.") All the music material has now been relocated to Diane Lederman's music classroom.

Books That Inspire Pride in the Community

No matter where our school was located, I would collect books set in our locale. It's no surprise that teachers and students often borrow such informational picture books as Kathy Jakobsen's *My New York* and Roxie Munro's *The Inside-Outside Book of New York City.* They borrow as well such pictures books as Erica Silverman's *Mrs. Peachtree and the*

Eighth Avenue Cat, Amy Hests's *Jamaica Louise James,* Maxine Rhea Leighton's *An Ellis Island Christmas,* and Lynne Barasch's *Old Friends,* stories all set in the heart of our city.

Books That Encourage Language Play

I've been seen racing down the hall with such books as George Shannon's *Tomorrow's Alphabet,* R. M. Schneider's *Add It, Dip It, Fix It,* Jon Agee's book of palindromes, *Go Hang a Salami! I'm a Lasagna Hog!,* Norton Juster's *As Silly as Knees, as Busy as Bees: An Astounding Assortment of Similes,* Remy Charlip's *Arm in Arm,* Marvin Terban's *Hey, Hay!: A Wagonful of Funny Homonym Riddles,* as well as picture books whose language play makes the story worth telling, as in Janet Stevens's *Cook-A-Doodle-Doo!* Children appreciate when every once in a while, the read-aloud time leaves them guessing, squealing in delight, and thinking differently about language. No doubt, they also share their new language discoveries with their families over the dinner table. (See related information in Chapter 10, "On Loving and Learning Language.")

Old Treasures

I take great pleasure in plugging old books. Our school is housed in a building that had previously been occupied by an elementary school that closed its doors due to declining enrollments. The contents of the school library had been divided up and distributed to other district elementary schools. During the first years of the school, I spent many wonderful hours scouring the building for forgotten treasures. Hidden high on shelves and in the back of dusty cabinets, I made some great discoveries. No one, apparently, wanted books written twenty or thirty years ago, faded, or bound in those gray or khaki green, hard pebbly covers. Much to my delight, I found several out-of-print poetry collections, including Richard Margolies' *Only the Moon and Me* and Marci Ridlon's *That Was Summer* (now reprinted as *Sun Through the Window*). How fortunate for me that these were left behind. They are not only filled with wonderful poems but with photographs and drawings that speak to diverse populations of children. They were truly ahead of their times. I also found classic early picture books by such accomplished writers as Maxine Kumin, Bernard Waber, Faith McNulty, and Margaret Wise Brown. Aileen Fisher's 1968 publication *We Went Looking* is as lyrical and content-rich, and with as many repetitive phrases, as the finest of early reading materials published today. Publishers of big books would be well advised to look for older books by fantastic writers to reprint in big-book format, instead of some of the watered-down texts that are frequently produced today in the name of shared reading. I also found many chapter books from the early 1950s and 1960s about such illustrious heroes as Beezus and Ramona, Betsey and Star, and of course the Bobbsey twins.

Books About Birthdays

Children who find me in my office when they bring me a cupcake from their classroom birthday party can also choose a birthday book to be read aloud. There are so many children's books written on this topic, every child can find one to please their taste as readers. Some of the childrens' favorites include Amy Hest's *Nana's Birthday Party*, Heidi Goennel's *It's My Birthday*, Pat Hutchins's *It's My Birthday!*, and Johanna Hurwitz's edited collection *Birthday Surprises: Ten Great Stories to Unwrap*.

Books That Inspire Acts of Kindness

After the tragedy in Littleton, Colorado, our PTA presidents invited Dr. Fred Kaesar, our district coordinator of health services, to talk about what parents can do to prevent violent behavior in children. Fred suggested that they all go home and make sure that the books they read to their children contain characters who show empathy. This is important advice for teachers as well as parents.

Yes, children who are disrespectful in the playground, get into fights on the school bus, tease classmates, or lose their cool during class discussions might benefit from listening and responding to such books as Phyllis Reynold Naylor's *King of the Playground*, Eleanor Estes' *The Hundred Dresses*, and Dorothea Lachner's *Andrew's Angry Words*, but all children all the time need to be surrounded by empathic characters, and to discuss ones who are not. Reading aloud from carefully chosen books remains my favorite way to be the school disciplinarian.

Books That Lead to Significant Conversations

We expect our students to voice confident opinions and ask honest questions. Sometimes I read a picture book and I am absolutely sure it will lead to talk about significant matters. Books such as *The Keeper of Ugly Sounds* by Eleanor Walsh Meyer, *The Hidden House* by Martin Waddell, *The Roses in My Carpet* by Rukhsana Khan, *Good Luck Mrs. K* by Louise Borden, *Horace and Morris but Mostly Dolores* by James Howe, *Hey Little Ant* by Philip and Hannah Hoose, and *Brass Button* by Crescent Dragonwagon can lead even very young children to talk about such issues as speaking in respectful tones, how things change with the passage of time, child labor and refugee camps, concerns over serious illnesses, the decision to kill an insect, gender stereotypes, and falling in love.

Books That Speak to the Parenting Experience

There are many reference books for parents in my office, including Arlene Silberman's *Growing Up Writing: Teaching Our Children to Write, Think and Learn*, Peter Stillman's *Families Writing*, Peggy Kaye's *Games for Writing: Playful Ways to Help Your Child Learn to Write*, Jean Grasso Fitzpatrick's *Once Upon a Family: Read-Aloud Stories and Activities That Nurture Healthy Kids*, Elizabeth Stone's *Black Sheep and Kissing Cousins: How Our Family Stories Shape Us*, Mary Pipher's *Reviving Ophelia: Saving the Selves of Adolescent Girls*, Bee Cullinan and Brod Bagert's *Helping Your Child Learn to Read*, and Jim Trelease's *New Read-Aloud Handbook*. I also shelve books on such important and sensitive topics as sex, adoption, drugs, foster care, stepfamilies, discipline, and having a new baby in the family. (See also "Special Interest Books on Significant Emotional Issues," on p. 19.)

Personal-Interest Books

Children need to know that when you are truly interested in a topic, you collect books on that topic. For me, it's baseball. My collection of baseball literature for children stretches across the windowsill ledges in my office. Some of my favorites for children include David Shannon's *How Georgie Radbourn Saved Baseball*, Paul Janeczko's poetry collection *That Sweet Diamond*, Ken Mochizuki's *Baseball Saved Us*, Peter Golenbach's *Teammates*, David Adler's *The Babe and I*, Ron Cohen's *My Dad's Baseball*, Helen Ketteman's *I Remember Papa*, and Lee Bennett Hopkin's selection of baseball poems entitled *Extra Innings*.

Books That Pay Tribute to Writers' Legacies

In the introduction to *Going Public*, I list many children's writers who have passed away since our school first opened. When children see these writers' works between the bookends in my office, they appreciate the legacy we have been left. Students know that they will not read any new novels by Pam Conrad or poems by Valerie Worth, but they can always reread their favorites.

Other Categories

At first, I thought of including an extensive bibliography of all the books that sit between the bookends on my shelves. But then I realized that readers would benefit more from discovering their own titles to meet any of the categories listed above, as well as from creating their own categories of books to meet the needs of their unique communities. The creation of such categories and the search for appropriate books would probably be a useful staff meeting activity.

Additional categories of books are listed below. They are closely connected to the teaching of writing in our school, and are therefore fully explored in the companion volume to this text, *Writing Through Childhood*.

- Books that brim with quality writing
- Books that contain accessible patterns for young writers
- Books that suggest new formats for young writers
- Books that offer lessons for notebook keepers
- Books that prove that informational writing can be breathtaking
- Books that are rooted in personal memories
- Books that are rooted in curiosity and news clippings
- Books that add to a favorite author collection
- Books that contain poems for children throughout the grades
- Memoirs, biographies, and autobiographies of writers
- Writers' reference materials

The Importance of Schoolwide Literacy Events, Rituals, and Traditions

If children are to believe they belong not only to a class but also to a school and a community, we have to live our lives accordingly. In *Going Public,* I describe our annual parade celebrating our return to school, complete with banner waving and poetry reciting. I also discuss our schoolwide study of one poetry anthology throughout the grades, our family literacy portfolios, our name-tag Thursdays, our search for books with names of students in the titles, our baseball reading and writing club, and our standing invitation to write to friends who have moved away.

We have several other schoolwide literacy events on the drawing board. Not all will be carried out, especially during the same school year. Special events are not special when they become routine and take too much time away from regularly scheduled work periods. If schools are to be tranquil places, no one should feel like they're squeezing in their teaching. The following are a few events we've either begun or have been meaning to get going.

Read-Aloud Reunions

Imagine a morning, perhaps midway through the school year, when all the children read aloud a short snippet of text to their teacher from the year before. Students can choose passages from their own writing or excerpts from published books. Fifth graders reconvene in their fourth-grade classroom, as do fourth, third, second, and first graders. Fifth-grade teachers whose students have graduated visit in the kindergarten rooms, helping teachers take care of this year's children, who serve as wide-eyed audiences for last year's returning readers. (Kindergarten children stay in their rooms, of course. They were not in attendance the year before. New students to the school in other grades can accompany their friends.) We can extend these read-aloud reunions to many grades, not just the grade from the previous year. Wouldn't every elementary student like to spend time showing their kindergarten teacher how much they've grown as readers? Sandra Cisneros's short story "Eleven" reminds us that when you are eleven you are also ten and nine and eight, and so on. In a similar way, we want our students to know that even though they have a fifth-grade teacher, they are still loved by their fourth-, third-, second-, first-grade, and kindergarten teachers.

Game Playing

Our students are responsible for their own entertainment during their recess breaks when the weather is awful. During those bitter cold, snowy days, the children rely on their rainy-day boxes and activity books. In addition, it seems worthwhile to ensure that students know a few of the pencil-and-paper games as well as the board games that require players to read, write, and play with language. I made a strong plug for family members to play with language at home. In part, a letter I wrote to families read,

Many of my warmest memories at home with my own children involved language play. We
played Scrabble and Boggle and Jotto. We answered riddles, made up puns, did crosswords,
word searches, and anagrams. We challenged one another with tongue twisters, stumped one
another while playing ghost, geography, and hangman. (If you've forgotten how to play these
games, send your child to me for a refresher course.) Playing with language, delighting in
language, is good for readers and writers . . .

I can easily imagine a school morning devoted to the playing of worthwhile word
games. We would put out a call for sets of Scrabble, Probe, and Boggle, as well as pads
for Jotto and Mad-Libs. We'd also gather lots of scrap paper and pencils for ghost, geography, and hangman. (This past school year, after much discussion of the violence taking place in schools across the country, I decided to eliminate "hangman" as the name of
that popular word game. The students and I now call it "beat the clock," and we have to
guess the word before a clock face, rather than a dangling person, is complete.) And then
the teach-in would begin. Teachers and parent volunteers would work with small clusters of students and teach them how to play the word games that filled their own childhoods. Students, familiar with these games, would of course be invited to explain game
rules as well. What a scene! Up and down the corridors, people teaching people all their
favorite word games. And what a payoff! Students expanding their word knowledge while
having so much fun and being better able to entertain themselves during indoor recess.

Sing-Alongs

I'm for bringing back the old-fashioned hootenanny and the "follow-the-bouncing-ball"
sing-alongs. We close the street to traffic in order to make space for the children to play
after lunch, and we close it for dancing; we should close it for singing as well. Once a
week in good weather, our kindergarten teachers form a kindergarten chorus. The three
classes sit on our front stoop and sing their favorite songs. Neighbors stop what they are
doing to watch the students' joyful faces and listen to their sweet soft voices. They also
seem to admire the teachers' seemingly boundless energy and pride in their students and
their work. Occasionally the neighbors hum, clap, sway, or sing along. I think the entire
school can be out there, one morning a year, singing the songs they know so well,
accompanied by our guitar-playing teachers. It would be quite a challenge to agree on a
list of songs that would represent our shared music heritage. I'd vote for a few American
folk songs, catchy Broadway tunes, (How can we be a New York school and not pay tribute to the "great white way"?) as well as songs taught to us by our students from many
lands. We probably don't sing often enough in schools. We certainly don't sing often
enough on the sidewalks of New York.

Letter-Writing Campaigns

Sometimes at workshops or summer institutes, I invite participants to write that letter
they've been meaning to write. Even the most reluctant adult writers come to appreciate

the assignment. They still may not enjoy writing, but they appreciate having written. I've never met anyone who can't think of a letter that they've been meaning to write to someone. I can easily imagine creating a periodic schoolwide letter-writing workshop in which everyone writes the letters they've been meaning to write. In preparation for the day, stationery, postcards, stamps, and addresses would be gathered. Children would have a chance to keep in touch with family and friends who have moved away. They could use the time to keep up their regular correspondence with grandparents, cousins, and folks from their old neighborhoods and former homelands. They could write to former teachers, pen pals, and even politicians. And of course, parents and teachers could do likewise. The morning would end with a walk to the corner to drop our letters in the mailbox. What a scene, hundreds of children lined up to drop their letters in the box. Letter writing is one of those lifelong literacies we care so much about at our school. Perhaps, if community spirit and pleasure are attached to writing letters, children as well as adults will choose to continue the activity on their own.

Rotating Read-Alouds

Joan Backer, one of our fourth-grade teachers, suggested when our school first opened that every teacher figure out a way to read aloud to every class. Now that our school has grown, it would be too time-consuming for everyone to read to every class, but we can devote a morning to this exchange. Every teacher would trade places with a colleague for a portion of class time. Imagine the conversations that would take place. Before the visits, teachers would talk about choice of text to read aloud and classroom routines. After the visits, teachers would share their learnings about students and their responses, as well as how their classroom settings seemed similar or different. (Teachers could probably swap writing workshops as well, although it's difficult to confer with children without knowing their histories). It would also be interesting to interview students about different teachers' style of reading aloud.

Guest Readers

Students are used to having visiting teachers as guests, but what about guests from the community? Once a year, the New York City Public Library hosts a celebrity read-aloud. We could do likewise, one morning each year, only our celebrities would not be famous actors, musicians, or politicians. Instead, we could devote a morning to read-alouds and follow-up interviews with neighborhood shopkeepers, grandparents, relatives of teachers, or people who work in our building who usually don't have a chance to read aloud, including our secretary, security guard, custodian, and kitchen workers. Children would think about these important people in new ways if they sat in their classroom rocking chairs with one of the class's favorite books in their hands. Occasionally teachers *have* invited such guest readers into their classrooms. I'd like to think that a schoolwide effort would add drama, magic, and extra importance to such moments.

Poetry Recitals

We paid tribute to children's literature expert Bee Cullinan when she generously donated five hundred copies of *A Jar of Tiny Stars* to our students. We invited Bee to spend a morning with us, and representatives from every class were invited to our staff room at set times to show their appreciation. I was struck by how many children chose to memorize poems as a way of saying thanks. In Minneapolis, Minnesota, there is a children's bookstore, Wild Rumpus, that hosts an annual summer "Read Till You Sweat" day. Children sign up to read aloud around the clock. Our plans would not be so ambitious, but I can imagine an annual get-together in which children and adults alike share memorized poems. When the wonderful British poet Michael Rosen visited our school and the children asked him to read one of his poems, he didn't need any of his anthologies. He knew his poems by heart. So too, we all could learn our favorite poems by heart and gather in our ballroom, taking turns reciting. It would be interesting to study the types of poems chosen and to invite parents in to recite poems from their own childhoods. How valuable it would be for young students to hear poems that have been in someone's head for thirty years or more. (For more on this subject, see Chapter 5, "Paying Tribute to Poetry.")

Poems on Hand

Several years ago I visited a school in Indiana, where the students, teachers, and administrators took Beatrice Schenk De Regnier's poem "Keep a Poem in Your Pocket," to heart. Everyone quite literally kept a poem in their pockets. I could imagine having a monthly ritual at our school, when everyone on a set day is required to have selected a poem to share. There is something enticing about having those poems on pocket-size slips of paper, always at the ready when you are stopped at any time, anywhere, to read or recite a poem. I could also imagine adding extra challenges to the task. Perhaps one month we could call for an original poem, or a poem in a different language, or a poem written before 1900, or a poem in a specified form—haiku, limerick, free verse, or ballad. Of course, teachers as well as children would be expected to participate.

Book Swaps

In the first year of our school, Julie Liebersohn's first and second graders organized a schoolwide swap of used books. The students prepared and distributed the flier shown in Figure 1.1. After Julie left our school, we never had another book swap. I'm sorry that her students didn't think to carry on the tradition. What a wonderful way to end the school year, with new "old" books for summer reading. That's a school tradition worthy of reinstating.

Commonplace Books

The Oxford English Dictionary defines a commonplace book as one "in which one records passages or matters to be especially remembered or referred to, with or without arrange-

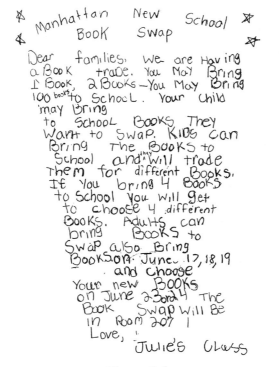

☆ Manhattan New School ☆
☆ Book Swap ☆

Dear families, we are having
a Book trade. You may bring
1 Book, 2 Books—You may bring
100 books to School. Your child
may bring
to School Books They
want to Swap. Kids can
Bring the Books to
School and will trade
them for different Books.
If you bring 4 Books
to School you will get
to choose 4 different
Books. Adults can
bring Books to
Swap also. Bring
Books on June 17, 18, 19
and choose
Your new Books
on June 23 or 24. The
Book Swap will Be
in Room 207.
Love,
Julie's Class

Figure 1.1

ment." If you read W. H. Auden's published commonplace book entitled *A Certain World,* you'll discover a rather incredible array of excerpts from Auden's extensive readings. I wish I had known about the concept of saving and savoring excerpts from my favorite books read over the course of my life. (For some reason, it doesn't seem satisfying to start at this late age.) No doubt, the passages I would have decided to save would have served as memoir, hinting at significant moments in my life. I'd love to see our students each begin a commonplace book. If money weren't an issue, we'd provide a huge bound scrapbook for all our students, encouraging them to add the passages that speak to them. The book would be too big to fill during their elementary years. The message would be clear: "This is a lifelong commitment."

Book Partners

Upper-grade students in many schools serve as book buddies for early-childhood students. Our children do as well. Many third and fourth graders have assumed weekly paired reading-aloud responsibilities in kindergarten or first-grade classrooms. Of course, such arrangements can be extended throughout the school, so that every child in the school has a book partner every year. Thoughtful teachers have extended the book partner experience.

Most begin by instructing older children about the basics of sharing texts with younger children, including how to choose an appropriate text, how to sit so that both students can see the page, how to read aloud naturally with expression, how to allow for time to talk about the story and the illustrations, how to point out the words, demonstrating the movement from left to right and top to bottom, and so on.

Some students are required to correspond with their book buddies. (Reading these letters, searching for a few to include in this chapter, was like staring at a box of Godiva chocolates. The decision was a most difficult one. They were all so appealing).

Sungho Pak's fourth graders sent process notes to Isabel, the kindergarten teacher, describing her students' involvement in each book buddy meeting. These notes, written on index cards (an example is in Figure 1.2), were then filed in each kindergartner's portfolio. No doubt Isabel learned a great deal about her students from reading the fourth graders' comments, and their observations informed her teaching.

Pam Mayer's kindergartners pair with Renay Sadis's third graders and each year the two classes work on a literacy project together. One year, inspired by an anthology put together by Sharon Taberski entitled *Morning, Noon, and Night: Poems to Fill Your Day,* the third graders interviewed their five-year-old buddies to find out their main interests and then met the challenge of creating poetry anthologies surrounding that interest. They picked appropriate poems and invited their young friends to work on the illustrations. The anthologies were formally presented in front of family members of all the students involved at an end-of-the-year celebration. Copies of the anthologies remained in the classroom libraries.

Another year, partners worked on "Read to me and I'll read to you" texts, inspired by Jacqueline McQuade's *Good Times with Teddy Bear* and *My Little House Book of Animals* and *My Little House Book of Family* adapted from the *Little House Books* by Laura Ingalls Wilder. In these books, each page contains a large-print topic and a one-line description of the topic in smaller print. This structure seemed like a natural one for our mixed-age

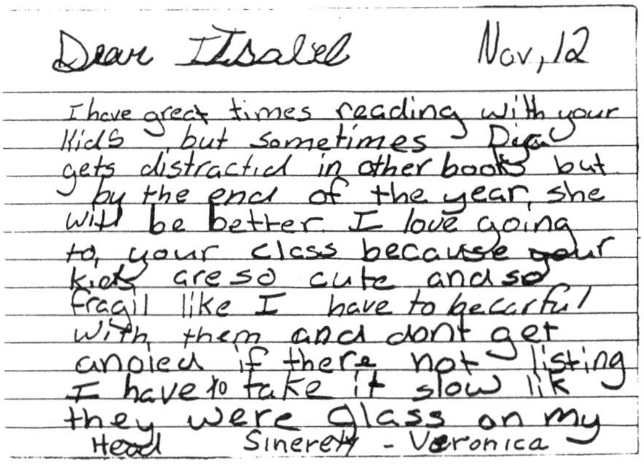
Dear Itsabel Nov, 12

I have great times reading with your kids but sometimes Diga gets distractid in other books but by the end of the year, she will be better. I love going to, your class because your kids are so cute and so fragil like I have to be carful with them and dont get angied if there not listing I have to take it slow lik they were glass on my Head Sinerely - Veronica

Figure 1.2

partners. We invited the pairs to create original picture books based on a common interest. The five-year-old wrote one word labels for each illustration and the older students wrote lyrical sentences that sat alongside the simple labels. Third-grade Ronnie and his younger buddy Jacob collaborated on a picture book entitled "Rainbows." On page one, Jacob wrote "Raining" and Ronnie added, "Drops of rain trickled down my forehead down to the edge of my face." Page two followed with the one word label, "Sunshower," and the sentence, "Magically, the sun bursts through the clouds to make a rainbow." The pair continued their book with pages devoted to each of the colors of the rainbow.

Other possibilities for book-buddy collaborations are listed below.

Counting Books   Older students create counting books based on the interests of their younger partners. Older students may need to pore over published counting books for inspiration. Younger children can be responsible for the invaluable illustrations in counting books.

Favorite Songs   Older students turn the kindergartners' favorite songs into picture books. Teachers may have to supply accurate and complete words. Each buddy can sing their tune at a classroom celebration of completed works.

Alphabet Life-Stories   Older students create an alphabet book based on the younger child's life. Older students might have to pore over some alphabet books for inspiration and will need time to interview youngsters. Writers may decide to cover such ground as My Buddy's Favorite Playthings, Things My Buddy Eats, Stuff in My Buddy's Bedroom, Places My Buddy Has Been, Authors My Buddy Likes, Things My Buddy Likes to Do, and so on.

Question-and-Answer Books   Younger students ask a series of those wonderfully "childish" "Why is the sky blue?" kind of questions. Older students have to find the answers and explain them in ways very young children can understand. Each question is asked, answered, and illustrated on a separate page of paper and slipped into binders, a copy for each classroom. If younger children have trouble asking questions, older children can interview family members of the younger children to discover questions they have asked at home. Older children can also tempt them by sharing questions from those big thick published books of questions like *Charlie Brown's Super Book of Questions and Answers* (Random House), *1000 Questions and Answers* (Scholastic), or *Highlights Book of Science Questions That Children Ask,* or *I Wonder Why I Blink and Other Questions About My Body* (Kingfisher Books).

"What Were They Thinking?" Photography Books   Older students surprise younger children by taking candid photographs of them during the school day. They then show the younger students the photographs and ask them to say what they were thinking when the snapshot was taken. (This idea is inspired by the "What Were They Thinking" column in *The New York Times Magazine*). Older children can then craft passages based on the students' responses. The finished product, including the photograph and passages, can be duplicated for both partners and a set can also be bound into a class book. (Later in the year, when younger children are more experienced writers, they can be invited to do the same for older children. Parents and student teachers can help snap the photos for the youngsters.)

In an article in *The New Advocate,* summer 1997, I summarized the benefits of such book buddy get-togethers. In addition to the obvious benefits of older children practicing their reading aloud and younger children learning from the more accomplished readers, I also cited additional ways these sharing experiences are particularly beneficial to the older children. These upper-grade students are learning about the teaching of reading, aspects of child development, as well as being reminded of all the personal pleasures attached to reading. I write, "Five-year-olds, for example, remind us all to be in awe of illustrations. . . . Young children also remind us of the sheer pleasure and value attached to rereading a favorite text. . . . In addition, our kindergartners continuously demonstrate what uncomplicated, authentic reader response is all about. . . . And finally, five-year-olds remind us how comforting it is to have rituals attached to our literate acts."

It should also be noted that book buddy sessions can be thought of as prime-time for teacher assessment. Teachers can walk the room (and the corridors, stairwells, etc.) and observe and eavesdrop on the work of the book buddies. Teachers can informally note students' abilities to read aloud, stay on-task, care for books, and so on. (For more on this, see p. 290.)

New-Student Welcomes
When you work in a community where people take it as a compliment when others borrow their ideas, we should expect that many individual class rituals and traditions will become schoolwide ones. Judy Davis and her fifth graders, for example, have prepared end-of-the-year, annotated summer reading lists for our fourth graders. It has occurred to me that all our students could do likewise. In June, every class could work on a list of recommended books for students about to enter their grade. All classes in the same grade could combine their lists to create a really substantial one that goes home to all the appropriate families. Of course, the lists need not be narrowed to traditional grade or "reading levels," rather to the interests of students of similar ages.

Other similar tasks come to mind. When my children were undergraduates they would share their university's "Critical Analysis" books with me. These contained brutally honest as well as funny student-composed descriptions of courses and professors. Rather than harsh critiques or rave reviews, students at the elementary level could offer specific and accurate information and advice about the grade, the classroom, and the teacher in the form of letters. Instead of suggesting that students spend time over the summer writing individual letters to children about to take their place, we could make it an annual in-school tradition. In June, members of each class could collaborate on a group letter that would be sent to every child in their teacher's new class. These letters could be attached to the formal letter we send students, announcing their new class placement. (See Chapter 3, "Discovering Real-World Reasons to Write," for examples of letters written to students who arrive midyear.)

Hellos and Goodbyes

Many teachers write "Welcome Back to School" letters each fall. It seems to me that children should be expected to do likewise. It would be a lovely tradition to ask students to present their teacher with a letter on the first day of school. The letter could contain the usual summertime chitchat as well as the child's hopes, expectations, questions, and areas of interest. This "passing of the envelopes" could take place again on the very last day of school. The teacher once again writes a letter to her class, or to each student, if the teacher is so inclined, and once again each child presents a letter to the teacher. These end-of-the-year notes would most likely contain reflections on the year, memorable moments, gracious comments, and wishes for a peaceful summer break.

Dialogue Journals

In *Going Public,* I noted that I occasionally keep dialogue journals with a few students. This is a joyful experience that can be shared with lots of members of the school community. All the adults in the school could take on one dialogue partner. They could decide if their dialogue journal would be limited to a shared interest or if it would be "anything goes." I'd love to see early-childhood teachers correspond with older students. I'd also love to see relationships grow between students and people who rarely get to know children as writers, including attendance teachers, adaptive physical education teachers, speech therapists, or guidance counselors. Then too, I think our custodian, security guard, school aides, and secretary would be great dialogue partners. Students of different ages could also serve as dialogue partners. Students who kept journals with me simply left them each morning in a specified spot in my office to be picked up the following morning. I would respond in the evenings to the student's letter. It was the most pleasurable school-related work I did in the evenings. (See samples in *Writing Through Childhood*).

Community Time

I have also been intending to gather students together in our ballroom on a regular basis. When we opened the school, I had a vision of starting and ending each day with a community gathering. As our school began to grow, I realized the impossibility of bringing hundreds of students and their teachers together twice a day. The movement to and from the fourth-floor meeting area would take up too much time, time that was precious to teachers with rigorous plans and students needing big blocks of time to carry out their commitments. Now that we have over 550 students, the challenge is even more foreboding. I'd still, however, like to devise a way for smaller numbers of classes to meet on a regular basis, perhaps once a month. Kindergartners and first graders could spend time together, as could second and third graders and fourth and fifth graders. I am not thinking of the traditional assembly that I can recall so well from my childhood. I don't remember what went on exactly at those meetings, only that they were always held on

Wednesday and that all students had to wear white blouses, blue bottoms, and red ties or bows around their collars. I have nothing so formal in mind. Instead, I can imagine starting each new month with a few favorite songs and poems, followed by an opportunity for people to share what they are hoping to learn in the weeks ahead and to listen to one another's published writing.

Inventing New Literacy Events

Creating new schoolwide events or beginning new traditions is not only up to the principal. In the following letter I invite second graders to join me in thinking of meaningful ways to look back on a school year.

> *June 27, 1994*
>
> *Dear children,*
>
> *I can hardly believe that the last full week of school for this year has arrived. Today, Monday, June 27, 1994, is the last Monday that you will meet as second graders. This is the last Monday that you will meet in room 201. Next year, you will make new friends, meet in new places, sit in new seats, and study new things. Don't you think the year has gone quickly?*
>
> *Perhaps you will set aside time today to think back on the past year. You might draw the outstanding scenes of the year and arrange them in a sort of patchwork quilt to be hung for next year's second graders to see in September. You might recall the important things that you studied this year and arrange them on a timeline that you will save forever. You might meet in small groups and list your top-ten favorite books of the year and then share your choices with the whole class.*
>
> *What other end-of-the-year celebrations can you think of?*
>
> *I look forward to hearing from you.*
>
> > *Love,*
> >
> > *Shelley*

School events fill our student's childhood memory banks. Ones celebrating or involving literate acts can influence children's reading and writing attitudes and behaviors. They are worthy of conversations at staff meetings, parent planning sessions, student council gatherings, and of course, in our classrooms.

Keeping Up with Children's Literature

After her first visit to our school, the wonderful children's writer Louise Borden sent me a pen inscribed with the words, "Some School!" I understood this literary reference to E. B. White's *Charlotte's Web*, as did the teachers and the students I showed it to. Good books are what we talk about, in class and out.

It's not unusual to hear teachers talk about books while they share their morning coffee, break bread together at lunch, or swap stories after school. Of course, they also talk about movies, families, relationships, clothes, dates, restaurants, exercise, and so on, but when you are passionate about books, you can't resist the urge to share a great one. Teachers don't hoard new finds. They talk about them, lend them, and even pick up an extra copy for a friend. There is no fear in the building that someone else will read aloud "your new book." We know good books deserve to be read time and again.

We are all stunned when a book we've never heard of wins the Newbery or Caldecott award. Since children's books are at the heart of all we do, we expect to be familiar with all high-quality books. But there are so many books published annually, it's nearly impossible to know them all. Keeping up with children's literature can be a full-time job, one none of us have the necessary time for. All of us at school have come to rely on one another, on outside resources, and on several schoolwide structures to make sure we don't miss out on any really fine books.

Becoming a Literary Traveler

I appreciate the St. Augustine quote that reads, "The world is a book and one who does not travel reads only a page." The same sentiment can apply to keeping up with children's literature. We need to leave our classrooms, leave our school buildings, and see what's out there. We need to visit one another's rooms and visit friends in other schools. We need to visit libraries and bookstores. We have to do a lot of browsing before we buy. Especially when funds are very limited, we have to be careful about our choices.

Extending Invitations to Students and Parents

Keeping up with children's literature needs to be a joint venture. Every member of your class can be considered a scout. Even if you simply ask every student to visit the public library and find one book they think no one in the class has seen, you will quickly learn about new authors and new titles. Of course, this can become a monthly ritual, guaranteeing a yearlong supply of information about children's literature. I can also imagine asking students to present the study of one author. They can be asked to line up books on the chalkboard ledge, prepare a complete bibliography of books written, offer biographical information, and choose an excerpt to read aloud. (See "Across-the-Grades Guide to Author Study" in Appendix 1.)

Claire, a fourth grader, was a devoted reader in need of an engaging literacy project. I challenged her to survey teachers throughout the grades and prepare a summer reading list to be distributed to every child. When she handed me a file complete with a cover letter to families, a list of titles, and a computer disk, I recall being struck not only with her competence and seriousness of purpose but also with her sophisticated know-how. It was such a grown-up act to hand over her complete file—disk and all. (I was also delighted that she thought to add my name to her lovely letter). Her cover letter follows.

June 25, 1999

Dear MNS families,

Summer is coming! As you know, MNS encourages summer reading. We have put together a list of books to read over the summer or any time.

MNS teachers from all six grades recommended books they believe children will enjoy. We hope you have the time to read some of them. Summer reading can be fun if you have plenty of good books and it will pay off when school starts in the fall.

Happy reading!

Claire Bulgar and Shelley Harwayne

(Not surprisingly, in the summer of 1999, J. K. Rowlings' *Harry Potter* books made it to Claire's lists for children in grades three, four, and five.)

Parents can be invited to participate in the search for great literature as well. Teachers need to let parents know the kinds of books they and their students are interested in. You never know which parents have a background in children's literature or which would be delighted to search the stacks at the public library. PTAs would do well to form Children's Literature Support Committees.

Discovering District Expertise

Our district asked me to chair a children's literature committee. We were asked to compile a bibliography of wonderful books throughout the grades. The district understood the challenge of keeping up with children's literature. It was right to ask teachers to help one another. What was more significant than individual titles, however, was the chance to meet other educators who were interested in children's books. There are thirteen hundred teachers in our district. I shouldn't have been surprised to meet so many experts, each with their own armload of classroom favorites, bibliographies, journal articles, and specialty areas.

As a committee, we struggled with the notion of compiling any list, for fear it would become a required reading list. We were not interested in mandating titles and creating uniformity in students' reading districtwide. We determined that any list would be accompanied by a clear statement explaining our hope that this list would be a way of helping teachers keep up with new publications. It might be used as a suggested reading list over holiday and summer breaks. It might be used as reference for purchasing new books for school and classroom libraries.

We brainstormed questions for a survey to be sent to every district teacher, making sure we tapped the expertise right here at home before we referred to outside sources. The explanatory letter and the survey we sent to all the teachers appears in Appendix 2.

We gathered a great deal of information simply by reaching out to our colleagues. The results of the survey appear in Appendix 3. In the end, we chose to recommend authors, not individual titles.

Tapping Community and City Expertise

Teachers who rely on real books, not textbooks, for teaching across the curriculum would make good use of a directory of all their city resources connected to children's literature. Imagine having a little book containing the names, addresses, and phone numbers of all the area bookstores, publishers, children's literature professors, libraries, members of children's literature professional groups, as well as educators and community members who consider themselves experts in this area. I think most of us would be surprised how thick that little book would become. It sounds like a great project for a teacher network to undertake. It also sounds like the kind of information that every school and public library should offer, presented electronically or traditionally, in book form.

Learning from Librarians

As mentioned, most public elementary schools in New York City do not have licensed librarians. That's all the more reason for us to depend on neighborhood public librarians. Unfortunately, it's very easy in a big city like New York to not take advantage of these local experts. "After all," most teachers think, "how much time can librarians give us, when they have so many classes visiting, and so many teachers, children, and parents needing their help? How can we possibly form close relationships with our local librarian?" You never know unless you ask, and if you're fortunate enough to connect with just the right one, it will be worth having been a little more aggressive. Perhaps, if the politicians realized just how much the public schools needed the help of public librarians, they would allot funds for more personnel and longer hours in our local libraries. Then too, the powers that be could reinstate the role of librarian in all our schools.

Bonding with Bookstore Owners

Throughout this country, I've met teachers who have come to rely on owners of children's bookstores. These shopkeepers have become local folk heroes of sorts. Teachers call these shopkeepers by their first names. They know their phone numbers by heart. And they trust their advice completely. Every teacher in Albany knows Frank Hodge and his Hodge-Podge Books just as every teacher in Denver knows Sue Lubeck from Bookies, and teachers in Minneapolis count on Collette Morgan of Wild Rumpus Books for Young Readers.

I've been to bookstores that host special evenings for parents and teachers and to many that arrange for guest authors to read aloud. I've met bookstore owners who read the same professional literature as teachers and others who skillfully prepare bibliographies as soon as they hear the topics being studied in schools. These bookstores not only offer teachers a chance to view all the latest books, buy a few, and create a wish list of others, they also provide settings worth emulating. Teachers often discover clever ways to arrange, display, and categorize books, as well as ways to provide comfortable and inviting places to curl up with a good book. It's also well worth adding your name to the mailing list of bookstores. Their mailings often contain informative newsletters, announcements of guest speakers, store promotions, discounts, and special events.

Teachers with less time to hang out in bookstores might simply do what our colleague Judy Davis used to do in her early days of becoming a literature-based teacher determined to buy a few surefire books for her sixth graders. She used to go into children's bookstores and ask the salespeople, "What are the books you keep running out of?" If Judy had limited funds, she wanted to make sure there were absolutely no duds on her shelves.

Maintaining University Connections

I can still remember with great fondness the undergraduate course I took in children's literature. I can even recall the day Maurice Sendak spoke in the college library. All I could think of at the time was how much he looked like his character Max. Even after we leave university settings, we need to remember that there are still experts a phone call away. We can also look to teachers who are enrolled in graduate programs and student teachers who are currently studying children's literature. We'd probably do well to carve out faculty time for these adult students to teach us what they're learning. Those of us who haven't taken a course in children's literature in over twenty years need to chat with current students or take a refresher course of our own.

Accepting All Donations

I never say no to book donations. Even sight unseen, I always say yes to parents, neighbors, and community organizations. I don't worry about storage space, condition of the texts, or even their quality. I much prefer to pick through a random pile than to give a hesitant or conditional thank-you to a caller with books to spare. Even just a few new titles are worth the effort. Good classroom collections are built one book at a time. When we look through these assorted shopping bags, totes, or cardboard boxes and discover books that we don't need at school, we are happy to give them away to children eager to start their own home libraries. Then too, if we discover books that are beyond repair, we know that they will come in handy in literary collages.

Being a Public Learner

The minute some people walk into a room you can tell they are totally obsessed with children's books. They are walking billboards, carrying bulging bags filled with literary treasures, wearing T-shirts advertising their favorite bookstores or buttons announcing their commitment to literacy. Their faces are always hidden behind the covers of children's books, and if you are lucky enough to catch their eye, they're happy to explain what they're reading.

People recognize my passion for children's books not by my appearance, but rather by my conversation. I let people know I want to know. I'm always asking, "What have you been reading aloud lately? Have you found any 'must-have' titles?" And I always have paper and pencil handy to jot down their suggestions. I've even bought one of those book lover's books made especially to keep lists of books to buy, borrow, or carefully lend to friends. (I've added a fourth section for "books to write," jotting down potential ideas whenever they occur to me.)

Public learners notice what children at airports and in doctor's waiting rooms are reading. They talk books to neighborhood children, visiting relatives, and children browsing the stacks in local libraries and bookstores. And people who are interested in children's literature are always delighted to meet other folks who share their obsession. They swap articles, ads, bibliographies, and news about book sales and discounts.

Posting a Literature Graffiti Board

One way of sharing information about books inside of school is to devote a prominent bulletin board to noteworthy announcements concerning literature—sort of a central clearinghouse for reviews, advertisements, and announcements of local speakers. Teachers are always interested to know which books are being banned, censored, and taken off shelves in different parts of this country. They are fascinated to discover that Beatrix Potter's works are used to teach English in Japan, that Jamie Lee Curtis's latest children's book has made the best-seller list, that Carolivia Herron's *Nappy Hair* has caused turmoil in a Brooklyn school, or that Dr. Seuss's widow plans a million-dollar tribute to the popular writer in his hometown. This display board might also be used by teachers to post themes being studied, wish-list titles, and the inevitable titles that have somehow disappeared from their classroom collections. This would also be a perfect place for children to correspond with one another, sharing recommendations of books throughout the grades that are too good to miss.

Relying on Professional Resources

There are many professional resources available to teachers interested in keeping up with children's literature. Subscriptions to journals, magazines, and reviews are a good place to begin. Individual teachers sometimes subscribe to publications that focus on children's literature; others are ordered through the school. Either way, they're only helpful if they are read, shared, and referred to when there is money to be spent. Just as with any professional text, the articles in children's literature journals are worthy of professional response. It's not unusual for staff members to suggest that we all read a provocative or informative article in *The New Advocate* or in *The Horn Book Magazine*. Then too, the bookcases in our staff room welcome donations of professional texts, including the children's literature textbooks we all read as college and graduate students. These books often contain detailed information on the history of children's literature as well as information on genres, award winners, author's lives, thematic groups of titles, and invaluable indexes of related books and periodicals. Of course, to keep up to date, we need to gather the most recent editions as well as purchase important and helpful professional books on children's literature.

Attending Conferences and Conventions

Whenever you see an incredibly long line in the book exhibit hall at a literacy conference, the chances are very good that a beloved author is autographing books. Teachers are more than willing to wait on long lines to meet their students' heroes, but they are also happy walking up and down the aisles, taking in all those new titles. Of course, teachers can't afford to buy all the titles they lust for, but they need to pass those titles on to librarians, parents, and principals. They also know to return to the publisher's booths at the very end of the convention to buy books at great discounts. Exhibitors don't want to travel home with those heavy loads, but teachers do. Teachers are also willing to carry home catalogs, a wonderful resource for sharing with colleagues who weren't able to attend a conference. Catalogs can also be put to other schoolwide uses.

Reading Catalogs

Catalogs enable colleagues to keep up with the latest titles, and they come in handy when book funds become available. Catalogs can also be used to let parents know the titles of books that would be appropriate to add to classroom collections. I could easily imagine teachers posting a, "We'd love to read . . ." board outside their classroom door, filled with clippings from catalogs. Parents and visitors would not only learn the titles of desired books, but the covers of the books would be firmly planted in potential donators' minds. Teachers passing by would, at the same time, become familiar with the new books. Catalogs can be picked up at conferences, and teachers and schools can easily be put on publisher's mailing lists.

Hosting Book Fairs

In the fund-raising section of *Going Public,* Chapter 5, "Reaching Out to Families," I describe our biannual book fair. Hardworking parents contact big publishing houses, survey the staff, select a wide range of appropriate books, and display them in the cafeteria. There is no easier way for teachers to keep up with new titles than to browse table-tops covered with new books. Not only can you see the new books, you can touch them and read their back covers and first pages, all without even leaving the building. In my many years as a staff developer, colleagues frequently asked me how they could get seemingly disinterested teachers to begin rethinking the teaching of reading and writing. My first bit of advice: "Help them fall in love with books again." In-house book-fairs are a great place to begin.

Valuing Book Clubs

Student book clubs not only expand students' personal bedroom collections and add bonus-point books to class libraries, they can also be valued as a way to keep up with what's hot in children's literature. Of course, we may not love all the books that students long to own, but those brief, easy-to-read listings are a quick way to ask ourselves,

"Have I heard of . . . ?" A teacher well versed in children's literature should also be able to advise students and their families about worthwhile purchases.

Organizing Bibliographies

Years and years of courses, workshops, and conferences means stacks and stacks of bibliographies of children's books. I longed for those handouts. I couldn't wait to see the list of titles the speakers had gathered, on an incredible range of topics. At the time, those bibliographies seemed so important. I shudder to think about the location and condition of those precious lists today. They're no doubt randomly scattered throughout my file cabinets and desk drawers. Some probably never even made it out of my conference tote bag. It's so easy to ask students to have good work habits and not have those very same habits ourselves. It would be ideal if all members of our staff contributed their collected bibliographies and filed them by topic in a central location. It's so frustrating when a topic arises and we remember once seeing a great list of appropriate titles but haven't a clue where that list is today.

Looking into Electronic Sources

Although I'm not an expert in using electronic resources, many of my friends, colleagues, and family members are. When I was recently asked to put together a bibliography for principals, I asked my editor Lois Bridges for help. She put out a call on her educator listservs and very quickly I had a wide range of responses from an incredible group of well-read educators. Not only did their responses help me to create a solid, up-to-date bibliography, I was also able to find out what such brilliant thinkers as Yetta Goodman, Susan Ohanian, and Linda Rief think a principal should read. You get an uncanny sense of tapping the whole wide world on its shoulder when you reach out to so many so quickly.

I must also admit that the first time someone downloaded a magazine article for me, I read it with the same sense of awe with which I ate my first microwave-cooked potato. How can anything work so quickly?

Then too, I remain amazed that my daughter so readily uses electronic retailing to get recommended titles for me, read reviews of those titles, and order them as well (see p. 236). I may not be an expert at electronic resources, but I am certainly reaping the literary rewards. Our young students and most of their teachers, on the other hand, are doing both. They understand the technology and they are enjoying the fruits of their labor.

Many of our students' favorite authors have Web sites, and many children have proudly shown me their e-mail correspondence with friendly authors. Our students in the upper grades periodically include book recommendations and reviews on our school's Web site, and this past school year Pam Mayer's multigrade early-childhood class worked with her friend Julie Rosemarin to add book reviews to Julie's Spaghetti

Book Club Web site (www.spaghettibookclub.org). The children read recently published books, wrote reviews with partners, and illustrated their reviews. Now their comments are available to our entire school community and beyond. Teachers know many helpful sites including those of publishers and literature journals, as well as such CD-ROMs as *The Horn Book Guide, Interactive,* containing over twenty-nine thousand critical reviews of children's and young adult books. (I wonder if the day will arrive when schools will have Franklin Rocket EB-500's, the literary equivalent of a CD player? By logging on to the Franklin Web site, readers can buy up to ten books online, download them onto their computer, and then upload them onto this portable electronic library.)

Honoring Expert Volunteers

Neighborhood volunteers can include retired librarians, storytellers, and children's literature professors. A small ad in a local newspaper might bring all the help educators need in their quest to keep up with children's literature. When our schools are volunteer-friendly places, we reap many rewards. Just as our science teacher Lisa Siegman invites scientists from the National Academy of Science to volunteer their expertise in matters scientific, we need to look to those who can offer literary expertise with pleasure. This volunteer crew can also include doctoral students with interests in literature, local authors, and book reviewers for local papers. (Of course, interested educators could also volunteer to write reviews for local papers, bookstores, and professional or parent publications. The reviewer's role brings access to many new titles. For more information on reviewing books see p. 225).

Assigning Designated Readers

Just as there are designated hitters in baseball games and designated drivers at Saturday night parties, in schools we can cultivate designated readers in different areas of children's literature. It's so hard to keep up with everything. Imagine if everyone on staff agreed to become well versed in just one area. You would know just the right person to go to when you needed to add energy to your poetry collection, or choose a nonfiction writer for an author study, or find different versions of a familiar fairy tale. We need to allow specialists to emerge in our schools and create school cultures in which sharing information is a way of life.

Designing Rituals for Sharing

Staffs determined to keep up with the latest in children's literature would do well to create rituals to guarantee that children's literature remains on their front burners. At every staff gathering, over an extended period of time teachers can be invited to share books. Some staffs begin or end every meeting with a ten-minute period set aside to share new literary discoveries. Books can be displayed, talked about, or passed around. Others announce hot topics prior to the meeting, asking people to share any or all books they own connected to such classroom studies as snails, butterflies, chicks, snow, skyscrapers, or whatever fever happens to be sweeping by. Other faculties rotate the setting of their meetings, hanging out in one another's library corners. A principal colleague told me that her staff has periodic BYOB ("bring your own book") parties, in which favorite nonfiction books, poetry anthologies, or chapter books are read aloud. I've even heard of staffs being asked to bring four titles to a meeting, including "something old, something new, something borrowed, something blue." ("Something blue" referred to an emotionally charged text, one that usually results in serious classroom conversations.) Some schools have added read-aloud rituals to their faculty meetings; others invite knowledgeable guest speakers. Schools with designated experts can carve out time to hear the latest from the pros. I've occasionally asked a student to survey all the teachers, finding out what is being read aloud on any one school day. These surprising results can be shared periodically at staff meetings. Teachers can also be asked to bring books to swap to staff get-togethers. Just like the rule some people apply to old clothes, "If you haven't worn it in two years, give it away," so too, "If no one in your room has read a particular book in two years, give it away." Perhaps those books just haven't been placed in the right readers' hands, and should be sitting in someone else's library.

Making a Lifelong Commitment to Literacy

When Judy Davis was putting together a yearbook for her graduating seniors, she asked me to collaborate with her in writing a letter to the graduates to include in the publication. Together we wrote the letter that appears below:

> *June, 1995*
>
> *Dear graduates,*
>
> *Although the following is a bibliography of shared books, let it serve as the biography of our times together. We trust that books will forever make a difference in your life.*
>
>
>
> *With love and respect,*
>
> *Judy and Shelley*
>
>

Journey by Patricia MacLachlan, because it was the first book we read as a class, and it launched us on our literary journey.

Joyful Noise: Poems for Two Voices by Paul Fleischman, because you guys never allowed anyone to speak alone.

The Giver by Lois Lowry, because one never knows how things turn out.

Oh, the Places You'll Go by Dr. Seuss, because we hope our senior trip to Washington, D.C., is just the beginning.

Little by Little by Jean Little, because that's how we hope you'll savor the world and like Jean Little you'll appreciate each small moment.

The Place My Words Are Looking For edited by Paul Janeczko, because we hope there will always be a place for your words in the world.

Webster's Dictionary because we hope that one day you'll finally know the difference between "there," "their" and "they're."

Shoebag, by Mary James, because like Shoebag, you're not leaving the same way you entered. You have undergone a metamorphosis.

The Pain and The Great One by Judy Blume, because each of you was a little bit of both, mostly the great one.

Lasting Impressions by Shelley Harwayne, because that's what you've left upon us.

Although our choices and comments were a bit tongue in cheek, we sincerely trust that books will make a difference in the lives of our students.

Not too long ago, I was leaving for work at my usual six-thirty in the morning. I was making my way down the long hallway toward the elevator in my New York City high-rise apartment, when a very elderly woman motioned toward me from the far end of the corridor. She was leaning on a wooden cane, still dressed in her nightclothes, and in a very kind, yet determined voice asked, "Can you help me?"

I assumed she had locked herself out of her apartment or needed some medical assistance. When I approached, she used her cane to explain her dilemma. She pointed to the floor where her daily copy of *The New York Times* had been delivered, "It's usually rolled up with a rubber band," she explained, "and I can use my cane to shuffle it into my apartment. I push it along straight into the living room and I get it close to my chair. Then when I sit down, I can bend to pick it up. There's no rubber band today. I can't scoot it in and I can't bend down so low to pick it up out here."

My neighbor's request was an easy one: to hand her her daily newspaper. When I got to work, I told my colleagues about this elderly woman. Of course, she made us wonder about ourselves. We imagined being that age. We imagined having to work so hard to pick up the newspaper. We imagined being so determined to read the newspaper at such a senior age. Then, of course, we thought about our students. Will they care about reading the newspaper when they are twenty, fifty, ninety years of age? Will they have a newspaper delivered to their homes? Would they work as hard to pick up their daily newspaper?

We'd like to think that the answer is "yes!" to all three questions. We'd like to think that we are working in such wise ways that our students will care about their own literacy long after they graduate. In fact, there is only one reason we work so hard to create such a beautiful and inviting literary setting filled with extensive collections, schoolwide literacy rituals, and ways to keep up with children's literature. We want our students to make a lifelong commitment to reading and writing. And so we begin by painstakingly caring about the literary landscape, and then we proceed to do the best literacy teaching imaginable, the subject of the remainder of this book.

RELATED READINGS IN COMPANION VOLUMES

Going Public (Heinemann, 1999) is abbreviated as GP. *Writing Through Childhood* (Heinemann, forthcoming), is abbreviated as WC.

Making schools look beautiful	**GP:** Ch. 2
Reading to inform your writing	**WC:** Ch. 5
Keeping up with children's literature	**WC:** Ch. 11
Valuing literature as a humanizing tool	**GP:** Ch. 4
Making a lifelong commitment to literacy	**GP:** Ch. 2, Ch. 7; **WC:** Ch. 1
Assigning cumulative portfolio tasks	**GP:** Ch. 6
Enriching content studies	**GP:** Ch. 6
Honoring languages	**GP:** Ch. 4
Displaying student writing	**WC:** Ch. 9

CHAPTER 2

REFLECTING ON THE TEACHING OF WRITING

Key Literacy Lessons

1. There is no one way to run a writing workshop.
2. Writing is important in children's lives because it enables them to pay attention to the world, make sense of the planet, improve the quality of their lives, and hold on to their childhoods.
3. The school culture can either support or hinder the teaching of writing. It is easier to write and teach writing when there exists
   - a caring social tone
   - a commitment to using time wisely
   - authentic uses for student writing
   - access to literature
   - a deep respect for language
   - a love of story
   - a genuine curiosity about the world
   - a passion for good writing
   - a deep respect for childhood
4. We must strive to keep the teaching of writing simple.
5. Traditional workshop structures continue to be innovated on by teachers of writing. Teachers bring their own personal style to minilessons, writing conferences, and whole-class shares.
6. Signs of a successful writing workshop include children writing for sustained amounts of time, children able to explain workshop routines to visitors, and children eager to share their work.
7. Students should be challenged to hone their skills in a writer's bootcamp—an environment that supports and demands high-quality work.

Several years ago I was asked to honor Donald Graves when he was given the National Council of Teachers of English's (NCTE's) Language Arts Educator of the Year award. I began my presentation by describing the "back to Bacon" game that has spread like wildfire throughout this country. Let's say I challenge you with the name of the actor Morgan Freeman. You have to figure out a way to get "back to Bacon," the actor Kevin Bacon, of course. If you were up on the latest movies and their stars, you might say, "Morgan Freeman was in the movie *Seven* with Brad Pitt. Brad Pitt was in *Interview with a Vampire* with Tom Cruise. Tom Cruise was in *A Few Good Men* with Kevin Bacon." You've now succeeded in coming back to Bacon. In the world of movies, it seems, all roads lead to Kevin Bacon. In the world of teaching children to write, all roads lead to Donald Graves.

In fact, much of our work in the teaching of writing can be traced back to the groundbreaking work done by Donald Graves and his colleagues at the University of New Hampshire. When our school first opened in the fall of 1991, staff members carried in many well-worn books written by Donald Graves, along with books by Don Murray, Tom Newkirk, and Jane Hansen. Of course, our heads were filled as well with the pioneering work of such luminaries as Nancie Atwell, Janet Emig, and Georgia Heard.

We have learned a great deal from the distinguished work of these researchers. Their theories and insights as well as their practical applications are the foundations upon which we have shaped the writing classrooms on East Eighty-second Street. Their footprints are in the snow that surrounds our literacy work.

We still believe wholeheartedly in the importance of topic choice, in having big blocks of regularly scheduled time to write, in the incredible power of audience response, and in the role that reading plays in the teaching of writing. Above all, we still believe that learning to be a good teacher of writing begins with learning to be a good listener. Thankfully, some things never change.

The Principal's Perspective: A Diverse Approach to Writing

There are twenty-two writing workshops in our school; each is hosted by a separate teacher. To my mind they are equally brilliant, equally successful, and yet incredibly different. They have different tools and routines, and they offer different writing challenges. When I think of these incredibly diverse workshops, I come to my first big teaching "Aha!" since opening our school. Teachers don't have to do it my way. There is in fact no one way to run a writing workshop. Yes, we all share common beliefs, we all value many of the same things, we are all gazing in the same direction, but we are clearly not clones of one another. I take real delight in seeing all the different ways teachers can create successful writing workshops. I marvel at the varied ways each teacher has discovered to bring out the best in his or her young writers.

I was recently at an airport yogurt stand and the woman in front of me asked for a waffle cone filled with low-fat strawberry and butter pecan swirled together. The young sales clerk responded, "I can't swirl them. Is side by side okay?" In our professional lives, principals can't attempt to swirl teachers of literacy together. Side by side is more than okay, especially if teachers have opportunities to learn from one another.

The literacy lessons I have learned as an elementary school principal are necessarily true to life and varied. I begin by sharing those broad lessons that will pave the way for the more specific ones to come. These include learning why writing is so important in children's lives, learning how the culture of schools can support or hinder the teaching of writing, and learning how to keep the teaching of writing simple and at the same time help children write in ways that move an audience. A fuller explanation of each lesson follows.

Why Writing Is Important in Children's Lives

After my daughter's first few weeks at law school, she called home to say, "Mom, law school is not for lawyers." What she meant, of course, was that law school should not be just for lawyers. "Everyone," she said, "deserves to know what I now know about my constitutional rights. Everyone needs to know this stuff to have a better life." I believe the same thing about writing. Everyone needs to know this stuff to have a better life.

Paying Attention to the World

I don't wear rose-colored glasses. I don't emphasize the teaching of writing because I think our students can rely on writing to solve all the problems they will face. I don't expect that our students will all grow up to be professional writers (but I wouldn't be surprised if a few do). When I say that writing can help students have a better life, I am first referring to the act of writing as a means of helping students pay more attention to their world. In *Going Public* I state that our job at the elementary level is to help kids see the richness of their lives. Writing is one very effective way to help students realize what a fascinating place their corner of the world is. You can see this in Figure 2.1, in which Luda, an immigrant from Russia, records a visit to a Japanese grocery with her mom.

Making Sense of the Planet

Then too, I care that children have many opportunities to write because writing helps them figure out how this planet works. That's their job. If we do things right, children will be naturally curious about zillions of things. Writing gives them opportunities to sort things out, play hunches, and explore possibilities. Richard Margolis, on the book jacket of his first book of poems, *Only the Moon and Me,* explains,

> These poems speak of the things children think about when there's no one around to interrupt. They aren't daydreams and they aren't explanations. They are or are supposed to be the honest notions of children trying to make sense of their green minutes on earth. As often as not they turn out to be jackpot questions. . . .

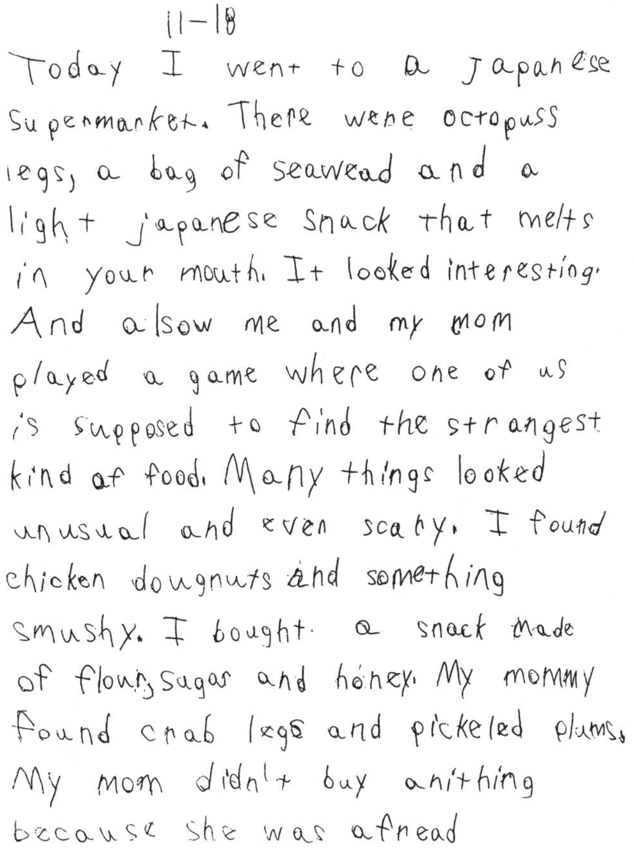

11–18

Today I went to a Japanese
Supermarket. There were octopuss
legs, a bag of seaweed and a
light japanese snack that melts
in your mouth. It looked interesting.
And also me and my mom
played a game where one of us
is supposed to find the strangest
kind of food. Many things looked
unusual and even scary. I found
chicken dougnuts and something
smushy. I bought a snack made
of flour, sugar and honey. My mommy
found crab legs and pickeled plums.
My mom didn't buy anithing
because she was afread

Figure 2.1

Growing up can be a lonely business, even when it's accomplished in the midst of a crowd, and much of it has to do with knowing how one feels. That is what many of the poems are about. The child surveys the day's events and comes to some definitive conclusions. . . .

He may also make some lasting judgments about the rest of the world. . . . These are more than merely cute conclusions. They are victories. They are also weapons which the child, to borrow Joyce's phrase, has forged in the smithy of his soul, and which he will wield another day.

We invite our elementary students to write because writing helps them "make sense of their green minutes on earth."

In Figure 2.2 Rosie uses writing to try and understand why so many people get off at the same bus stop. She begins with the practical and moves to the childlike possibilities. In Figure 2.3 Alexandra uses writing to help her make sense of grown-up behavior. In the excerpt following, Chelsea uses writing to announce what she has determined to be grown-up behavior.

You know you're an adult when you can swallow an aspirin whole. You know you're an adult when wine isn't gross. You know you're an adult when the news is something you enjoy watching on television.

You know you're an adult when you can charge stuff on your credit card. You know you're an adult when you have a paycheck to spend. You know you're an adult when you're the one giving the presents.

You know you're an adult when you can make your own decisions. You know you're an adult when you don't delay on doing the dishes. You know you're an adult when you eat anything put in front of you and you don't fuss.

You know you're an adult when you squeeze the toothpaste from the bottom. You know you're an adult when you're satisfied with just a birthday card.

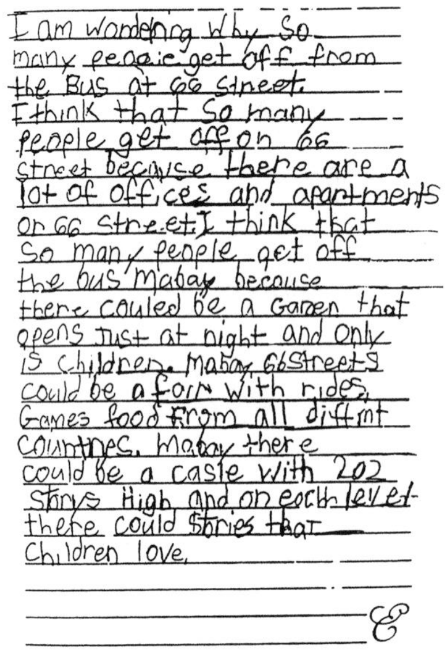

I am wondering why so many people get off from the Bus at 66 Street. I think that so many people get off on 66 Street because there are a lot of offices and apartments on 66 Street. I think that so many people get off the bus maday because there could be a garden that opens Just at night and only is children. Maday 66Streets could be a fair with rides. Games food from all diffmt Countries. Maday there could be a casle with 202 Storys high and on eorth level there could Stories that Children love.

Figure 2.2

Dad

if my dad is on the phone and you talk he snaps at you

Snap!

it makes me feel like a dog!

Figure 2.3

These three young girls have learned to use writing to help them figure out how their world works. They have learned to write in the summer and on school vacations. They don't write because writing is a school subject or because they receive a grade in writing on a report card. They write because they have learned that writing is one of life's pleasures.

Improving the Quality of Their Lives

If we do things right, if children take personal pleasure from writing and never associate it with punishment or failure, they will choose to write when they are adults. Not only will they write for personal pleasure, they will write to improve the quality of their lives. (See Chapter 3, "Discovering Real-World Reasons to Write.") We really are offering our families lifetime guarantees. We really are planting deep roots.

Holding on to Their Childhoods

I always encourage children to save every scrap of their writing, forever. "Someday," I suggest, "You'll be able to look back at these papers and remember who you were and what you thought about when you were very young. Writing will enable you to save and savor your childhood." (Of course there are many children living through unhappy childhoods. They too, however, deserve a chance to revisit their thoughts if they choose to.)

Someday, Kris will be grateful to look back on the piece of writing he did when he was ten, even though the history of the world has changed the look of Dubrovnik forever (see Figure 2.4). There's no doubt that Kris's piece qualifies as a family heirloom.

(See *Writing Through Childhood* for a fuller explanation of how children can capture their childhoods.)

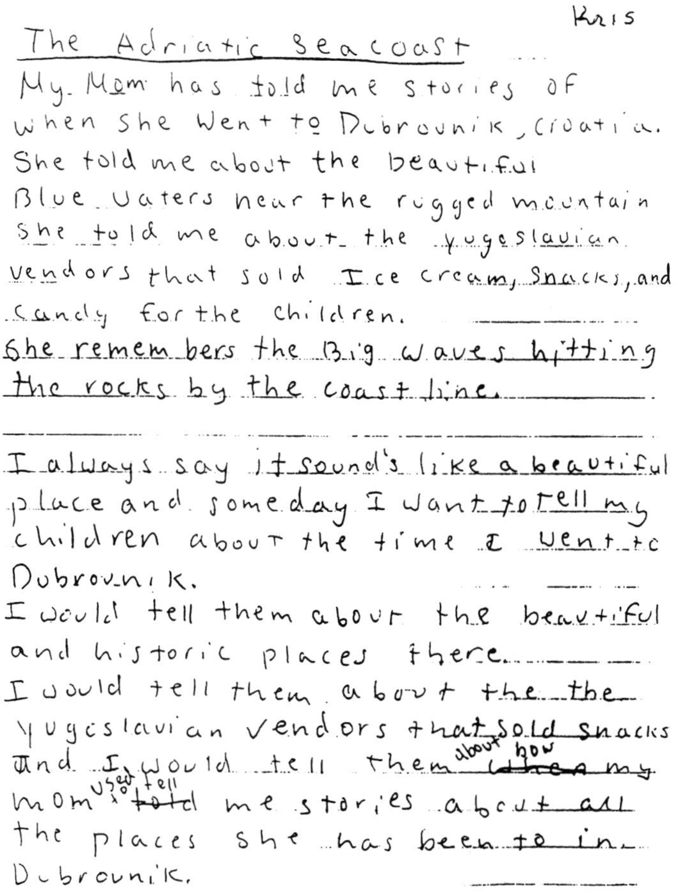

Kris

The Adriatic Seacoast

My Mom has told me stories of when she went to Dubrovnik, Croatia. She told me about the beautiful blue waters near the rugged mountain She told me about the yugeslavian vendors that sold Ice cream, Snacks, and Candy for the children.
She remembers the Big waves hitting the rocks by the coast line.

I always say it sound's like a beautiful place and someday I want to tell my children about the time I went to Dubrovnik.
I would tell them about the beautiful and historic places there.
I would tell them about the the yugeslavian vendors that sold snacks and I would tell them about how my mom used to tell me stories about all the places she has been to in Dubrovnik.

Figure 2.4

How the School Culture Can Support or Hinder the Teaching of Writing

Educators intent on improving the quality of literacy teaching in their schools probably need to begin by asking themselves if they can lead literate lives in their own schools. If the answer is no, those schools are probably not very easy places for children to lead literate lives. The adults in our school can take care of their own reading and writing for the very same reasons that our children learn to read and write so well. And the adults in our community *want* to lead literate lives. We don't pretend to like spinach and asparagus in order to get children to eat their vegetables. We really do love vegetables. So too, we don't pretend to care about reading and writing because we want to inspire children. Members of our school community really care about reading and writing and are growing as readers and writers because the culture of our school supports their efforts. (See Chapter 6, "Non-Negotiables in the Teaching of Reading.") Our community does this in numerous ways.

A Caring Social Tone

It's a lot easier to take your writing seriously when there exists a caring social tone. Writing is risky business. If children are going to poke fun at one another's attempts, students will not write. Young writers need unconditional respect to permeate the walls of their writing classrooms. (See *Going Public,* Chapter 4, "Making the Social Tone Top Priority.")

A Commitment to Using Time Wisely

It's also easier to take your writing seriously when a sufficient number of hours are devoted to the task. Students, just like adults, need big blocks of uninterrupted time to really make their writing the best it can be. You can't work in a whole language way if you never have your whole class together. The doors have to stop opening and closing during our writing workshops. Our students have abundant appointments to write, and we make sure they keep those appointments. The teachers on staff who write regularly do so on weekends, school holidays, and summer breaks because they too need big blocks of time for this important work.

Authentic Uses for Writing

When children write every day for considerable amounts of time, they are able to get their writing momentum going. Each day's work capitalizes on the preceding day's. When divorced people begin to date again, they often complain that they feel awkward because they haven't dated in such a long time. They've lost their stride as people who go out on dates. How much easier it is to feel comfortable on a date when dating is something you do regularly and with confidence. So too, when it comes to writing, people who write regularly begin to feel comfortable and confident. They therefore become more productive.

Our students also write well because their writing is put to authentic personal, school, and community uses. Our students don't write primarily for portfolios and bulletin boards. They write for people. They write to make a difference. They write to do good work in the world. (More on this in Chapter 3, "Discovering Real-World Reasons to Write.")

Access to Literature

Our love of literature and the abundance of texts we have on hand make it easy for children to apprentice themselves to fine writers. Students feel at home holding fine pieces of literature in their hands, rereading them, talking about what makes them effective, and attempting to do what their unknowing mentors have done. (See *Writing Through Childhood* for a full explanation of this reading/writing connection.)

A Deep Respect for Language

Writers love words, their sounds and their arrangements. When we paint the words *bano, bagno, toilette,* and *loo* on our restroom doors, we're not simply doing it to be clever. We know that writers are fascinated by the sounds and study of languages. When we label bouquets of flowers with their exact names, we're not simply teaching sight vocabulary. We know that writers need to know the precise names of things. The celebration and study of language—all languages—is central to our school's existence and to the growing of fine writers. (See more on this in Chapter 10, "Literacy and the Second Language Learner.")

A Love of Story

In *Going Public* I describe my pleasurable role as school troubadour. Knowing one another's stories changes relationships and improves the social tone in a school, but it can also be said that those stories become grist for the writer's mill. We care about stories from life because we've learned that writers need to put people on their pages. We listen for telling details, universal truths, and the way well-told stories make the ordinary seem extraordinary. We also care about swapping stories, because other people's stories help us realize that we have stories too. We learn that our own lives are worth writing about.

A Genuine Curiosity About the World

The children and the grown-ups in our school find the world a fascinating place. They are wide awake. They are genuinely curious. They find things interesting. They ask hard questions. They have an insatiable need to take it all in. And this kind of wide-awake stance is part of what it takes to be a good writer. Folks who have taken a long car ride with a chatty and alert preschooler know what it means to have an insatiable need to know. These young children are forever asking such questions as, Why are the stop signs always red? Why do all cars have four wheels? Why does grandma live in a different city? Why do the trees look different when we drive by quickly? We can tire of answering all their questions, but we must also bear in mind that it is this type of puzzling about the world that will work to their advantage when their teachers ask them to write. The challenge for educators is make sure that children keep on making those observations and asking those questions about the world.

I used to joke about why children have such short necks. The punch line was, "From all that shrugging of their shoulders." You ask what's important to children and they shrug their shoulders. If they're from New York City, they also mumble, "I dunno" while shrugging their shoulders. "What's on your mind?" "I dunno." "What are you thinking about?" "I dunno." "What are you learning?" "I dunno." Well, that joke wouldn't make any sense in our school. The children don't shrug their shoulders. They are not filled with "I dunno."

I read with interest Regie Routman's interview with Don Graves in the November 1995 issue of NCTE's *Language Arts* journal ("Donald Graves: Outstanding Educator in the Language Arts"). In it, Don compliments our school and the Center for Teaching and Learning. Don says, "In these schools, teachers are instinctively bringing kids in touch with the land. They are getting to know everything that's moving and breathing and living, where they are." Don has so eloquently described a teaching truth for us. In the last eight years, I have realized, from watching teachers who really care about young children and the quality of their writing and the quality of their lives, that we spend more time talking to children about paying attention to their world than we do about fixing up their drafts. We have discovered that when the first is in place, the second becomes much easier. This discovery has been big news for me, the kind of news that carries strong classroom implications.

Jennifer Clement's poem "Lemon Tree," appearing in Naomi Nye's collection *The Tree Is Older Than You Are,* speaks volumes as to the kind of rich, supportive, and stimulating setting we are trying to create for our young writers. She writes,

> If you climb a lemon tree
> feel the bark
> under your knees and feet,
> smell the white flowers,
> rub the leaves
> in your hands.
> Remember,
> the tree is older than you are
> and you might find stories
> in its branches.

We don't have lemon trees in New York City, but if we did, our students would be climbing them, feeling the bark, smelling the flowers, rubbing the leaves, and finding stories in their branches.

When children are encouraged and inspired to put all their senses to work when they walk down the streets of Manhattan, it's no surprise Judy Davis's eleven-year-olds are able to construct pieces like those in Figures 2.5 and 2.6.

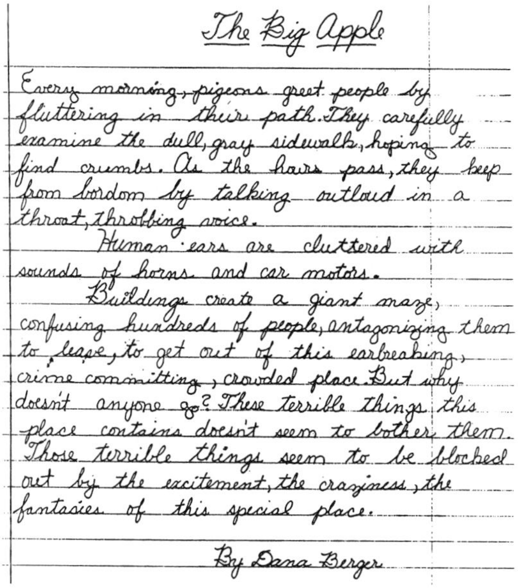

The Big Apple

Every morning, pigeons greet people by fluttering in their path. They carefully examine the dull, gray sidewalks, hoping to find crumbs. As the hours pass, they keep from bordom by talking outloud in a throat, throbbing voice.

Human ears are cluttered with sounds of horns and car motors.

Buildings create a giant maze, confusing hundreds of people, antagonizing them to leave, to get out of this earbreaking, crime committing, crowded place. But why doesn't anyone go? These terrible things this place contains doesn't seem to bother them. Those terrible things seem to be blocked out by the excitement, the craziness, the fantasies of this special place.

By Dana Berger

Figure 2.5

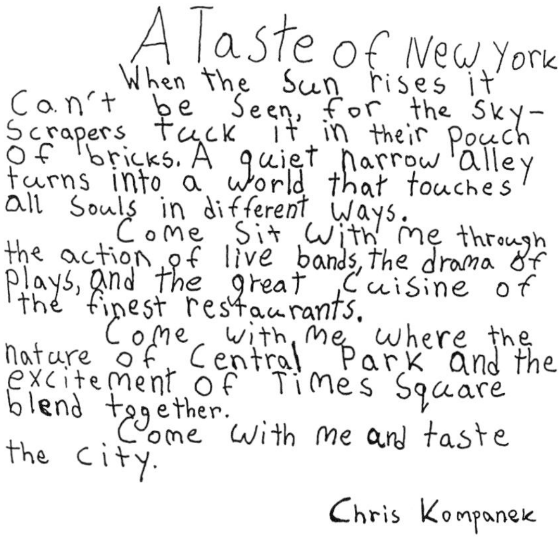

A Taste of New York

When the Sun rises it can't be seen, for the Sky-scrapers tuck it in their pouch of bricks. A quiet narrow alley turns into a world that touches all Souls in different ways.

Come sit with me through the action of live bands, the drama of plays, and the great cuisine of the finest restaurants.

Come with me where the nature of Central Park and the excitement of Times Square blend together.

Come with me and taste the city.

Chris Kompanek

Figure 2.6

A Passion for Good Writing

One year our students wrote pen-pal letters to the children at the Center for Teaching and Learning in Edgecombe, Maine. We knew our students' letters were going to be read by students who were working with such accomplished writers and teachers of writing as Nancie Atwell, Susan Stires, Donna Maxim, and Susan Benedict. You can be sure nothing was mailed until we served as final editors. We wanted those letters to be moving, memorable, and filled with voice. We wanted the punctuation, grammar, spelling, and handwriting to be worthy of applause as well. We raised our standards when we knew our work would be in the hands of people who really care about good writing. (See example of a student letter on p. 123.)

Our school, as well, is filled with people who care about good writing. Caring about good writing has become a way of life in our school. People talk about quality writing, share good writing, and attempt to do their own good writing. This kind of attention to quality can be contagious within a close-knit community. People are more than a bit self-conscious when colleagues read their writing. And this is as it should be.

As I walk around our school, there are signs everywhere that the grown-ups make a deliberate effort to write well. For example, a PTA request for goods for an upcoming flea market begins with a catchy lead. It reads,

Remember the candlesticks given to you by Great Aunt Mabel as a wedding present, the ones that have never been out of the box, or out of your closet? The Manhattan New School PTA is giving you an opportunity to dispose of these and other treasures, as well as a means to contribute to your child's school.

I always appreciate it when other people point me in the direction of good writing. One day Regina Chiou, a second-grade teacher, asked me, "Have you seen a copy of the poem Pat gave her children before the winter break?" I made sure to climb to the fifth floor, our penthouse, to see what she so admired. Pat's gift to her third graders read,

To My Class on This Winter Vacation

I wish you . . .
days of opening your eyes at 7:00 a.m. and then
closing them right up again,
a book so good you finish it in one day,
and then you find another one just as good,
time to take a walk in the park,
time to play Monopoly, or Boggle, or Clue, or anything
with your friends and family,
time to look in your math packet and maybe try one,
drawings you just have to share
and many moments you just must jot down in your notebook.

Thank you for filling my days with joy,
Love, Pat

I also took great delight one summer in receiving a postcard from a family that was traveling across the country (see Figure 2.7). The father, Sam Blank, did the actual composing of this note. I loved getting mail from a school family during the summer and I loved that the letter was filled with so many rich details of their trip. Most of all, I loved Sam's postscript. "How's my writing?" is a very telling question. I suppose all members of our community are just a little self-conscious about their writing, because they know the value we place on it.

One spring, when I noticed that many children were arriving late for school and families were lax in picking up their children on time at afternoon dismissal, I sent a note home that began as follows:

Dear families,

Somehow the beautiful sights of spring—parks filled with children, yellow daffodils in bloom, birds returning to city perches—always remind us to do some spring cleaning at home. The cluttered closets and overflowing drawers begin to gnaw at us, begging to be straightened up.

> *At school too, it feels like time to do some spring-cleaning. We've begun to redecorate our classrooms and hallways, hanging up fresh posters and poems, student art and writing. We've begun to rearrange furniture, reorganize files, and rethink school routines.*
>
> *And with the weather finally warming up, the school routines that are most on my mind are the arrival and dismissal procedures. Please pitch in with our spring-cleaning efforts and review the attached procedures with your children . . .*

If we expect students and teachers to care about the quality of their writing at school, administrators need to rethink those voiceless memos, the ones labeled "To: From: and Re:"—we, too, must catch the good-writing fever.

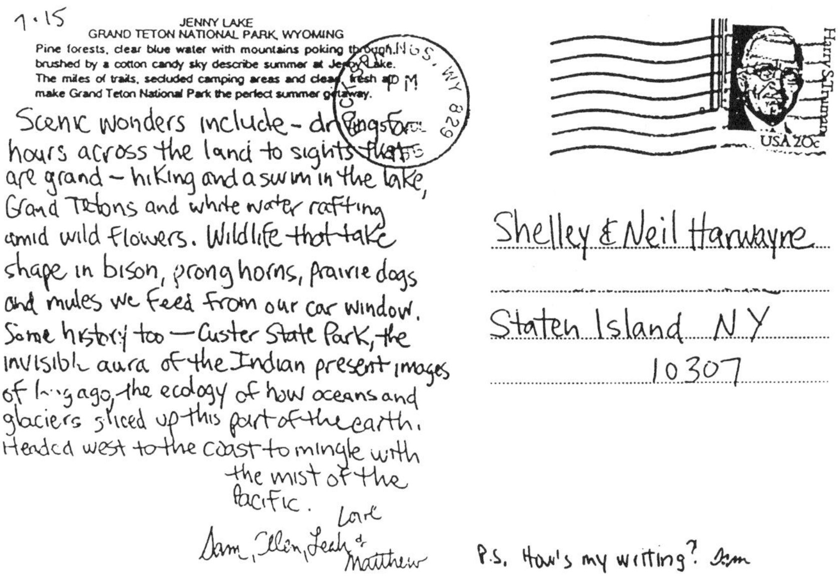
7·15

JENNY LAKE
GRAND TETON NATIONAL PARK, WYOMING
Pine forests, clear blue water with mountains poking through, brushed by a cotton candy sky describe summer at Jenny Lake. The miles of trails, secluded camping areas and clean, fresh air make Grand Teton National Park the perfect summer getaway.

Scenic wonders include – driving for hours across the land to sights that are grand – hiking and a swim in the lake, Grand Tetons and white water rafting amid wild flowers. Wildlife that take shape in bison, prong horns, prairie dogs and mules we feed from our car window. Some history too — Custer State Park, the invisible aura of the Indian present images of long ago, the ecology of how oceans and glaciers sliced up this part of the earth. Headed west to the coast to mingle with the mist of the Pacific.

Love
Sam, Ellen, Leah & Matthew

P.S. How's my writing? Sam

Shelley & Neil Harwayne
Staten Island NY
10307

Harry S Truman USA 20c

Figure 2.7

A Deep Respect for Childhood

A final ingredient that permeates the air we breathe at school is a deep respect for childhood. This element is so central to the teaching of writing that it serves as a fulcrum for the companion volume, *Writing Through Childhood.* There I strongly suggest that when teaching writing at the elementary-school level, we never forget that we are teaching children to write, and as such, we need to pay careful attention to our expectations, assignments, materials, teaching techniques, and even the language we use. People who have been on the planet fewer than ten years deserve special recognition and consideration. If we ran a cooking class for children, we would not ask them to prepare soufflés, crepes, or creme brûlée. Instead, we would probably begin a dessert course of study with fruit salad, sugar cookies, and ice-cream sodas. So too, in running a writing workshop for children we need to let the needs, interests, and gifts of childhood serve as the candle that lights our way.

Keeping the Teaching of Writing Simple: The Basics

We value simplicity in the teaching of writing. We try not to complicate our lives by continually inventing new and elaborate or more and more sophisticated routines, genres, ways of responding, or forms of publishing. The teaching of writing has always been one of the most joyful times during the school day and we aim to keep it that way. (I am determined that the current stress attached to the much dissected teaching of reading will not tarnish the teaching of writing. In fact, many teachers of reading would do well to return to their own confident selves and simplify their teaching of reading. More on this in Chapter 6, "Non-Negotiables in the Teaching of Reading.")

When we do try something new in the teaching of writing, it usually works to simplify our teaching and writing lives. We put our trust in creating calm, joyful settings with simple, clear routines. (Even though children read during the writing workshop and write during the reading workshop, Manhattan New School teachers still set aside clearly demarcated reading and writing workshops. This adds to the clarity and effectiveness of our teaching.) We get to know our children well and then we invite them to write. And as they write we get to know them even better. Our job is to listen, and when appropriate to laugh, hug, sigh, and then of course to teach. If we listen well, the children will show us what we need to teach. And that teaching can be done effectively and elegantly because the basics are in place. These basics are outlined below.

Accessible and Abundant Supplies and Materials

We spend our money wisely, teach children about the proper care of materials, and keep up with children's literature. Each classroom has a rich library feel and teachers have models of good writing in all appropriate genres at their fingertips. Each classroom is equipped with at least one up-to-date computer, many kinds of writing paper and writing instruments, overhead projectors in good repair, wipe-off boards and markers, staplers and staples, and bottles of correction fluid. Also available for schoolwide use are machines that duplicate, bind, and laminate. We even have a machine that enlarges text into poster-size presentations.

Clear and Effective Workshop Routines

Each teacher has the freedom to create his or her own workshop procedures. Many rely on traditional workshop components, but all have innovated and experimented with ways to streamline those routines to work best in individual classrooms. What cuts across all classrooms is that students know what is expected of them and fully understand how their writing workshops operate. There are no day-to-day surprises in class-room routines. Surprises only appear in students' writing. (See writing workshop structures beginning on p. 62.)

Supportive Schoolwide Structures and Beliefs

Our teachers take full advantage of their decision-making powers. For example, they are free to carve out a full hour each day for students to write. A few daily agendas appear below:

Isabel Beaton's (kindergarten)	**Paula Rogovin's (grade 1)**	**Sharon Taberski's (grade 2)**
Book Time	Research Workshop	Reading
Reading	Math Workshop	Meeting
Story Partner	Science	Reading
Physical Education	Reading	Writing
Morning Meeting	Writing Workshop	Lunch/Recess
Center Time	Lunch/Recess	Math
Handwriting	Meeting: Read-aloud	New York Study
Cleanup	Poetry	Cleanup
Lunch	Singing	Science
Story Time	Center Time	
Writing Workshop		
Show, Tell, and Teach		

Joanne Hindley's (grade 3)	**Sharon Hill's (grade 4)**	**Judy Davis's (grade 5)**
Meeting	Physical Educ.	Meeting:
Spelling	Read-aloud	Class Journal
Story Time	Writing	Words We Love
Writing	Reading	Read-Aloud
Story Time	Lunch	Shared Reading
Math	Social Studies	Independent Reading
Lunch/recess	Math	Word Study
Reading	Homework	Lunch
Science Research	Cleanup	Writing
Home	Dismissal	Math
		Social Studies

(For more detailed information on how the day runs in these classrooms see Joanne Hindley's *In the Company of Children;* Paula Rogovin's *Classroom Interviews: A World of Learning;* Sharon Taberski's *On Solid Ground,* and forthcoming books by Judy Davis and Sharon Hill.)

Teachers are also free to choose the genres they would like to teach as well as the amounts of time to devote to each. Our teachers are also relatively free of the obstacles that often prevent writing teachers from doing what they know best. (I say *relatively* free, because we do take part in all standardized assessments). For example, our school has no contradictory writing messages. We don't have edited pieces due in the principal's office every Friday. We don't assign writing as punishment and we don't mandate participation in every essay contest that arrives in the mail. (See additional information about how these basics support the writing teacher's ability to confer with students in *Writing Through Childhood.*

A Deep Understanding of the Writing Process Approach

All classroom teachers on staff have studied the writing process approach. They have attended summer institutes, taken graduate courses, read and responded to professional literature, and worked with expert colleagues. In addition, they keep up with research findings by taking advantage of our well-stocked professional library, attending conferences and other professional development opportunities, and making time to visit and learn from colleagues. Many conduct their own classroom-based studies as well.

Writing Workshop Structures: Innovations on Traditional Forms

As principal I have the wonderful opportunity to take part in many writing workshops. Although each workshop has been personalized by teachers who throughout the years have reinvented the writing hour, traditional workshop structures remain.

Minilessons

Our teachers have confidence in their teaching. They believe they have worthwhile information to share with students about a range of important topics. They never hesitate to offer guidance in such areas as the following:

- topic choice (strategies for discovering topics that matter)
- choice of genres (options available; ways to study specific genres)
- revision strategies (techniques for rethinking and reworking your writing)
- elements of quality work (close study of effective writing)
- ways of responding to one another's work (peer conferring; response group)
- management of the workshop (rules, routines, care of materials, editing)

- editing (specific skills)
- publishing (classroom procedures and options)

Our teachers also have flexibility in how they go about their teaching. Although they all value giving explicit information to their students through minilessons, they deliver that information in a variety of ways. Information about writing is presented in any or all of the following forms:

- five-to-fifteen-minute whole-group gatherings at the beginning of the writing workshop. (These are still the most typical minilessons, with teachers often displaying texts on the overhead projector to support their teaching.)
- direct teaching at the end of the writing workshop as children share their writing. (When students share their work in progress or their finished work, teachers are not afraid to highlight elements and make suggestions that would benefit the whole class.)
- information presented in the middle of the writing workshop. (As teachers work the room they are continually assessing students' needs. On occasion teachers stop the writing workshop in order to make a point or share a student breakthrough.)
- information gleaned from the literature students are reading during their reading workshop, which serves as a transition to the writing workshop. (At the end of the reading workshop, the teacher invites children to the meeting area. Her closing comments on the literature they are reading serves as the content of the writing workshop minilesson. This works most effectively when students are reading the same genres they are writing and when the reading workshop precedes the writing workshop.)
- responses to student literature assignments. For homework, students are asked to read literature selections and annotate them with respect to the quality of the writing. The traditional "checking homework" ritual that begins the schoolday serves as a minilesson for the writing workshop to follow.

Teachers not only offer writing lessons to their students in these varied ways, they also offer them with varied frequency. I have seen teachers who craft minilessons every day and those who limit this direct whole-group teaching to only a few times per week. What individualizes these lessons even more are the resources the teachers rely on to help design them. I have seen breathtaking minilessons in which teachers make use of any or all of the following:

- student writing (teachers display current student work on the overhead projector as well as share pieces from previous students. Both are done with permission, of course)

- their own adult writing
- stories from their own lives
- professional texts
- children's literature

(See *Writing Through Childhood* for detailed examples of minilessons.)

I have also seen teachers who ask guest speakers to present minilessons, including children from other classes and colleagues with specific areas of expertise. In addition, I have seen teachers who help accomplished writers in their own class take on the responsibility of teaching classmates the writing lessons they need to learn.

Although minilessons are as diverse as the teachers who conduct them, there are several elements that cut across these instructional times. These include:

- Content based on felt needs. (The teacher's choice of content is related to the work the children are doing or not doing.)
- Information explicitly presented. (This information is not elicited from the students but the workshop leader has more of a, "Here's what I know, I think it will help you," attitude.)
- Opportunities for children to interact with the information. (Children have opportunities to respond either in short discussion times immediately following the presentation of the information or when they leave the whole-group session to put the information to good use in their own writing.)

I have long thought that students should take turns recording minilessons in a class scrapbook. Literature excerpts and student writing could be mounted alongside student summaries of what was presented in the lesson. Imagine the value of having all that information available for students to revisit. Absent students could catch up. Teachers could refer to the content of past lessons as they conferred. Colleagues could dip into one another's treasure chest of teaching ideas. Then too, the collection would be a great source of data for the teacher interested in researching the power and effectiveness of her minilessons. Not to mention the inherent value of children being responsible for taking the kind of notes that would enable their classmates to remember important suggestions.

Writing Conferences

My favorite time to walk into a writing workshop is when children have left the meeting area and gone off to write and confer about their writing. Children are scattered throughout the room, seated at round oak tables or long rectangular ones (we have no desks in our school), gathered in the carpeted meeting area with clipboards, writing folders, or writer's notebooks in hand. (See *Writing Through Childhood,* chapter on "Rethinking Our Use of the Writer's Notebook," for a full explanation of this writing tool.) Some are huddled in the library area, referring to published books for help with their own work in progress. Others have spilled out into the corridors (with teacher's permission), seeking perhaps a quieter and more private spot to work on their writing. Most children use this time to simply write, although you can hear a soft hum of voices coming from those children who have chosen to confer with classmates, student teachers, or teachers. I can easily join in on the teaching, pulling up alongside a student to talk about the work in hand.

In each classroom, teachers have established their own way of organizing for conferences. Some remain in a stationery spot in the room, with a schedule of conferences posted. Others prefer to wander the room, stopping to confer and coach students in need. Many arrange for periods of small-group instruction during this workshop time, bringing together students with common needs. (For more detailed information on the content of conferences see *Writing Through Childhood*.)

Whole-Class Shares

Many writing workshops end with a time for a few students to share the work they accomplished during the period. Again, teachers have varied procedures as well as varied reasons for orchestrating these moments of sharing and responding to finished work as well as work in progress. Some teachers always end with a share meeting; others only announce them a few times a week. (Some intend to have them frequently but often lose track of time and must escort their children to gym, art, or lunch before anyone has shared. I try to see this as a good sign; children are getting lost in their writing! In these classrooms, the approximately fifteen-minute share time often takes place when children return to their classrooms after their visit to a specialist or the cafeteria. Perhaps the break even affords young writers a bit of distance on their writing.)

Some teachers select particular children to share because of breakthroughs they have made or struggles they are dealing with that apply to large numbers of children. Some welcome students to share, without any predetermined teaching goal in mind. They take a "come what may" stance to student sharing. Some encourage small-group sharing or buddy shares so that every child has an opportunity to participate and receive feedback each day. Others invent their own very unique ways of bringing closure to their writing workshops. Joanne Hindley Salch periodically invites children to read to a circle of classmates, with no hand-raising or responses allowed. This sacred time permits children to feel the power of their own words as well as the cumulative effect of many voices speaking on many topics, one right after the other. Yet other teachers invite informally trained parents, on a once-a-week basis, to host small-group shares so that every child is sure to share with an adult regularly.

Teachers arrange the kind of share meetings that best suit their purposes and ways of living in their classrooms. The same applies to their guidelines for student response to pieces read aloud. Some teachers take a very active role in share time, using their adult voices to add energy and focus to these sessions. Others take a backseat, trusting that children will find unique ways to help one another. (I can't resist being an active participant in share meetings. They provide so many teachable moments.) All the teachers I visit, however, make sure that these share meetings add up to meaningful instructional time. They make sure that this important component of the writing workshop provides a time for all children to learn, not just those whose turn it is to share.

The Signs of a Successful Workshop

When I visit writing workshops, I sense that they are going well when I see the following telltale signs:

- Children are writing for sustained amounts of time. They seem engrossed in their work.
- Unless there is a whole-class genre study taking place, there are many kinds of work in progress.
- There is a soft hum of voices. People are conscious of others at work.
- Children eagerly and proudly share their work with me or any visitor who might enter.
- Student writing is true to the spirit of childhood. (This point is explored in detail in the companion volume *Writing Through Childhood*.)
- Children can be spotted huddled together, sharing their work respectfully.
- Children are referring to literature during the writing workshop.
- Children understand the routines and are able to explain how their workshop runs.
- Children can retell the minilesson, if any has been taught that day, and they understand why the teacher chose to teach it.
- The teacher is hard to spot because her voice is soft and she's at eye level with her children. She's also engrossed in her work and doesn't look up when visitors enter.
- There are no long lines of children waiting to speak to the teacher, nor are there children interrupting her to ask for a conference, a stapler, or a spelling word.
- At the end of writing many children are eager to share, they encourage their classmates to share, and they listen and respond respectfully, not halfheartedly. There are no robotlike or auto-pilot responses to student work. (I have a particularly hard time when children ask a question of the author and don't really listen to the answer, or when they ask a limited number of set questions over and over again, regardless of the piece of writing.)

- The content of the teacher's minilessons and conferences indicate that he or she has realistic and clear goals in mind.
- The students understand the importance of editing and have the know-how required to edit their writing.
- The students have many options for frequent publishing.
- The quality of the students' writing is getting better all the time.

Toward a Writer's Bootcamp

The last point above, "The quality of the students' writing is getting better all the time," is an essential one. Children, just like adults, will lose interest in writing if they don't believe they are improving as writers. Good work inspires more good work. Everyone takes delight when their words move an audience. The quality of students' writing at the Manhattan New School is always improving because teachers are always re-examining their teaching practices. (See *Writing Through Childhood.*)

With all the basics in place, it's no surprise that my colleagues and I can spend time thinking about improving the quality of students' writing. One of our parents, Kate Manning, describes our school as a writer's bootcamp. A writer herself, Kate appreciates our rigorous writing workshops in which we are not afraid to suggest big challenges, insist on high-quality work, and even post due dates if necessary. In *Writing Through Childhood,* I explore the main ways my colleagues and I help students craft high-quality work. These teaching practices are summarized below:

- We help students lead more attentive and observant lives.
- We confer in honest and purposeful ways.
- We use carefully chosen literature (including our own writing) in wise ways.

(Although early-childhood teachers also rely on the above practices, working with kindergarten through second-grade students does offer some unique challenges. This topic is likewise explored in *Writing Through Childhood.*)

The information on the teaching of writing in the following chapters focuses on genres that seem most appropriate for elementary-age children. These include many forms of real-world writing, nonfiction, and poetry. Alastair Reid, in an article about Robert Graves in *The New Yorker* magazine, wrote, "His life and his writings so interact that they cannot be unraveled: writing was how he lived." I like to think that the writing in our school is likewise interwoven with the way we live our lives, the one influencing and informing the other. Writing is how we live. How we live and how that living informs the teaching of the genres listed above form the basis of the three upcoming chapters.

Related Readings in Companion Volumes

Going Public (Heinemann, 1999) is abbreviated as GP. *Writing Through Childhood* (Heinemann, forthcoming), is abbreviated as WC.

Understanding the importance of writing	**GP:** Ch. 2
Creating a caring social tone	**GP:** Ch. 4
Honoring childhood	**WC:** Ch. 1, Ch. 2
Creating a deep respect for language	**GP:** Ch. 4
Nurturing a love of story	**GP:** Ch. 2
Celebrating curiosity	**GP:** Ch. 7; **WC:** Ch. 3
Developing a passion for good writing	**GP:** Ch. 5; **WC:** Ch. 5
Carving out big blocks of time for writing	**GP:** Ch. 1, Ch. 6
Making reading/writing connections	**WC:** Ch. 5, Ch. 7
Keeping the teaching of writing simple	**WC:** Ch. 2, Ch. 6
Responding to student writing	**WC:** Ch. 4, Ch. 6
Creating effective minilessons	**WC:** Ch. 5; **WC:** Ch. 7
Taking a closer look at writer's notebooks	**WC:** Ch. 3
Crafting high-quality writing	**WC:** Ch. 3, Ch. 4, Ch. 5
Re-examining teaching practice	**WC:** Ch. 11

CHAPTER 3

DISCOVERING REAL-WORLD REASONS TO WRITE

Key Literacy Lessons

1. Writing improves the quality of life in a school and teaches the following lessons:
   - A safe environment leads to honest and emotional writing.
   - Writing for the school audience can change relationships.
   - Writing for the school audience produces a wide range of genres.
   - Readers appreciate writers with voice.
2. Real-world writing benefits the entire community by building morale, spreading energy, accomplishing real goals, providing many opportunities to excel, encouraging social and collaborative moments, tapping the resources of adults, instilling pride in the school, including second-language learners, and improving the quality of the work.
3. We must encourage students to take part in real-world writing.
4. Writing that is fed by the world feeds the world.

I've been reading in our local papers that more tourists have been coming to New York City lately because the quality of life here is on the rise. Some folks would attribute our gain in popularity to such things as the presence of more police officers on the streets, improvements in mass transportation, the reopening of the Children's Zoo in Central Park, the revitalization of the theater district, more sidewalk sweepers, and even etiquette training for taxicab drivers. These strategies have been offered as deliberate and concrete efforts designed to make our city a more welcoming and inviting place.

In the last eight years I have been asked to take part in many initiatives—reading, writing, math, and science being at the top of the list—but I've never been asked to participate in a quality-of-life initiative. I've often wondered what a full-scale, board-of-education-supported quality-of-life initiative in our schools would look like. I'd like to think that in some very real ways we have already begun one of our own.

There are many ways in which we have improved the quality of life in our school. Enter the main reception area and smell the fresh flowers, listen to the classical music, and taste the home-baked delicacies that frequently sit on the center table. Roam the halls and see the comfortable places to sit and chat, the framed art along the walls, and the carefully chosen books tastefully displayed. Peek into classrooms and spot the rocking chairs, the stained glass windows, the cushioned couches. Listen to the calm voices. Notice the absence of public-address announcements. Visit the restrooms and enjoy the framed posters and photographs, the baskets for paper towels, and the ceramic dishes filled with specialty soaps. All these little things do add to the quality of our school life, but through the years I have learned that there is yet another way to make life a little calmer, richer, and joyful. I learned this lesson from our first custodian, John D'Antonio; he taught it to me through his writing.

Lessons Learned About Everyday Writing

The lesson is quite simple: Writing improves the quality of life in a school. Of course, for many years I had been leading workshops, delivering keynotes, and writing chapters about providing children with real reasons to write, but here was a firsthand opportunity to put theory into practice, all-encompassing, long-term practice. In years past, I had not been living in the schools I had been talking about. I was merely a visitor, an itinerant staff developer, or a consultant about to catch the next flight out of town. Now I was being held responsible for the quality of life in a school. Now I had an opportunity to look at a school as a whole, over a long period of time. Now I had John D'Antonio leaving notes on my desk, taping reminders on my door, and slipping letters and stories into my mailbox. I had better days at school because of John's writing and he pushed me to wonder if other people in school had better days because their students, colleagues, and administrators had taken pen to paper. The following are big lessons we learned from John's bulging portfolio of notes:

- The gift of words can change relationships.
- A safe environment leads to honest and emotional writing.
- Writing for the school audience enriches the school.
- Writing for the school audience produces a wide range of genres.
- Readers appreciate writers with voice.

Each lesson is further explored below.

The Gift of Words Can Change Relationships

John reminded us how powerful the gift of words could be in a school community. John often paid tribute to people in the school by writing notes to them or about them. Whenever he did so, the note was shared at staff meetings, hung on the main office announcement board, or simply passed from one teacher to another. Children and parents alike heard about John's gracious gifts. I like to think that John started an important trend. Now children often write kind notes to one another and to their teachers. Family members write gracious letters to teachers. As principal, I write letters, observations, and even poems to honor teachers. Then too, teachers write notes and tributes to other staff members.

Pat Werner, our reading teacher, sent me this note soon after she was hired.

Dear Shelley,

This thanks has been sitting in my heart since you said over the phone, "Okay, so it's set then, you'll teach reading." You couldn't see the catch in my throat or the wet in my eyes, and I thought, surely I heard wrong. If you hadn't said it twice on the phone I would have known I'd heard wrong. It was what I wanted to hear and surely I put those words there.

Every morning I thank you for giving me this opportunity.
Every month I am thankful for book talks.
Every Wednesday afternoon I am thankful for teacher talk.
I am thankful for being surrounded by books, being asked to review books, being included
      in book conversations.
I am thankful for your teacher's open doors.
I am thankful for the quiet and the calm.
I am thankful for the diligent, yet joyful students.
I am thankful for your ever ready-ness to discuss
      reading, writing, teaching, books.
I am thankful for being surrounded by master teachers
      and being able to watch them work.
I am thankful for the opportunity to prove myself and
      the offers of support and tools.
I am thankful for your, "How did your day go?"
I am thankful for your deliberate words that create pictures in my head

> *and send me off with new ideas.*
> *I am thankful for you letting me know your books and their places.*
> *I am thankful for being included in the conversation.*
>
>
> *To be continued . . .*

Truly,

Pat Werner

A Safe Environment Leads to Honest and Emotional Writing

John stood over six feet tall, was a great fan of wrestling, could move furniture on his back, fix a teacher's flat tire, and repair the school's boiler. He also understood the value of writing from the heart. And when he shared his feelings about his work and his colleagues, he changed relationships on staff. People treated one another differently after receiving a note like the one shown in Figure 3.1, a thank-you note in response to an Elvis tie the staff gave him.

Shelley AND Staff,

Thank you very much for the beautiful tie! It is simply a teriffic gift. It is a gift I will cherish till the day I take my last breathe! My heart did flips when I saw it!! It dazzled me more than the day I got hit in the head with a ceiling fan!

I have to say it was very nicc working with all of you this year. you all influenced me in many ways Not only did you teach the children, but you also taught me many things, you all did such a profressional job, it motivated me to want to do a profressional job. But what really impressed me was the dedication to →

The children. The way things are in this day in age children need love and attention. you all were there for the children and that's why I'm proud to say I work with you people. You have earned my respect AND adhiration. I look foward to working with all of you in the future.

I must say I never meant to hurt or offend anyone. I only bust chops because where I come from its a way of telling people you like them.

IN any event have a great vacation. Be healthy AND happy.

with love, Respect, Adhiration

John

Figure 3.1

Writing for the School Audience Enriches the School

John always wrote with an audience in mind, and his audience was usually our school community. Of course, much of John's writing could be called "writing to get the business of living done"—the expected custodial reminders and requests. But he did so much more. One year, John wrote a personal narrative about an orphan child he befriended one Christmas when he was in the service, stationed in Europe. He titled the piece "Greatest Christmas of All" and spoke of being away from home, missing his family, and how a young child he met touched his heart and reminded him what Christmas was all about. John didn't tuck this piece into his desk drawer but shared it with the staff at holiday time.

Our children do the majority of their writing at school, but unless we announce it as a priority, they don't automatically write with the intention to use their writing as a way to enrich the life of the school. We, of course, can design ways to make this priority a reality.

Writing for the School Audience Produces a Wide Range of Genres

John wrote reminders, warnings, thank-you notes, requests, editorials, political commentaries, instructions, explanations, personal narratives, birthday messages, a picture book about the boiler room, and even a humorous excuse purportedly written by his mother. (It read, "Please excuse my son John the janitor this afternoon. He will be attending a janitor's meeting at P.S. 104. Sincerely, Mrs. Ann D'Antonio.) He also wrote the sentimental goodbye note shown in Figure 3.2 when he accepted a position in another school closer to home.

John sent separate farewell messages to the parents and to the students as well.

Readers Appreciate Writers with Voice

John chose his words very carefully, always staying true to his spirit. His writing is so filled with his voice that I can easily bring his image to mind when I look back at all the notes he sent me over the years. Often I find myself laughing out loud because his writing is as funny as his hallway banter. Once when my office radio mysteriously disappeared, John wrote the note in Figure 3.3 to accompany the gift of a new radio from John and his assistant James. He couldn't resist teasing me about the classical music that is always on in my office.

Then too, John's letters could also be filled with passionately serious statements. At one point our district was considering privatizing the custodial services. In other words, rather than hiring custodians through the current union procedures, the services would be contracted to outside private agencies. John sent me his response, shown in Figure 3.4, entitled "Feelings and Thoughts About Privatization."

John's presence in our school during those early formative years had a profound effect on our school. His words changed the social tone of the school. His words changed relationships. His words were infectious. He helped us to see that all of us, including the

From tne desk of :

JOHN D'ANTONIO
Custodian
Manhattan New School

Shelley + Staff,

I would like To Thank you all for making my stay at the M.N.S. a great experience. I have been very blessed AND fortunate to be in such great company!

I have learned great respect for what each and everyone of you perform on a daily basis. As shelley once told me, John, it's not what you do but more in the spirit it is done. In the name of our children, you have performed with excellence!!

To The Teaching staff, the ❖ true unsung

From the desk of :

JOHN D'ANTONIO
Custodian
Manhattan New School

heroes, you have all earned my admiration and respect. In these Times, you are not only Teachers but you are a "Second parent", friend, whatever void is called upon not only to teach, but help keep a child on The "right track". And may I Say you all have performed this Task with great love for our children, not half heartedly. The children of this school are very very fortunate. I thank you from my heart for Taking care of the people I love most, OUR CHILDREN!

To my Two assisiTianTS! I Thank

From the desk of :

JOHN D'ANTONIO
Custodian
Manhattan New School

You very much. I have received many compliments on the building. But To Say I deserve the credit is foolish. You are the Two gentlemen that deserve the credit. For it is your blood AND sweat that made this building what it is today. A custodian is only as good as his help. For the sake of the children I hope you keep up the great work!

Figure 3-2

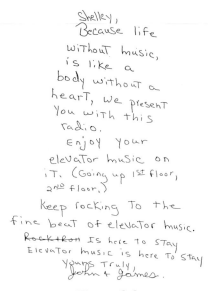

Shelley,
Because life
without music,
is like a
body without a
heart, we present
you with this
radio.
Enjoy your
elevator music on
it. (Going up 1ST floor,
2ND floor.)
Keep rocking to the
fine beat of elevator music.
Rock+roll is here to stay
Elevator music is here to stay
Yours Truly,
John + James.

Figure 3.3

THE MANHATTAN NEW SCHOOL 311 East 82 Street, New York, N.Y. 10028 (212) 734-

FEELINGS AND THOUGHTS FROM THE SLOP SINK
John D'Antonio, Custodial Engineer

Shelley,
on this piece of paper please find
one persons feelings about privatization.
As you read this article please note this
is the human side, not political side to
the story.
Building this building up is
much like bringing up a child to me.
Four years ago we (yourself, myself,
the teachers, James, Gonzalo) brought a child
into this world. Together we watched the
child learn how to crawl, then eventually
walk. We showed the child much love
and support. We became very proud of
the child and watched him/her become
very strong. The child became everything, we
lived for. Our hearts beat for this child.
Now I'm told, I may no longer
be a co-parent tho this child. I'll have
to look in from the outside. I feel like a
big part of my heart was taken away from
me. although I'm told "it's not personal"
my heart and mind tell me; it is personal!
Sincerely,
John

Figure 3.4

children, could be doing the kind of writing that he was doing. We discovered many ways that this kind of writing benefited the community, particularly the students in our community. In addition, our desire to invite students in on this wide world of writing options led to valuable thinking about the kind of instructional practice that would promote such real-world work. These two points are elaborated upon below.

Why Real-World Writing Benefits the Entire School Community

Several years ago I spoke at the Australian Reading Association in Melbourne. I suggested that literacy in the new millennium requires us to dream the impossible dream. I wrote, "We need to conjure up images of schoolhouses the world over, in which children, teachers, and parents are surrounded by quality texts, eager to put pen to paper, able to ask hard questions, and willing to listen to many voices. We need to create schools that are judged not by the students' scores on reading tests, but by the students' investment and delight in reading and writing for real-world reasons." I have conjured up an image of such a schoolhouse and of course it exists on East Eighty-second Street in Manhattan. When students do write for real-world reasons, the positive effects are evident.

Building Morale

What could be more uplifting than to read a letter from the local homeless shelter thanking our students for all their holiday greetings? Or to see kindergarten children chorally reading poems written for them by fifth graders? Or to see third graders help reunite a wayward cat with its owner, by plastering detailed descriptions of the cat all over the neighborhood?

When childrens' words go out into the school community to do good work, everyone is reminded how lucky we are to be together. Teachers are reminded just how important their chosen profession is and students are reminded that the work they do is real and valuable.

Spreading Energy

It's not enough for students' work to merely fill folders and portfolios. We run the risk of students becoming bored with writing. Years ago, when students seemed to be losing interest in writing, I used to think about small ways to add energy to the writing workshops. I spoke of changing the tools, inviting guest speakers, or having a publishing party. These strategies may be temporarily helpful, but the most long-lasting way to add energy to a writing workshop is to ensure that students know how to send their work out into the world of the school, their families, or to the wider community. There is nothing like getting real-world feedback or payoff to inspire students to keep on writing. When Josh and Thiago send a note to the president and get a response on White House stationery, you can be sure many other children would like to do the same. When Dominique wins the grand prize for her essay about New York City, you can be sure many students want to enter other contests. When Nicole's list of complaints about the condition of the restrooms is read at a student council meeting and actions to improve the restrooms result, you can be sure that Nicole and her classmates will continue to use writing to improve the quality of their lives.

Accomplishing Real Goals

It is a fifth-grade rite of passage in our school to allow our seniors to go out to lunch on Fridays. With parent permission and a few dollars in their pockets, our students go to the local pizzeria, Chinese restaurant, Greek diner, or bagel shop. Members of the staff often eat in the same restaurants at the same time. We're then able to observe the appropriateness of our students' behavior, including the tip they leave for the waitresses that serve these often lively clusters of children. Our fifth graders know how to leave a 15 percent tip.

There is no finer way for mathematics teachers to help students understand percentages and value mental math abilities than to enable the students to eat in a real restaurant and put their mathematics abilities to real-world use. The same line of thinking applies to the teaching of writing.

Yetta Goodman reminds us that we are not preparing children for citizenship "someday"; the time is now. Rex Brown reminds us that "another reason we don't get the educational results we want is that we've been mistaking means for ends. We've been teaching kids all about the hammer and nothing about how to build with hammers." Our students understand what writing is for. Our teachers understand that students' attempts at real-world writing demand follow-through. They know that student letters must be mailed, petitions signed, and poems performed. This kind of stance toward student work is not like watching five-year-olds put on tuxedos and gowns in the dramatic play corner of kindergarten. It is not pretend, fantasy, acting-grown-up work. It is real. It demands results. Because they write, our students know that their problems get solved, their causes get attention, their viewpoints get aired, their opinions get counted, their information gets shared, and their lives become richer.

Providing Opportunities to Be Excellent

Years ago, I worked in the black townships of South Africa, inviting students to tell the stories of their lives. The writing was incredibly moving and powerful. The students had important stories to tell and were grateful to have been asked. It pains me to think about the many generations of South African students who never had an opportunity to develop their full potential to become poets, dramatists, journalists, or novelists. Jacques d'Amboise and the National Dance Institute has been working with our fourth graders for the last four years. Some Friday mornings when I watch the children and Tracy, their instructor, at work, I can't bare to think about the children who graduated before this powerful program entered our lives. Who among those early graduates might have been an incredible dancer? It likewise pains me to realize that I'll never know.

I learned a long time ago that children need lots of ways to shine in a writing workshop. If all children are ever asked to do is craft personal narratives, we may never discover who the talented poets, journalists, or dramatists are. So too, unless children are invited to write for a wide range of real-world reasons, we may never discover the children who are very effective at using writing to get the business of living done. In South Africa, I not only invited students to tell the story of their lives, I also encouraged students to write the speeches, letters, and news articles that would improve the quality of their lives.

We must ever be on the lookout for children who invent their own formats for writing. One day when I entered my office there was a large, colorful, two-sided drawing of an alien on my desk. On the front side of the creature appeared the words "Come In." On the back were the words "Don't Come In." Several third graders in Joanne Hindley Salch's class had created it and left an explanatory note on my desk (see Figure 3.5).

Joanne creates the kind of classroom in which children feel safe to invent new genres. She then encourages and supports students' efforts to produce high-quality work.

Laura, another student in Joanne's class, proudly shared the summary of musicals that appears in Figure 3.6. This third grader decided to write a brief synopsis and critique

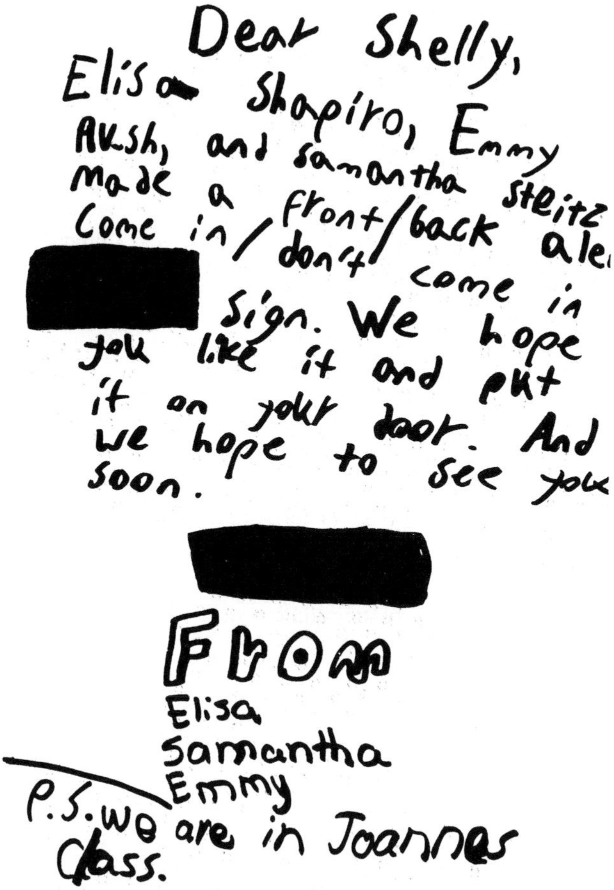

Figure 3.5

Musicals.

Have you ever seen a musical? I've seen 15. I liked most, hated some, in between for the rest. [For an opinion,you have to see one!] So,read this,see one,tell me what you think! See you coming out of the theater!|I hope!|

Ones playing now|from this list|

_____

BIG.
Grease.
CATS.
Guys and Dolls.
Beauty and the Beast.

_____

Beauty and the Beast:Taken from a movie,the view of the show <u>and</u> people changed a little.i.e. They added songs and in the fighting seans,used fake blood.   Moral: be kind.

_____

Bye-bye Berdie: Good story.Bad Elvis immatation.After all,Elvis Presaly and Conread Birdie are 2 different people!   Moral:don't cheat your steady.

_____

BIG:Great music! Great acting! Great backdrops! Great Giganticness!Great musical![Great intermission!][HaHa!]Listen,you may have seen a good musical but BIG was great! Moral:Your age is enough!

_____

CATS:jelickle cats, to be exact.Anyway.There was no plot! Moral:Memory

_____

.Fiddler on the roof:Songs,okay.Plot,okay.Acting,okay.Moral:Free choice.

_____

Guys and Dolls:Listen,have you ever gambeled?If so,you'll like this better.There was a good plot,good music and good acting. Moral:Love through difference

_____

Grease:First,the movie version.Favorite song:Your the one that I want. The movie had more action than the play.The seane of s-e-x was desugsting![There were no naked people,even so.]Now for the play. There was no s-e-x in this one.[The people proboly didn't want to do it in public.] Moral:Doesn't matter how you look,only whats inside.

_____

Godspell:OK,guys this is realy,truely,strait out of the <u>Bible</u>.It has the whole <u>Bible</u> story here! Moral:The Moral Of The <u>Bible</u>.

_____

Into The Woods:<u>Someone</u> has been fooling with our fairy tales,folks.Well,It is weird!After all,have you ever heard of the Baker who was friends with Jack?Or his Wife,who got killed by the giant that Jack Killed's wife?Neither had I before this!Moral:Your life is hardenough!_____

_____

So,how aout taking your dad to Grease?Or your mom to BIG?Or your friend to CATS...

Figure 3-6

of all the Broadway musicals she had seen. Laura certainly writes with voice, honesty, and awareness of audience. Perhaps we should send this piece to the New York City Tourist and Visitors Bureau.

Encouraging Social and Collaborative Moments

When writing is done for real-world purposes and audiences, the writing often takes on a social dynamic. When students write picture books to be read by the kindergartners, poems to be performed by first graders, or original lullabies to be sung by parents to their children, the work in progress usually demands personal response in order to meet the need of the targeted audience. Then too, the finished work is often shared in social, celebratory gatherings. When children are doing the kind of writing that gets the business of living done (letters, petitions, signs, surveys, et cetera), these kinds of writings often have a social component. Sometimes students huddle together to collaborate on the piece of writing. They meet to negotiate, listen to one another's opinions, seek clarification, prepare a draft, get feedback, and revise their work. Even if a child is working independently and individually on a piece of functional writing, once sent out into the world, the student hopefully receives responses from a wide range of people, not just the students in his or her classroom. Real-world writing demands real-world response.

Tapping the Resources of Adults

When students' choice of writing formats goes beyond personal narratives and includes a very wide range of possibilities, including those that many people do in their everyday lives, our pool of mentors grows by leaps and bounds. Teachers, school aides, security guards, custodians, secretaries, kitchen workers, nurses, and parents with hundreds of occupations, perform very different kinds of writing tasks. Students who choose to write letters of request, plans for a party, inventories of their collections, or toasts for their parents' anniversary can turn to many adult conference partners. Teachers are not the only folks in a school who can help young writers.

(In addition, when members of the adult community share their writing interests, we discover who takes their own poetry, short story, or nonfiction writing seriously. The kitchen worker who writes menus, recipes, and food orders all day may also be a writer of poetry at night. The secretary who types letters, surveys, and purchase orders may have a novel tucked away in her bureau drawer at home. The mother who tucks notes into her kindergartner's lunchbox may also be an accomplished journalist. In other words, the nonpedagogical staff might be a rich resource for all kinds of student work.)

Instilling Pride in the School

Our fifth graders have read Sandra Cisneros short story "Eleven." They understand that when you are eleven you are still ten, nine, eight, seven, six, five, four, three, two, and one. When Kate, a ten-year-old in Judy's fifth-grade class, shows me her latest piece of writing, she wouldn't be surprised to hear me ask, "Have you shown it to Pam, Paula, Regina, Kevin, and Sungho?"—all her teachers in past grades. Of course, previous teachers take pride in former students' accomplishments, but I'd like to believe that all of the teachers, along with all of the students and parents in our school, take pride in any one student's accomplishments.

As a school community we are always designing additional ways for the work of students to be valued throughout the building. We must. A school that expects students' writing to do good work in the life of the school community requires many forums for people to appreciate student work. You can expect to hear student work being performed, posted in public places, sent to community readers, and reprinted in school publications. Not only do students receive feedback from wide audiences, they are once again reminded that they belong to a school, not just a class.

Including Second-Language Learners

Because our community is a multilingual one, we are always searching for ways to make sure that the student who is just beginning to learn English is able to take part in all aspects of school life (see Chapter 10). Occasionally our older students begin writing in their first language and their bilingual classmates serve as translators, but fairly soon after they arrive in our school, students who speak English as a second language begin writing lists, labels, and letters. They are frequently seen labeling hallway displays, creating purposeful signs, composing invitations for school events, writing captions for family photo albums, crafting bilingual dictionaries, creating titles for works of art, and so on. These kinds of writing are particularly helpful for the child learning a new language because they are so wedded to context and so clearly attached to visual supports. In addition, the real-world feedback they receive encourages them to keep putting their language learning to real uses.

Improving the Quality of the Work

Jennifer, a second-grade teacher in her first year of teaching, asked me about the possibility of introducing writer's notebooks to her seven-year-olds. When I asked her why she was interested in this tool, which I usually consider to be for older students (see *Writing Through Childhood*), she talked about her desire to raise the quality of the students' work. When I visited her workshop to further understand her thinking, I appreciated her desire but suggested she postpone the writer's notebook and instead focus more on the purposes and audiences of her second-grade writers. When children have real reasons to write, the quality of their writing improves. For example, the young child who starts to create an original alphabet book and begins to lose interest at around the letters *J, K,* and *L,* will no doubt become more invested knowing the kindergarten teacher will be adding the text to her alphabet book collection. The second grader who is writing about the leeches she found on some box turtles will work more rigorously and carefully if she knows that the piece will be used by the science teacher to begin a conversation about interdependency among life forms. The child who is writing a book entitled "How to Make Coffee" will double-check his information as well as his punctuation if he knows that his instructions will hang alongside the staff room coffeemaker. (By the way, the first two pages in six-year-old Miles's instructions read, "Get money from the cash machine. Then you go buy the coffee at the store.")

There are many ways to lift the quality of student work including the wise use of wonderful literature as well as the importance of helping students lead attentive and observant lives. These are presented in detail in *Writing Through Childhood.* There, I note that writing improves when students pay attention to their world and have ways to discover topics they are committed to. I also suggest, in the section on conferring, that students need to understand what writing is for. Student writing will improve when students have answers to such questions as, "Where in the real world does this piece belong?" and "How can this piece improve the quality of our lives at school or our lives at home?"

I always hope that the pieces of writing I see in students' portfolios are copies, because the originals have been sent out into the real world. Students shouldn't be writing to fill portfolios, but for all the reasons that you and I write. Students will understand the need to do their best work when the work they do makes a difference in their lives and in the lives of people they care about.

Encouraging Students to Take Part in Real-World Writing

The phrase *real-world writing* refers to more than just the kind of writing that gets the business of living done, like toasts, speeches, letters, surveys, and signs. I'm also referring to the ways students' poetry, nonfiction, and personal narratives can do good work in the world. When we intend for student writing to find authentic audiences and receive real-world feedback, we necessarily have to think about all aspects of the writing workshop, from its launch on the first day of kindergarten straight through to graduation day some six years later.

Launch Writing Workshops Toward Purpose and Audience

I'd like to think that if you stopped any student in our school and asked him why he writes, his answer would have something to do with the power of words. Our students know that their words can serve many purposes. They can inform classmates. They can entertain kindergartners. They can persuade kitchen workers. They can make requests of custodians. They can keep in touch with friends who have moved. Their words can become gifts for friends and family members. Their words can provide personal and private solace.

Our students understand the reasons people write because on the very first day they enter our school, we demonstrate the wide range of reasons people write. (See *Writing Through Childhood,* chapter on "Working with Our Youngest Writers," in the section on "Launching in the Primary Classroom.") Students need to hear this message more than on their first day of kindergarten. Each and every year, we need to begin our writing workshop by reminding students that they are not writing for grades on report cards or to fill a portfolio. Instead, they need to realize that we ask them to write because their writing can do good work in the world. I might even launch a class of older students by asking them to list their most memorable pieces of writing. Then I would ask, "Where are those pieces today?" I would hope that many of those texts are shelved in classroom library collections, enlarged on oak tag to be used as shared reading material in lower-grade classrooms, permanently bound in school anthologies, published in magazines and newspapers, framed and hung in their grandparents' homes, kept in a special box reserved for family treasures, mailed to family members in other cities, and so on.

Surround Students with Mentors

Many years ago, in my early days of teaching, scratch-and-sniff books became very popular. Young children loved scraping those aromatic swatches of paper and smelling the chocolate cookies or apple pies baked by the children in the story. It shouldn't have surprised me to find, tucked into student writing folders, bags of ground cinnamon or pine needles hidden in tiny homemade envelopes. The students were attempting to create their own fragrant picture books. The same held true with pop-up books. I'd frequently find students folding little accordion-shaped papers to make their characters spring to life when the pages of their books were turned. Most young writers will write with the image of what impresses them in mind. Our job, of course, is to make sure that what impresses them includes a wide range of writing.

Principal as Activist/Mentor   One of my New Year's resolutions last year was to become more vocal about issues of concern. In other words, I was going to find the time to write letters about community issues that really tick me off. One Saturday morning I whipped off two very strong letters of complaint. The first was to the management of my apartment building expressing outrage at the tenants who allow their dogs to urinate right in front of the building in the early morning. I got tired of jumping puddles at 6:30 A.M. The second was to the New York City Transit Authority describing an unsafe bus driver who, besides driving too slowly in the express lane, drank a soft drink while he drove and read at every red light. Now, I lead a pro-reader life, but this driver didn't stop reading when the lights turned green! As a true New Yorker, I have a very low tolerance for sitting in traffic unnecessarily, especially with an unconcerned driver. Not only did I inform our older students about the letters I had written but I made sure to share the responses I received. Students need to see how powerful writing can be. (See "Take a Deliberate Stance Toward Raising Activists," p. 95.)

Teachers as Mentors   Teachers can also become part of the mentor pool. Our students need to know that Michael Miller, our popular physical education instructor, composed a touching eulogy for his grandmother's funeral, which included a childhood image of his grandparents holding hands as they slept. And they need to know that our bilingual learning disabilities teacher, Drina Saldias-Rigau, wrote a letter to the editor of *The New York Times* about one of our students who bravely and politely asked a passenger not to smoke in the subway because she was polluting our planet Earth and harming her own health and others'.

Every minute we are at work has the potential for demonstration. Joanne Hindley Salch becomes quite the activist when neighborhood residents park their cars in the few spots reserved for teachers in front of our school. Her students read the signs that she plasters on the windshields of those cars. So too, when teachers empty the paper tray in the duplicating machine and don't refill it or empty the roll of toilet tissue in the restroom and don't replace it, Joanne's students read the strong yet collegial notes that Joanne posts.

Sharing Posted Material with Students   Over the years, I have seen teachers frequently share with their students texts that have been posted on a bulletin board in the main office. The following words, written by parents, visitors, and teachers became a resource for writing workshop minilessons.

Tamara Nikolic was an assistant in our science workshop. She was an immigrant from the former Yugoslavia whose two daughters were enrolled in our school. On every payday, she left sweet treats for the staff members and when she left to help her husband open a bakery, she wrote a poem as a thank you. She prefaced the poem with the following words: "Your school gave me comfort and love when I needed it the most. It is very hard being in a new country. Thank you again."

Sound of Harp

A darkness of a night,
Like a womb,
Warm and protective
Covers me.
I start remembering.

Floating in the universe of light,
My memory healed
Its wounds.
Projections of eternity
Dismembered the pain.
Throughout all of life's holocausts,
I heard the most sensitive,
The most delicate,
Godlike sound
Of harp.

Revolving through my dreams,
Its sound rings

And leads me ahead.
Sudden bright light,
A sharp sound,
I cry.

And I am with new friends,
New school, new places, New York.
But the ever present, everlasting
Is this sound in me.

The same beautiful,
Godlike sound
Of harp.

Roberta Pantel Rhodes, our resource room teacher as well as the chapter chairperson of the teachers' union in our school, wrote the following poem in tribute to our school community. I hope many teachers lifted it off the wall and copied it to share with their budding young poets.

Last Day of School

On the last day of school,
pink, yellow and white flowers
with streaming ribbons flutter
in the wind.

Like Nureyev admirers, mothers
hurl bouquets at
teachers' feet.

Words swim in their children's heads,
poems burst forth from their
sons and daughters.

Bravo, bravo!

How many weeks until
the first day of school?

Several years ago, after returning from leading writing workshops in the black townships of South Africa, I delivered several speeches about my teaching and learning in such a complex and controversial country. I commented on what was called "praise poetry," verse written to be performed in tribute to people at funerals, rallies, and other celebrations. Roberta has written a praise poem in tribute to her colleagues, their students, and their families. So too, young writers can be invited to write their own praise poems, to be performed at special occasions. All that our children need are the right mentors to inspire and inform the work they do. (See "Ode to Two-0-Six," p. 103.)

Visitors as Mentors   Over the years we have received many memorable notes from visitors, and we always hang them on the front-office board so that all members of the staff can appreciate our visitors' comments. The response we received from Karen Ernst, author of *A Teacher's Sketch Journal* and *Picturing Learning,* however, was impossible to hang. Throughout her visit to our school, Karen filled her sketch journal with drawings and words. When she returned home, she beautifully duplicated, mounted, annotated, laminated, and bound the pages of her journal and sent them to us as a means of helping us understand what she had learned from her visit. The book couldn't be appreciated with just a quick glance. Oh no, teachers needed time with this incredible work. They needed time to take the book home, read it leisurely, and marvel at the power of Karen's art and insights. And then they needed time to share the book with their students. Karen unknowingly became a mentor for our students as well as our teachers. All of us now think about giving feedback to colleagues and classmates in new and powerful ways. (I wondered about the possibility of preparing observations of untenured teachers with annotated sketchbook pages. What a wonderful way to breathe new life into this required task.) Karen's sketch journal taught us all about paying attention to details, about reflection and imagination, about taking pride in your work, the importance of presentation, and the power of a really beautiful work of art.

Parents as Mentors   I have seen teachers elevate parents' writing in order to inspire students to write for new audiences and reasons. Pam let her entire kindergarten class know about the notes Kate's mom leaves in her lunchbox each day. She asks, "Are there people who would love to receive a little surprise note from you each day? Where would you leave them? What would you write about?"

Bari's dad writes tooth fairy letters, getting totally absorbed in the persona of this imaginary character. Jessica's mom writes an annual holiday letter summarizing the year's happenings for family and friends. Matthew's mom writes a news flier for the PTA. Teachers can introduce all these kinds of writing, or better yet all these writers can serve as guest speakers during writing workshops, explaining their process, products, and reasons for working so hard.

Our older students were particularly interested in the following letter sent home by two mothers who were appalled at the energy with which some of our students played with water guns during a street fair.

Dear MNS Parents,

In response to the recent tragic events at high schools around the country, a group of parents are forming around the issue of encouraging better understanding of the use of guns and issues of nonviolent conflict-resolution in our children.

> *At the school picnic on June 17th, we would like to offer the children of MNS an alternative to toys that resemble guns. A collection has been taken up to purchase water squirters in the forms of animals or plant sprayers to replace the popular assault-style water guns currently on the market. The children will be presented with the option to play with these or even water balloons. Our intention is simply to reduce the association of play objects with objects similar to those used to inflict bodily injury and death. Please encourage your child not to bring such "toys" to the school picnic . . .*

Persuaded to swap their water guns for more peaceful squirters, many children left the picnic with small plastic dolphins and elephants in bold neon colors.

Students as Mentors   When students become impressed with the power of sending words into the world, they will write for their own authentic reasons. And when they do, we need to highlight their literate activism. When students write a protest letter to the cooks in the school cafeteria kindly suggesting that meatloaf surprise and sloppy joes are a bit too surprising and too sloppy, and the cafeteria workers respond with a school survey about likes and dislikes, this sequence of events needs to be highlighted at class meetings.

When Angelina sent me a carefully documented letter of protest about an inappropriate bus driver (see Figure 3.7), I took her complaint seriously, investigated the sit-

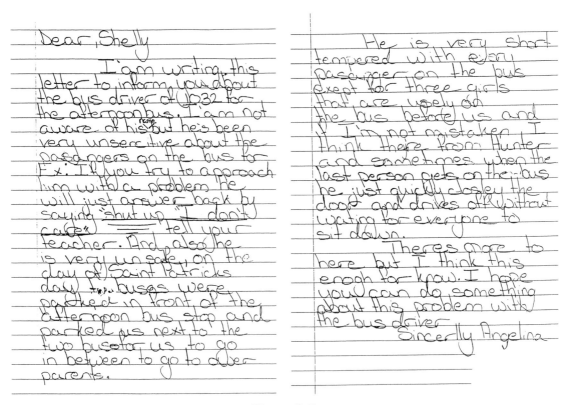

Figure 3.7

uation, and contacted the appropriate agencies. I let Angelina's peers know how effective her specific details and straightforward and thorough style were. She then became a mentor for her classmates. A writer who needs to work on homophones, standard spelling, and proofreading, Angelina is nevertheless apt to be an eager learner, since she has grasped the understanding that writing can be a powerful communicative tool.

Establish Writing as a Way of Life

Writing is a way of life in our school, an almost automatic response to practically every occasion. Students are encouraged to write, throughout the school day, for the same various reasons you and I write. When children tell their teacher they have changed their afternoon travel plans, the teacher is most likely to say, "Have you sent a note down to the office?" When a student requests adding a computer software order to the class's monthly book orders, it's no surprise the teacher responds, "Can you write a note explaining this new order form to families?" When a child is worried she will forget to bring a snack when her turn rolls around, the teacher is likely to suggest the first grader write a reminder note. When a student complains about a broken hook in the classroom clothes closet, it's no surprise that she is asked to put her request in writing and leave it in the custodian's mailbox. Our students quickly learn that writing is a tool that helps you get things done.

It comes as no surprise then that children begin to write on their own without teacher prompting. When kindergartners are sent to borrow snacks from another class and the five-year-olds find a box of cheese crackers in an empty room, they know to leave a note. When second grader Mark is frustrated with how his soccer career is going he sends a "retirement" announcement to our physical education instructor. When fourth grader Lindsay wants her class to view *All My Children,* a soap opera in which she is appearing, she leaves a letter of request on my desk. When second grader Sam doesn't know which restroom the boys on the fourth floor are to use, he automatically sends me a note, complete with check-off boxes for my response (see Figure 3.8).

There is an extra bonus to all this real-world writing. When children use their writing for real purposes, they understand why they need to edit their work. They become serious about checking their spelling, punctuation, and grammar and even using their best handwriting.

Over the last seven years, I have kept all the children's letters in scrapbooks. They make for some wonderfully entertaining and nostalgic reading. Someday I should probably categorize their contents. I could imagine creating separate sections for requests, complaints, "love letters," birthday and holiday greetings, tributes, reminders, and one entitled "Writing Our Wrongs," filled with all the letters containing explanations, apologies, and promises to never repeat wrongful acts.

The latter is the kind of writing we ask children to do when they have forgotten about gracious living and the need to resolve conflicts in a just and peaceful way. Classroom misbehavior is relatively rare, but bus rides and lunchroom and playground times

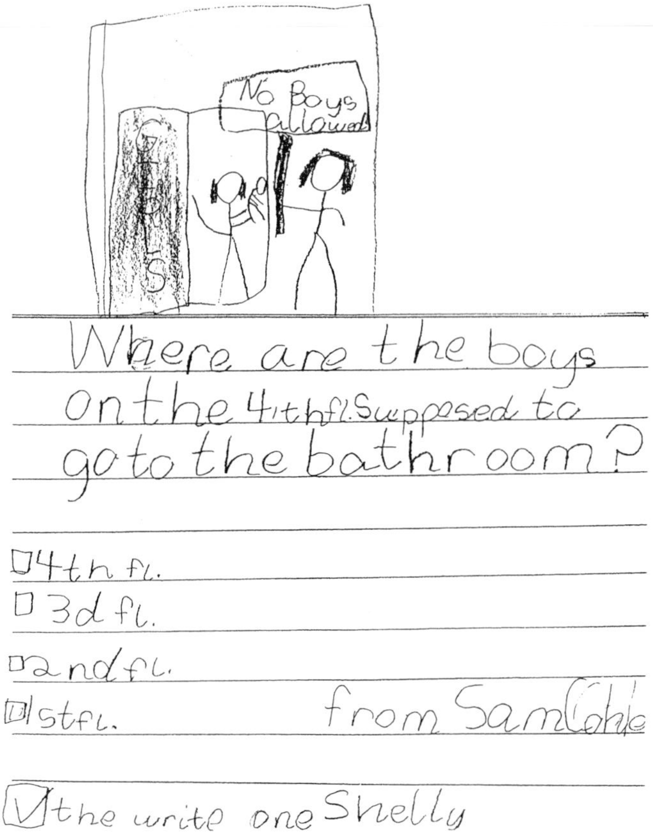

Figure 3.8

seem to bring out the feistiness, daring, and mischief we could easily live without. There have been times when I wished I could dramatically whip out a cellular phone, just for the effect, and announce to the rascal in front of me, "I'm calling your mother!" More times than not, my first response is to ask children to cool off by writing an explanation of what went wrong. (See Figure 3.9 for one such explanation, written by a second grader.)

Last year, my mother had to go into the hospital for surgery. When the orderly was wheeling her out of the room I heard him ask her, "What are you here for?" When she told him she was having her gallbladder removed, he responded, "Oh, that's just a misdemeanor." As it turns out, her surgery was complicated, much more than a misdemeanor. So too, children's moments of misbehavior are often just their own childhood "misdemeanors," but we do need to take them seriously. We never know when they might be attached to much more complicated issues. Asking children to write the story of the incident that prompted their misbehavior helps us to get a handle on the child's motives, feelings, and reactions.

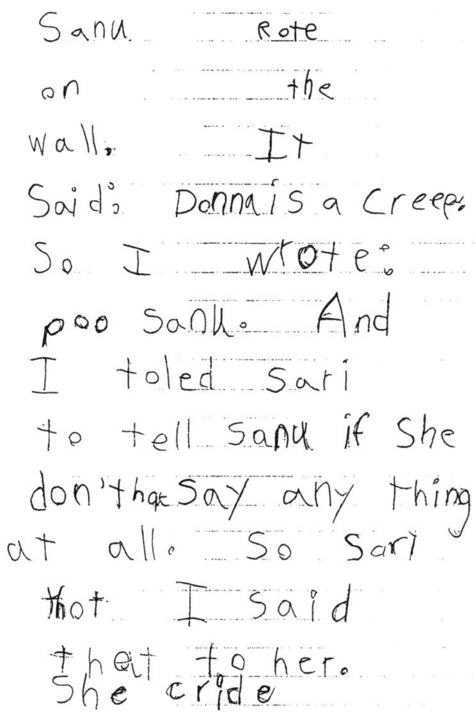

> Sanu Rote
> on the
> wall. It
> Said: Donna is a creep.
> So I wrote:
> poo Sanu. And
> I toled Sari
> to tell Sanu if She
> don't hae Say any thing
> at all. So Sari
> thot I said
> that to her.
> She cride

Figure 3.9

Although this kind of explanatory writing is valuable, I much prefer looking back over the writing that suggests more positive school moments. For example, I'm always delighted when graduating seniors decide to write tributes to the school. (It might be a very lovely graduation ritual to *require* each senior to write a tribute to the school. These could be placed in a separate three-ring binder and added to each year. It would make for some very fine nostalgic reading.)

Commit to Delegating Jobs to Students

Someone once shared with me the guidelines Rex Brown and his team of educators developed for P.S. 1 in Denver, Colorado. One of their statements especially hit home for me. The author suggested that no adult should do jobs in a school that a child could do and learn from doing. This sentiment has always been a way of life in our school.

I once began a workshop by asking the teachers gathered to list the specific reading and writing tasks they had to do during an average school day. I then asked them to check off the ones they could give away to students. I reminded teachers that they might have some extra time if they were willing to give some of their jobs away. (I'm able to spend time in classrooms only because I'm willing to give many jobs away.) All this requires of course that you trust children (and that I trust my colleagues and support staff), and that you are willing to let them have a go at some of the tasks usually reserved for those of us with licenses to teach. These include writing curriculum updates for family members, creating class calendars, designing homework packets, and so on.

Throughout the school, we make sure that children take advantage of a wide variety of writing opportunities. We buy no commercial signs. Students make all the signs and posters we need, everything from "Open Door Slowly," to "No Smoking," to "Visitors Sign In Please." When classes are away from their room, we don't have those teacher-made-and-decorated paper plates with little arrows fastened to the center that point to the class's possible whereabouts. Instead, students hang their own informative signs on classroom doors.

Kindergarten teachers at the start of the school year do much of their class's real-world writing because most of those students are just beginning to write. But by midyear many are ready to join in on the responsibility and the fun. In March, we took down the welcome sign Pam had written to hang outside her door way back in September. I suggested to her enthusiastic writers that it was time for them to craft their own welcome messages. Several appear below:

AV O NOS DY VOZTRS	Have a nice day visitors
WELCOM TO AER SOOL	Welcome to our school
MAK YOUR SEL AT HOM	Make yourself at home
BE COMFORDEBL	Be comfortable
I HOP YOU HAD A GOD TAYM	I hope you had a good time
CUM BAK A NUTHR DAY	Come back another day

Following this successful writing opportunity, I suggested that Pam give the snack message board hanging outside her door over to the young writers. This board is used for family members to sign up for weekly snack donations and Pam usually decorates the board with box tops from the children's favorite snacks as reminders to the families. Now the children were ready to write their own list of suggested snacks. Several appear below:

CHEZ AND CRAKRS	Cheese and crackers
BAGLS AND KREM CHES	Bagels and cream cheese
CHOCLT TDE GRAMS	Chocolate Teddy Grahams
KARETS	Carrots
PRETSLS AND GRAPS	Pretzels and grapes
FROT ROL OP	Fruit Roll-ups
KRAKRS AND PEN BTTR	Crackers and peanut butter
GRNOL BRAS	Granola bars
APLS AND RNGS	Apples and oranges

Early in the history of our school, I became aware of just how monumental a pile of lost-and-found items could become. I was at my wit's end trying to think of a sensible way to encourage children and parents to retrieve lost goods. I decided to ask two first graders to write a description of each item so that we could compile a list to send home to families (see Figure 3.10). I then attached the following letter to the children's list.

> *Dear families,*
>
> *Attached are two lists of lost-and-found items written by young writers in what is known as "invented spelling." Know that as the year progresses, these children will be learning standard spelling, but we delight in these early attempts. I've included some standard spelling equivalents to help you through the lists.*
>
> *scke=ski*
> *howd, hod=hood*
> *blow=blue*

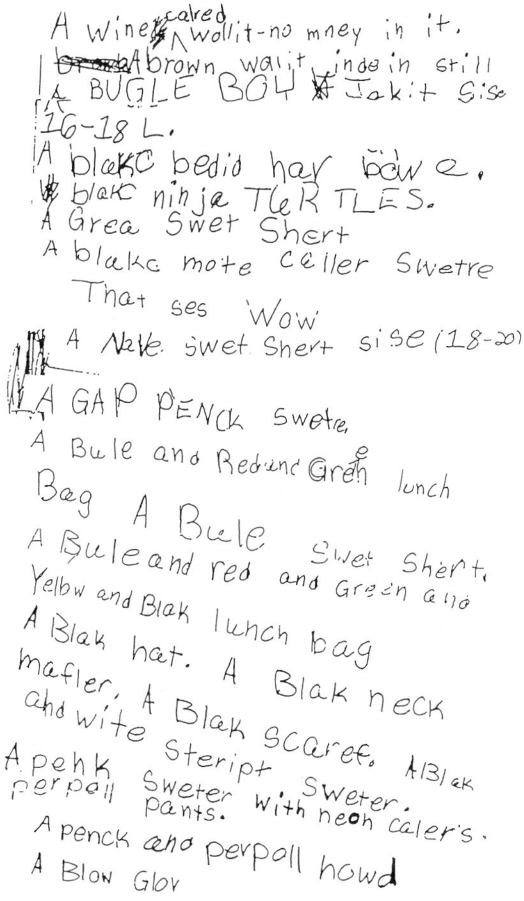
A wine calred wollit-no mney in it.
A brown walit inde in still
A BUGLE BOY Jakit Sise 16-18 L.
A blakC bedid hay bowe.
blakC ninja TleRTLES.
A Grea Swet Shert
A blakc mote celler Swetre That ses Wow
A Nake swet Shert sise (18-20)
A GAP PENCk Swetre
A Bule and Redand Grene lunch Bag A Bule
A Buleand red and Green and Yelbw and Blak lunch bag
A Blak hat. A Blak neck mafler, A Blak scaref. A Blak and wite Steript Sweter.
A penk perpall Sweter pants. With neon Caler's.
A penck and perpoll howd
A Blow Glov

Figure 3.10

blakc, blak, =black

oun=one

steript=striped

penk, penck=pink

nave=navy

grea=gray

perpoll=purple

calred=colored

indien still=Indian style

bedid=beaded

har bow=hair bow

mote caller=multi-colored

skaref=scarf

Please come to school to claim your items. We will be giving the unidentified goods to charity at the end of next week.

Not only did the lists help families retrieve lost items, they also helped them appreciate and marvel at invented spelling. It was a very practical way to get two jobs done. And the added bonus was that the children enjoyed the challenge.

Another lost-and-found writing opportunity comes about when children post messages about misplaced treasured possessions.

A lost earring message was written by Bailey in grade three (see Figure 3.11). Note how precise her description is.

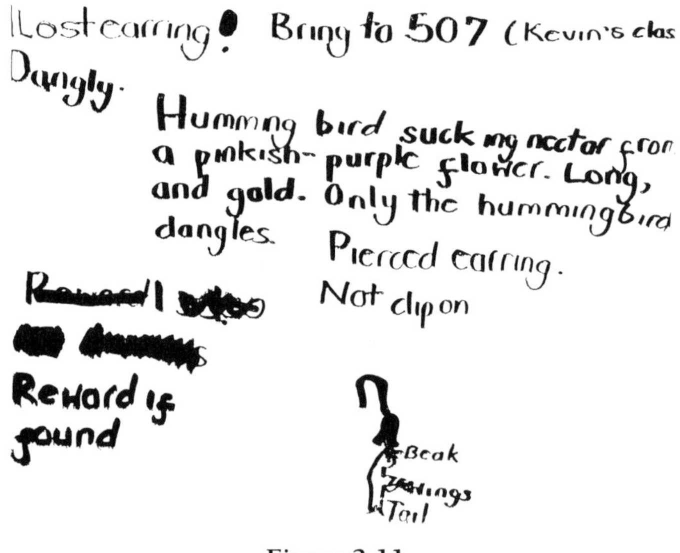

Figure 3.11

Most school buildings have display cases and ours is no exception. We have only one glass-enclosed case, hanging very close to the main office. Over the years I have taken responsibility for its contents, changing the displays as the seasons change. In the autumn I fill it with welcome-back-to-school poems. In the winter I create my sculpture of lost mittens and gloves surrounded by winter poems. In spring it becomes a tribute to the baseball season, complete with banners, baseball caps, news clippings, book jackets, photos, and poems. Toward summer, I display lists of recommended summer reading as well as book jackets filled with summertime events. I probably should step aside and give the job of filling this display case to students. I can easily imagine them coming up with worthwhile uses for the cabinet, ones that would encourage a wide range of writing formats.

The cabinet might be the perfect location to present the results of school surveys, which our students are always so eager to give out. For example, in honor of the eightieth birthday of the Oreo cookie, Layne's first graders surveyed our community for our favorite way of eating an Oreo. They could have filled the cabinet with the news story about the Oreo birthday, their procedures for creating the survey, and of course their results, which read as follows:

229 kids twist their Oreos.

107 dunk their Oreos.

116 eat their Oreos whole.

452 kids answered our survey.

Most people in the Manhattan New School twist their Oreos.

Other classes might decide to use the cabinet to follow sports events, elections, or local new stories, all topics of interest to the entire school community and each filled with opportunities for a wide range of writing formats. Students would also be faced with the challenges attached to presenting information in public displays.

Students at the Manhattan New School also create the school map, the visitors' guide to neighborhood restaurants, and interviews with school personnel that get published in the school newsletter. They write their own permission slips to eat out and to take walking trips in the neighborhood. They write their own notes to explain absences and changes in their transportation arrangements. Older students can also be called upon to participate in creating those administrative type documents required by the central board of education, including procedures for fire drills, a plan to improve attendance, and the school's discipline code.

Take a Deliberate Stance Toward Raising Activists

In *Going Public*, book one in my Manhattan New School trilogy, I state that we are raising activists in our school. I suggest that one of our big curriculum goals is to help students use their literacies to make this world a better place. When this belief permeates a school you can expect a great deal of real-world reading and writing to be done. After all, if you want to know what is happening in your community, you read the newspaper, interview residents, take field notes, read original documents, gather supporting materials, and so on. And if you want your voice to be heard you write letters, start petitions, post signs, craft speeches, mail letters to the editor, and so on. (For more on this, see Chapter 4, "Paving the Way for Nonfiction Study.")

When children begin using their writing to make a difference within the safe environment of their school, they are more likely to reach beyond the four walls of the schoolhouse and write for social action in their neighborhood, city, state, and country.

For example, Avram wrote to the commissioner of baseball as well as to the major television networks, protesting the late hour that baseball games were broadcast on television. They were shown way past this eight-year-old fan's bedtime. And Isabel's kindergartners wrote to the Lego company complaining that there were more boy than girl figures in their Lego sets. The company's written response suggested that the figures were gender-free. This unsatisfactory answer inspired Isabel and her students to survey students' response to the figures. They asked many students if the Lego figures were male or female. Results showed that our students did *not* think the figures were gender-free.

Students in Sharon Hill's fourth-grade class, calling themselves the City Readers Book Club, hung the announcement shown in Figure 3.12 throughout our school. They were determined to raise money for the three causes listed. They held their bake sale outside of school in Central Park on a half day of school. The sale raised money for one very personal cause. The crisis in Kosovo greatly affected our community, since we have both ethnic Albanian and Christian Serb children in attendance. Many children wrote letters requesting donations for their wartorn homeland.

Paula Rogovin's first graders took a one-thousand-dollar summons issued to the father of some of our students to heart. Anthony Avellino and his three daughters, all students at the Manhattan New School, had been approached by an officer in Central Park because the girls were climbing a tree, which, unbeknownst to this law-abiding family, is forbidden in the park. When Anthony asked the officer, "How would I know that you aren't allowed to climb trees? There aren't any signs." The flip officer countered, "Well, there are no signs outside a bank telling you not to rob it!" (You might recognize this story, as the entire family was invited to appear on *The Rosie O'Donnell Show,* and their photographs appeared in all the newspapers.) Paula's students got busy designing appropriate signs to hang in the park and sent them off to the parks commissioner.

Josh, Thiago, and Carmen wrote to President Clinton, sharing their concerns about their grandparents and encouraging the government to preserve benefits for senior citizens. The president sent the children a detailed list of his commitments and closed by saying, "I will continue to work with Congress to guarantee that our nation keeps its compact with older Americans into the twenty-first century. I appreciate your interest in these important issues and welcome your involvement." There is nothing like receiving

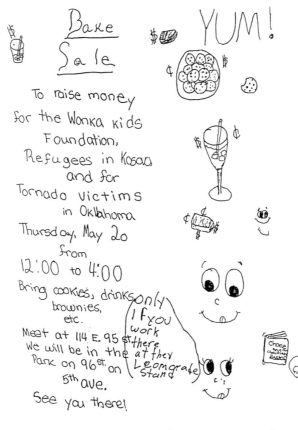

Figure 3.12

a letter with the return address 1600 Pennsylvania Avenue to inspire young students to keep on writing to improve the quality of their lives and the live of others.

Provide Appropriate Tools

The first year Sharon Taberski joined our staff, she created a letter-writing center in her classroom. On a small table she placed a basket filled with necessary supplies—stationery, postcards, pens, markers, and so on. She completed this special writing area with the addition of a beautiful reading lamp. What child could resist the opportunity to work in this very private area of the classroom? Many children were inspired to try their hand at letter writing because Sharon had provided the necessary tools. Had her students been older, perhaps she would have added student directories, telephone books, catalogs of free materials, lists of public officials, and so on. Had our school been wealthier, perhaps she would have added a laptop or even a fax machine. The tools in our classrooms, common areas, and corridors say a lot about the kinds of writing we hope our students will be doing.

I've placed a large wooden suggestion box on a low oak table in our main reception area. Because the box exists and is easily accessible to both young and old, children as well as adults frequently drop handwritten notes into the carved slot. (I created the box out of an old teachers' union ballot box I found in an old dusty closet in our 1904 building.) A kindergartner wrote the suggestion in Figure 3.13, in his very best invented spelling, complete with the logos for both the Yankees and the Mets baseball teams.

Providing students with evocative tools can inspire them to do quite imaginative things. I've always wondered what a classroom of children would do if each were given his or her own personal Rolodex; the alphabetical cards need not be used for names, addresses, and telephone numbers, but for any collecting or cataloging the children were interested in. Children would, no doubt, invent quite novel uses for these compact cards. What would parents think to see a Rolodex added to the beginning of the year school supply list?

Thinking About Schoolhouse Tools   You might ask yourself the following questions as you take a walking tour of your school. They are designed to promote richer uses of writing tools, ones that will enable students to discover additional reasons to write.

Figure 3.13

- Do early-childhood classrooms have a variety of paper placed in each learning center? In other words, is there music paper on the piano? Clipboards next to the guinea pig cage? Oak tag strips for signs in the block area?)

- Do all classrooms have sufficient library collections containing samples of work in many genres? (In other words, are there real-world artifacts such as surveys, brochures, and maps, in classroom collections?)

- Do students have opportunities to respond to work displayed in the hallways? (Are response sheets and writing tools provided?)

- Are mailboxes easily accessible to students? (Can they drop a note to a former teacher?)

- Are addresses of children who have moved away available to former classmates?

- Are children seen with clipboard in hand, interviewing and observing people around the building?

- Is space provided for students to post announcements, requests, complaints, and so on?

- Are baskets of notepaper and pencils readily available for the recording of wonderful ideas?

- Are appropriate contest announcements, calls for manuscripts, and lists of publishers of student writing kept in a prominent place?

- Do older students have adequate access to word processors in order to prepare their finished work?

- Does the school have ample supply of a wide range of papers? (Big enough for banners and posters, small enough for reminders and notes, medium size for signs and letters, and high quality for durable homemade greeting cards?)

- Do the waiting areas provide children with access to paper and pencil? (Nurse's waiting room, offices, inclement-weather congregating areas?)

- Are wipe-off boards hung low enough for children to post reminders, announcements, requests, and so on?

- Are blank books available for children to publish their work in durable formats?

- Does the school have such equipment as poster-printer, binding, and laminating machines?

- Do teachers have sufficient access to duplicating machines so that student work can be distributed in plentiful and appropriate ways?

- Does the computer software enable students to get feedback on their writing from students outside their classroom?

Celebrate Student Initiative

Several years ago, I clipped a photograph from a magazine that showed two young naked preschoolers being carried by police officers. One of the young boys had been

Dear Oma,

How are you? I am fine. I am making a book about my aunt (your daughter) and would like if you would tell me the following: What did you do the day she was born? And what did you do the day she passed away? What were her hobbies? What did she like to do best? How old was she when one passed away? This book is going to be dedicated in memory to her. If you want I will send you a copy of the book.

With Love Lauren

P.S. Was she like me?

Write back soon

Figure 3.14

riding his tricycle very early in the morning and the other was carrying a pad and pencil. The caption under the photograph revealed that the children had left home while their mother was asleep. The boys explained to the police officers that they had been giving out parking tickets. I've always admired this story. It reminds me of the power of demonstration. Clearly the young boys had watched someone issuing tickets. The story also delights me because I so appreciate children with initiative.

When I worked in staff development and would visit schools periodically, I knew I had to work in ways that guaranteed that lots of learning would occur when I was *not* there. So too, when working with young students, what happens when we are not present often says more than what happens when we are. I take great delight when students show initiative and share with me their unsolicited work. Lauren asked me to photocopy a letter to her grandmother that appears in Figure 3.14. Later I told David, her teacher, how lovely the letter was. He hadn't even known that she had written it. Lauren had learned how to use writing independently to get the information she needed.

I was amused to find the following notice plastered on our schoolhouse walls:

Sports Card Rally

You and anyone you want to bring is welcome to come during recess this Thursday the 7th. You must have at least 10 cards. There will be wrestling—just kidding, we don't want any cards or people to get in bad condition.

This will be hosted in room 506

Carey, in fourth grade, sent me a request to begin a question-and-answer column to be displayed in the school cafeteria (see Figure 3.15). Abby, in third grade, tried to help me when I launched a campaign to have every child bring in a shoebox filled with "stuff" to entertain themselves during recess in inclement weather. She wrote the letter that appears in Figure 3.16.

One day, while visiting David Besancon's fourth-grade class, I was surprised to discover a flier sitting atop a bookcase, which read as follows:

Looking for a book that's neither in the classroom nor at your house? Just go to us, at Claire and Sofia's Library, because we have most of the books that you don't. Tell us the name of the book, we'll go home, see if we have it, and if we do (which is likely), we'll bring it back to school the next day. You can keep the book for a week.

Buy a library card for the low price of only $1.00! 15 cents a book (if you don't want a card) and only 15 cents a day overdue.

The notice charmed me, until I got to the second paragraph. There are, of course, city regulations prohibiting the use of a public school building as a profit-making business, no matter how adorable the entrepreneurs!

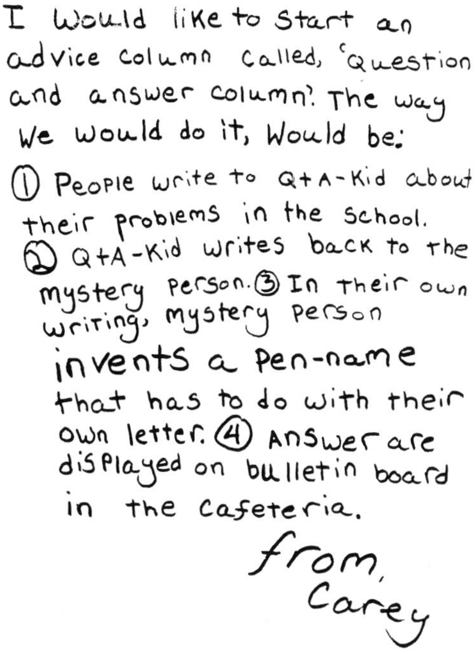

I would like to start an advice column called, 'Question and answer column'. The way we would do it, would be:

① People write to Q+A-Kid about their problems in the school.
② Q+A-Kid writes back to the mystery person. ③ In their own writing, mystery person invents a pen-name that has to do with their own letter. ④ Answer are displayed on bulletin board in the cafeteria.

from,
Carey

Figure 3.15

Dear boys and girls,

Please bring your rainy day box in by Monday the twenty-fifth if you have not yet brought it in. Please do this right away you were supposed to bring it in three weeks ago. If you do not know what to bring in here are a few suggestions.

Playing cards
Baseball cards
travel games
paper and pencils
crayons markers
auotgraph books
a book
comic books
crossword puzzles
Activity books

Thank you

from Abby in Joannas class

Figure 3.16

Confer About Purpose and Audience

Conferring can help children understand what writing is for. When teachers continually ask, "Where in the real world does this piece of writing belong?" students appreciate that their words can make a difference to the people, places, and causes they care about. Students revise their writing keeping in mind the destination they envision for their work. If I suggest to a child that her writing has potential to become an article for the school newspaper, a text to teach reading in the first grade, or an appropriate gift poem for a teacher who is about to have a baby, they often approach revision more purposefully. If they understand the constraints of the chosen genre and audience, they can establish clear ways to make their work the best it can be. (For more on conferring see *Writing Through Childhood*.)

Elevate the Genres Particular to Schools

Each year, our fifth-grade teachers have to write recommendations for middle school for each of their students. Kathy Park, in her first year in our school, helped me to see what a unique genre this kind of writing could be. She wrote her recommendations with tremendous flair, voice, and surprise, as shown in the example below.

> With her vivid imagination and spark of optimism, Anna handles everything with a the-atrical flourish. As a writer, she seems at ease with all genres—especially fiction. Anna is an expert when it comes to breathing life into her stories with her cleverly designed plots and quirky characters. Anna is also an avid reader, who has probably read virtually every book

on our library shelves. Her reader responses are often full of insight and intelligent commentary well beyond her years. Socially, Anna works beautifully with any child, in both small- and large-group settings. Mostly, she's an expert in pinpointing other students struggles and articulating their needs for them, if they aren't able to do so themselves. Her empathy for other students is in this way remarkable. Without a doubt, this quality would make her a treasured participant in any classroom community.

Sam is the perfect candidate for a specialized program geared for the sciences. In math, Sam is an eager participant who can introduce new and insightful strategies for other students. Whenever he sets off to tackle any math problem, regardless of its complexity, Sam will regard this experience with relish—almost as if he were playing a video game. During reading, I often see Sam completely enamored in the Eyewitness books. Even though Sam is often shy to admit it during book talks and other such class discussions, he can probably name and give a detailed explanation about the arachnid family and its habitats. Given the proper setting, I believe Sam could excel in both learning about and articulating his scientific pursuits.

Kathy's writing reminded me that the life of a school produces many kinds of writing that are exclusive to scholarly communities.

At the end of each school year, I am asked to contribute to the yearbook for the graduating seniors and occasionally to individual classroom yearbooks. Last year I contributed the following ode to Pam's K/1 class, which met in room 206. (The young readers were appreciative of this simple rhythmic chant.)

Ode to Two-0-Six

Caroline, Jacob, Jeanine, and Maeve
Two-0-Six
What a mix!
Allie, Amanda, Petrit, and Reese,
Two-0-Six,
Nothing to fix!
Chelsea, Jenna, Stephen, and Ray,
Two-0-Six,
Solid as Bricks!
Hadley, Aldin, Alexander, and Danielle,
Two-0-Six,
Their friendship sticks!
Jordana, Emily, Keely, and Catharine,
Two-0-Six,
It's real, no tricks!
Devon, Danielle, Sara, and Sam,
Two-0-Six,
It really clicks!
Charlie, Karla, and especially Pam,

Two-0-Six,
Parks and picnics!
Caroline, Jacob, Jeanine, and Maeve,
Two-0-Six,
Book reviews and chicks!
Allie, Amanda, Petrit, and Reese,
Two-0-Six,
Top of the picks!
Chelsea, Jenna, Stephen, and Ray,
Two-0-Six,
Go Yankees and Knicks!
Hadley, Aldin, Alexander, and Danielle,
Two-0-Six,
Go get your kicks!
Jordana, Emily, Keely, and Catharine,
Two-0-Six,
The clock really ticks!
Devon, Danielle, Sara, and Sam,
Two-0-Six,
Nothing to fix!
Charlie, Karla, and especially Pam,
Two-0-Six,
What a mix!

The following is a list of many other kinds of writing I encounter because I am working in a school:

- welcome notes
- school brochures
- tenure toasts
- phone messages
- bus schedules
- floor plans
- journals on plant and animal growth
- birthday greetings
- get-well messages
- goodbye messages
- personal planners for assignments
- congratulatory notes
- pen-pal letters
- dialogue journals
- interviews
- curriculum guides
- permission slips
- supply lists
- class lists
- reading recommendations
- invitations and programs for school events
- resumes for school jobs
- application letters
- speeches for school causes

- procedural writing
- minutes of meetings
- yearbook pages
- thank-you notes
- late passes
- school newspaper articles
- letters to families
- toasts for school events
- banners and congratulatory notes
- bulletin board announcements
- surveys about school issues
- classroom signs
- self-evaluations
- mailbox messages
- checklists
- narrative reports
- school brochures
- visitor's guides
- environmental print labels
- substitute instructions
- homework assignments
- daily agendas
- plant and animal care suggestions
- procedural writing for use of school equipment
- inventory of supplies
- attendance records
- fire drill procedures
- captioned photo albums
- labeled map of the school
- good news announcements
- help-wanted postings
- school calendars
- cafeteria schedules
- bus schedules
- discipline codes
- assessment forms
- schedules for use of the auditorium and cafeteria
- teaching plans
- program cards
- custodial requests
- observations
- nurse referrals

The question remains, "How many of these genres can be introduced to students?" All, I would imagine, in one appropriate form or another. Some have already been learned by children in their home settings.

For example, thank-you notes are perhaps one of the first genres parents ask their children to write. Some forms of writing are more unexpected. One afternoon a prospective family arrived at school with child in hand. I'm very used to the parents bringing a list of must-ask questions, but this time the child carried his own list. His questions included, Who are the second-grade teachers? Where and what time do we get the bus? What are the specialists? Do you have to bring your lunch? What Manhattan New School kids live around 96th and Columbus and/or 106th and Broadway? What time do you start and let out? Needless to say he was my kind of kid. We must never underestimate what children can do. Children can learn to write significant interview questions, as they can learn many of the genres listed above. Some would require very little instruction, others might deserve brief, whole-class genre studies.

Years ago I attended a reading conference in Perth, Australia. Each participant received a letter of welcome, tucked into the registration material, from a local schoolchild. It was a delightful way to learn about the city, the schools, and the life of a child. I could easily imagine asking students in our school to prepare welcome letters to be handed out to new parents, students, student teachers, and all visitors.

Whenever a child joins our school in midyear, I make it a practice of stopping to check on the child in the lunchroom and playground during those first few days, just to be sure the child is making friends and becoming part of the school community. It's a custom that has served the students and me well. (I get to know the new children and the new children appreciate the extra transitional support.) Similarly, children can take on some of these welcoming behaviors. They can provide tours of the school to a new student, be assigned as temporary playground partners, and of course they can write individual letters of welcome to new arrivals. Regina's students did, in fact, do just that when seven-year-old Jahan moved to New York from far-off Bombay (see Figures 3.17 and 3.18).

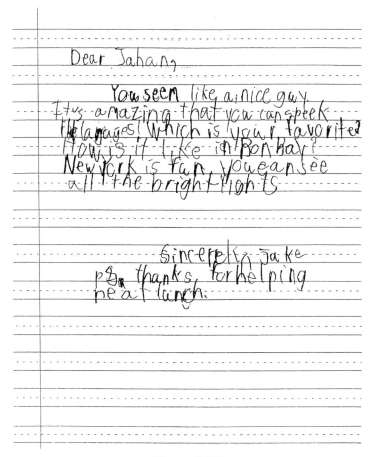

Figure 3.17

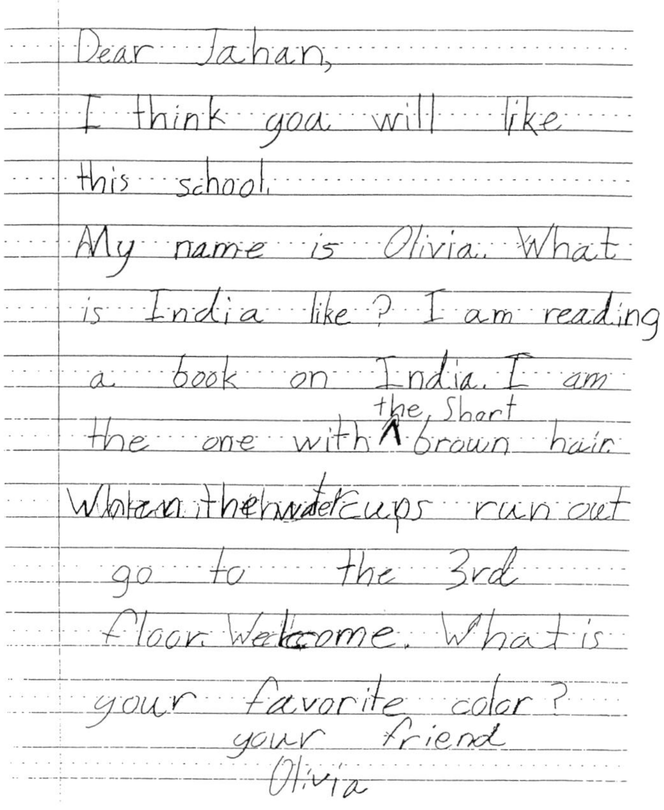

Dear Jahan,

I think goa will like this school.

My name is Olivia. What is India like? I am reading a book on India. I am the one with the, short brown hair

When the water cups run out go to the 3rd floor. Welcome. What is your favorite color?

　　　　your friend
　　　　　Olivia

Figure 3.18

Select Inspirational Literature

There are many children's books in which the main character takes their writing seriously and the writing contained provides demonstrations for new and functional genres. The following is a list of titles in which genres are modeled within the texts.

Mr. Lincoln's Whiskers, by Karen B. Winnick—letter writing.

Toot and Puddle, by Holly Hobbie—travel postcards.

Keepers, by Jeri Hanel Watts and Felicia Marshall—the recording of family stories.

Snapshots from the Wedding, by Gary Soto—Photo-captions.

All Around Town: The Photographs of Richard Samuel Roberts, by Dinah Johnson—captions.

Brown Angels, by Walter Dean Myers—poetic captions for photo albums.

Charlie's Checklist, by Rory Lerman—ads, letters, checklists.

The Signmaker's Assistant, by Tedd Arnold—signs.

Bluewater Journal: the Voyage of the Sea Tiger, by Loretta Krupinski—travel journal.

A Sign, by George Ella Lyon—signs, letters.

Paddington Bear: My Scrapbook, by Michael Bond—scrapbook.

Big Jim and the White-Legged Moose, by Jim Arnosky—wildlife sketchbook.

Night Letters, by Palmyra LoMonaco—nature notes and letters.

(See *Writing Through Childhood* for minilessons attached to titles that inspire young people to write.)

Similarly, there are nonfiction texts that encourage students to write (and take other forms of action) to accomplish real-world goals. These include *Take a Stand,* by Daniel Weizmann, and Barbara Lewis's books *What Do You Stand for?: A Kid's Guide to Building Character, The Kid's Guide to Social Action,* and *The Kid's Guide to Service Projects.*

Newspaper articles that showcase children who have used their writing to improve the quality of life in their community also inspire older students. We shared the column about the young girl who wrote a pamphlet to help children who must stay in the hospital and the one about the young girl in Sudbury, Massachusetts, who challenged the law prohibiting ice-cream trucks in her town. Students were also impressed with the ten-year-old girl who realized that when the pencils carrying the slogan "Too Cool to Do Drugs" were sharpened, their message turned negative. It became "Cool to Do Drugs," and finally, "Do Drugs." The pencil company had to recall the batch of pencils and reprint them with the words appearing in the opposite direction.

Publish in Authentic Ways

Educators need to make sure that there are many occasions for students' writing to do good work in the real world. We need to continually simplify the notion of publishing, taking away the extravaganza feel by creating everyday vehicles for going public with student work.

In Charles Frazier's novel *Cold Mountain,* Ada, one of the central characters, picks apart a thistle, looking for the "thistle dwellers." The author explains, "Her thinking was that since every tiny place in the world seemed to make a home for some creature, she would discover who the thistle dwellers might be." Similarly, as I walk around the school, I've begun to expect student writing to dwell in every tiny place. I expect students' writing to find comfortable homes in all the nooks and crannies of our school. Nothing delights me more than to see student writing put to significant use in the school building.

It's no surprise that in our writing community, Ricardo's notebook comments about teasing form part of a guidebook on student behavior, Chloe's piece on box turtles is shared in the science class, Zach and Emmy's big book of original tongue twisters was given as a gift to the kindergartners, and Bailey's rhyme about roller coasters became a chant for the young students across the hall. Karen's second graders wrote mathematical word problems, and when they were satisfied with their efforts they posted a sign-up sheet for other classes. They wanted to arrange appointments to share their work with children who were learning these same mathematical concepts (see Figures 3.19 and 3.20).

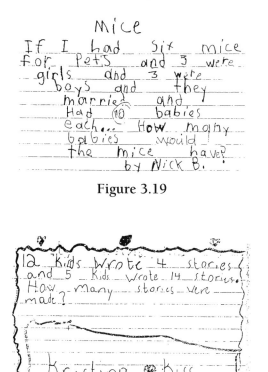

Mice

If I had six mice for pets and 3 were girls and 3 were boys and they married and Had 10 babies each... How many babies would the mice have?

by Nick B.

Figure 3.19

12 kids wrote 4 stories and 5 kids wrote 14 stories. How many stories were made?

Kristina Kiss

Figure 3.20

I was impressed with the quality as well as the simplicity of this project. Karen's presentation was also memorable. She backed each problem on beautiful colored paper, mounted them on index cards, punched a hole in the corner of each, and slipped a large ring through the corner holes. Karen clearly intended to add these problems to her permanent collection of mathematics materials. Children will do their best when their work is put to real use in the community they know best.

This notion of sending writing to the places in the school where the writing can do the most good extends of course outside the school community. When children write about toys, restaurants, hotels, amusement parks, shops, and libraries, we need to send copies of their work to the people who would most appreciate reading about their reactions. One never knows where such contact might lead.

Celebrate At-Home Writing

Every once in a while a parent proudly shows me a piece of writing that a child did at home, without being asked to. Children who derive a great deal of satisfaction in writing write poems and picture books as they sit in their doctor's waiting room, spend an afternoon with a friend, or pass a rainy weekend. They also invent ways to use their writing to tend to the business of living. Parents have shown me such artifacts as:

- signs hung on bedroom doors detailing who can enter
- rules for neighborhood clubs
- supermarket shopping lists
- place cards for family dinners
- instructions for new baby-sitters
- letters to grandparents
- telephone messages
- instructions for playing homemade games
- table-clearing schedules
- invitations to birthday parties
- family surveys of favorite meals and television shows
- tooth-fairy thank-you notes
- calendars for playdates
- letters to Santa
- photo album captions
- homemade telephone directories
- greeting cards for every occasion
- family and neighborhood newspapers

The most natural way to encourage children to attempt some of these very at-home formats is to simply share them publicly, with permission. If you encourage family members to bring in these writing samples and then you ask students to share the story of how these pieces came to be written, no doubt many classmates will be inspired to try these kinds of writing or invent additional ones. A collection of these at-home pieces would also make a grand across-the-grades bulletin board display.

Weave Writing into Thematic Studies and Community Projects

Over the years I've been tempted to lead professional-development workshops for elementary teachers based solely on young people's attraction to animals. I've never met a young person who wasn't deeply touched by John Reynolds Gardiner's *Stone Fox.* I've never met a young person who didn't want to write about a pet he has had or a pet he has dreamed of having. I've never met a young person who didn't want to read, recite, and perform Alice Schertle's poems in *Advice for a Frog,* or those by Barbara Juster Esbensen in *Words with Wrinkled Knees.* At our own school, even the most squeamish city kid still wants to observe the rabbit, chameleon, guinea pig, and turtles on the shelves in Lisa's science lab.

Stephanie Wilson, then a second grader, handed me a business card. It was hot pink and read, "Stephanie Wilson's Gerbil Ranch." It was adorned with a sketch of Stephanie in full western attire saddled onto the back of a larger-than-life gerbil, gleefully

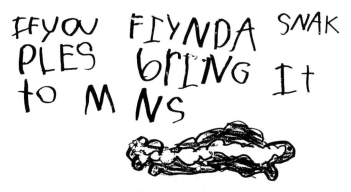

Figure 3.21

riding through a cactus-dotted stretch of landscape. Business cards are perhaps a surprising kind of writing for young people to be doing, but a love of animals has motivated our young people to do many varied kinds of writing. A few examples follow.

Visitor's Guide to Animals in the Building Our students listed the animals found in each classroom, their names, the best time to visit, as well as what you might bring to feed the animals. It was through this writing that I discovered that most of the turtles had Shelley-like names. Get it? Turtles? Shells? *Shelley!*

Signs for Lost Class Pets The lost-animal sign shown in Figure 3.21 (a classic example of invented spelling) is the kind I frequently find on school walls. The news report in Figure 3.22 was included in Regina's class newsletter to families.

Hamster!!
Hamster!! News Report

At M.N.S. (Manhattan New School)
in Regina's class has lost a hamster
A hamster is a little rodent, simalar
to a gerbil But lets get on
with it They got the hamster on Jan. 9th
1995. It is quite new. They are getting
worried. Please tell Regina Chow if you
see a little furry rodent, and when it
sleep it looks like a pinecone.

Thank you Zara Stern
Frazier, Tabuzia Jones,
Marsha Thopson, and Amy
Hanrahan

Thank you. Zara Stern
Frazier, Tabrizia Jones, Marsha
Thompson, and Amy Hanrahan.

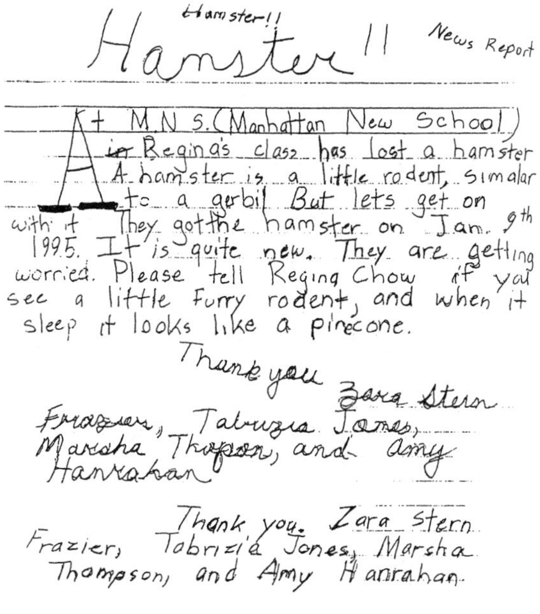

Figure 3.22

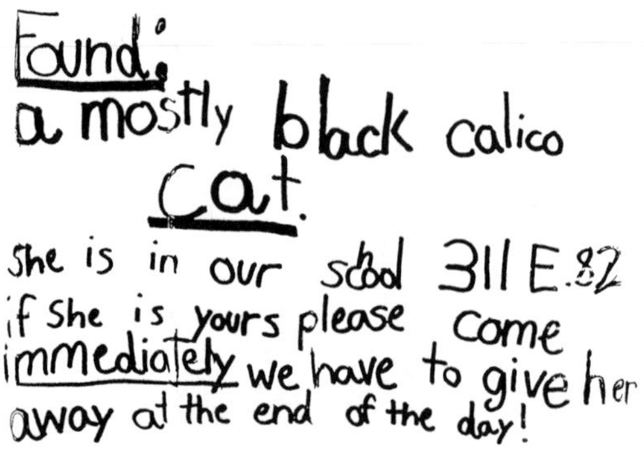

Found:
a mostly black calico
cat.
She is in our school 311 E.82
if she is yours please come
immediately we have to give her
away at the end of the day!

Figure 3.23

Lost-and-Found Signs for Neighborhood Pets   Then too, I sometimes find student writing *outside* of school. The sign in Figure 3.23 was plastered on lampposts and trees in the neighborhood. The students received a response to this plea. We found the note in Figure 3.24 taped onto the schoolhouse door. (These notes are the kind of seed material that could make for a great short chapter book à la the *Polk Street School* series.)

Observation Journals   Molly, a kindergartner, studies the class snails and records her observations on a specially designed paper created by her teacher Isabel Beaton (see Figure 3.25). In his science log, shown in Figure 3.26, a first grader recorded his observations about slugs. Sometimes children attach timelines of growth to their science

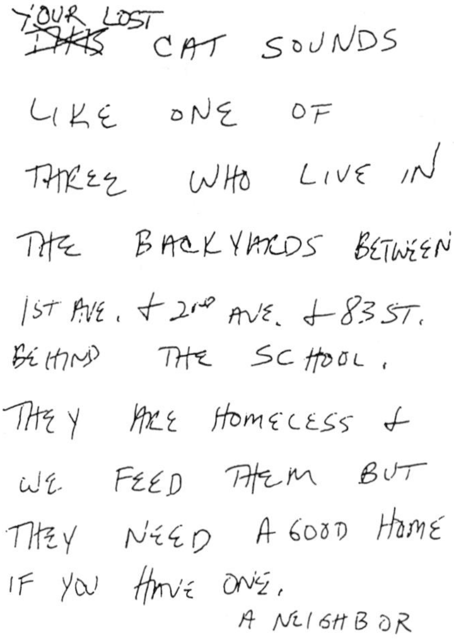

YOUR LOST
~~THIS~~ CAT SOUNDS
LIKE ONE OF
THREE WHO LIVE IN
THE BACKYARDS BETWEEN
1ST AVE. + 2ND AVE. + 83 ST.
BEHIND THE SCHOOL.
THEY ARE HOMELESS +
WE FEED THEM BUT
THEY NEED A GOOD HOME
IF YOU HAVE ONE.
                    A NEIGHBOR

Figure 3.24

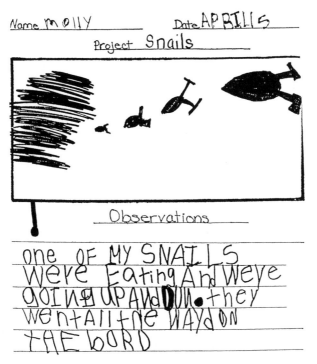

Figure 3.25

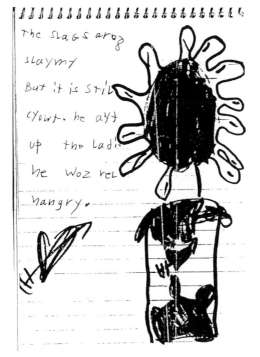

Figure 3.26

observations, especially when they are recording the hatching of chick and duck eggs or the metamorphosis of butterflies.

Other Writing Formats Connected to Students' Love of Animals   When students are invited to indulge themselves in their love of animals, the possibilities for literate moments are seemingly endless. An array of writing formats follow:

- signs, background information, and schedules for animal care to hang on cages and tanks
- care instructions for families that take animals home over vacations
- staff and student surveys concerning allergies to animals
- letters to protest animal abuses
- invitations, rules, and regulations for school clubs devoted to animals
- contest instructions to name school pets
- request notes for information or books on animals
- all-about books devoted to favorite animals
- odes to pets
- Did You Know . . . ? pieces about researched animal (see p. 143)
- research reports (see migration templates on p. 144)

(See related information in Chapter 4, "Paving the Way for Nonfiction Study.")

Other Content Studies   Animals, of course, is not the only topic that seems to cut across grade levels in our school. Many students, along with their teachers, are interested in such diverse subjects as skyscrapers, computers, basketball, cooking, and Broadway shows. If we put our minds to it, we can tease out many worthwhile writing tasks connected to any of these subjects.

Each teacher and group of students, as well, find their own passionate areas of inquiry. Paula's children create and care for a window box garden in the front of our school. Lorraine's children study architecture in the community. Regina's children visit the senior citizen home. Layne's children collect pennies to save the rain forest. Teachers need only to think through the possibilities and extend the invitations and students will be crafting labels, requests, posters, petitions, letters, schedules, maps, directions, and signs. Not to mention the poetry and prose that can be sent or performed in tribute to the people and places connected to these projects. Paula's students, in fact, paid tribute to the men and machinery at a local construction site, and the workers displayed the students' art and poetry under sheets of Plexiglas surrounding the site. (Read more about Paula Rogovin's techniques for getting to know members of the community in her book *Classroom Interviews: A World of Learning.*)

Any school project or event, in fact, can lend itself to a wide range of writing opportunities. One day I received a surprising letter from two second graders who had a plan to raise money at our fund-raising street fair known as the Fest with Zest. Their letter appears in Figure 3.27.

Attached to it, next to the directions "Peel off," was a homemade Band-Aid carefully crafted from tissues, loose-leaf paper, and tape. I was charmed by their inventiveness but worried about the unsanitariness of unwrapped homemade Band-Aids. I scheduled a meeting with the two young girls and suggested that they first survey their classmates to find out if anyone would buy such an item. When they discovered that no one would use such bandages for cuts and bruises, the young girls shifted their marketing and announced that they would sell their creations as "Band-Aids for Dolls!"

Assign Schoolwide Writing Tasks

Many of the schoolwide literacy events and rituals described in Chapter 1, "Designing the Literary Landscape," encourage students to write for new reasons, new audiences, and in new formats. Our students have designed school maps, listed adults and their job titles, recorded words to songs, and drawn floor plans. Similarly, their writing challenges include letter-writing campaigns, book partner correspondence, new-student welcomes, hellos and goodbyes, and dialogue journals.

When I accepted the role of deputy superintendent in my district, all the students at the Manhattan New School were asked by their teachers to write me a letter. These 550 notes were mounted and bound by two hardworking parents. This schoolwide

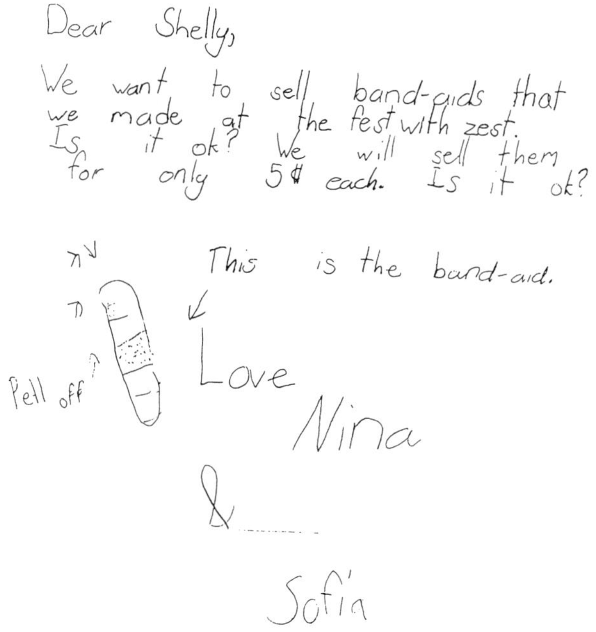

Dear Shelly,
We want to sell band-aids that we made at the fest with zest. Is it ok? We will sell them for only 5¢ each. Is it ok?

This is the band-aid.

Pell off

Love
Nina
&
Sofia

Figure 3.27

assignment helped me to realize anew just how powerful the written word is inside a school community. Some of the letters made me laugh. Others touched such a deep chord that my voice cracked when I attempted to read them aloud at our staff end-term party.

> Danielle told me she will miss me a million times and even more than that.
>
> Arieta wrote that I am like a nice cat looking at the sun.
>
> Caroline told me that I was good at smiling.
>
> Daniel said our school without me is like chicken soup without any chicken.
>
> Arjeta said I smell like a real principal.
>
> Kathy told me that the roses are dying when I walk out the door and that when I come bursting back in again they will come back alive.
>
> Georgie said I make people feel like they can do anything.
>
> Morgan said I am the nicest principal she ever met and the only principal she ever met.
>
> Driton asked if I could visit on my lunch break.

Design Community-Service Assignments

Community-service assignments come about in a variety of ways. All fifth graders are expected to perform community service as part of their graduation requirements. Many classroom teachers create their own community-service requirements depending on the age of their students. I frequently put out calls for students to volunteer for jobs that need doing. Some individual assignments are given to students who are in need of bigger challenges or boosts to their self-confidence. Sometimes they are given to students who have in one way or another taken away from or disrupted their community, as a means of reparation.

Classrooms have changed a great deal since I went to school, and therefore so has the role of the class monitor. Interclass e-mail has eliminated the need for a student to be knighted the class messenger. Wipe-off boards and markers have put students who used to clap chalk dust off the erasers and wash the slate blackboards out of business. Gone too are the days when teachers would look only to boys when chairs needed to be folded or books carried. Classrooms and school common areas still require helpers, however, and children still love to be selected. Parents often tell me how surprised they are that the same child who doesn't want to clean his room, clear the dinner table, or care for his baby brother is often eager to become the class librarian, lunch monitor, or a helper in the kindergarten playground. All I need do is post a "help wanted" sign and I find application letters or resumes in my mailbox.

Recently, as part of their senior community-service requirements, a cluster of Judy's fifth graders sent the following note to all teachers:

Dear teachers,

Vicky, Jason, Lia, Darryn, Sheila and Sean D. from Judy's fifth-grade class are updating the teacher photograph board. We will be taking your picture with the digital camera. Be prepared to answer the following question in a <u>short</u> quote. The question will be, "What do you like about teaching at the Manhattan New School?" We will be coming around next week.

Thanks for helping us,

V, J, L, D, S, SD

Students took photographs, collected quotes, and created the display that now hangs at the foot of our main staircase. A few of the collected quotes follow:

Regina's reads, "It's a place of possibility where teachers ask interesting questions and listen to the wisdom of children."

Tammy's reads, "This school reminds me of an old quilt . . . warm and comfortable."

Eve's reads, "There's a hug waiting around every corner you turn."

Joanne's reads, "Buddies come in all sizes."

Pat's reads, "This is the home that knows me by heart."

The quote next to my own photo reads, "My only regret is that my own children didn't get to attend this wonderful school. I love everything about teaching here."

In *Going Public,* I described the African concept of *ogbo,* according to which people of different ages are assigned certain village responsibilities. I suggested a similar set of responsibilities for schoolchildren at different grade levels. I could easily imagine assigning specific grade levels to the following writing tasks, all carried out for the good of the whole community.

- Third graders could be asked to write commentaries for the monthly menu posted in the cafeteria. Other students would refer to this explanation and critique when deciding whether or not to order school lunch.
- Fourth graders could be asked to craft written instructions for physical education activities and exercises and games. These would be given to new students and to students who need additional support.
- Third graders could be asked to prepare a written summary of all the events listed in the school calendar. Their notes could be given to all new families.
- Fifth graders could be asked to serve as a get-well crew, responsible for sending cheerful notes to anyone who is absent for an extended period of time. One year, when I was home recuperating from a bout with hepatitis, Judy's fifth graders sent me a collection of original aphorisms. Their messages of course brought a smile to my jaundiced face. How could I not hurry back to work when children wrote such gems as the following?

To be with Shelley or not to be with Shelley . . . There is no question.
—Emma

Without Shelley there is no pal in principal.—Maude

The day Shelley leaves we stop seeing our reflections in the mirror.—Nina

Shelley, oh Shelley. Where for art thou Shelley?—Sarah

MNS without <u>Shelley</u> is like peanut butter without <u>jelley</u>.—Josh

- Fifth graders could be asked to serve as roving reporters, regularly crafting columns for the school newsletter. (See Chapter 4, "Paving the Way for Nonfiction Study.")
- Fourth graders could be asked to write for specific areas of the school. For example, Sharon Hill's fourth-grade class took it upon themselves to solve the school problem of children being disrespectful and sloppy in the restrooms. Their collaboratively written poem appears below.

Think Twice

Don't be in a rush
Always flush.
No spit balls
They mar the walls.
Don't flood the floor
Or you're out the door.
Writing on the wall?
You're not on the ball.
Wash your hands,
But no headstands.
Leaving a mess?
We're in distress.
Think Twice.
It's just not nice.

I added a few more verses to their beginning efforts.

No trash in the bowl,
Or you'll stuff up the hole.
Use the soap,
Sparingly we hope.
If you can't be neat,
Wipe the seat.
Peeking in the stall?
It's rude, that's all.

- Fourth graders could also hang signs reminding people to use soft voices in the halls. They could create posters reminding students to clean up after themselves in the school cafeteria. They could hang warnings about the dangers of play fighting turning into real fighting.

Other worthwhile community-service assignments to be offered to specific grade levels include:

- teaching local senior citizens in the community how to use a computer and surf the Internet
- recording books on tape to add to listening centers
- typing texts into the computers for use with struggling students who might find it helpful to separate passages as they read and interact with the text in an ongoing way. (See Chapter 9, "Providing Safety Nets for Struggling Students.")

Host Real-World Events

In *Going Public,* I describe many of the curriculum-related celebrations in our school. We also celebrate inside of school many of the events that you and I celebrate outside of school. During the last eight years, our school community has celebrated several engagements, weddings, births, graduations, book publications, tenure, and countless birthdays. Each get-together invites many forms of writing. Our students have gotten quite good at crafting announcements, invitations, congratulatory and thank-you notes, speeches, and even songs. When Joanne Hindley Salch got married, her students even wrote wedding vows and toasts for their in-school celebration.

Sometimes the events are sorrowful occasions. In the last eight years we have attended the funerals of parents of three of our children. On each occasion our students wrote comforting words to their friends in mourning. I've often been struck by how often tragic deaths of historic figures take place during the summer months when we are apart from our students. To be honest, I'm often relieved that we are not in a position to explain the untimely deaths of people like Princess Di and John F. Kennedy, Jr. Had these unfortunate accidents occurred during the school year, I'm sure that many of our students would have asked for addresses to send kind words to the grieving families. No, we wouldn't have asked our young students to write traditional condolence notes, but I'm sure their words from the heart would have been well received.

Expect Artwork to Be Accompanied by Text

There is very little white space on the walls of our school. Every inch seems decorated with student work. Just as museum pieces are accompanied by titles, placards with background information, and brochures describing the work and the artist, so too children's work in a school deserves to be treated in the same elegant fashion. (I can even imagine asking older student to periodically prepare a walking tour of the school on tape to be given to visitors who want to tour the hallways on their own.) Perhaps less ambitious, but nonetheless valuable, would be to require that every piece of art in the hallway have a title (or at least an "untitled" notation), a description of the media used, and background on the student/artist. Other writing possibilities would be procedural notes so that other students can learn the techniques used, reflections by the artist on his work, and blank paper to encourage written response by viewers.

Figure 3.28 is a first grader's explanation of how to make marble paintings. Not only do viewers learn from this piece of writing how to do their own marble paintings, but Esther's teacher can appreciate which spelling patterns this student needs to learn.

Weave Writing into Student Government

In *Going Public,* I introduce our school's student council. This group of students (one representative from every class) meets with me every two weeks. Our mission is to acknowledge the people and events worthy of celebration and to attend to the problems that need to be solved. Following the half-hour gathering, representatives share their notes with their individual classes. Not only does this structure allow for quick sharing of information with the entire student body, it also enables students to take on leadership roles in the school. In addition, this structure leads to all kinds of writing tasks. In the upper-grade classes in which students actually vote for their class representative, some children even prepare promotional materials encouraging their friends to vote for them.

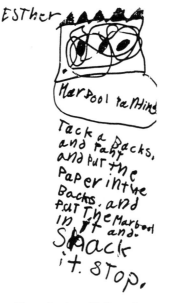

Figure 3.28   *Text Translation: Take a box and paint and put the paper in the box. And put the marble in it and shake it. Stop.*

Most of the writing, however, takes place at our meetings or in response to our meetings. First, all students take notes on the discussions. Even the kindergarten children find a way to record key points (see Figure 3.29). Then too, children's conversations about the good things happening in the school and the problems yet to be solved inevitably lead to some real-world writing. They write thank-you notes, congratulatory banners, and good news announcements. They've also written many letters to the custodian requesting repairs, reminder signs for hallway decorum, and posters for a neighborhood "curb your dog," campaign. Their writing brings to mind the Gallatin Writers' Project of Bozeman, Montana, in which writers examine local issues and try to come up with solutions. Likewise, our students use their literacies to improve the quality of life at school. Dominique and Jhordan sent the note in Figure 3.30 to our custodian James. Note their "c.c." to me. The younger children at the student council were fascinated by this device and in fact began adding a "c.c" to their writing and sending carbon copies to their parents and teachers.

Provide Opportunities for Students to Teach

In Chapter 4, "Paving the Way for Nonfiction Study," I suggest that every child be considered a potential teacher. When children do have occasions to teach they can become familiar with a host of new writing genres that facilitate their presentations and inter-

Figure 3.29

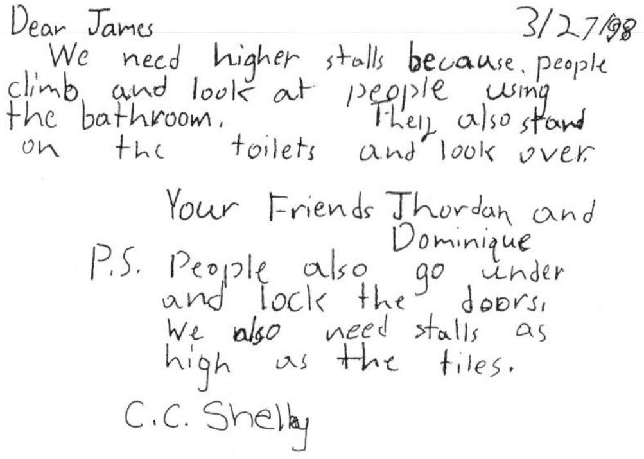

Dear James   3/27/98
   We need higher stalls because people
climb and look at people using
the bathroom.   They also stand
   on   the   toilets   and look over

        Your Friends Jhordan and
                        Dominique
   P.S. People also   go under
        and lock the doors,
        We also need stalls as
        high as the tiles.
      C.C. Shelby

Figure 3.30

actions. Children can learn to use the overhead projector well, to make helpful diagrams, charts, and displays, to jot notes on a wipe-off board, and distribute outlines, glossaries, and bibliographies.

Last year Lorraine's first-grade students invited children, teachers, and family members in to view a formal presentation of a dream neighborhood they had constructed, complete with parks, fountains, playgrounds, and benches. In addition to crafting invitations and labeling their constructions, individual children prepared welcoming remarks, brief lecture notes, and closing statements. Lorraine sent photographs of their exhibit to the Making Our City Livable Foundation sponsored by the New York Foundation of Architecture. These young children learned to study their surroundings closely and make thoughtful suggestions. Most of all, they learned to expect their work to be taken seriously and treated respectfully. (See related information in "A Commitment to Putting Students' Nonfiction Writing to Good Use," p. 142.)

Create Classroom Newsletters

When children know that there is a predictable, formal vehicle for publishing their writing they often write toward that publication. In several classes, parents assume the responsibility of putting together a biweekly or monthly class newsletter. They include all the information parents need to know, including updates on curriculum, a calendar and description of upcoming trips, book recommendations, and supplies needed. In addition, most leave ample space for student writing and artwork. Parents are eager to tuck in students' poems and short stories, but the newsletter format invites children to try their hand at more newsy genres. Children in fact can take over for the parents. Youngsters can be asked to write their own accounts of what is happening in their class and school as well as their own lists of supplies needed, calendar dates, and curriculum happenings. (For more information on schoolhouse publishing see *Writing Through Childhood*.)

Encourage Keeping in Touch with Friends

I always encourage students to keep in touch with friends who have moved away. The possibilities of using electronic mail have made keeping in touch even more popular. Children write to former classmates as well as to children they have never met. Regina's students write pen-pal letters to children from her former teaching assignment in Brooklyn, and the teachers arrange for the children to meet. David requires all his fourth graders to select someone in their lives that they can write to on a regular basis. Monthly letter writing is built into their writing workshop schedule.

As noted earlier, in the early years of our school our students wrote pen-pal letters to the students at the Center for Teaching and Learning in Edgecombe, Maine. They thought about the quality of these texts much the way they thought about the poems and picture books they'd been writing. Cineca wrote the first introductory letter to her pen pal (see Figure 3.31).

At the end of some school years, I have given out self-addressed stamped postcards with my summer address printed on the front. The message was clear to students: I expected them to keep in touch over the summer break. They did, and do.

Similarly, I always tell our graduating seniors to keep in touch. And I mean it. Sometimes they send us letters. Recently they've begun to send rather clever e-mails (see Figure 3.32). Other times, they show up in person. The letter in Figure 3.33 was left on my desk by a graduate who stopped by when I was out of the building.

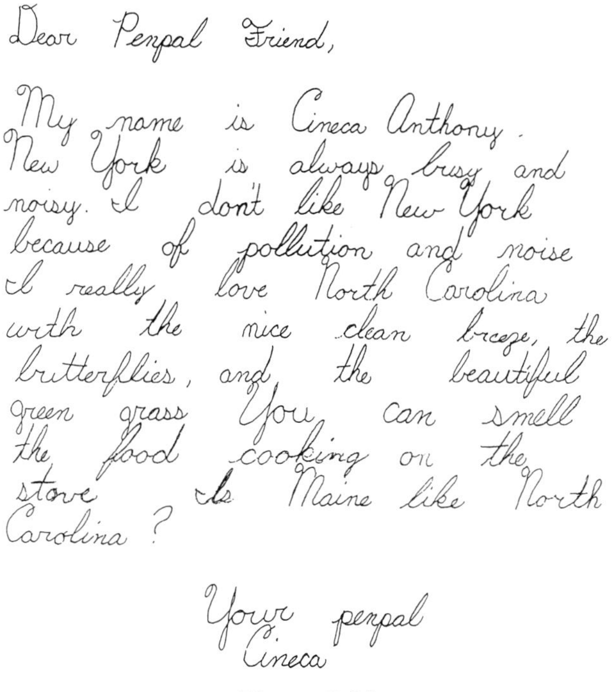

Dear Penpal Friend,

My name is Cineca Anthony. New York is always busy and noisy. I don't like New York because of pollution and noise I really love North Carolina with the nice clean breeze, the butterflies, and the beautiful green grass You can smell the food cooking on the stove Is Maine like North Carolina?

Your penpal
Cineca

Figure 3.31

```
>Hi!!!!!!!!!!!!!!!!!!!!!!!!!!!!!!!!!!!!!!!!!!!!!!!!!!!!!!!!!!!!!!!!!!!!!!!!!!!
>!!!!!!!!!!!!!!!!!!!!!!!!!!!!!!!!
>
>!!!!!!!!!!!!!!!!!!!!!!!!!!!!!!!!!!!!!!!!!!!!!!!!!!!!!!!!!!!!!!!!!!!!!!!!!!!!!
>!!!!!!!!!!!!!!!!!!!!!!!!!!!!!!!!
>
>!!!!!!!!!!!!!!!!!!!!!!!!!!!!!!!!!!!!!!!!!!!!!!!!!!!!!!!!!!!!!!!!!!!!!!!!!!!!!
>''''''''''''''''''''''''''''''
>
>!!!!!!!!!!!!!!!!!!!!!!!!!!!!!!!!!!!!!!!!!!!!!!!!!!!!!!!!!!!!!!!!!!!!!!!!!!!!!
>!!!!!!!!!!!!!!!!!!!!!!!!!!!!!!!!!!
>
>(Sorry if I was a bit redundant.)
>
>How's everything going at M.N.S.? Has anything happened since I left? I
>really, really, really miss going to M.N.S.. (I also really miss being
>able to wake up at 7:20.) Even though I have to wake up early, I really
>like LAB. I hope that everybody's having a wonderful year so far.
>
>
>-                                                           Love,
>
>
>Adar-
```

Figure 3.32

Dear ⬥ey,   3/7
                                   Friday

    I am having the greatest
time just looking at your office.
It's always been the greatest
I've ever seen. I feel bad I
couldn't see you. M.N. looks
great! The walls are
decorated from head to toe, (ceiling
to floor) and even when there
isn't anybody in the classrooms
or on the floor, I can still
feel the wonderful, supportive,
fun atmosphere that you are so
too lucky to "live" in. You
had the most wonderful idea to when
start you decided to start this
school and I, along with millions
of kids are glad you had that
great idea and made it come
to life. It's made a "Lasting
Impression; (a book by the wellknown
and loved Shelley Harwayne) on me.
I wish I could come back!
    Love,
    Dana, from the graduating
class of 1995

Figure 3.33

Feeding the World

This chapter has been filled with ideas on creating opportunities for children to engage in writing with real-world payoffs. In addition to inviting students in on the kind of writing that gets the business of living done, I have also suggested ways to put students' more literary efforts to good use in a building. All of the above requires, of course, not just determined teachers but a supportive principal and probably a supportive custodian and parent body. This kind of writing begs to leave the four walls of any one classroom, and students will need adults to pave the way for their words to be heard in the real world.

Years ago, I was very moved by Don Murray's notion that if our work is fed by the world it may in turn feed the world. I have come to believe that if our work is fed by the world it *must* in turn feed the world.

RELATED READINGS IN COMPANION VOLUMES

Going Public (Heinemann, 1999) is abbreviated as GP. *Writing Through Childhood* (Heinemann, forthcoming), is abbreviated as WC.

Changing relationships in schools	**GP**: Ch. 4, Ch. 5
Writing to improve the quality of life at school	**GP**: Ch. 4; **WC**: Ch. 9
Inviting children to write for many reasons	**GP**: Ch. 4; **WC**: Ch. 7
Inviting children to write in many genres	**WC**: Ch. 4; **WC**: Ch. 7
Launching writing workshops	**WC**: Ch. 3. Ch. 6
Designing community-service assignments	**GP**: Ch. 4
Arranging celebrations	**GP**: Ch. 4
Raising student activists	**GP**: Ch. 1, Ch. 7
Selecting inspirational literature	**WC**: Ch. 5
Delegating jobs to students	**GP**: Ch. 1
Conferring about purpose and audience	**WC**: Ch. 4
Publishing in authentic ways	**WC**: Ch. 9

CHAPTER 4

PAVING THE WAY FOR NONFICTION STUDY

Key Literacy Lessons

1. Children are interested in such a wide range of topics that the elementary years seem custom-designed for nonfiction studies.

2. Children and teachers can do their best nonfiction research when the following elements are present in the school culture:
   - A feeling of belonging to a school, not just a class
   - An appreciation that everyone is a teacher
   - A willingness to engage the wider community
   - A deep-felt belief that the world is a fascinating place
   - A commitment to providing big blocks of uninterrupted time
   - Priority given to literacy acts with lifetime potential
   - A determination to build nonfiction libraries
   - A set of realistic goals for nonfiction reading and writing
   - A shared interest in writing among school specialists
   - A commitment to putting students' nonfiction efforts to good use

3. If students are to engage in a successful nonfiction writing course of study, teachers must address the following issues in clear and explicit ways:
   - discovering a topic
   - collecting data
   - thinking new thoughts
   - choosing appropriate formats
   - learning from nonfiction literature read-alouds
   - using the special features of nonfiction writing
   - reading nonfiction independently
   - modeling nonfiction writing

4. Nonfiction studies are important to students as well as to their family members.

Childhood is the time to be intensely interested in figuring out how this world and everything in it works. In Richard Russo's novel *Nobody's Fool*, Sully's grandson Will demonstrates this point. The author writes,

> Will was ready. He'd finished his cereal and was engaged in a scientific experiment with a few remaining Cheerios in his bowl. In the beginning they floated. You could hold a Cheerio under the surface of milk for a long time, but as soon as you removed the spoon, it floated right to the top. You could break it in half, and then the two halves floated. Break the two halves in half and all four floated. But when you broke them into smaller pieces, they bloated up, lost their buoyancy, turned to brown muck in the bottom of the bowl. Without arriving at any conclusions as to what this phenomenon might mean, Will nevertheless found it interesting. It was nice to be able to think such thoughts in peace.

Will got lost in scientific phenomena, whereas Digger in David Malouf's *The Great World* became passionate about geography. The author writes,

> When Digger was in third grade at primary school, and the teacher allowed them for the first time to take home books, he had for several months been obsessed with atlases and maps of every sort. Kneeling up at the kitchen table to get closer to the lamp, he would screw his eyes up so that he could read even the smallest print, and making himself small, since whole towns in this dimension were no larger than fly-spots, would try to get a hold of what it was here that he was dealing with, the immensity of the world he had been born into, but also the relation between the names of things, which were magic to him, and what they stood for, towns, countries, islands, lakes, mountains.

Children: Custom-Designed for Nonfiction Studies

Young children certainly have a lot on their minds. If no one stifles them, they notice and question every little thing. One day, Suzy asked our science teacher, "When lightning hits water, do the fish fry?" Children also love to offer possible answers and explanations, experiment with possibilities, and teach others what they're learning. They love to hang out shingles, proclaiming themselves experts at something.

In the unedited writer's notebook entry in Figure 4.1, Patrick boasts that his friend Griffin is "packed with a lot of knowledge," about sharks.

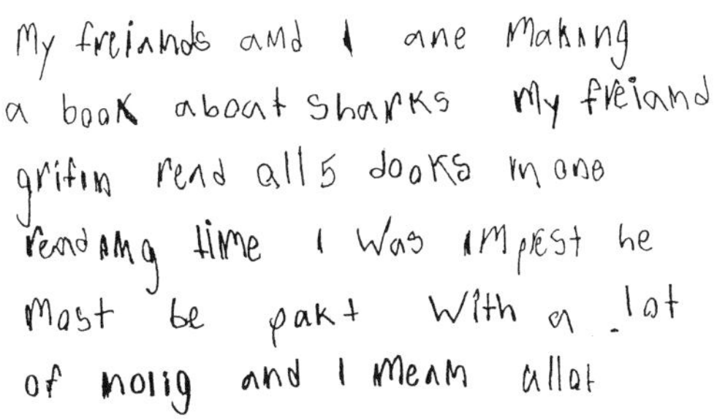

My freiands and I are making a book aboat sharks my freiand grifin read all 5 books in one reading time I was impest he most be pakt with a lot of nolig and I mean allot

Figure 4.1

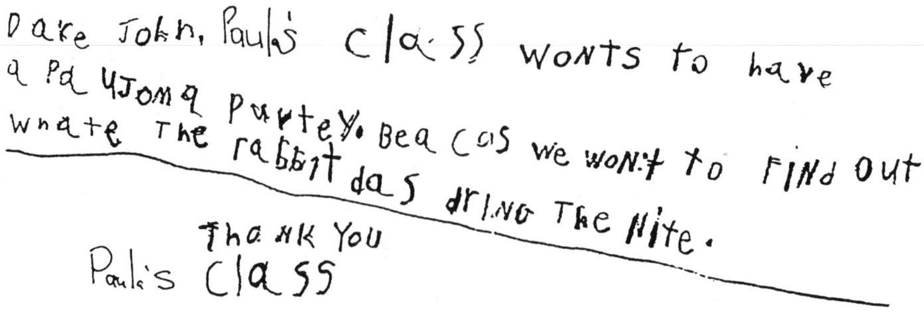

Dare John, Paul's class wonts to have
a pd yjom q purtey. Becaus we wont to find out
whate the rabbit das dring the nite.
                    Thank you
Paul's class

Figure 4.2

The naturalist Edward O. Wilson claims to have never outgrown his bug period. We are lucky enough to be living with hundreds of children who are going through their bug period, along with their dinosaur, cat, kite, bridge, frog, airplane, shell, whale, gemstone, shark, UFO, and a gazillion other periods. Our custodian John received the note in Figure 4.2 from Paula's first graders. Her students were going through their rabbit period. It's not surprising to find similarly inquisitive notes all over our school.

Children are interested in such a wide range of topics that the elementary school years are custom-designed for nonfiction studies. As building principal, I am always asking myself how I can support teachers' efforts to engage children in frequent and meaningful nonfiction reading and writing projects. In other words, I ask myself, "What needs to be in place in the culture of our school so that teachers and students can do their best nonfiction work?"

I want to lead a scholarly school. I want to know how to make such a school possible.

Toward a School Culture That Promotes and Supports Nonfiction Studies

In earlier works and earlier in this work, I have presented several aspects of our school's culture. Here, I will describe how these cultural beliefs, attitudes, and school practices specifically support nonfiction work. I will also introduce several additional aspects of our school culture that directly promote and enrich nonfiction reading and writing.

As fully explained in *Going Public,* ours is a school community in which curriculum decisions are made by people whose lives are touched by those decisions. In other words, our teachers have the flexibility to let children's voices, needs, and interests be heard as they make decisions about what will be studied in the areas of science and social studies. Teachers also have opportunities to bring their own areas of expertise and passions into their classroom inquiries. This does *not* mean that we ignore state mandates and city policies in regards to curriculum studies. It does mean that we sift through possibilities thoughtfully and use our time wisely so that our students are prepared for whatever challenges face them when they leave elementary school. At the same time, we have found ways to let children follow their own inquiries, oftentimes during their reading and writing workshops. This flexibility in curriculum is one of the most crucial factors in supporting teacher efforts to create content-rich, nonfiction-rich classrooms.

The following elements in our school's culture also promote and enrich nonfiction studies.

A Feeling of Belonging to a School, Not Just a Class

We have a very content-rich corridor life in our school. Children spend lots of time reading the walls of our hallways, gathering information as they go. They can see permanent artistic displays of time zones all over the world, the names of all their government leaders, and the location of all their home countries on world maps. Bulletin boards are lined with American history timelines, murals offering the precise names of local trees, and newspaper articles about immigration issues in New York City.

In addition, children know how to crisscross those corridors, tapping resources in all the classrooms. They have the flexibility to talk and work alongside someone who is not in their class, to read a book that does not sit on their shelf. Our school has very few multigrade classrooms (see *Going Public* for details). Instead, I like to think that all our children feel like they belong not to any one class nor to any one grade, but to the school. I like to think that our students feel at home in any classroom in the building.

Anne Lamott's book on writing, *Bird by Bird,* takes its title from the advice her father gave her brother as he plowed through a research report on birds. Her father consoled the frustrated young writer by saying, "Just take it bird by bird." When our students conduct research, I'd like to think they are given the advice, "Just take it room by room."

Schools, if they are to become scholarly communities, need to create structures so that children have access to the experts and the information they need. Our job is to create networks, to serve as switchboard operators who help young people make connections. Children who love baseball should know all the other baseball fans in the building, and there should be structures in place that allow children with this common interest to read, write, think, share, discuss, and argue baseball together. If a student is writing about the arrival of a new baby in the family and needs more information on the topic, he should be able to talk to other students in the school who are going through the same experience. Children need to know that there are people and places in the school that can answer their most mundane as well as their wildest questions. Children need to know that the community thinks highly of children with interesting and honest questions.

These schoolwide structures might include an open-door policy for children hunting down information, public files of experts within the school community, a current list of schoolwide research topics and nonfiction writing being done (imagine if teachers brought all pieces of nonfiction writing to a staff meeting, and the topics were sorted and students with shared interests were introduced), nonfiction reader-response groups formed around students' interests and across grade levels, and opportunities for children to teach one another (see below).

An Appreciation That Everyone Is a Teacher

Donald Graves once commented that it was a good thing the children at the Manhattan New School were short, otherwise it would be hard to tell the children from the teachers. We like to think this is so. One year when Matthew was just in kindergarten, he looked up at me on March 10 and asked, "Right, Shelley, there are 264 hours until spring?" I was rather stunned by his comment and asked him to explain his thinking. "Oh," he said rather matter-of-factly, "My mom told me that spring begins on March 21, so I took eleven twenty-fours." How many concepts is this five-year-old juggling? How many can he share with his friends?

Children are tapped for their areas of expertise, but never as often as they probably should be. The days seem to go so quickly. I'm always thrilled and at the same time saddened when I discover that a student has an outside specialty that I knew nothing about. How could I not have known all along that Deyan sings with Pavarotti? That Jason is a champion soccer player? That Masafumi played the violin at the White House? That Joseph is an accomplished gymnast?

It's no surprise that when I needed a new bulletin board display for our main reception area I put out a rather simple call. I sent the following letter to all families.

> *Dear families,*
>
> *Rumor has it that your child _____ is an expert at _____. Won't you send in a photograph demonstrating this expertise and write a brief explanation of how this interest got started and developed? I am planning a bulletin board display so that all members of our community appreciate our students' unique areas of interest.*

Teachers filled in the blank when they were aware of a child's outside interests, but families were asked to tell us about areas of expertise that might not have been known to us. Similar to other bulletin boards described in this text, this display interested passersby, especially because the photographs enabled them to match children with the story of their interests. And as with other schoolwide bulletin boards, teachers, parents, and support staff couldn't resist adding their own hitherto unknown areas of extracurricular expertise.

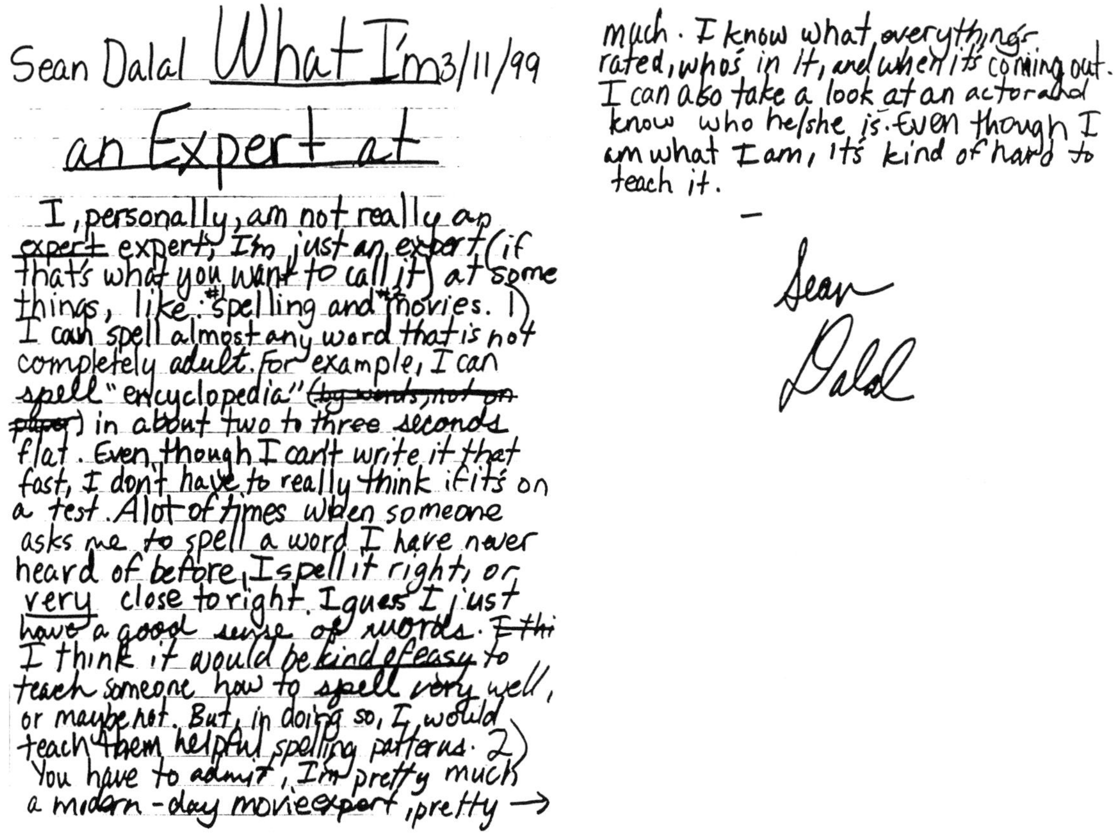

Sean Dalal <u>What I'm</u> 3/11/99

<u>an Expert at</u>

I, personally, am not really an ~~expert~~ expert; I'm just an expert (if that's what you want to call it) at some things, like: #1 spelling and #2 movies. 1) I can spell almost any word that is not completely adult. For example, I can spell "encyclopedia" ~~(by words, not on paper)~~ in about two to three seconds flat. Even though I can't write it that fast, I don't have to really think if it's on a test. A lot of times when someone asks me to spell a word I have never heard of before, I spell it right, or very close to right. I guess I just have a good sense of words. ~~I thi~~ I think it would be kind of easy to teach someone how to spell very well, or maybe not. But, in doing so, I would teach them helpful spelling patterns. 2) You have to admit, I'm pretty much a modern-day movie expert, pretty →

much. I know what everything rated, who's in it, and when it's coming out. I can also take a look at an actor and know who he/she is. Even though I am what I am, it's kind of hard to teach it. —

Sean
Dalal

Figure 4.3

A few student responses from our "The Experts Are Coming! The Experts Are Coming!!" board are included here. The response of Sean, a fifth grader with humility, is in Figure 4.3. Without the photograph attached to the response shown in Figure 4.4, it might be difficult to appreciate third grader Sofia's special expertise. As is our usual custom, when these experts' displays were taken down, the exhibit was turned into an anthology by slipping each response into a three-ring binder.

Children need ample opportunities at school to share their areas of expertise. They know stuff, and we need to acknowledge that knowing. Some days they surprise you with the stuff they know, like the time Lisa asked a kindergarten class that was studying geology, "What's deep under the rocks?" Very confidently, Charlie called out, "Hell." More times than not, children can be considered authorities when they have devoted great amounts of time to thinking, reading, asking questions, observing, role-playing, and collecting artifacts related to the pirates, dinosaurs, and skyscrapers of their dreams.

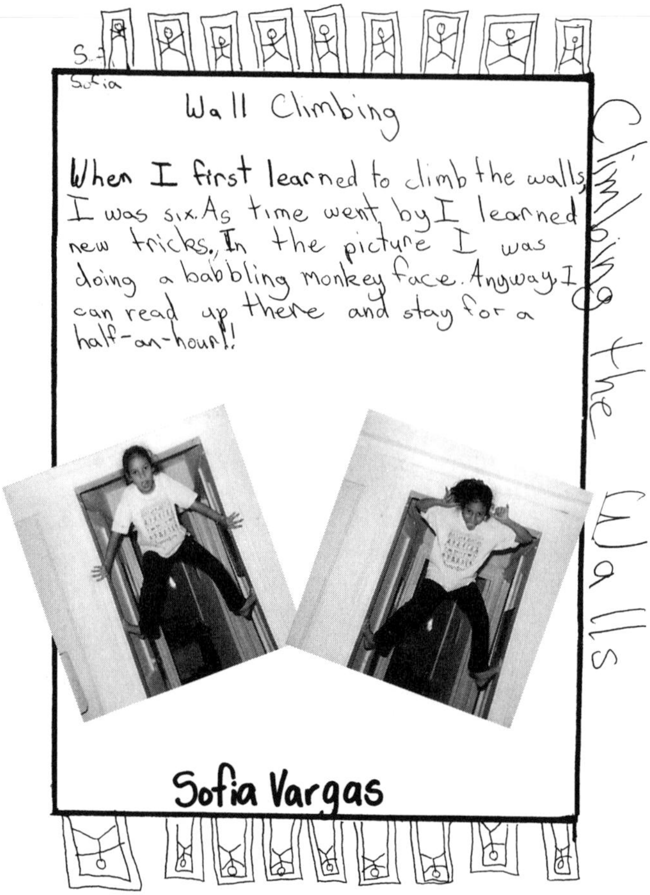

Figure 4.4

One year I received a birthday card created by two six-year-olds (see Figure 4.5). How wonderful that children would think of giving information as a birthday gift. That card has remained one of my all-time favorites.

I've framed the scrap of paper in Figure 4.6. I found it on a tabletop in a hallway. I never discovered who wrote it, but it serves to remind me that children need to be part of the teaching pool in schools.

A permanent invitation sign hangs in our main lobby. It reads,

Please share your area of expertise.
Arrange a lunchtime meeting to teach your friends.
See Shelley to arrange a time and place and a guest list.

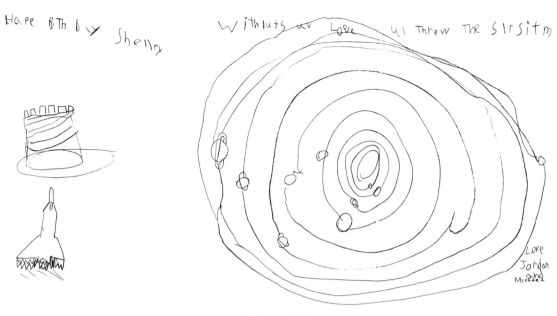

Figure 4.5

Over the years, children have taught such diverse subjects as French, origami, hair braiding, and soccer. I ask them how many students they would like to host and then we pick an appropriate time and place. The teaching sessions usually take place on the gray leather couch in my office and students invite classmates and occasionally teachers. Included here are some of the requests from students who wanted to share their expertise.

Figure 4.7 is a request from two kindergartners. Figure 4.8 shows the announcement for Mark's 12:30 hockey class, followed by several of the visual aids he used during his presentation. If you didn't know this was a hockey lecture, would you be able to make sense of this six-year-old's invented spelling? When children know we are excited about their hobbies, talents, obsessions, and the like, they never say, "I have nothing to write about." Our students know that areas of expertise can provide a lifetime of writing topics.

a liccuid is carfy.1
a Gas isa clowd2
a SAlid isa Ice

Figure 4.6

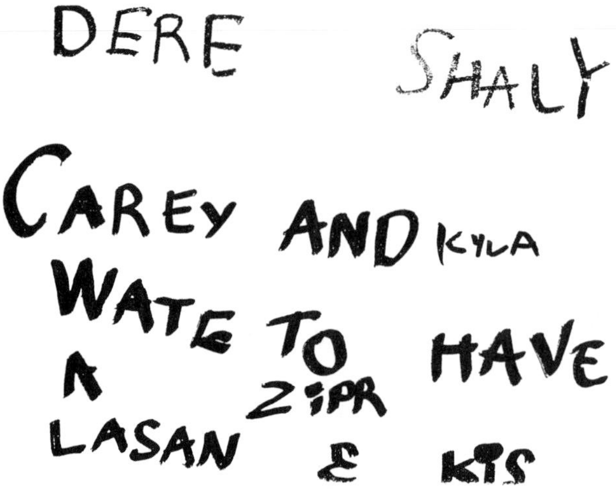

DERE   SHALY

CAREY AND KYLA

WATE TO   HAVE

A   ZIPR

LASAN   E   KTS

Figure 4.7 *Text translation: Dear Shelley, Carey and Kyla want to have a zipper lesson—3 kids.*

HOOKING

SLASHiKI

SMBUE

PUITAE PRAISS

Figure 4.8 *Text translation: Hooking, Slashing, Penalty, and Zamboni.*

Teaching someone else what you know and care about serves to crystallize your thinking and helps you discover areas in which you are still lacking sufficient information. Think about the last time you were asked to present information to your faculty or to your district colleagues. You literally get your act together before leaving the house. As a yearlong course in law school, my daughter taught constitutional rights to a class of seniors in a Washington, D.C., high school. You can be sure that this was a very effective way to guarantee that she deeply understood the Constitution.

A Willingness to Engage the Wider Community

Our students know the feeling of belonging to an entire school as well as to an entire community because they have had so many experiences that help them appreciate that the neighborhood of the school is an extension of the school. In addition to the more than 550 children and their family members who belong to this school, as well as the 30 teachers and the dozen members of our support staff, our children know that they can tap community resources. Observing and interviewing neighborhood residents provides our students with firsthand information that surfing the Internet cannot. Paula Rogovin's first graders interview more than 40 people each school year. Imagine what our fifth graders could do. They could write a local history, investigate how the local shopkeepers rely on science, math, and literacy to keep their businesses running, or write articles about neighborhood residents with interesting stories to tell.

Our students need opportunities to be out of doors sketching, jotting, observing, talking, interviewing, and analyzing, and neighborhood residents need opportunities to be indoors lecturing, showing slides, demonstrating techniques, telling stories, and answering questions. Eve Mutchnick, one of our kindergarten teachers, hangs a sign on her classroom door each year. It's the classic shopkeeper's red-and-white metal sign that reads, "Come In, We're Open." We need to roll out the red carpet and make way for the park rangers, chefs, museum curators, greengrocers, bagel bakers, and cabinetmakers whose places of work are in walking distance of our school.

Eventually, we want our children to realize that all of the city's resources are at their disposal. I'm never surprised to see a note on a classroom door (written by a student, of course) that reads, "Gone to the Empire State Building. Be back at 12:30." I'm also never surprised when teachers take their classes on sleepovers to the Liberty Science Center in New Jersey, an environmental center in Connecticut, or to Washington, D.C. As children grow older, their sense of community widens and their sense of responsibility grows, as do their nonfiction topics and range of nonfiction formats.

A Deep-Felt Belief That the World Is a Fascinating Place

I can easily imagine beginning a nonfiction course of study by reading aloud Susan Bonners's short novel *The Silver Balloon,* in which a young boy begins a correspondence with an older man. Each time they write, they include a mystery item to be identified by the receiver. Readers get vicarious pleasure as the young boy employs all kinds of research methods to identify an arrowhead, a rose hip plant, a grain of wheat, and an ancient saber tooth. The main characters in this novel do indeed find the world and everything in it quite fascinating. Students hunger to have mystery items of their own to identify. Although novels like this one (as well as picture books like *Archibald Frisby* by Michael Chesworth and *Weslandia* by Paul Fleischman) can inspire children to roll up their sleeves and lead wide-awake lives, so can real-life members of the school community.

Earlier I described the insatiable need to know which characterizes the adults and children in our school. The grown-ups are as eager as the children to recognize one another's languages, to locate one another's countries on a map, and to taste one another's foods. They are as excited as their students when the chicks hatch, the snails give birth, and the turtle lays an egg. They read the newspaper voraciously, travel whenever they can, and have their own areas of expertise apart from teaching. They look at the world with eyes of wonder and so do their students.

A school filled with curious people is fertile ground for nonfiction writers. When one of our students was involved with the lowering of the ball in Times Square on New Year's Eve (see *Writing Through Childhood*), the children began wondering about all the people involved in the celebration. How do you become the confetti lady, the balloon blower, or a member of the cleanup crew? When our good friend and mentor Jacques d'Amboise announced his ambitious plan to fulfill his lifelong dream of hiking the Appalachian Trail, our students and their teachers were eager to ask him about how he was preparing for the trip, what records he would keep along the way, and how he would share the experience when he returned. Jacques's contagious energy for the project made us all passionate about the Appalachian Trail. When teachers shared the news stories about the Nabisco Company not being allowed to sell crackers in the same shape as the famous Pepperidge Farm Goldfish crackers, children wanted to understand how there could be laws attached to brand names, what law suits are all about, and who gets to make the final decisions in these cases.

At MNS, no area of inquiry is too bland or too bizarre. Children are never told not to stare, ask hard questions, or voice their opinions. Quite the opposite. We want children to take in their world, make sense of it, and share their discoveries with everyone in their scholarly community.

A Commitment to Providing Big Blocks of Uninterrupted Time

Throughout this book as well as in the previous volume, *Going Public*, I have stressed the need to rethink the use of time in our schools and to eliminate busywork and needless interruptions. Nowhere is the need for big blocks of time more apparent than when children get hooked on a nonfiction inquiry project. It takes a great deal of time to become a student of your subject. Several years ago, in an article entitled "Chutzpah and the Nonfiction Writer," in *Pen in Hand: Children Become Writers,* edited by Bernice E. Cullinan, I noted, "Nonfiction writers do not simply sit at their desks with pen in hand or word-processor at the ready. They' re out there taking in the world, aggressively trying to learn more." Nonfiction writers need time to discover topics and dwell in topics, before they even begin to share their learnings. If children are to do serious nonfiction research and publication, teachers have to feel okay about inviting children to read related nonfiction during their reading workshop time. They have to feel okay about discussing inquiry topics during class meeting times. They have to feel supported when they schedule related field trips. They have to not be asked to hand in finished work at arbitrary intervals. It takes a lot of time to live the life of a nonfiction writer.

Priority Given to Literacy Acts with Lifetime Potential

Many adults readily admit to spending the greatest portion of their reading time with newspapers, magazines, and nonfiction bestsellers, mainly travel books, biographies, and self-improvement texts. We know that nonfiction reading and writing will be of prime importance throughout our student's lives as well. They too will pass many hours reading pertinent informational texts. In addition, they will spend time following instructions, filling out forms, studying maps, writing letters of request and complaint, composing thank-you notes and condolence cards, participating in surveys, using catalogs, directories, and encyclopedias, reading fliers, menus, and brochures, and conducting Internet searches. It should come as no surprise, then, that we think it's essential to build these types of activities into our regular reading and writing workshops.

A Determination to Build Nonfiction Libraries

Nonfiction writer Marjorie Facklyn has said, "Nonfiction used to be like underwear and hot water tanks—you only buy them when you need them—not for pleasure." Thankfully, times have changed, and we can now provide students with quality books on an incredible array of topics, in varying formats for all stages of readers. If we do things right, students should be able to name their favorite nonfiction writers along with their favorite poets and chapter book writers. (Have all your students heard of Milton Meltzer, Kathryn Lasky, Gail Gibbons, Seymour Simon, Patricia Lauber, Jill Krementz, David Macaulay, and Jennifer Owings Dewey?) Older students should be selecting appropriate works of nonfiction to share with their younger book buddies. Teachers should be reading nonfiction aloud as easily they do other genres. Summer and vacation suggested reading lists should include nonfiction works. Multiple copies of nonfiction works should be available for guided-reading lessons as well as reader-response get-togethers.

Then too, teachers must invite children in on all the formats nonfiction writing can take and the special techniques used by nonfiction writers so that young people become better readers and writers of nonfiction.

It would probably be very helpful to survey the staff members in any school to discover the topics that are particularly intriguing for children at different ages. No doubt many lists would contain such topics as dinosaurs, horses, space travel, cats, dogs, the body, vehicles, building houses, babies, zoos, farm life, and sports. It would then be interesting to survey classroom libraries to see if the books on the shelves support students' interests. If not, why not?

We have recently turned our nonfiction reading room into a nonfiction research room. This room houses print and nonprint reference material. Each year we purchase additional titles, and similar to our classroom collections, only much more vast, we have books connected to our science and social studies curriculum, as well as a wide range of books and magazines dealing with issues elementary children frequently inquire about. In addition, this room houses a lending library of nonfiction multiple copies for readers throughout the grades. It is our intention that teachers will borrow these for guided-reading lessons during their reading workshops. (See p. 200 for more information on guided reading in small groups.)

When children pay their weekly visit to the nonfiction research room, one half of the class is scheduled to use the Internet to study the science topics they are studying in science workshop. (Our technology is not viewed as an end in itself but is used as a tool to support children as they carry out their studies.) The other half utilizes our growing collection of nonfiction trade books. In this way, we have doubled the amount of time our students spend with their science teacher, who also oversees their research and technology studies.

Leslie Carr, a parent writing about our science/technology studies in the school newspaper, observed the following:

> On the fifth floor, there is a science room of the sort most of us remember: a messy place for experiments and discoveries where animals and plants and simple machines reside. On the third floor, there is the new-this-year Research Room, a technology center with ten computers (Windows and Mac) networked to a Windows NT server. It too is a place for discovery, but of an informational, rather than physical kind. . . . Also part of the research program is the nonfiction library, where children can look up topics of interest and gain experience learning to tease out the most salient, surprising, and interesting facts among those they have gathered, by creating "Did you know?" books [see p. 143].

Children working with the Internet are not merely downloading information, just as the children who are reading books are not merely copying out passages. Instead, all students in this nonfiction research room are expected to sort through the information, evaluating it to determine what is valuable and what is worth saving and sharing with others.

A Set of Realistic Goals for Nonfiction Reading and Writing

In *Writing Through Childhood*, I suggest that short genres are magical at the elementary level. The range of very short formats is particularly rich in the nonfiction arena. Among last year's Pulitzer Prizes, writers in the world of journalism received awards for such distinct formats as commentaries, criticism, investigative reporting, beat reporting, breaking news reporting, editorial cartooning, international reporting, national reporting, editorial writing, explanatory journalism, and feature writing. There are all kinds of ways to share information.

In "Chutzpah and the Nonfiction Writer," I suggested that nonfiction writers know their options. I wrote, "They have an image of where they are headed. They ask themselves, 'Who is my audience? What might I do with this information? Is this article suited to one of those airline magazines or would it do better in a technical journal? Or should I try crafting it as a picture book for young children?' Once they've made a tentative decision about form, they begin reading that genre with vigor."

The same is true for children. They need to know their options. They need to know that their nonfiction information can be turned into a picture book, a nonfiction poem, a newspaper article, a photographic essay, an annotated timeline, a published interview, a speech, a book review, a case study, a biographical sketch, a brochure, a letter to the editor, and so on. And then they too need to read these genres with vigor.

The sky must be the limit when it comes to discovering the best form to support students' nonfiction content. We must even be ready to design new formats. A case in point follows.

Several of the nonfiction books in our class libraries contain supplemental information in the back under headings such as "Biographical Notes," "Historical Notes," or simply "Notes." These brief pages usually provide very useful background information about the people and/or places mentioned in the text. It occurred to me that our students could write needed background notes for books that do not provide such information. I suggested that Judy's students begin with *Celebrate America in Poetry and Art* edited by Nora Panzer. In this anthology, which pays tribute to different geographical sections of America as well as to different historical time periods, each poem is published with a great amount of white space bordering the text. The publishers seem to invite students to prepare background notes for each poem, taping these directly alongside the poems. How much richer a student's reading of Emily Dickinson's "To Make a Prairie," or R. P. Dickey's "Santo Domingo Corn Dance: Santo Domingo Pueblo, New Mexico," when they have some context for the setting and its role in history. In addition to background notes for poetry anthologies, students can prepare such material for informational picture books and historical fiction. Not only will students receive practice in preparing succinct, accurate notes, they will easily appreciate how their writing can enrich the work of the class.

Parents frequently ask me if their children will leave our school prepared to write the kind of research reports that students are usually asked to write in middle school, high school, and college. I can't imagine how they could be more prepared. After all, if a student has had experience creating timelines, writing up interviews, and crafting photographic essays, he or she will be able to weave these formats into the traditional research report. And chances are their products will be well-written. (See "Modeling Nonfiction Writing," p. 154.)

A Shared Interest in Writing Among School Specialists

The reading and writing of nonfiction takes place in our regular classroom workshops and also when our students go off to study with the specialists in our school. No doubt, some of the richest reading and writing of content area materials takes place when our students collect research data in the science lab, take notes on an art history slide show in our art studio, search for background information on composers in our music room, prepare summaries of health-related articles for their physical education coursework, or prepare presentations on different countries for their Spanish as a second language class.

It becomes clear then, that school specialists must be well-versed in the way classroom teachers teach reading and writing. Students who use writer's notebooks, double-entry ledgers, and learning logs when they study immigration or the Revolutionary War can use these same tools and techniques when they study the human body, Paul Klee, or Mozart. Content area teachers need to know how to respond to requests for spelling, understand grade-level editing expectations, and fully appreciate revision. And our specialists need to share the ways they support children's writing of nonfiction, especially in the limited blocks of time that are characteristic of once or twice a week schoolhouse specials. In fact, at staff meetings, our science teachers have been asked to share the templates students use when they craft nonfiction texts associated with their science studies. These creations necessarily led to very professional talk about how templates scaffold students' ability to share what they are learning across many disciplines.

Esther's "Did you know . . . ?" passage, a very popular way for our students, working with Lisa Siegman in the research room, to quickly share what they have been learning, appears in Figure 4.9. Figure 4.10 contains a sample of a template designed by a cluster of teachers to facilitate the fifth graders' ability to share what they were learning about migratory animals. Students decided upon the categories of information and the space allotments for each. The template seemed to make it easier for children to know what was expected of them and to fulfill the requirements of the assignment. (Of course, there was always room for innovations and variations.) Mindy Gerstenhaber, teaching science to our youngest writers, provided similar supports. Using a simple alphabet book template, Iliana shaped her information on moths and butterflies (see Figure 4.11, p. 145).

A Commitment to Putting Students' Nonfiction Writing to Good Use

Several year ago, I shared a newspaper clipping with our oldest students. The headline in *The New York Times* read, "A Child's Paper Poses a Medical Challenge." Our students were proud of the eleven-year-old girl from Colorado whose science fair research paper challenged the medical community's use of therapeutic-touch techniques. The children were proud, but not particularly surprised. After all, our school community works hard to take their nonfiction efforts seriously and find ways for their hard work to get real-world feedback.

Children's efforts at nonfiction writing need to be put to good use, or students will wonder why they bother to work so hard. Students realize that they can not add to the

DID YOU KNOW? By Esther Shusho
That the biggest whale ever is the Blue whale, even a Bull
elephant can even stand on the Blue whale's tongue!

THE WORLD'S BIGGEST BABY

When a Blue whale baby is born it is
already the size of an elephant!!!!!!!

HUNTING
Whalers usually hunt for Baleen whales, because their skin can
make oil for lanterns.
So the government decided to pass a law, "whoever hunts for
whales, will have to pay a fine."
Some whalers broke the law ...So year after years there were only
a few Blue whales left.
Still Blue whales are one of the most popular whales ever!

Figure 4.9

body of knowledge the way a reporter for *National Geographic* can, but school communities must offer legitimate ways for students' beginning efforts to become school resources. When students see their efforts making a difference in the world of the school, they are more likely to continue publishing high-quality nonfiction materials. (See Chapter 3, "Discovering Real-World Reasons to Write.")

The following are a few ways that students' nonfiction (informational writing, teaching texts, etc.), can be used wisely in a school:

- Their work can be slipped into teacher resource packets on topics that are studied year after year. When second-grade teachers begin their course of study on the history of New York City, they should be able to turn to all the published materials written in years past by second graders. Likewise, third-grade materials on immigration should be available for all the third-grade researchers yet to come. (See *Going Public,* pages 216–219.)

- Their work can be slipped into professionally published picture books on the same topic and read as companion material.

- Their work can be added to the nonfiction shelves of lower-grade class libraries and used as independent-reading material. I can easily imagine sharing

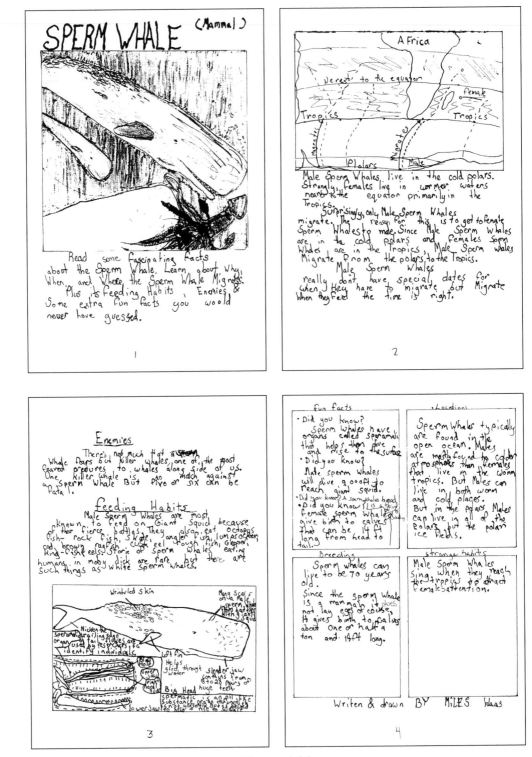

Figure 4.10

Name: by Eliana

A	B
An African Migrant butterfly.	The Bogong moth.
C	D
Camouflage,	Day flying moths.

Name:

E	F
The Esses Emerald butterfly.	Flightless Mother.
G	H
The Ghost moth is Year big.	The hermit butterfly

Figure 4.11

seven-year-old Hejoo's short paragraph listing the attributes of crickets, with children who are just beginning to read nonfiction (see Figure 4.12).

- Their work can be added to the nonfiction section of the school library (in our case, to our nonfiction reading room), and students prepare audiocassettes as read-alongs. (In the last several years Paula's first graders have interviewed and then written books about the lives of over two hundred people. Copies of those books should be on our permanent reference shelves.)

Crickets
Crickets are special to Chinese people. They make music and bring luck. There are not very many crickets around New York City. Crickets live where grass and trees grow. Cricket are pets in China. Crickets sometimes make children fall asleep. Thir music sounds like violins.

By Hejoo

Figure 4.12

- Their work can be used as English as a second language teaching materials, especially those with significant visuals attached.
- Their work can be included in school newsletters to inform parents about the range of content being studied. In Figure 4.13, first grader Zara writes about her class's interview with Ida, our security guard. (See *Going Public* for background information on this interview and Paula Rogovin's *Classroom Interviews: A World of Learning.*)
- Their work can become part of their own classroom library, and copies can be kept from year to year to be used as models as well as resource material for incoming students.
- Their work can be added to content area text sets, bringing together fiction, poetry, and nonfiction pieces on the same topic.
- Their work can be translated into Spanish and added to our Spanish library.
- Their work can be shared at formal presentations that bring to mind openings at museums and galleries. (See Lorraine's students' seascape presentations in "Art That Enriches Content Studies," p. 10, "Provide Opportunities for Students to Teach," p. 121, in Chapter 3, "Discovering Real-World Reasons to Write," and Karen's second graders' biographies in *Writing Through Childhood,* "Adding Energy to the Writing Workshop Through New Genres, New Projects, and New Audiences.")
- Their work can be prepared as thematic teaching calendars with information and illustrations or photographs for each month and distributed to teachers, friends, and family members with similar interests. (See *Writing Through Childhood,* "Adding Energy to the Writing Workshop Through New Genres, New Projects, and New Audiences.")

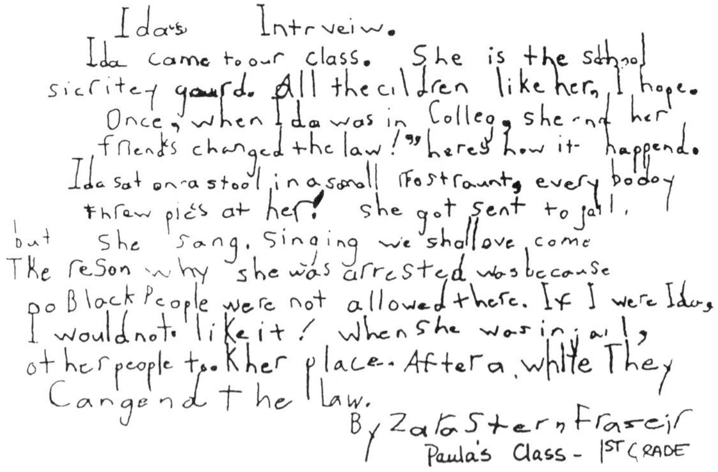
Ida's Intrveiw.
Ida came to our class. She is the school
sicritey gaurd. All the cildren like her, I hope.
Once, when Ida was in Colleg, she and her
friends changed the law!" here's how it happend.
Ida sat on a stool in a small rostraunt, every body
threw pies at her! she got sent to jail,
but she sang. Singing we shallove come
The reson why she was arrested was because
no Black People were not allowed there. If I were Ida,
I would not like it! when she was in jail,
other people took her place. After a while They
Cangend the law.
By Zara Stern Fraseir
Paula's Class - 1ST GRADE

Figure 4.13

Engaging Students in Nonfiction Writing

No matter the grade level, when I walk in and out of classrooms, I expect to see classroom libraries brimming with nonfiction texts. I always look at the amount of space devoted to nonfiction as compared with poetry and fiction. I expect teachers to choose nonfiction books as they read aloud throughout the day. I poke into book pots and baskets as well, wondering if there are any maps, brochures, surveys, or nonfiction picture books included, ones that are appropriate for the ages and interests of the children in the room. (All this has strong implications for the purchase orders I sign. I must ask myself, "Are we spending substantial amounts of money on documents, newspaper and magazine subscriptions, reference materials, and nonfiction trade books?")

I expect that in any one classroom, during any writing workshop, some children will be working on pieces of nonfiction. (Although true stories about their lives is of course nonfiction writing, I am referring here to children writing about content area subjects in which they consider themselves experts or are in the process of becoming experts.) I therefore expect to eavesdrop on interesting informational conversations. It never comes as a surprise to me that amid the poems about loose teeth, family celebrations, and new pets written by first graders in Paula Rogovin's classroom are pieces about construction workers, steel miners, medical professionals, and child labor laws. These are the subjects of students' inquiry during the rest of the school day, and they naturally spill over into the writing folders of six-year-olds. Students should be teaching their classmates, schoolmates, and family members what they are learning.

I also expect that occasionally, especially as we move up in the grades, teachers host whole-class, nonfiction genre studies. When I enter the writing workshop during these genre studies, I expect there to be minilessons devoted to the issues described below.

Discovering a Topic

I deliberately use the word *discovering* here rather than *choosing*. If children are keeping writer's notebooks, they might discover important nonfiction topics when they reread the pages of their notebooks. When Jenny's fascination with clocks, for example, surfaces in her writer's notebook, the young writer might ask her teacher if she could do a project connected to her interest in clocks. The teacher might capitalize on the student's discovery and make the story of her intentions the subject of a minilesson. In this way Jenny lets her classmates know that she has a lot to say about clocks, as well as an eagerness to learn more.

Making Plans to Proceed   The teacher might use mini-lesson time to publicly share strategies for how a child such as Jenny might proceed. Together they list:

Collect more information, thoughts, questions, images, reflections.
Create a project folder or envelope to store additional artifacts.
Duplicate the needed pages from writer's notebook, placing in folder.

Decide on a genre, choosing the form that bests supports the content.

Study examples of that genre.

Create a first draft, aiming for a strong voice

Confer with teacher and friends.

Revise draft if needed.

Edit according to classroom expectations and procedures.

Find a way to go public with your writing.

The classroom teacher might design follow-up minilessons to clarify any of these important components. (See sections below.)

These procedures could apply to any writing project, not just a nonfiction one and the same procedures might apply even when the whole class is involved with an assigned topic, (see comments below.)

When Topics Are Assigned   In "Chutzpah and the Nonfiction Writer," I discuss the practicality of occasionally involving beginning writers in a broad whole-class "umbrella" topic, one which lends itself to lots of individually chosen subtopics. This type of assignment is particularly attractive in settings in which children have limited possibilities for researching on their own outside of school. I summarize these benefits as follows, "There is much to be said for whole-class projects: they lead to a real sense of community; they punctuate the school year by giving a dramatically different feel to the writing workshop; they prompt detailed exploration of topics as children go off in different directions; they show students what it's like to really dwell on, probe, and stick with a topic; and most of all they provide students with a safety net against failure." In other words, if all the children in the class are selecting one aspect of city animal life to investigate, the teacher can use minilesson time to provide many of the supports needed. She can share needed resources (books, movies, tapes, CD-ROMs, magazines, photographs, etc.), invite appropriate guest speakers, and provide her own background knowledge. Then too she can step away from small lessons and arrange the necessary field trips, guaranteeing that all children will have access to rich amounts of firsthand information. (Teachers can also suggest an array of possible writing formats for children as they begin to shape their data into finished pieces, or they can assign one particular format, as described below.)

Teachers can design more concentrated minilessons when there is an umbrella topic and/or when there is one format of nonfiction being studied. For example, when Karen challenges her second graders to write biographies, her minilessons during that time period can be devoted exclusively to the writing of biographies. Since all her children chose different people as subjects, she would not be able to provide all the content information needed during minilessons, but she could use minilesson time to talk about ways to get information, take notes, organize notes, use the template she provided, read aloud biographies and learn from published works, model her own writing of a biography, and so on. (See *Writing Through Childhood* for additional information on this biography course of study.)

Similarly, if a teacher invites children to study annotated timelines, she could begin by sharing a collection of published ones, demonstrate her own writing of one, collaborate on a whole-class timeline, and then invite children to create original ones. Teachers often introduce this format by asking children to create rather personal timelines on such topics as "A History of My Firsts" (first word, first step, first bike, etc.), "Teachers I've Had Through the Years," or "My Growth as a Reader." Later, teachers might ask children to select topics with no umbrella focus, the only criteria being that the topic can be appropriately represented by a timeline. For example, children have chosen such topics as, "The Growth of Video Games," "The Development of Television," "The History of Baseball," "Coins in the United States," and "Mayors of New York City." (See additional information in "Choosing Appropriate Formats," p. 151).

Collecting Data

Teachers often devote minilessons to exploring strategies for collecting additional information. These include recalling all that you already know about your topic, letting the world know that you are looking for more, doing firsthand observations, interviewing people with expertise, reading for more information, surfing the Internet for additional resources, and following up leads with e-mail, letters, phone calls, and faxes.

I'm always pleased when I'm sorting the mail and I discover letters addressed to our students or when the secretary announces that a fax has arrived for a student. I'm equally as pleased when I introduce a student to a visitor and the child quickly gets the visitor talking. Our children have learned how to get information from people.

Strongly connected to collecting data is teaching children how to take notes, whether those notes are based on reading, observing, interviewing, or experimenting. Taking notes is rather idiosyncratic; just look around at the next conference you attend. I've discovered that the best way to teach children how to take notes is to ask them to do so, and then confer with them, offering suggestions on how they can improve. Their initial attempts give you a starting place. I also suggest that children's early attempts at taking notes be attached to something purposeful. For example, Judy Davis's fifth graders take turns at taking notes on the day's happenings and each student writes up the notes for a class journal. Students are asked to take notes at my student council meetings; the notes form the basis for their reports back to their classmates. Paula's students take notes during classroom interviews and the results are turned into class books.

One day, Bee Cullinan brought the wonderful children's poet Rebecca Dotlich to our school. She gathered the students in Pat Werner's third-grade class and shared her poems and her ideas about writing poetry. I sat off to the side of the meeting area, near Wilbert, one of the students. I noticed that Wilbert was taking notes in his writer's notebook during the entire conversation with Rebecca. And the best part was that no one had asked him to. He was doing what made sense to him, jotting ideas down so he wouldn't forget this special day. I asked him to share his notes with the entire class and he did so proudly, teaching other students an important lesson in how to capture the essence of an experience with just a few memorable phrases. His notes appear in Figure 4.14.

Thinking New Thoughts

Teachers design minilessons that demonstrate the importance of developing a strong voice, an original angle, or a surprising perspective. Bruce Brooks, in the introduction to *The Red Wasteland: A Personal Selection of Writings About Nature for Young Readers,* comments about nature writing, suggesting the stance writers must take. He writes,

> Because as a writer I must tell you: Behind every paragraph lurks an attitude. That's what's interesting, really, for us writers and us readers. In describing how a weaverbird makes its nest every spring, one writer can reveal that he thinks nature is holy and birds are our equals in importance and we shouldn't mess with them and the grasses they weave, while another writer can reveal his belief that man is the rightful master of the earth and ought to try copying those weaving techniques and making hats to sell at resorts even if it means swiping the grasses used by the birds and leaving them homeless and eventually dead, while another shows her feeling that the nest "means" nothing—it almost hasn't even happened—until someone has taken it into a laboratory and disassembled it and counted the strands used in its construction and analyzed where the bird probably picked up the nine different varieties of fiber it combined in the weaving. . . .

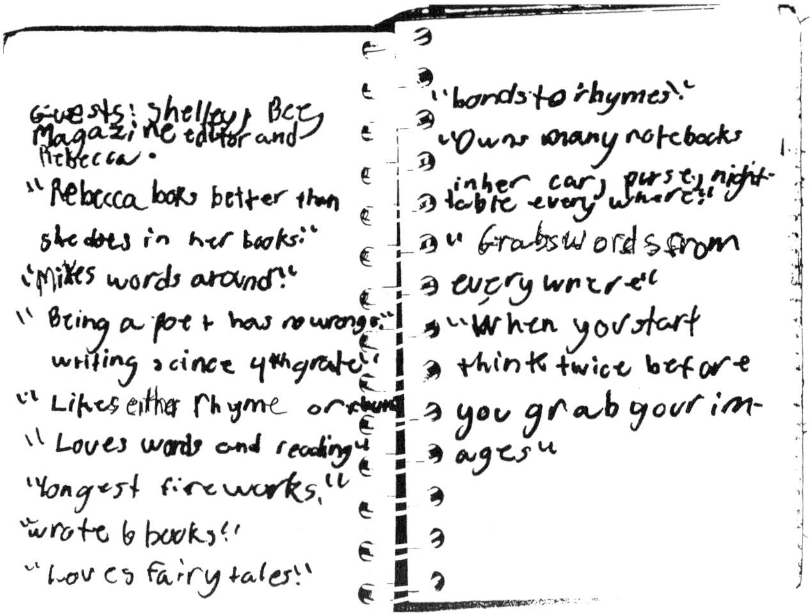

Figure 4.14

If students can't add markedly new information to a field, they can at least look at established information in new ways. They too can have an attitude. To help students discover unique ways of presenting their information, teachers remind students to not just take notes, but to make notes. They remind students to read and then respond to their reading, to ask themselves questions based on their reading. They remind students that it's okay to have opinions, to take a stance when they write nonfiction. They remind students how important it is to talk through your ideas with your friends and to allow seemingly unconnected, surprising thoughts to inform the work at hand. Most of these points are made clear through the use of powerful nonfiction texts or the teacher's own attempts at writing nonfiction.

When Jenny decided to write a picture book about different kinds of clocks, her draft pages were filled with brief histories of grandfather clocks, digital clocks, alarm clocks, cuckoo clocks, clock radios, wristwatches, and so on. Her illustrations showed the same child gazing at each clock and reporting how that particular kind of clock made her feel. She wrote,

> The grandfather clock is big and carefully carved from wood. It makes me feel like reading a long book or baking a cake from scratch.
>> The digital clock shines bright and neon. It makes me feel like being an astronaut and flying to the moon.
>> The clock radio sits on my night table like a treasure chest filled with songs. It makes me feel like tapping my feet or singing along.
>> The wristwatch is delicate and gold and makes me feel grown-up with an appointment to keep.

Jenny got the idea to include her feelings because she had an opportunity to share her work in progress. When a classmate began talking about which kind of clock she preferred, Jenny responded that she would like to own one of each because each made her feel different. She had never realized that before and decided to use that angle to make her clock book different and original. It is essential that students have opportunities to share their works in progress and receive response through individual conferring or small- or whole-group meetings.

Choosing Appropriate Formats

Teachers make sure students are aware of genre possibilities. They might teach minilessons that help students select the best form to deliver the desired content. Students ready to decide on format might be asked to share their content and to list publicly the publishing formats they are considering. The teacher can help students think through the benefits or appropriateness of the choices made. Once she is clear on her meaning, Jenny, for example, could decide if her jottings should be shaped into a timeline on the history of clocks, a how-to book on learning to tell time, a photographic essay on the placement of clocks in public places around New York, a letter to the custodian requesting synchronization of the clocks throughout the school, an article for the school newspaper on the advantages and disadvantages of digital clocks, and so on. Jenny, of course, could decide to pursue several of these options, depending on her commitment to her topic and her abundance of raw material.

Learning from Nonfiction Literature Read-Alouds

As part of their study of geographic formations, David's fourth graders were asked to begin with dictionary definitions of the various formations they were about to create on a huge classroom mural. When Bari and her classmates read the definitions, they were a bit depressed by the lackluster style of writing used in dictionary entries. The children chose to write their own more literary descriptions of the chosen terms. Bari's presentation on mountain peaks appears in Figure 4.15. As you can see from this example, this student understands the literary voice and has high standards for the nonfiction texts she reads and writes. No doubt Bari has heard a great deal of quality nonfiction read aloud.

Teachers read aloud nonfiction material during their regular read-aloud moments as well as at the start of many writing workshops. Since our nonfiction classroom libraries are plentiful, teachers and students have many books to choose from. Sometimes their choice is based on content, when the children are anxious to learn about a

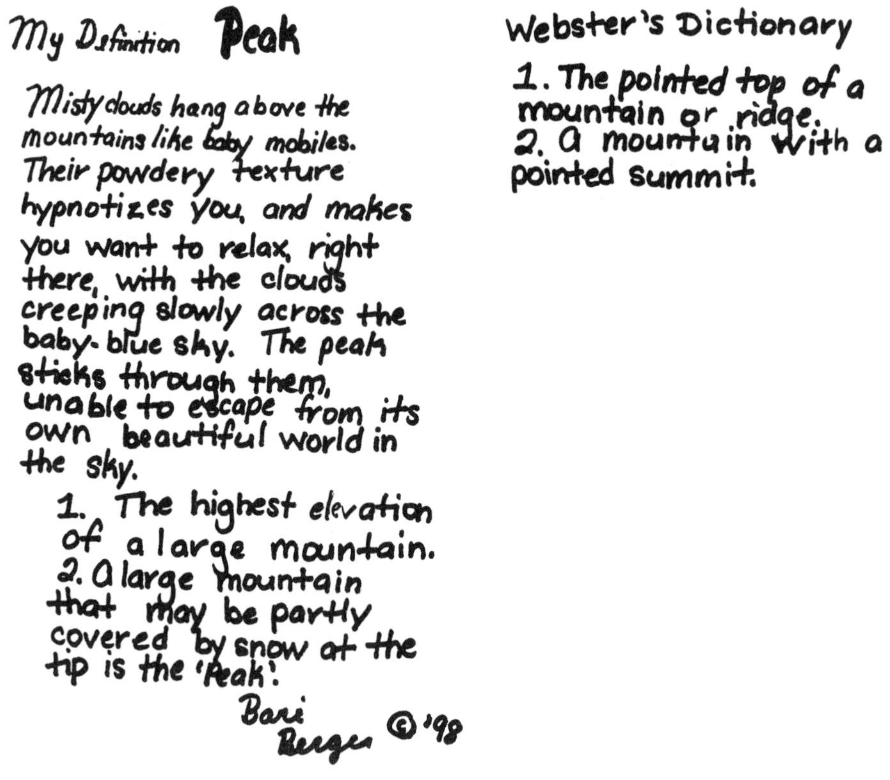

> **My Definition Peak**
>
> Misty clouds hang above the mountains like baby mobiles. Their powdery texture hypnotizes you, and makes you want to relax, right there, with the clouds creeping slowly across the baby-blue sky. The peak sticks through them, unable to escape from its own beautiful world in the sky.
>
> 1. The highest elevation of a large mountain.
> 2. A large mountain that may be partly covered by snow at the tip is the 'Peak'.
>
> Bari Berger © '98
>
> **Webster's Dictionary**
>
> 1. The pointed top of a mountain or ridge.
> 2. A mountain with a pointed summit.

Figure 4.15

particular topic. Other times their choice is based on some literary technique the teacher is interested in sharing. Then too, teachers might share insights from the autobiographies of beloved nonfiction writers in order to help young writers understand the process of researching and crafting nonfiction topics. For example, *On the Bus with Joanna Cole: A Creative Autobiography* by Joanna Cole with Wendy Saul (part of Heinemann's Creative Sparks series), brims with important lessons for young writers.

At yet other times, the teacher presents all the work by one particular nonfiction author in the hopes of inspiring serious mentor relationships. Teachers want children to take writing lessons from these accomplished authors and develop their tastes as nonfiction readers. They want to demonstrate the possibility and desirability of having favorite nonfiction authors.

I frequently join in on the fun, sharing informational picture books written by a few of my own favorite informational authors. For example, I might share a few texts by Mick Manning in the hopes that students will comb the library shelves looking for more. When I read aloud his *A Ruined House,* the students are as enthralled as they would have been if I had chosen to read aloud an adventure story. This book details the changes that take place when a house becomes abandoned. Filled with facts about plants, animals, and the weathering of construction materials, this tour of a sixteenth-century English farmhouse offers many lessons for young writers. In addition to the power of a strong lead ("This is my favorite house. I like it because it has gone to rack and ruin"), precise verbs ("The weather broke through the windows"), and a richness of details, the book illustrates for young nonfiction writers the advantage of creating an intimate, conversational voice, using sidebar information, and selecting unusual topics for study.

I also share Manning's *The World is Full of Babies! How All Sorts of Babies Grow and Develop,* another nonfiction picture book, this one cowritten with Brita Granstrom. The topic is a naturally engaging one for children, and in addition to many of the qualities listed above, this one offers an accessible pattern for children to borrow. On the left-hand side of each double-page spread, the authors describe the activities of human babies, and on the right-hand side they offer the animal equivalents. So while the human baby takes about six months to learn to crawl, on the animal page we learn that, "If you were a baby rat you would be an adult in three months with a family of your own, and you could have twenty babies every six weeks." Students easily spot the pattern in this text and even note that different fonts are used to present the human and animal facts. They also note the repeated refrain, "If you were . . ." which leads to talk about the effect of patterns and repetition in nonfiction texts. (For more examples of qualities to highlight in informational books, see *Writing Through Childhood,* "Reading to Inform your Writing.")

Of course, the nonfiction writing students need to be immersed in cannot be limited to picture books. If we invite children to write photo essays, interviews, speeches, and the like, these too must become part of our read-aloud moments. With older students, I have shared a timeline describing our city sanitation department entitled, "Great Moments in Waste Management," our president's Inaugural Address, and Ted Kennedy's eulogy for his nephew John (all taken from *The New York Times*), excerpts from Carrie Boyko and Kimberly Colen's *Hold Fast to Your Dreams: Twenty Commencement Speeches,* and passages from Anna Quindlen and Nick Kelsh's photographic essay book entitled *Naked Babies.* Even ten-year-olds appreciated the sentiment in the following line from this last book's jacket. Quindlen writes, "The next time you are sitting in a meeting after three cups of coffee, badly needing to go to the bathroom but instead doodling dutifully, crossing your legs and watching the clock, remember that if you were a baby you would have gone by now, and no one the wiser." Then too, there are nonfiction collections that contain a range of nonfiction formats, as in Bruce Brooks's previously sited book *The Red Wasteland,* which contains poems, essays, and short observations.

Using the Special Features of Nonfiction Writing

Nonfiction texts often contain very special tools including glossaries, indices, italicized words, headings, subheadings, appendices, captions, graphs, diagrams, insets, maps, keys, and sidebars. Teachers devote minilessons to explaining the uses of these tools so that children will get the most out of their nonfiction reading as well as feel at home using these techniques to enrich their own writing of nonfiction. In fact, when responding to students' attempts at nonfiction writing, teachers encourage young writers to rely on these tools to make their meaning clear.

Reading Nonfiction Independently

Then too, teachers devote time to demonstrating to children the special reading strategies needed to get the most out of reading nonfiction texts, including paying attention to the above-listed tools as well as all the previewing, skimming, and note-taking that goes along with making sense of nonfiction. Teachers of upper-grade students often place newspaper articles from *The New York Times'* science section on the overhead projector to demonstrate their own strategies for reading nonfiction. They also distribute copies of carefully selected magazine articles related to the students' social studies topics to provide opportunities for students to mark up texts. Students turn into active readers when they write in the margins, highlight key thoughts, star important passages, and circle key words. (See more on active reading in Chapter 9.)

Modeling Nonfiction Writing

Judy Davis and her students began a course of study on writing photo essays. We shared several carefully selected pieces from newspapers to give children an idea of what's possible. Over the years I have clipped a series of photos accompanied by a short paragraph or two of written text on varied topics including the underground world of subway riders, dogs dressed in fancy garb on the sidewalks of New York, decorations hung on New York City fire trucks, and billboards with larger-than-life images. These served as helpful models for our fifth graders, who we thought could prepare text of equal length and about similar topics.

We also brought in several coffee-table type gift books that qualify as photo essays. We sensed that children needed as many examples as possible of what photo essays could look and sound like. The children began selecting topics and snapping photographs. They chose such accessible and interesting issues as churches in New York, scenes in Central Park, poverty in New York, and surprising store windows.

When children brought in their early drafts, Judy worried that her students still weren't developing cohesive texts with essay-like qualities. She was right. Her students were writing captions for individual photos related to their theme, rather than a well-crafted essay in response to the cumulative effect of the photos they had taken.

Judy invited me in to talk to the children and brainstorm ways to redirect the students' efforts. My thoughts went to providing more powerful demonstrations. I suggested that every one in the room, including the teacher, principal, student teacher, and all the students, attempt to quickly get the feel of an essay by writing one then and there. Judy had a series of black-and-white photos hanging on her bulletin board. They were snapshots of her students at work, taken by first-grade teacher Lorraine's husband, Herb Shapiro, our resident photographer. Everyone was asked to study the photos and write an essay that spoke to the overall feeling of the images. In essence, I was encouraging students to see a pattern, discover a unifying angle, or find a thread that brought these photos together. I was trying to take Stephen Jay Gould's comments on essay writing to heart. He has said, "My talent is in making connections. . . . Can you see a pattern? I'm always trying to see a pattern in this forest and I'm tickled that I can do that. . . . I can sit down on just about any subject and think of about twenty things that relate to it and they're not hokey connections. They're real connections that you can forge into essays."

My rough attempt appears below. I wasn't after twenty connections, just one to use as a demonstration for these ten-year-olds.

School—What Really Matters

Some people think that the quality of a school depends on the lessons taught, the books read, or the tests taken. For me, what really matters in a school are none of the above. Instead what really makes a school are the people in it and their relationship with one another.

Teachers and children alike need to work collaboratively together. They need to teach, help, comfort, and even hug one another. They need to create a nurturing and nourishing scholarly community, one that reads together, solves problems together, and even builds works of art together. They need to huddle together, coach one another, and form think tanks in all four corners of the classroom.

Yes, schools are made up of clusters of people. Of course, you could read at home, write at home, paint and solve mathematical problems at home, but there is something extra special about taking part in these activities when you are in the company of other scholars.

After listening to the beginning of my essay as well as those of their teacher and student teacher, the students finally understood the difference between writing a photographic essay and labeling photos. The grown-ups once again learned to not ask children to do things we ourselves had never done. We had shown the power of demonstration.

Judy's students worked diligently revising their essays, and their photographs and words have adorned our stairwells for many years, as permanent tributes to our city, to the children's writing and photography talents, and to the expertise of their teacher. (See Josh's essay on vendors below.) Judy even assigns clusters of her students to work collaboratively and periodically craft photographic essays about school life. These too are on permanent display, atop a red easel, in our second-floor corridor. Children have selected such across-the-grades topics as poetry, mathematical problem solving, and parent involvement. Since the arrival of our digital cameras, I expect more classes to get involved in producing photographic essays. In fact, they seem like a prime way to keep parents informed about school happenings.

Life on the Streets: Vendors in New York City

Whether it's your traditional green-and-white-striped cart of an immigrant with a stand trying to make a living, they all go under the same occupation of vendor. Neither sleet, nor rain, nor snow will stop them from going to work on the streets of New York.

As Mr. Shoshkovitch set up his "Central Park Snack Shop" he tells me of how he left Russia for America to gain a better life. He was a teacher once he said, but the pay was poor. When he came to America there wasn't much he could do since he spoke so little English. So he got a license as a vendor and laid his life on a cart outside the Metropolitan Museum of Art. I wondered as we left about his family. If he had one, how could he support them?

I don't think I would be able to be a vendor. Standing out there for long hours, handing out a pretzel on command. "Too stressful," my mom, brother, and I agreed. One yawning vendor who sold hats said he was there since four in the morning until seven at night. "Geez," Zach said, which seems like the only way to describe it.

Vendors must be one of the most helpful sources to New York City. Think about it. If a kid has just come from the park on a hot summer day, what's better than getting a cool soda from a vendor? Or what if a lady has lost her hat on a windy day, a vendor is there to supply her with a new one. Think about it. Vendors are one of those little things that make New York City, New York City.

As I walked home the other day on 86th Street, I saw a car with a freezing vendor waiting inside for business. On it, I saw a small bumper sticker. It read, "I LOVE NEW YORK," and New York loves its vendors, I added in my mind.

Family Members and Nonfiction Study

Early in my teaching career, I was assigned to teach a "gifted and talented," fourth-grade class. My colleague next door offered me friendly advice. She told me to send the students home talking excitedly about something. "That's what makes the parents happy," she added. As a new teacher, I was certainly concerned with keeping the parents of my students happy. The very first day of school, I recall filling a bucket of soapy water and dramatically dipping some rather unusual plastic bubble makers into the liquid. They were various geometric frames, built from thin tubes with long handles attached that allowed for dipping. When you slowly removed the constructions from the water, the soap film adhered, forming interesting designs and actually replicating the shape of the triangle, square, or rectangle. In other words if you lowered the hollow square into the water, when you raised the frame, a three-dimensional soap film square appeared, suspended inside the plastic frame. The children all wanted a turn and buzzed about why this was happening. They certainly went home talking.

I've learned a great deal about teaching since those very first days. First, of course, it's not just the children who have been labeled "gifted and talented" that must find schools rewarding and stimulating. All children deserve such experiences. All children should be going home excited about what they're learning. Secondly, I've learned that I need not bring in buckets of soapy water and create special events to engage my students. Every evening, children should have stories to tell at the dinner table because *so many* engaging and interesting things are taking place on a regular basis. That's where nonfiction studies really rise to the surface. All classrooms must be content-rich. Children love to consider themselves experts and be able to teach the grown-ups in their family something they never knew.

And finally, I've learned not to fret over keeping parents happy. Our job is to teach in ways that engage students, inspiring them to dig deeply, getting thoroughly lost in the work at hand. Then students will be happy and the rest will fall into place.

In T. H. White's *The Once and Future King,* Merlyn, when speaking to young Arthur, advises, "The best thing for being sad . . . is to learn something. That is the only thing that never fails. You may grow old and trembling in your anatomies, you may lie awake at night listening to the disorder of your veins, you may miss your only love, you may see the world devastated by evil lunatics, or know your honour trampled in the sewers of baser minds. There is only one thing for it then—to learn." It's no surprise then that students at the Manhattan New School seem so happy. After all, they are always finding answers to issues that concern them and they are learning in slow, thoughtful and personal ways.

RELATED READINGS IN COMPANION VOLUMES

Going Public (Heinemann, 1999) is abbreviated as GP. *Writing Through Childhood* (Heinemann, forthcoming), is abbreviated as WC.

Raising student activists	**GP:** Ch. 1. Ch. 7
A commitment to providing big blocks of time	**GP:** Ch. 1, Ch. 7
Designing a curriculum that responds to community needs	**GP:** Ch. 7
Paying attention to the world	**WC:** Ch. 3
Having realistic writing goals	**WC:** Ch. 2, Ch. 7
Putting student writing to good use	**WC:** Ch. 9

Choosing writing topics	**WC:** Ch. 3, Ch. 6
Selecting writing formats	**WC:** Ch. 4, Ch. 7
Editing student work	**WC:** Ch. 10
Writing biographies	**WC:** Ch. 7
Learning from mentors	**GP:** Ch. 2; **WC:** Ch. 5

CHAPTER 5

Paying Tribute to Poetry

Key Literacy Lessons

1. We want to teach in such a way that our students will have lifelong and positive poetry memories.
2. Poetry adds value to children's lives in many ways; in its ability to change relationships, launch children's interests in learning, inspire them to lead wide-awake lives, and provide lifelong comfort and nourishment.
3. There are many ways poetry can be used by members of a school community, throughout the school day and throughout the school curriculum.
4. School cultures that support the reading and writing of poetry have a caring social tone, are word loving, and value reading aloud and performance.
5. Creating a poetry-friendly school community supports the work of teachers and students.
6. Principals play an important role in promoting the reading and writing of poetry.
7. Administrators can use poetry to enrich school life.
8. Many schoolwide structures, rituals, and activities can center on poetry, and there are many ways to put poetry to real school uses.
9. We are raising children who will experience the privilege of knowing and loving poetry throughout their lives.

When I first came upon Virginia Hamilton Adair's poem "Asbury Park, 1915," I knew that the poet's childhood image would inform my thinking about poetry in the life of an elementary school. The poem made me wonder about the poetry memories our students will have. It reads:

> I am two-and-a-half-years-old,
> hand and hand between my parents.
> "What is that big thing?"
> "A cannon?" says my father.
> The cannon sits on its two wheels and tail
> in a sea of red flowers.
>
> "Roses," I say.
> "No," says my mother, "those are cannas."
> In a burst of delight I chant,
> > "She looked at the canna
> > and jim-jamma-jane."
> It is my first poem.
> My mother wants to know,
> "Do you mean 'cannon' or 'canna'?"
> But on the picture-postcard of my mind,
> cannons and red flowers
> are forever one.

I want to educate children who will delight in remembering their very first poem. Not too long ago in the Metropolitan Diary section of *The New York Times,* I read about a six-year-old who described the very New York image of a dog walker surrounded by dogs as a "bouquet of dogs." I hope someone told that young child that she was beginning her very first poem.

Giving Children Lifelong Poetry Memories

My earliest childhood poetry memory contains a simple never-ending chant that my mother shared with me. It went,

> My name is John Johnson.
> I come from Wisconsin.
> I work as a lumberjack there.
> When I walk down the street,
> All the people I meet,
> Say, "Hello. What's your name?"
> And I answer,
> "My name is John Johnson . . ."

I fondly remember thinking how clever the verse was, and how clever my mother was for sharing a poem that could go on forever. (My standards weren't that high fifty years ago.) I have no recollection of learning any poems by heart at school, and my first memory of having written a poem wasn't until junior high school. In *Lasting Impressions*, I talk about the poem I wrote for a math project. It began:

> What is? What Is?
> What is it to me?
> What really is geometry?
> I think it is of no use
> To know a triangle from an obtuse . . .

I want to educate students who will have much richer poetry memories than I. To that end, I know we need to start earlier, start with the best and invite children to live with poems in ways that have the potential to last a lifetime. Every day of the school year, I am conscious that we are responsible for creating rich poetry memory banks. Some say April is National Poetry Month. We know that every month needs to be poetry month. It's no surprise that on our front door hangs the following anonymously written poem:

> Come in, come in, wherever you've been. . . .
> This is the poem in which you're a part,
> this is the home that knows you by heart.

The Value of Poetry in Children's Lives

Poetry makes us pause and appreciate the gifts that surround us. In Bogotá, Colombia, poets are hired to perform their poems on public buses in order to relieve stress in workers' lives. (Copies of poems are distributed when people get off the bus). Poetry enriches our lives because fine poets fill us with moments of compassion, awe, humor, reverence, solace, truth, and beauty. I want nothing less for our students. When a colleague retired, I discovered James Berry's "Retirement Poem" at just the right moment. What could be more perfect than to toast my friend with these lyrical lines?

Retirement Poem
For teacher, Maisie Carter

> Years, after years
> and years after years
> she wakes with shoes on
> and goes
> hugging books, pens, folders,
> off to scatter words
> in the growing of girls and boys.
> Will she kick her shoes off now?

Children too need to take part in the delights of discovering just the right poem, the thrill of sharing that poem at a public occasion or offering it as a private, intimate gift to a loved one. Poetry does indeed provide comfort and nourishment for all ages.

When our colleague Meggan Towell Friedman got married she presented each of her bridesmaids with individually selected, handcrafted poetry books. We want to educate students who could imagine doing likewise.

We showed our students a newspaper article about David Oliveira's portraits of contemporary poets for the *Poet Cards All Star Series*. We want to educate students who would as easily collect cards with Lucille Clifton, Gary Soto, Eve Merriam, and Donald Hall on them as they would Derek Jeter, Paul O'Neill, Andy Petitte, and Darryl Strawberry.

We want to educate the kind of students who are just as likely to hang announcements about poetry readings and poetry festivals on their refrigerator doors as they would announcements about upcoming rock concerts, discount theater tickets, and restaurant reviews.

We have lofty poetry goals for our students and for ourselves. All this requires, of course, that we live our lives accordingly. In the remainder of this chapter, I will share the steps we have taken to make sure that our students feel at home in the world of poetry. (For specific ideas on the teaching of poetry writing see *Writing Through Childhood*.)

The Uses of Poetry at School

Several years ago I wrote a foreword for Marci Ridlon's poetry anthology *Sun Through My Window*. I also worked with Bee Cullinan, the children's literature expert and acclaimed poetry editor, to divide the poet's work in this volume into appropriate categories. My criteria for grouping the poems had to do with the ways teachers might use them. (Of course, poems are not written with "uses" in mind. They are all meant to be read aloud, reread aloud, listened to, performed, and responded to. I do not mean to trivialize them by categorizing them, but in a school community it is often helpful to note the distinguishing features of poems and use them accordingly to help students meet their academic and social goals.)

In both my professional and personal life I have come to depend on poetry. Upon rereading *Going Public* with my poetry antenna extended, I realized once again that eight years later and with an entire school in the palms of my hands, I frequently looked to poetry to enrich the life of that school. Throughout the pages of *Going Public,* the reader will find poems that, in addition to being wonderful pieces of literature to share with students, can be used to support the specific school goals. See Appendix 17, *Putting Poetry to Many Uses*.

In this current chapter, poetry will take center stage and I will share the importance of creating a school culture that supports poetry, suggestions for creating a poetry-friendly environment, administrative uses of poetry, schoolwide rituals, structures and activities involving poetry, individual students and classroom poetry projects, and the place of poetry in the teaching of reading and writing.

Creating a School Culture That Supports Poetry

Robert Pinsky, the poet laureate of the United States, recently wrote an article for the op-ed page of *The New York Times*. It was entitled "Writers Who Could Be Teachers" and was written in response to a poetry slam in which youngsters shared their work after having been taught by a group of special poetry instructors from the D.C. Writerscorp. Pinsky goes on to suggest that there should be more opportunities for master of fine arts graduates to become writing teachers in our nation's schools. I couldn't agree more. Our schools should be filled with adults who can demonstrate their passion for poetry. When adults love rock and roll, their children usually grow up with an interest and ear for rock and roll. When adults love newspaper reading, their children grow up with the background and comfort level it takes to become newspaper readers themselves. So too, when adults care about poetry and are knowledgeable about poetry, the children in their care look to poetry for nourishment, pleasure, and consolation. Most of our schools do not have special poetry instructors. Every classroom teacher needs to take on that role and every administrator needs to find ways to support those teacher's efforts.

Just as there is something appealing about the world of Greenwich Village in New York City that makes it such a hangout for artists and writers, so too we can create a school world that supports budding poets and the adults who are mentoring, instructing, and guiding them. Poets need uninterrupted blocks of time, realistic goals, abundant libraries, and an appreciation that the world is a fascinating place. So too, they need their finished work to be put to real-world uses. Poets often take risks when they write, and the school community needs to wrap these writers in support. Interestingly enough, not only do poets need a caring social tone, but carefully selected poetry can be used to build a caring social tone. (See *Going Public*, Chapter 4, "Making the Social Tone Top Priority.")

The poet's life is also marked by a love a language. Poets care about words, their meanings, sounds, and arrangements. Poets profit from being in a word-loving community. (See Chapter 10, "On Loving and Learning Language.")

Poets also benefit from a community that values performance. Poems are meant to be read aloud and schools that elevate the role of performance pave the way for poets to do their best work. In a recent op-ed page cartoon in *The New York Times*, Victoria Robert listed "The Six Steps to Subway Etiquette." The last panel suggests that travelers *not* read aloud the poems that line our subway walls, poems displayed as part of our city's "Poetry in Motion" campaign. Our students would think it poor etiquette to read the poems silently, keeping all the pleasure to themselves. (By the way, these subway poetry posters are so enticing, we have several hanging in our school corridors. They have become so popular, they are available for sale in postcard format, published by the New York City Transit Authority in cooperation with the Poetry Society of America.)

Creating a Poetry-Friendly Environment

Below are a few poetry landmarks that might appear on a walking tour of any poetry-minded school.

Poets-and-Their-Poems Matchup   In our school, this bulletin board display is filled with copies of thirty different poems written by thirty different poets. Each is enlarged so that even young children can see the poems hung high on the board. Each is mounted on colorful paper. The perimeters of the bulletin board are trimmed with folded-down slips of paper. On each is the name of one of the poets. Hidden inside the slip of paper, and fastened down with a paper clip, is the title of the poem corresponding to the poet. It's hard to pass by the board and not try to guess who wrote such classics as "Things," "Sea Fever," "Song of Myself," "Stopping by Woods on a Snowy Evening," and "April Rain Song."

Poetry Giveaways   In some New York restaurants, you'll find a display case offering free postcards published by various commercial enterprises. Teachers are notorious for taking whole class sets of these free items, for school use of course. I've often thought how wonderful it would be to create a similar school display, but this one would offer poems to passersby. Just as you can tear the name of a word processor for hire off the wall of any college corridor, so too you'd be able to tear off the copy of any poem you appreciated as you walked down the school hallway. Simply prepare multiple copies and line the wall with thumbtacked stacks. It would be interesting to see which poems disappeared first.

Restroom Anthologies   I'm always interested in ways to beautify our student restrooms. People take better care of pretty places. Our turn-of-the-century student restrooms are far from pretty. The floor to ceiling tiled walls invite decorations. Why not poetry? Ask upper-grade students to record their favorite poems on restroom walls and accompany each with an artistic response. The tiled walls can be divided into four-tile rectangular units (depending on the size of tiles), to allow for sufficient space to record poems and illustrations. The allotted spaces can be sectioned off with black permanent marker. These framed areas are then ready to be filled. The poems can alternate with illustrations, forming a checkerboard effect. No doubt, children will be reading poems every day.

Poster Poems   One of our most useful hardware investments was a machine that turns small sheets of paper into poster-size presentations. The machinery comes with several plastic sleeves for display purposes. Anyone looking up and around when they visit our school will spot our students' original poems enlarged and mounted in our hallways.

Found-Poems Board   I can easily imagine setting aside a small bulletin board with the simple heading "Found Poems" to inspire others to always be on the lookout for poems in the environment I'd hang poetical newspaper ads, headlines, cookbook listings, menus, and so on. I'd even hang a note I found on a counter where parents were stuffing envelopes for a school mailing. The note read, "Stamped, Stuffed, Not Licked." I'd hang snippets of poems found in the environment and invite all the other members of our community to do likewise.

Newspaper-Clipping Poems   Another form of found poems is actually composed from phrases found and cut from newspaper headlines. When composed with thoughtfulness, these bold printed words in various colors, fonts, and sizes make a memorable exhibit. One of mine read:

Big Day
Big Apple
MANHATTAN **NEW** SCHOOL
ANY ROOM
Drafting
Struggling
Ups and Downs
Stronger Words
So Much Ink
READ THE POEM
perfect time
CELEBRATE

Students seem to enjoy this change-of-pace composing activity and many are reminded how rich in inspiration most newspapers are.

Favorite-Poems Display   Invite children across the grades to copy down their favorite poem and post it along with a photo of themselves and their explanations about why they chose that particular poem. When the board comes down it can be the start of an ongoing school anthology of favorites.

Poems in Fresco Works of Art   Pam Saturday, our talented art teacher, invited students to create permanent three-dimensional "installation art," made out of plaster of paris. Our stairwell landings are studded with sculpted and painted hands and masks, as well as student-designed books and writing instruments. On one open-page book I couldn't resist entering the words to a poem. I selected Lilian Moore's "In the Park." All the children in our school can probably recite that poem because they pass it every day and have been doing so for several years.

Display of School Poems   A very engaging wall of poems can be quickly created by gathering poems from anthologies devoted to the school experience. Select your favorites. Copy and mount them. Be sure to leave blank paper nearby and dangle some pens and pencils so that teachers, students, and parents can respond to these school images. Some poetry anthologies devoted to schoolhouse experiences include:

School Supplies: A Book of Poems, selected by Lee Bennett Hopkins

Somebody Catch My Homework, by David Harrison

If You're Not Here, Please Raise Your Hand: Poems About School, by Kalli Dakos

Don't Read This Book Whatever You Do: More Poems About School, by Kalli Dakos

The Bug in Teacher's Coffee and Other School Poems, by Kalli Dakos

Mrs. Cole on an Onion Roll and Other School Poems, by Kalli Dakos

Geese Find the Missing Piece: School Time Riddle Rhyme, by Marco and Giulio Maestro

The Goof Who Invented Homework and Other School Poems, by Kalli Dakos

Lunch Money and Other Poems About School, by Carol Diggory Shields

Back to Class, by Mel Glenn

All We Needed to Say: Poems About School from Tanya and Sophie, by Marilyn Singer

Did You See What I Saw? by Kay Winters

Poetry Maps   Hang a world map or map of the United States. Invite members of the school community to search for and post poems related to different geographic locations. Be sure to start them off with a few to demonstrate your intention.

Poetry Shades   Poems could be hand painted onto the dull beige window shades that are standard fare in our classrooms. On sunny days when the shades are lowered, some treasured verses would appear. Teachers and students need to select poems with care as they no doubt will last for a very long time.

Poet Tributes   Imagine each month of the school year paying tribute to a different poet on a bulletin board. There are ten months in a school year, and if ten new poets are picked each year, a student could become familiar with sixty poets in the course of his or her elementary school stay. The assumption behind this requires that all teachers appreciate school bulletin board displays as worthy instructional "field trips." When each bulletin board collection is removed it can be slipped into a permanent home in a three-ring binder for easy future reference. This growing collection could be housed in the poetry room described below. It would be interesting to attempt to list sixty poets worthy of study at the elementary level.

Poems About Poetry   Whenever I come across a poem about poetry I slip it into a file folder. Every once in awhile I decorate a board in our poetry reading room by mounting and hanging this collection by a wide variety of poets. (See p. 192 for specific titles).

Welcome Poems   Students in every class are asked to carefully select poems to hang on classroom doors. The poems serve to welcome visitors, hint at curriculum, or express shared values.

Poetic Magnetism   Refrigerator doors are not the only perfect home for the flood of small strips of magnetic words, commercially sold as Magnetic Poetry. The Catch the Poetry Bug Campaign, sponsored by Volkswagen and the Magnetic Poetry of Minneapolis has sent a few Volkswagen beetles covered with fifteen hundred magnetic stickers to schools across America. (People who recently bought Volkswagen beetles also received a copy of the American Poetry and Literacy Project book, *Songs of the Open Road,* a sixty-one-page anthology with such classic travel poems as Robert Frost's "The Road Not Taken" and Alfred Lloyd Tennyson's "Ulysses.") There is, of course, no need to have students composing on car hoods. Every metal file cabinet in a school building can be covered with these easy-to-use poet's tools. Our classrooms are filled as well with blank magnetic strips for children to add their own words. These come in particularly handy when children are thinking about line breaks and the shape of their poems. (See *Writing Through Childhood.*)

Poetry Reading Room   If you peek under the handmade sign that announces you have found our small second-floor poetry reading room, you will find the black lacquered words "Medical Suite." Instead of a full complement of medical offices, this main floor suite of small rooms does house our school nurse, along with my office, my part-time administrative assistant Tara, and our poetry reading room. The room is filled with assorted mismatched bookcases, all filled with poetry collections. One wall is devoted to collections for adults. (We don't expect children to do things we don't value ourselves.) The other bookcases boast books for children. Poetry books also sit atop the old piano that fills one wall of this great literary hangout. In fact, the piano has three carved panels across its front and these natural frames have become a popular place to hang original poems written by our children. The room also contains a magnetic board covered with small magnetic words for poets seeking inspiration. The walls are covered with poems written by students, as well as lists, announcements, cartoons, and newspaper clippings all pertaining to poetry. Setting aside a separate reading room for poetry certainly signals the importance we have given to this genre. (We also have reading rooms devoted to fiction and nonfiction. If we had the luxury of space, we would probably want to have smaller reading rooms devoted to such nonfiction formats as newspapers and maps. That's how significant we consider these genres to be.)

Over the years, I have created several charts suggesting ways to enjoy the poetry reading room and the poets and poems contained therein. For example, on one wall hangs a chart labeled, "Things to Do with a Poem." It reads,

> Read it aloud.
> Memorize it.
> Choral read it with friends.
> Give it as a gift.
> Illustrate it.
> Copy it into your notebook.

Write in response to it.

Collect others to read alongside.

Turn it into a picture book.

Set it to music.

Read it softly to yourself.

Start your own anthology.

Read about the poet.

Translate it into other languages.

On another wall hangs the chart below.

Things to Do with a Poetry Anthology

Browse and enjoy.

Read preface if any to understand the anthologizer's intentions.

Reflect on how reading a poetry anthology is different from other reading experiences.

Copy your favorites into your writer's notebook.

Select poems as gifts for family and friends.

List ten moods and match ten poems to them.

Reorganize poems into new categories and explain your decisions.

Select poems that resonate with novels you've read, art you've created, and collections you've gathered.

Suggest additional poems that belong in the anthology.

Create a poetry calendar, choosing a poem for each month.

Select poems for homemade greeting cards.

Find other poems by these poets. Create a parallel anthology.

Select poems that lend themselves to choral readings. Perform them.

Read multiple copies of the anthology with a cluster of friends.

Comment on the title of the anthology

Reflect on what you have learned about reading poetry from having read this anthology. Do the same for writing poetry.

(Judy Davis has created similar tasks for students who are studying the same anthology as well as one for students who are studying one poet intensively.)

Poetry and the Principal's Role

Bee Cullinan has sent mail to me at school, addressing the envelope, "To the poetry principal." I suppose it is very obvious to Bee, one of our favorite visitors, that I really do love poetry and that I believe that it is an essential genre at the elementary level along with nonfiction and real-world writing. It becomes obvious to all visitors that I love poetry. There are signs everywhere.

I mount carefully selected poems in fitting settings. I've hung Lilian Moore's "Where I Live It Never Snows" (a clear explanation of being aware of what you know and what you don't know about a topic) on the science room door, Shel Silverstein's "Band-Aids" on the door to the nurse's office (a tribute to Band-Aids, whether or not one has a need for one), Pablo Neruda's "Ode to My Library" on the door to our poetry reading room, and Barbara Esbensen's "Friends" (a declaration of friendship accomplished through the description of a drawing) on the art room door.

Perhaps the most public sign that the principal appreciates poetry is the morning ritual begun by Paula Rogovin and her band of roving first-grade troubadours. A small group of Paula's first graders find me early every morning to start my day with one of the many poems they regularly learn by heart. (Paula steeps the children in such frequent recitations, they can't help but memorize their favorites.) I often encourage people standing by to stop what they're doing and glory in the performance. Many grown-ups in the building now know many poems by Marilyn Singer, Monica Gunning, and Langston Hughes by heart. When I was home sick, Paula called and six-year-old Mia recited Hughes's "April Rain Song" over the phone. A morning ritual is a morning ritual. (When I accepted the role of deputy superintendent in our school district, Paula and her students gave me a most thoughtful going-away gift—an audiocassette recording of all those poems recited by the entire class, as well as a big book filled with illustrations and titles of all the poems on the tape, in the exact order. My morning ritual can continue.)

Throughout the grades, the writing of poetry requires the reading of poetry. The more children read, reread, discuss, listen to, perform, memorize, dramatize, choral read, and so on, the more successful they will be as poets. Likewise, the more teachers read, reread, discuss, listen to, perform, memorize, dramatize, and choral read, the more successful they will be as teachers of poetry and as poets themselves. (See *Writing Through Childhood* for details on the poetry workshop.)

Quite frequently, the books I long to share with young writers are collections of poetry. I know fine poets have lessons for all writers, not just for other poets. In other words, it doesn't matter what genre the children are studying, I can be sure that the writing lessons gleaned from carefully crafted poetry can be applied to all genres. In addition, in my role as principal of a kindergarten-through-grade-five building, I can put my trust in sharing the same poetry anthology throughout the school. One volume is likely to contain poems and poetry lessons for writers of all ages. I take great pride in toting one magical volume and discovering the different ways it resonates with children throughout the grades.

I also frequently choose to share poetry because I never want to overstay my welcome. Poetry allows me to read and reread aloud for a short duration of time and still have time for student response as well as time to highlight literary techniques. In other words, my minilessons can feel complete in a short amount of time. I do not have to feel guilty if I cannot return to this particular class for several days. I have thereby rationalized my "disruptive behavior." A few of my favorite anthologies to share with elementary school children have been Susan Marie Carlson's *Getting Used to the Dark,* Kristine O'Connell George's *The Great Frog Race and Other Poems,* Alan De Fina's *When a City Leans Against the Sky,* Richard Margolis's *Only the Moon and Me,* James Stevenson's *Pop-Corn,* and Marci Ridlon's *Sun Through the Window: Poems for Children.* All these titles imply that ample funds must be allocated to provide rich poetry collections. This is perhaps a fundamental way for principals to support the reading and writing of poetry. (See *Writing Through Childhood* for a longer list of anthologies as well as specific minilessons attached to their use.)

How Administrators Can Use Poetry to Enrich School Life

There are, of course, many more ways that administrators can use poetry to enrich the life of a school. All require, however, that principals get in the habit of browsing anthologies. There are no short cuts here, nor should administrators want any. We work hard. We deserve to unwind at night in the company of a few good poets.

The following suggestions were written with the school administrator in mind but of course can be followed by classroom teachers as well.

Include Poems in Everyday Correspondence   Let people come to expect poems to accompany fliers, newsletters, lunch menus, family letters, and school calendars and be disappointed when they are not included. Students, teachers, and family members will begin to look to poetry to enrich their own written work.

Feature Poems in Special School Events   Each year when the city announces the "Take Our Daughters to Work" event, I post a copy of Myra Cohn Livingston's "Working with Mother" along with the announcement. Similarly, it's not hard to find poetic tributes to the first day of school, the first snowstorm, the arrival of a new year, the opening of baseball season, and of course graduation and summer vacation. I have even discovered poems that connect to our fund-raising walkathon to the Forty-second Street Library, our annual school picnic, our seemingly endless test-taking season, our Dancing in the Street event, and Grandparents and other Grand People's Visiting Day. Last year members of our PTA selected first grader Ben's poem about the moon to appear in the advertisement for their fund-raising auction (see Figure 5.1). The auction's theme always celebrates the lights of our city so his poem was a perfect choice.

When children understand the value of tucking appropriate poems into all these happenings, they too will look to poetry to toast the special occasions and people in their lives in school and out.

Use Poems in Administrative Documents   Include poems alongside administrative information given to teachers. Imagine the possibilities of attaching appropriate poems

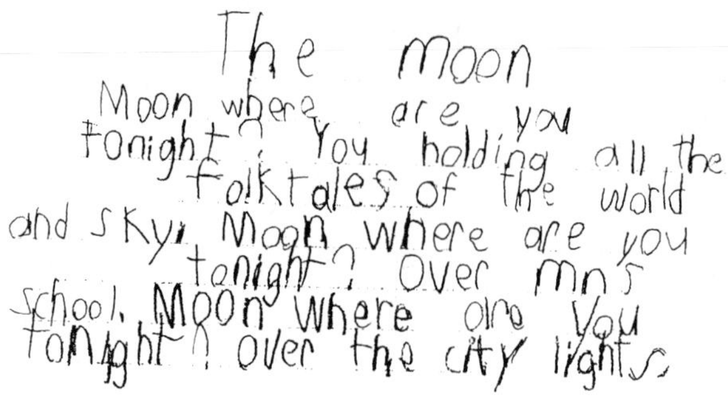

The moon
Moon where are you
tonight? You holding all the
folktales of the world
and sky, Moon, where are you
tonight? Over mn's
school. Moon where are you
tonight? over the city lights.

Figure 5.1

to such administrative documents as attendance plans, discipline codes, goals and objectives, safety plans, and so on.

Last fall, my back-to-school packet for teachers included the following note attached to several poems.

Dear friends,

I couldn't think of a better way to start the year than by sharing some poems that remind us what it's like to be a child. I found them in Naomi Nye and Paul Janeczko's anthology I Feel a Little Jumpy Around You, *Gary Soto's collection* Canto Familiar, *and Liz Rosenberg's anthology,* The Invisible Ladder. *I look forward to hearing your responses. Enjoy!*

Love,

Shelley

Open Meetings with Poems   Whenever I'm at a loss for how to start a formal meeting, I reach for my poetry anthologies. Many times, families and staff have heard me say, "I'm going to begin by sharing an appropriate poem." For example, I once launched a conversation about grading and parental pressure at a PTA meeting with the following simple yet powerful anonymously written poem.

> Dad says that at
> least my rotten
> marks at school
> prove that I
> haven't been cheating.

(See *Going Public,* Chapter 5, "Reaching Out to Families," for additional information on sharing poetry with adults.)

Initiate a Poem-of-the-Week Ritual   Initiate a poem-of-the-week ritual for staff members. In our weekly logbook someone once wrote the label "Poem of the Week." My choices have included Constance Levy's "Color the Tiger" and Marge Piercy's "To Be of Use."

Highlight the Work of School Poets   Be on the lookout for any poems written by adults in the community and design ways to showcase them. (See Tamara's poem on p. 85 and Roberta's on p. 86.) When conditions are supportive, the writing of poetry can be contagious. (Of course, we must showcase children's poetry as well (see *Writing Through Childhood.*)

Keep Poetry Files   Keep accessible files of poems that demonstrate what is valued in your community. For example, in our school, teachers would appreciate poems that build camaraderie, poems that elevate city life, poems that honor language learning, and so on. I also rely on my across-the-grades file of poems for spur-of-the-moment coverages. Mine include ones that are perfect for choral readings, ones that inspire the telling of family stories, ones that the children don't quite understand (so that plenty of conversation takes place), and ones that inspire children to write in response. Carefully selected poems can take children in surprising directions, no busywork needed.

Serve as a Poetry Mentor   Serve as a mentor, demonstrating your own involvement with poetry. In addition to reading poems aloud to students, try writing alongside young poets in a writing workshop. (See *Writing Through Childhood,* "When Principals Are Willing to Write Poetry.")

Start a Poet Reference File   Begin a reference file of poets in the community. Invite poets to visit and serve as mentors. When Bee Cullinan escorted Indiana poet Rebecca Dotlich to visit our school, the two were not expecting such a grand reception. Students greeted the poet with bouquets, murals in response to their favorite lines of poetry, and a trail of beautifully mounted poems leading to their classrooms. The children recited her poems by heart and even set them to music. When Bee asked them how they felt about memorizing poems, the childrens' poetic responses included, "I become the poem," "I become the poet," and "The poem stays with you through the seasons." It is always worth the effort to invite a fine poet to spend time in a school.

Publicize Poetry News   Post all poetry-related newspaper clippings, neighborhood announcements, anthology reviews, publisher news, and journal and magazine articles in a central location. (Of course, this job can be shared with an older student or parent who is willing to read the daily newspaper with their poetry antenna extended.)

Emphasize Professional Growth in the Teaching of Poetry   Keep the study of poetry on the front burner at staff meetings by:

- reading and responding to professional books on the teaching of reading and writing poetry
- discussing ways to launch a poetry course of study throughout the grades
- selecting evocative and accessible professional poems to share with children
- discussing ways to establish mentor relationships with professional poets
- creating schoolwide structures for students across the grades to share original poetry
- sharing ways to weave together poetry reading and writing workshops
- establishing a video library of poetry minilessons, conferences, share meetings, and publishing celebrations
- inviting students to staff meetings and publicly conferring about poems in progress
- listening to such professionally published poetry readings as *The Best of Michael Rosen* (Wetlands Press) and *The Words of True Poems* by Georgia Heard (Heinemann) and thinking through classroom uses of such audiocassettes.

(For an additional way that administrators can put poetry to good use in schools, see "Using Poetry to Teach Content Studies on p. 192.)

Schoolwide Poetry Structures, Rituals, and Activities

I am not alone in my love of poetry. Staff members at the Manhattan New School form a like-minded, poetry-minded community.

Schoolwide Anthologies

If you were to visit our school, you would find children participating in many schoolwide structures, rituals, and activities that involve poetry. Some have had a profound influence on the life of our school. Bee Cullinan's donation of a schoolwide poetry anthology for every child to keep, described in Chapter 1, "Designing the Literary Landscape," led to many new practices. Several are described in a letter I sent to families. In part it read:

> No doubt our teachers will design brilliant ways to use these books in their classrooms. My hope is that they will also be used well in your homes. Perhaps the children will even be assigned family poetry homework. I can imagine children and family members:
>
> - *reading aloud to one another as a bedtime ritual*
> - *setting poems to favorite family music*
> - *reading chorally, with different family members taking different lines*
> - *selecting poems for homemade greeting card messages*

- *illustrating poems to give as gifts to out-of-town relatives*
- *memorizing poems to be shared at family gatherings*
- *preparing read-aloud tapes to give as holiday or birthday gifts*
- *translating poems into other languages*
- *gathering books from the library by your favorite poets in the collection*

Please keep these special gifts in a safe place. Please see that they are brought back and forth to school when they are being used for class study. Please let us know your family's response to the book, as well as any new ways you have discovered to enjoy the book. If you'd like to drop Bee a thank-you note, I'd be happy to send it to her.

We will also be having a special celebration at the school to honor Bee and to appropriately thank her by inviting her to watch all the wonderful ways our children and our teachers have delighted in A Jar of Tiny Stars. *It is our hope that wonderful benefactors will come along to make this gift of poetry available again next year and the year after that, and the year after that and . . .*

Bee's donation did inspire Di Snowball, an acclaimed literacy educator and author from Australia, to do likewise. In the following year, Di and her husband, Greg, donated over five hundred copies of *Morning, Noon and Night,* an anthology created by our colleague Sharon Taberski.

Each year we paid tribute to our poetry benefactors by inviting them to a schoolwide celebration in their honor. Children performed many of the poems for our invited guests. They read aloud, recited, dramatized, and chorally performed the poems. They set poems to music and sang the lyrics. They prepared art in response to the poems. They translated the poems into their first languages. They shared original poems written in response to the published poems.

These poetry gifts gave us our first opportunity to develop a dramatic schoolwide literary heritage. Brothers and sisters, neighbors and classmates were all reading the same poems over an extended period of time. When the Yankees won the World Series in 1996 I was awakened by a communal scream coming from the courtyard below my apartment window. I hadn't witnessed such a shared joyful emotion since the spring I celebrated the Passover holiday in Israel. There, when I stood at an open window during the traditional seder ceremony, I heard all the neighbors singing the same songs at approximately the same time. It was an incredible experience. I am uplifted in the same way when I walk through the corridors of our school and over five hundred children are reading, responding, and reciting the same collection of poems.

Some of the following poetry events take place regularly, others only occasionally, and many are yet to be carried out. No school can or should carry out *all* these ideas. Time is precious for students and teachers alike. No one has time to plan, organize, and carry out all the activities suggested. I learned a long time ago that good ideas are a dime a dozen in a school. (If only thinking hard and coming up with good ideas burned calories! Most of the educators I know best would be svelte, never having to worry about diets and exercise.)

The questions that need to be asked about all these good ideas include:

- Which activities make the most sense for our community right now?
- Which should be schoolwide?
- Who will parent schoolwide projects?
- Which should involve small clusters of classes?
- Which should be carried out by individual classes?
- How can the community at large benefit from classroom projects?

School Poet of Choice   Sharon Olds became the New York State Poet in 1998. This news led naturally into a discussion of the students' choice for a school poet. Who are the poets that our children most admire? How can they narrow their selection down to one? How can they pay tribute to their selected poet? Is there a way to contact the poet?

Poetry Recitals   Just as young pianists perform at piano recitals, so too we can schedule periodic recitals of memorized poetry. Years ago Branch Rickey suggested that a struggling Dodger pitcher memorize poetry to improve his concentration. Perhaps it would have the same effect on young children. When Michael Rosen, the acclaimed British poet, visited our school, the children naturally asked him to share some of his wonderful poems. A student began to hand him one of his anthologies, but of course Michael knew his poems by heart. After his visit, students longed to listen to his recording, *The Best of Michael Rosen,* in order to take lessons from their favorite poetry performer.

Poetry in Motion Campaign   Earlier I mentioned the Poetry in Motion campaign in the New York City subways and buses. How about our own Poetry in Motion campaign? We can purchase white T-shirts in bulk at discount prices and ask the children to copy their favorite poems on the front of the shirt in large bold print. On the back they can artistically respond to their poem. If all the students wore their shirts on the same day, we would have a real Poetry in Motion parade.

Monthly Poet Study   Similar to the monthly "poet tribute" corridor display described earlier, a classroom project could totally immerse children in the study of one poet each month. Children, student teachers, and parents could take responsibility for preparing study packets for each child, complete with background information on the poet, a bibliography of published books, and a set of sheets filled with an array of poems. Children could browse the sheets, share their favorites, perform in small groups, share with their families, select one to give as a gift to a particular person, and be prepared to explain their choice, talk about any distinctive features, and have a go at imitating the author's style.

Poetry Picture Book Exchange   Older students can each be asked to search for a poem that can be prepared in picture book format to ceremoniously give to a kindergartner, first, or second grader. Students would need to study a few poems that have been professionally published as picture books and create a list of criteria.

Poetry Postcards   Knopf publishers has a wonderful series of postcards entitled *Poems to Go!* These beautiful cards contain a photograph of the poet and one of his/her poems. (NCTE also has poetry postcards.) Students can certainly create a child-size version of this project, using original poems (no copyright problems) and photographs of themselves. We could even have the postcards professionally printed and the series sold at our fund-raising street fairs.

Poetry Experts Day   Each member of a class can be asked to select a poetry specialty. Students can then "hang out a shingle," letting their classmates know they are interested in collecting such items as shape poems, language play poems, jump-rope rhymes, list poems, haiku, and so on. On a red-letter day, the class can become a poetry emporium, with each student and teacher sharing their expertise. Collections can be bound and added to class libraries.

Poetry Gift Day   When our fourth graders wanted to thank Tracy, their dance instructor from the National Dance Institute, and William, the pianist who accompanies her, I couldn't imagine a better gift than poetry. We searched for poems connected to dance and those connected to piano playing. The children illustrated the poems and we boxed each in a Lucite frame. It was a memorable tribute. Imagine a day marked on the calendar in which every member of a class is expected to give a poem to every other student in the class, as well as to their teacher and former teachers (and principal, of course), and explain their choices. I can easily imagine a staff meeting devoted to browsing anthologies and finding just the right poem for each child in a class.

Themed Poetry Readings   When I worked with teachers in Durango, Colorado, they treated me to an evening of cowboy poetry readings. The poems were as varied as the poets who shared them. Some were serious, others quite comical. Some poets played music, others did not. Some rhymed, many did not. All, however, spoke to the cowboy experience. I can easily imagine encouraging students to prepare a poetry reading related to a shared interest. Students could share original poems or ones they admire written by professional poets. In our community, poetry readings devoted to city life, love of animals, and restaurants would be easy to create.

Poetry Birthday Celebrations   Instead of cupcakes, family members can be encouraged to purchase a poetry anthology in honor of their child's birthday. As part of the celebration, the honored student can inscribe the book and share their favorite poems. Teachers might keep a running list of anthologies they'd love to have in their class library.

International Poetry Share   In our community, a sharing of poems from many lands would be fairly easy to orchestrate. Family members can be asked to read or recall poems from their own childhoods. Patriotic songs, lullabies, street rhymes, and even drinking songs can be shared. Teachers, students, and family members can also consult such anthologies as Naomi Nye's *This Same Sky* to gather additional poems.

Choral Performances   Classes on the same grade level can be given the same poem to perform. Perhaps with a week's preparation time, children from each class could decide on a choral performance and then the school community could meet to see the variety of orchestrations for the same poem.

Poetry Dances   Tracy Straus, our National Dance Institute instructor, does ask our fourth graders to select poems to which they can choreograph a dance. The children have powerful models for this because each year they learn dances connected to pieces of literature. This past year the children danced to Marci Ridlon's poem "City, City." Students can be asked to develop criteria for selecting other poems worthy of a dance interpretation.

Poetry Partners   Just as older children are paired with younger students to read books together, so too younger and older children can be assigned as poetry partners, devoting their weekly meetings to the sharing of poetry.

Special Poetry Collections   Imagine a small placard hanging alongside each classroom door, announcing the name of a few poets. The placards would indicate classrooms in which poetry collections by individual poets were housed. Everyone would know where to go if they wanted to study the work of Langston Hughes, Karla Kuskin, John Ciardi, and so on. Of course, poems by these poets would sit on the shelves in many classrooms, but how helpful to know that the bulk of their work is in a set location, just waiting for readers. Wouldn't it be lovely to hear a student bragging that their new classroom had all the books by Lee Bennett Hopkins?

Poetry/News Matchups   Last year I came across a photograph in the local newspaper showing a group of small children studying the rings in the stump from a large Norwegian spruce that had been cut down to adorn Rockefeller Center for the holiday season. I hung it alongside Elaine Cusack's poem entitled "Short Thought," in which the poet suggests that if humans had rings marked in their bodies they wouldn't be accused of lying about their ages.

Students can be asked to select newspaper photographs or articles and display it with a poem that resonates with the content. Students can also be asked to explain their choices.

Summer Picture Book Project   Over the summer, students can be given a stack of picture books from their upcoming class library as well as a few poetry anthologies. The students would be challenged to find poems to accompany each picture book and slip copies of the poem into the library pocket in the back of each book. Students would enter their new class familiar with a portion of the class library and prepared to explain their pairings.

Poetic Lullabies   Invite all students and their families to send in the words to their favorite bedtime lullabies, no matter the language. These tunes can be collected in a school anthology and then copied for distribution to all families. Of course, the collection could be launched at a schoolwide performance, preferably in the evening, around the children's bedtime. Imagine a school auditorium with parents, grandparents, and baby-sitters taking turns singing bedtime songs to their young children. The lullabies could also be recorded on cassette and distributed to families, with sing-along words. Back in class, older students could be asked to note differences between poems and songs.

Poetry Collages   A long bulletin board outside our music room is covered with a life-size mural, created in a collage style. It is the scene of an audience watching an orchestra. You only see the backs of the heads of audience members as all are facing toward the stage. Fourth graders worked very hard to find fabrics and other materials that could serve as hair textures and colors. (These included, yarn, leather, corrugated cardboard, steel wool pads, etc.). In their sketchpads, other fourth graders drew musicians at work and then enlarged them to fit the size of this hallway mural. Next to each member of the orchestra is a music stand. And on each music stand sits a poem, a poem about music. Poems are periodically changed, but the mural has been up for several years. Right now the poems include such appropriate texts as Daniel Slossberg's "Why I Didn't Practice My Violin Today," April Halprin Waylan's "Taking Violin at School," Kristine O'Connell George's "Choir Tryouts", and Karla Kuskin's "Lewis Has a Trumpet." Most were gathered from such anthologies as Michael Strickland's *My Own Song and Other Poems to Groove* and *Poems That Sing to You* and Myra Cohn Livingston's *Call Down the Moon: Poems of Music.*

Poetry Commonplace Books   Earlier in this book I described the practice of keeping a commonplace book (See Chapter 1, "Designing the Literary Landscape"). I can easily imagine devoting a commonplace book exclusively to poetry. I do have several bound blank books filled with the poems I love, but I wish I had started this collection in my childhood. How much richer my collections would be. How much I'd learn about myself from rereading the poems that touched me at different stages of my life. I can't recreate those earlier books, but I can invite the children I know best to start their own.

Poetry Archives   Robert Pinsky, the poet laureate of the United States, initiated the Favorite Poem Project in celebration of the millennium. He has built an audio and video archive of recordings of ordinary Americans reciting poetry. Schools could join his effort by encouraging students, parents, and teachers to participate. (A parent has already recorded our fifth graders before they graduated). Schools can continue this important idea, asking every student to add his/her favorite poem to a grand school collection. Multiple copies of these tapes can be made and placed in a lending library.

Poetry Walking Tours   Each day our students walk through the corridors and stair-wells of our school, moving from their regular classrooms to their specialty rooms (art, music, science, technology, and physical education) and on to lunch, recess, and dismissal. In addition to the poetry landmarks described on pages 165 to 169, imagine if students enlarged and hung wonderful poems in strategic places and then produced poetry walking-tour guidebooks to be given to each teacher. Who could resist stopping to read poems en route if you received an invitation such as the following?

> *Dear teacher,*
>
> *If you are escorting your class from the second floor to the fifth floor today via stairway #2, be sure to leave a little extra time. You'll want to gather your class in front of John Ciardi's "Summer Song" on the second-floor stairwell landing, Valerie Worth's "Safety Pin" on the third-floor landing, Myra Cohn Livingston's "Kittens" on the fourth-floor landing, and Lilian Moore's "Recess" on the fifth-floor landing.*

Different classes could assume responsibility for changing the poetry displays periodically and sending out the guided tours. Poems could be chosen at random, as those presented above, or related to a theme or form of poetry being studied.

Rolodex Rhythm and Rhyme   When children need to give back to the community because they have taken away from the community spirit (by behaving disrespectfully or disruptively), I like to have worthwhile tasks on hand. A large old-fashioned Rolodex intended for phone numbers has come in handy. Children search through poetry anthologies for poems they think others in the building would appreciate and hand-copy them onto large-size Rolodex cards. These are entered alphabetically by the poet's last name. Teachers are free to flip the cards looking for new poems to share.

Poetry Council   In Chapter 3, "Discovering Real-World Reasons to Write," I mentioned our student council, representatives who meet with me to decide schoolwide causes for celebration and discuss problems to solve. It has occurred to me that this sort of one-room-schoolhouse, across-the-grades collection of children would make a wonderful poetry writing workshop. It would be an interesting challenge to discover the information, poets, and poems that satisfy this multiage group. It would also be fascinating to hear if our poetry discoveries could be shared with the participants' classmates the way that student council announcements are regularly reported.

Putting Poetry to Real School Uses

One early June day, a parent named Joan Brenner shared with me an anthology of poems her daughter Erika had written in middle school. (Erika had graduated from our school the previous year.) The minute I glanced at the poems I knew that Erika had helped me write my upcoming graduation speech. I began my address to the latest group of graduates by talking about Erika's gift of poems. I told the new graduates that

that moment was very significant for me. "First," I said, "I love that Erika still keeps in touch and I expect all of you to do the same. Second," I continued, "I love that Erika still takes her writing very seriously and I expect all of you to do the same. And finally, I love the meaning in her poems and I'd like to end my brief comments by sharing a few."

I then read the following poem, having received Erika's permission.

Lingering Spirits

Your spirit is still here,
Hovering around
Where your possessions still lie.

We haven't moved anything
It's just the way you left it.
All still here
Cluttering the walls.

You couldn't bare to visit,
Too many memories.

But I wanted you to know
It's all waiting here.

I then told the audience, "We can't promise you that we won't move your things. Things, in fact, probably won't be the way you left them. But your spirit will be here. And we do want you to visit, because we know the memories will be great ones."

I ended with Erika's poem entitled "*All*."

Some people follow in the footsteps of their parents.
Some try to get as far away as possible.
Some start off wanting to be a lawyer or doctor.
Some stray from this path to pave their own.
To find what it is they want in life.

Maybe they'll find it.
Maybe they'll get lost.
They might regret wandering
From the traffic of people.
Or they might be happy
With what they choose.

But all in all,
The journey is everything.

After reading her poem I commented, "The journey *is* everything. And we wish each of you a wonderfully joyous and successful journey."

Erika attended graduation that year as an honored guest. When I began to read, she slid down into her chair, a bit embarrassed to receive the attention and to hear her words read aloud. But I knew it was the greatest compliment I could offer her and I know she will keep on writing.

When Judy, Joan, and Joanne collaborated on a writing celebration in honor of Father's Day, they put the students in charge. The children began by preparing a workshop explaining how they use the jottings in their writer's notebooks toward publication. Children used the overhead to show their writing process and then read finished pieces aloud. They even answered questions from the audience. The parents gathered were impressed by the students' ability to share what they were learning and by the quality of their writing. More than one dad choked up when fifth grader Dana toasted the fathers who attended with the following poem she had written:

> The plump hands of a little girl hold a peach.
> She sits on a log enjoying the taste,
> Letting the sticky juice trickle down her arm.
> She looks down at her bare feet.
> The soles are dirty from running wildly,
> Not even knowing where she was headed.
> Her father comes down the path,
> Cracking sticks and crunching leaves with his shoes.
> He sits down next to her.
> He holds the half-eaten peach up to his mouth.
> He takes a bite.
> She smiles.
> And they share the rest together.

(Here's to fathers who share peaches and special times with their children.)

Whether students deliberately write poems for school occasions or someone discovers that the poems they've written are a perfect match for a school event, all students, those that have written and those that serve as audience, will reap the rewards. Poetry invites us to laugh together, cry together, smile, sigh, gasp, stare, chat, and sing together. Most of all, poetry reminds us to pay attention to one another and to take care of one another. When children's poetry is used to enrich their lives at school they are more likely to use poetry to enrich their lives outside of school.

Assigning Poetry Tasks to Individual Students
Occasionally children enjoy being asked to do things that no one else in the school is asked to do. There is something to be said for children carrying out projects indepen-

dently, adding their personal touches, and demonstrating how much initiative and per-severance they have when given a personal assignment. The following tasks all involve poetry.

I asked second grader Madeline to assume responsibility for creating an A-Z poetry anthology. She sent the letter appearing in Figure 5.2 to all staff members.

Madeline received many responses to this letter and twenty-six slips of paper were eventually hung on my office door. As the responses came in, Madeline listed the names on the appropriate sheet. It was interesting to watch the growing clusters for each letter of the alphabet. Eloise Greenfield, Monica Gunning, Nikki Giovanni, and Donald Graves made the "G" list. There were many names on the "H" list including Lee Bennett Hopkins, Georgia Heard, Langston Hughes, Mary Ann Hoberman, and Patricia Hubbell. Eve Merriam, Lilian Moore, and Richard Margolis topped the "M" list. Naomi Nye, Ogden Nash, and Pablo Neruda made for an interesting mix on the "N" page. Shel Silverstein appeared with Gary Soto and Robert Louis Stevenson on the "S" page.

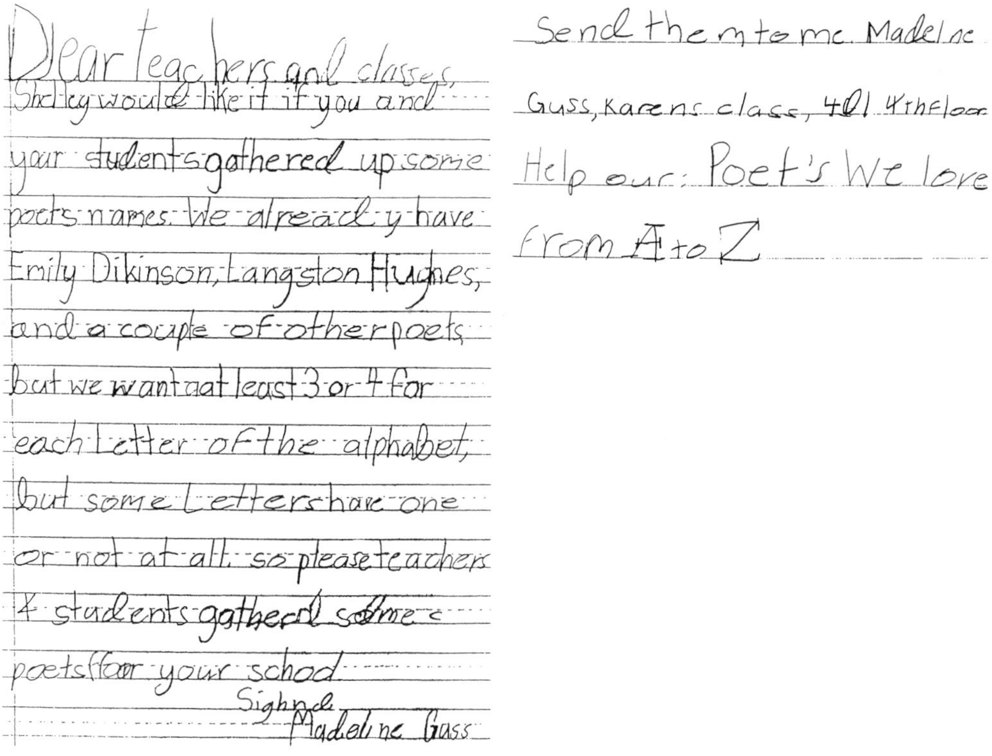

Dear teachers and classes,
Shelley would like it if you and
your students gathered up some
poets names. We already have
Emily Dikinson, Langston Hughes,
and a couple of other poets
but we want at least 3 or 4 for
each letter of the alphabet,
but some letters have one
or not at all. so please teachers
& students gatherd some
poets for your school
                    Sighnd,
                    Madeline Gass

Send them to me. Madeline
Guss, Karens class, 401 4th Floor
Help our: Poet's We love
from A to Z

Figure 5.2

The project took on several more layers as poems were selected for each poet and alphabet letters with no representative poets were researched. Upon completion, this anthology will become a unique school resource.

When Aaron asked if I could put a story into the school newspaper about the huge rubber-band ball that he and his classmate J. P. were collecting, I turned the challenge back to him, asking him to write up the story of their ever growing ball. He surprised me with the poem that follows, explaining that his entire family got in on creating this rhyming news story in poetic form.

Rubber-Band Ball

You probably think,
"Seen one, seen them all."
But I bet you won't find
One like this at the mall;

You'll find basket,
And bowling,
And soccer too.
But you'll never believe
How much work
We had to do.

It took J. P. and Aaron
And 3000 bands, and
We did it all
With our own bare hands.

It started with a crumpled
Piece of paper
In November of '95
It's now '96
And to keep it alive,
we're still adding rubber bands
Just J. P. and I.

So don't get scared
If it comes rolling
down the hall.
It's just the
Manhattan New School's
Rubber-band ball.

McKinley, a fifth-grade student, wanted to apologize for an inappropriate note she had sent during class. Her parents suggested she write me a letter, and she surprised me with the following poem.

An Act

An act of irrationality
May be quite fatal
And is not to be discussed
Around the dinner table.

Teachers stand around in awe.
Pondering what they heard and saw.
Hoping that paper airplane
Was just a bird.
The teacher opens the flying note.
What it said I will not attempt to quote.

An act of irrationality
May be quite fatal
And is not to be discussed
Around the dinner table.

Although McKinley's poem was certainly not assigned, there are many independent poetry challenges that could be assigned to students as a means of enriching the community as well as the life of the student. A few possibilities follow.

Poetry Anthologizer   Copies of all student poems published in a school can be sent to one student responsible for adding these poems to growing chapters in a huge school anthology. (They would probably need to be collected in a three-ring binder for easy organizing and reorganizing.) How wonderful it would be to have an archive of all the poems students in our school have published over the last eight years. What popular reading material it would become for all young writers. It would also be interesting to see the range of topics and kinds of poems produced. A new student anthologizer can be selected every year, each ceremoniously passing the binder to his/her successor.

Poetry Scout   An avid poetry reader can be asked to become a poetry scout, keeping the staff informed about the latest poetry books published. With a family member's cooperation and permission, the student can be asked to make monthly visits to local children's bookstores and libraries to report the titles of any new "must-buys." The student can be given a small notebook labeled "Potential Poetry Purchases," and then be taught how to record the ISBN number and the price in addition to the title, author, and publisher and a brief comment on the content and any illustrations. This is work that has real-world payoff.

Poetry Researcher   A student can be asked to research the amount of poetry in each classroom library. The student can be responsible for creating a data bank of titles, so that all teachers are aware of the school's resources. This collection would also become a needs assessment for future purchases. It would be interesting to note which titles appear in which grade-level classrooms and if poetry is equally available to students of all ages. In addition, the student can record the possibilities for gathering multiple copies of titles for special projects.

Poetry Muralist   A student interested in poetry as well as art can be asked to search for poems that could serve as the centerpiece for hallway murals. The student would need to find poems that speak to the central interests of the school at large (immigration, language learning, environmental concerns, skyscrapers, etc.). The student would then design and carry out a mural that contains the selected poem. A series of poetry murals, each assigned to an individual student, could then line a main lobby or school corridor.

Poetry Historian   Individual students can be challenged to gather poetry that speaks to the local history. In addition, students can be asked to write original historical poetry. The gathered works can be added to resource packets for the teaching of social studies in the school and neighboring schools in the community. Teachers, parents, student teachers, volunteers, and especially senior citizens in the neighborhood can be particularly helpful in suggesting resources, providing information, and guiding students to significant places of interest.

Instituting Poetry Practices in the Classroom

In *Going Public,* I noted how Judy Davis is able to actively involve parents of upper-grade students by inviting them to roll up their sleeves and chorally orchestrate and perform poems with their children. Likewise, earlier in this text, I describe how Pam and Renay extend their book-buddy activities by challenging the older children to create poetry anthologies based on the younger students' areas of interest. At upcoming staff meetings, it wouldn't be unusual for me to ask teachers to describe these projects to their colleagues. Far too often, teachers aren't aware of all the marvelous things taking place in one another's rooms. I take on the Johnny Appleseed role when I encourage teachers to spread the wealth of ideas. Asking teachers to humbly share their latest projects or inviting colleagues to participate in the "Have you seen . . . ?" ritual previously described, reminds teachers of the value of stopping by one another's classrooms. The following classroom poetry rituals and projects are worthy of admiration and or replication:

- Regina Chiou's children regularly follow Caroline Feller Bauer's suggestion and announce a poetry break. I have seen children respectfully ask for their classmates' attention during a reading or writing workshop by holding up a large sign announcing a poetry break. The child stands atop a low table and recites or reads a poem aloud.

- Pat Werner's third-grade students slip their finished poems into stand-up Lucite frames which serve as centerpieces for all the round tables in Pat's classroom. A different poem is slipped into each side, like the dessert menus in some diners. No matter where children sit, they can appreciate their classmates' work.

- Isabel Beaton's friend Doris Levy is a weekly guest poetry teacher in her kindergarten class. Doris shares many poems, always reading them aloud twice. Alumni of this class would never dream of reading a poem aloud only once. Doris has taught them well that once is never enough to appreciate the sound and meaning of most poems.

- Renay Sadis taught photography to her third graders. Children then wrote short poetic images in response to the neighborhood photographs. The photos and words were mounted on sturdy boards and sold at our fund-raising street fair. They were very popular items and easy to duplicate for multiple sales. Examples appear in Figures 5.3 and 5.4.

- Kindergarten teachers prepare poetry folders containing students' favorite poems. The children illustrate the poems and take them home regularly to share with parents.

Who lives in this house?
I wish I did.
The beautiful brown door,
the beautiful green vines,
I wish I did.

William Jackson

Figure 5.3

In the park
there are benches.
Empty benches
waiting to give
comfort
to the tired.

Samantha Defeo

Figure 5.4

- Joan Backer's fourth-grade students take turns preparing closing words for each day of school. Poetry is a natural for inclusion in such a ritual.

- Judy Davis invites her students to participate in so many poetry activities that I have been nudging her to write a book about her teaching. The corridor near her classroom is covered with elegantly framed student poems as well as collaboratively written poetry prepared on large chart paper. Enter her room and you will become immersed in students' original and year-long poetry anthologies, content-area poetry performances, and cleverly designed choral performances. We all eagerly await her book.

Using Poetry to Teach Reading

Many, many years ago, when I was just beginning my teaching career, I recall a sense of relief when a poem appeared amid the controlled and contrived stories that filled the required basal readers. These poems were a breath of fresh air. They usually had fewer worksheets to accompany them, fewer vocabulary lists to "pre-teach," fewer follow-up questions to make sure the children "got" their meaning, and probably less vocabulary constraints to stunt their meaning. And because they were usually quite short, they didn't require the snail's pace of attention the teacher's manual suggested for most of the longer stories.

It's hard for me to admit, however, that when a poem came up, I thought it was a day off. In my naïve state of mind, I didn't really believe I was teaching reading. Those poems were too much fun, too short, too much of a break from the serious work at hand. To me they were mere new-chapter decorations. I couldn't have been more mistaken. Today I realize that poetry is a powerful genre for the teaching of reading across all ages of readers, including us grown-ups.

I once copied a poem by Johann Wolfgang von Goethe off a subway wall. It was part of the Poetry in Motion campaign mentioned earlier. It read,

> One should . . . listen to a little song,
> Read a good poem, or look at a fine painting
> Every single day,
> And if possible say something sensible about it.

It seems to me that this poetic advice is perfect for the teacher of reading. If you were to weave in and out of classrooms at the Manhattan New School during reading workshops, you would be sure to stumble upon copies of poems in children's hands, on chart paper, or on overhead projectors. Children would be reading poetry and no doubt saying sensible things about it. Poetry is one of the most popular genres for teaching children what they need to know about reading, including skills, strategies, and sensibilities as readers.

Most of all, carefully selected poetry enables very young children to believe they *can* read, and inspires older children to want to read for the rest of their lives.

Then too, children throughout the grades are encouraged to talk about what appeals to them in poems. As Joseph Brodsky suggested, "There is only one way to develop a sound taste in literature—read poetry!" When immersed in fine poetry, our students come to expect that *everything* they read will be filled with precision, detail, and attention to the sounds of words and their arrangements, all distinguishing features of fine poems. When reading a picture book, they come to expect strong images, a satisfying design, and inclusion of essential words, more distinguishing features of memorable poetry. Likewise, when they read a novel they come to expect to be surprised, moved, and inspired to think new thoughts, because poetry has developed their tastes as readers.

Poems About Reading

I have a fairly thick file of poems about the reading experience; most are meant for children, some are more appropriate for adults. I use them during workshops and speeches and for inspiration at school. A few of my favorites are listed below.

> Aileen Fischer's "After the End," in *Always Wondering*
>
> Linda Pastan's "Recess," from *Realms of Gold*
>
> Gary Soto's "Eating While Reading," from *Canto Familiar*
>
> Billy Collins's "First Reader," in *Questions About Angels*
>
> Karen Fiser's "Teaching Myself to Read," in Naomi Nye and Paul Janeczko's *I Feel a Little Jumpy Around You*
>
> David McCord's "Books all Open," in *One at a Time*
>
> Jean Little's "After English Class" in *Hey World, Here I Am!*

Poetry Anthologies Devoted to Reading

Lee Bennett Hopkins's *Good Books, Good Times*

Bobbye Goldstein's *Inner Chimes*

Using Poetry to Teach Writing

Piri Thomas has said that "every child is born a poet and every poet is a child." I have to admit that every piece a child reads aloud to me in the name of poetry doesn't always confirm this idea. Over the years I have met very few children who seem to be born poets; most need information from their teachers as well as mentor relationships with practicing poets in order to develop their poetic sensibilities.

In *Writing Through Childhood* I describe how the writing of poetry changes as our students grow. Sometimes our five- and six-year-olds write such fresh, surprising things

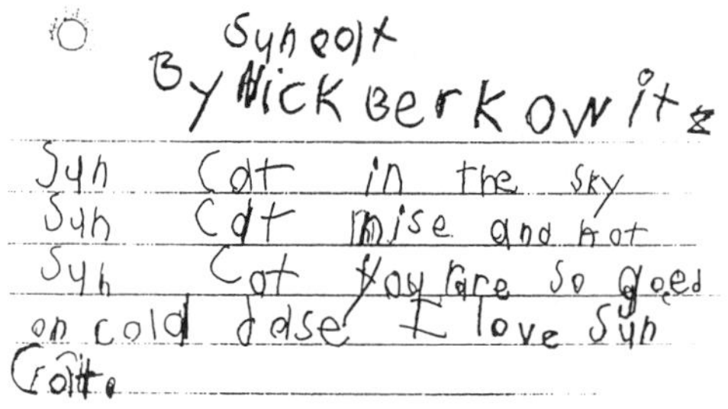

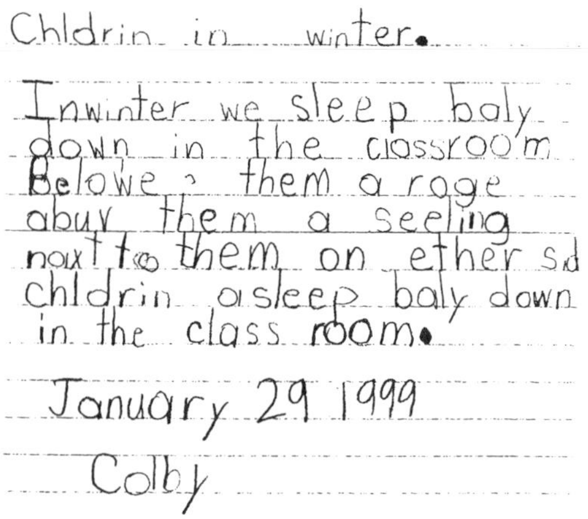

Chldrin in winter.

Inwinter we sleep boly
down in the classroom
Belowe them a rage
abuv them a seeling
naxt to them on ether sd
chldrin asleep boly down
in the class room.

January 29 1999

Colby

:O
By Nick Berkowitz
Syn eojx
Syn Cat in the sky
Syn Cdt mise and hot
Syn Cot You are so goed
on cold dase I love Syn
Cott.

Figure 5.5   Figure 5.6

that it is easy to call their words poetry. Paula Rogovin, a first-grade teacher, knew I would love the words written by her two very young writers that appear in Figures 5.5 and 5.6. As we move up the grades, however, we know that there is rich poetry content to teach. Formal poetry courses of study at the Manhattan New School emphasize the following:

- surrounding students with a wide range of poems and reading them aloud over and over again
- filling classrooms with poetry collections and anthologies and inviting students to make their own poetry discoveries
- carving out time for students to share their discoveries as they begin to develop their tastes as poetry connoisseurs
- providing structures for students to save and savor favorite poems
- helping children find their own words to talk about poetic techniques, avoiding clichés that inhibit thinking
- encouraging students to reread their writer's notebooks with a poet's eye
- making sure that students understand that any topic can be handled in poetic form, not just things such as lovely daffodils in the spring
- making sure students know that poems don't have to rhyme
- teaching children about different kinds of poetry
- inviting children to shape their thoughts into poems
- providing students with a rich toolbox of poetry techniques
- encouraging students to establish mentor relationships with favorite poets
- providing time to share their rough poems in order to receive honest feedback and get needed help

- ample time for students to revise their poems to their own satisfaction
- ample time to write dozens of poems
- tools and time to make their poems look like poetry
- ample time for performance and celebration of poems

Since our teachers take the teaching of poetry so seriously, it comes as no surprise that our upper-grade students are able to produce very effective poems. Elliot, a fourth grader, wrote the following beautifully surprising poem about poetry.

Fishing for an Image

Sitting on a plank
In swampy, humid climates
With a rod,
Catching images.

Baby poems
Drifting about
Waiting
To be adopted.

Hoping
To be called into action,
Hoping
To be hooked.

Gina, a fifth grader, crafted this powerful verse.

A Woman on the Street

There's a woman on the street
  I see her all the time.
She takes flowers from the park
  And puts them into a black garbage bag.
She weaves those flowers into bouquets and wears them
On her head.
She yells out $3.00 for a bouquet, $3.00.
Later a man sees her lying shivering in the street.
The stranger puts a blanket over her.
She refuses to take it.
She struggles to get up.
She takes her bag and walks down the street calling out
$3.00 for flowers, $3.00.

Poems About Writing

Whenever I browse poetry anthologies, I always slip a bookmark into the page that offers a poem about writing in general and about writing poetry in particular. The following poems all have lessons for elementary writers.

Ralph Fletcher's "A Writing Kind of Day," in *Water Planet*

Karla Kuskin's "Write About a Radish," in *Near the Window Tree*

Zaro Weil's "How to Get an Idea," in *Mud, Moon and Me*

Eve Merriam's "Rainbow Writing," in *Rainbow Writing*

Jean Little's "Writers," in *Hey World! Here I Am*

Alice Schertle's "Writing Past Midnight," in *A Lucky Thing*

Alice Schertle's "Right Here," in *A Lucky Thing*

Mary Jo Schimelpfenig's "A Geography of Lunch," and W. S. Merwin's "The Unwritten," in Nye and Janezcko's *I Feel a Little Jumpy Around You*

Louise Borden's "Writer/Author" in *The Reading Teacher* (Nov. 1992)

Poems About Poetry

Pat Mora's "One Blue Door." in *This Big Sky*

Salih Bolat's "My Share," in *This Same Sky*

Kalli Dakos's "Our Custodian's a Poet," in *The Goof Who Invented Homework*

Frank O'Hara's "Autobiographia Literaria," in *The Collected Poems of Frank O'Hara*

Douglas Florian's "Read This Poem," "Poem for Rent," and "Bad Poem," in *Laugh-eteria*

Linda Pastan's "Elegy," in Nye and Janeczko's *I Feel a Little Jumpy Around You*

(There are of course many poems about reading and writing that are more appropriate to share with teachers. Perhaps my favorite are those of Billy Collins's, including "First Reader," "Reading Myself to Sleep," "Cliché," "Purity," and "The Norton Anthology of English Literature" in *Questions About Angels* and his "Marginalia," "Silence," "Journal," "In the Room of a Thousand Miles," "Japan," and "Taking Off Emily Dickinson's Clothes" in *Picnic, Lightning*.)

Using Poetry to Teach Content Studies

I take real pleasure in slipping content-related poems and anthologies into teachers' mailboxes. I'm delighted to be able to support teachers' efforts by finding just the right poem at the right moment to enrich a class study of such wide-ranging topics as immigration, jazz musicians, dinosaurs, subways, and architecture. When our part-time colleague Lamson joined our staff, he told me that his mailbox felt like a Christmas stocking because he always found worthwhile treasures inside it. My Santa Claus sack brims with poetry.

There are no textbooks used in our school. Students, teachers, and family members understand that none could compare with the up-to-date informational books written with literary grace that fill our classroom shelves. They understand that no textbook map could possibly keep up with our ever changing world. Teachers and students depend upon a wide variety of sources of information. We look to the Internet, newspapers, magazines, resource people, primary documents, and—perhaps surprisingly—poetry.

Great conversations and inquiries have begun when provocative poems have been put on the overhead projector or into the hands of students. I recently shared J. Patrick Lewis's poem "In Books Are Bugs" with a group of third-grade readers. The poet speaks of microscopic mites that eat the pages of books. Leonela asked, "Is it true? Can bugs eat books?" "Yes, I think so," I replied. "But you should double-check with Lisa; she proba-bly knows more about that." I directed Leonela to Lisa, our science teacher, and the third grader returned quite proud to have discovered dozens of facts on the Internet about bugs, which do indeed thrive on paper.

Individual poems can support teaching and learning, and so can entire anthologies. Teachers can enrich the teaching of science and social studies with such poetry collec-tions as Lee Bennett Hopkins's *Spectacular Science: A Book of Poems* and *Hand in Hand: An American History Through Poetry.*

In addition to reading poems connected to areas of study, students can be asked to write content poems in order to crystallize their thinking and share their learnings with others. It becomes particularly important to remind children that poems do not have to rhyme. Students need to know that poems have rhythms, strong images, surprising metaphors, precise sensory language, and many have repetition, but they do not neces-sarily have to rhyme. When students attempt to write rhyming poems in the content areas, they usually cannot make their meaning clear because they are so determined to rhyme words with such terms as *revolution, migration,* and *division.* (Recall my junior high school attempt at a rhyming math poem on p. 162. For further information on the writ-ing of poems, see *Writing Through Childhood.*)

Raising the Poetry-Privileged

Several years ago, I visited Wales and brought home a framed placard that read, "To be born Welsh is to be born privileged. Not with a silver spoon in your mouth but with music in your blood and poetry in your soul." Similarly, I can proudly make the case, "To graduate from the Manhattan New School is to graduate privileged. Not with a sil-ver spoon in your mouth, but with music in your blood and poetry in your soul." When I walk the school corridors today and witness all the ways students are involved with poetry, I can't imagine these same children not taking the time to browse, read, share, write, and respond to poetry when they are grown. When Szilvia was in second grade

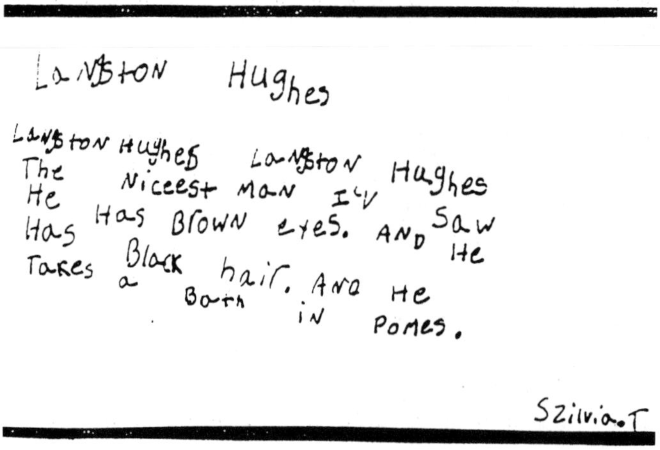

LANGSTON Hughes

Langston Hughes Langston Hughes
The Niceest man I'V
He Has Brown eyes. And Saw
Has Black hair. And He He
Takes a Both in Pomes.

Figure 5.7

she wrote the tribute to Langston Hughes that appears in Figure 5.7. If we have done our jobs right, Szilvia and all her Manhattan New School friends will be bathed in poems throughout their lives.

RELATED READINGS IN COMPANION VOLUMES

Going Public (Heinemann, 1999) is abbreviated as GP. *Writing Through Childhood* (Heinemann, forthcoming) is abbreviated as WC.

Sharing poetry to change relationships	**GP:** Ch. 4
Using poetry to inspire attentiveness	**GP:** Ch. 5; **WC:** Ch. 3
Creating a supportive social tone	**GP:** Ch. 4
Promoting a love of language	**GP:** Ch. 4; **WC:** Ch. 5
Using poetry for a range of school purposes	**GP:** Ch. 2, Ch. 3, Ch. 4, Ch. 7
Having realistic writing goals	**WC:** Ch. 2, Ch. 6, Ch. 7
Enriching the environment	**GP:** Ch. 2
Covering classes	**GP:** Ch. 2
Serving as mentor	**GP:** Ch. 2; **WC:** Ch. 7
Providing professional development	**GP:** Ch. 7; **WC:** Ch. 11
Celebrating student writing	**WC:** Ch. 9
Schoolwide literacy rituals	**GP:** Ch. 4; **WC:** Ch. 9
Educating parents	**GP:** Ch. 5
Enriching content studies	**GP:** Ch. 6

CHAPTER 6

NON-NEGOTIABLES IN THE TEACHING OF READING

Key Literacy Lessons

1. There is no one right answer to the question "How do we teach reading?" There is no one way to run a reading workshop.

2. Teachers in any one school can have shared hopes, expectations, and philosophical underpinnings and still run their reading workshops in markedly different ways. Even so, common teaching practices can be noted. These include reading aloud, independent reading, one-on-one conferences, shared reading, small-group guided reading and reader response groups, demonstration of reading strategies, matching students and books, word study, recording children's growth, needs, and interests, student response, using writing to inform reading, literacy modeling, and planning for the teaching of reading.

3. Prescriptive approaches to the teaching of reading cause anxiety in the profession and thwart the teaching process.

4. The following requirements need to be in place if schools are to succeed at raising committed readers:
   - a set of beliefs about how children learn to read
   - beautiful settings in which to read
   - real reasons to read
   - big blocks of time
   - high-quality books and plenty of them
   - a schoolwide stance that reading is "cool"
   - powerful models
   - well-informed teachers

One May, a few years back, two newspaper articles about our school appeared during the same week. One headline read "Milk, Cookies and a Couple of Plot Lines," the other, "Public Schools Are Making the Grade." The first had a bold caption reading "Sophisticated Kids Are Now Starting Their Own Book Clubs," and told the story of some of our fourth graders who were meeting on Friday afternoons in one another's homes to talk about books they had read. The caption on the second article read "The Cream of the Crop," and listed all the top-scoring schools on that year's standardized reading and math tests. The article reported that our students ranked in the top ten out of seven hundred city elementary schools. (This past year, a computer printout tells me that over 91 percent of our children were reading at or above grade level and over 96 percent of our students performed at or above grade level on the math exam.) Two articles about literacy, and our telephone didn't stop ringing. Unfortunately, all the calls, mainly from prospective parents and real estate agents, were in response to our reading scores and not about children starting their own out-of-school book clubs.

I have worked in New York City public schools long enough to understand why prospective parents were calling. Family members pay careful attention to the standardized test scores that are listed in rank order in our daily newspaper. The word is out that high test scores at the elementary level make it easier for students to attend rigorous middle and then high schools. I suppose parents even align high test scores at the elementary level with future SAT scores and acceptances into fine universities.

I want parents to understand, though, that children who choose to join an extracurricular book club on Friday afternoons are well on their way to academic success. High test scores do not guarantee that children love to read, know great authors, can get lost in a book, feel comfortable talking about texts, or value reading for pleasure. Those crucial elements don't show up on a standardized test. They do show up at a Friday after-school book club.

I read in the *Wall Street Journal* about a California restaurant with a sixty-five-dollar-a-plate Thanksgiving dinner. The expensive tab, however, included leftovers. The restaurant owners promised each customer some turkey and trimmings to take home. I like to think that we are serving leftovers with our literacy work. The children will take their reading home on weekends, holidays, and at such gatherings as Friday afternoon book clubs.

I really don't mind when folks call because they've heard good things about the literacy work we do, but when they ask about our rankings and our standardized-test scores I think they are asking the wrong questions. The really essential questions prospective parents should be asking about our teaching of reading include:

- How do you teach reading?
- What does a school need to teach reading well?
- How do your teachers keep up to date in the teaching of reading?
- How do you help a child who struggles with learning to read?
- How can families become involved in literacy learning?

The remainder of this chapter addresses the first two questions. The issues connected to teachers' professional growth are addressed in Chapter 7. The issues connected to family involvement are discussed in Chapter 8. The issues connected to the struggling reader are addressed in Chapter 9. (See Appendix 4, Content Rich Newsletter, for a list of questions frequently asked by family members who have become a part of our community.)

How Do We Teach Reading?

This is a good basic question, one I wish prospective parents asked more often. And yet it's a question for which I don't have a simple answer. No two reading workshops are run in exactly the same way. How could they be? Different teachers run them. They are filled with different students. (See *Going Public* for a description of our first-grade teachers' distinct methods of teaching reading.)

Jerry Harste has described our school as a bed-and-breakfast where other schools are Hiltons. I love this metaphor. Ours *is* a bed-and-breakfast. No two rooms look the same. We don't have matching furniture. We don't have required reading lists and packaged minilesson commandments. Instead, every classroom and every nook and cranny is informed by each teacher's unique passions, strengths, needs, and interests, combined with those of their students. We don't have any one Good Housekeeping Seal of Approval way of doing things. Sharon Taberski and I participated one year in an NCTE teleconference on the teaching of reading, entitled "Reading Instruction: What's It All About?" The broadcast overview suggested that "this program is based on the belief that teachers are the decision makers and not simply technicians who follow the script of a prescribed program." There is no one ideal way to run a reading classroom.

Shared Hopes, Common Practices

Each teacher throughout our school works in a different way, but all share a set of common beliefs about how children learn to read. We have shared values, hopes, and expectations for our students, even though each teacher has his or her own way of reaching these goals. These shared beliefs include the best of what is described as whole language teaching. You will find no watered-down texts in our school, no isolated-skill-and-drill work, no basal readers, no phonics workbooks, no textbooks at all.

Despite differences in style, organization, time schedules, classroom design, and manners of achieving common goals, all teachers value having predictability within their reading workshop. In other words, however teachers and students decide to run their classrooms, the routines are known to all and they are consistent, day after day. Then too, all teachers have effective classroom-management techniques. It's hard to teach reading if children are interrupting conferences, leaving books around, misplacing log sheets, using loud voices, and so on.

In addition, there are many teaching practices that all teachers support. On any given day, teachers throughout the grades can be seen engaged in any or all of the following activities. (Of course, each teacher brings his or her own unique ways of working to these activities.)

Reading Aloud

Teachers read aloud throughout the day and choose varied genres including fiction, non-fiction, and poetry, written by published writers, students, and themselves. Teachers value this time to build community, introduce new genres, authors, and titles, demonstrate fluent oral reading, suggest ways of responding to texts, make connections to student writing, model ways of working in smaller book-talk groups, and otherwise engage children in what it means to be a reader. (See p. 246 and Appendix 9 for additional information on reading aloud).

Independent Reading

Visitors often remark that our students seem to be given such big blocks of time to "just read." We think nothing can be more important than students throughout the grades having abundant time to reread familiar texts and get lost in new books with just the right amount of supports and challenges. How else can students practice the strategies they are learning? How else can teachers tend to individual or small groups of students? When students take their independent reading time seriously, the classroom teacher is free to conduct the essential reading conferences, small-group reading lessons, and word study sessions described below, without interruptions. (Teachers must devote time to demonstrating to students why this time is so valuable and they must provide students with suggestions and strategies for staying on-task during independent reading time. Of course, the prime strategy is providing appropriate texts for students.) Teachers can listen well to one student or to a small cluster of students when the rest of the class has appropriate books in their laps, is engaged in reading, and knows what is expected of them. During independent reading time, our students appear content and on-task and so do their teachers.

One-on-One Conferring

During reading conferences teachers assess students by listening to them read aloud as they record the results (running records), asking students to retell the content of their reading, discussing the material read, and engaging students in conversations about themselves as readers (their likes, dislikes, etc.). The teacher might also use this one-on-one time to help students choose appropriate books (see "Matching Students and Books," below), apply strategies taught (see "Demonstration of Reading Strategies," below), accept ambitious reading challenges, or comment on students' record-keeping and written response to their readings (see "Recording Children's Needs, Interests, and Accomplishments" and "Student Response," below). These individual conferences are essential because they help the teacher make wise decisions about all other aspects of her reading instruction. In other words, what a teacher learns by conferring with students informs her read-alouds, shared readings, guided readings, and so on. Effective confer-ring requires, of course, exquisite classroom management so that teachers can really tend to one student at a time. Teachers can't be like those rotating electric fans that sweep the room, continuously turning their heads to be sure that every child is on-task. They must be able to give undivided attention to the child sitting alongside them.

Sharing Reading with Students

The very popular label *shared reading,* refers to times when the students are looking *at* the text as the teacher reads it aloud and are invited to join in on multiple readings. Although this activity is very common, particularly in our early-childhood classrooms, we try not to get too caught up in labels. In other words, if you ask a teacher what she is doing, she is much more likely to respond, "I'm sharing a great poem" than "I'm doing shared reading." In early-childhood classrooms, texts frequently include carefully selected big books (some published ones are not worth reading), enlarged poems, songs, and chants.

Although the teacher chooses the text with a purpose in mind, on every occasion students are first invited to treat the piece as literature, offering genuine reader response and discussion. In other words, our teachers understand that although a text may be a perfect resource for highlighting a spelling pattern or some aspect of punctuation, it must first be enjoyed for the purpose it was written, as a poem, story, chant, et cetera. I worry a great deal when joyful teaching moments, such as sharing a poem with children, are institutionalized to such a degree, in the name of teaching skills, that they become joy-less occasions, led by educators who are fearful of sharing in the wrong way. We must keep in mind that the notion of providing shared reading experiences in classrooms has its roots in replicating the natural sharing of books that takes place between a parent and a young child. Certainly Don Holdoway never expected his joyful and exhilarating man-ner of sharing enlarged-print books with children to become associated with so many procedures and so many rights and wrongs.

In most early-childhood classrooms students also learn a great deal about reading when teachers share such everyday environmental print as schedule boards, class news stories, the calendar, and weather charts. In Pam's kindergarten, the reading of the sched-ule board became so popular that Carey sent the note in Figure 6.1 to her teacher. In the upper grades, texts are also prepared for display on the overhead or opaque projector. (Some complex and carefully chosen big books might also be shared in an upper-grade classroom, although their use in our school is infrequent.) For detailed information on shared reading with older students see pp. 237–238.

Small Group

When children are having difficulty learning to read, we do *not* label them and place them in year-long reading groups (the old bluebird and crow categories). Instead, teach-ers form flexible reading groups (popularly called "guided reading" groups), based

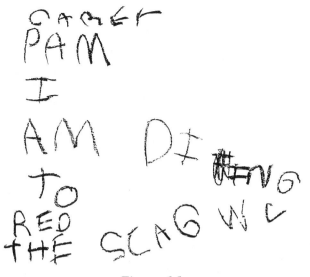

Figure 6.1

around specific needs and intended for a limited amount of time. In order to do this well, teachers must first understand the strategic behaviors that mark a good reader (See pp. 202, 206, 254–255, and 304). Then they must be able to assess the readers in their class, answering the question, "What does this child need to learn to do readily and efficiently to be a better reader?" Once that is decided upon, the teacher is ready to form temporary small groups in need of learning and practicing the same strategic behavior.

For example, children who do not pay attention to punctuation may be brought together, or those needing to understand the special challenges of reading mysteries or those who get confused by dialogue may be placed in the same group in order for the teacher to guide them through the new strategies they need to grow as readers. The teacher selects the kind of material that will help her meet the needs of the children gathered. Teachers' decisions are based on careful and ongoing assessment of students' needs primarily through individual conferences.

A caveat regarding small-group teaching is in order. I have on occasion visited schools throughout this country in which the work of a small group of children huddled together with their teacher seems effective only from afar. As I approach, I hear the tense voice of the teacher, who is hesitantly proceeding as if mechanically following a script. Just as in shared reading, working with a small group of readers must remain a joyful occasion. It's healthy for teachers to reflect on the work they do, but it's not healthy for teachers to proceed with so much caution that their efforts are weakened. It is likewise unfortunate when these small-group sessions serve as nothing more than round-robin sessions.

In our school, meeting with small groups also refers to the many occasions in which the teacher sits in on small reader-response groups (book clubs) within the reading workshop. Teachers attend initially in order to instruct students who have chosen to read the same text on ways of creating a successful reading-response group. Later, the teacher might want to assess the workability of the groups, the quality of the talk, and the participation of the members, as well as to extend the students' discussions. In our school, teachers rarely form small, independent reader-response groups before grade three.

Demonstration of Reading Strategies

These demonstrations are usually done during whole-class gatherings at the beginning of reading workshops, as the content of reading-workshop minilessons. (Demonstrations of reading strategies can also take place during read-alouds or during shared reading.) Teachers decide on what strategy to teach based on their assessment of students' needs.

Teachers usually choose to highlight just one reading strategy at a time, making sure that the strategy they choose fits with the belief that reading is a meaning-making process. (See "A Set of Beliefs About How Children Learn to Read," p. 207.) Strategies might include such acts as recalling what you know about a subject prior to reading, previewing a text by looking at titles, subheadings, and photographs, marking up a text as a means of selecting important information, rereading, stopping to ask questions of the text, and so on (see additional strategies on pp. 206, 254–255, and 304). Teachers remind students that although they are highlighting only one strategy at a time, fluent readers usually use many strategies during any one act of reading. Teachers also convey to students that when fluent readers are reading easy material they are usually not even aware of what strategies they are using, since strategies have become an automatic part of reading. When texts are more difficult, fluent readers realize they need help and therefore make deliberate moves, calling upon particular strategies in order to make meaning.

Strategies taught are not merely added to a class chart. Instead, teachers demonstrate their usefulness, guide children in their use during small-group meetings, and remind children of their importance in individual conferences. The point is not to have a laminated list of strategies hanging on a classroom wall, but for students to become strategic readers. (See Chapter 7, "Professional Growth in the Teaching of Reading," for additional strategies.)

Matching Students and Books

This is so crucial to students' growth as readers that the topic is often the subject of our weekly staff meetings (see p. 241). Teachers are determined that students read the kind of material that allows them to use all the strategies they are learning. Teachers don't hesitate to say to a child who has selected a too-difficult book, "No, I'm sorry, not right now." If students are to become strategic readers they need to have problems they are ready to solve as they read. (I've long wondered, especially in schools in which many students seem to have serious difficulties in learning to read, if books are inappropriately placed. Perhaps if we carted the second-grade library into the third-grade rooms and the third-grade collection into the fourth-grade rooms, and so on, more children would be learning to read fluently.)

At the Manhattan New School, teachers in the primary grades study texts closely so that they can suggest books that have adequate supports and appropriate challenges for young readers. They direct children to specific series, book pots, baskets, and shelves.

In the older grades, as well, teachers help children select books that allow the readers to use all the strategies they have been taught. They avoid books whose structure, concepts, or vocabulary load would prevent the child from making meaning at that point in time. Paul Jennings, a very popular Australian author, has said, "If a child hasn't learned to read, it means he hasn't found the right book yet." We can't agree more. Teachers recommend the kinds of books that allow children to experience real reading.

This does not mean that children are demeaned by or even conscious of "leveled" books (see p. 235). I'm always surprised when a child in our school mentions levels of reading. They might admit that they're "not ready for those harder books over there," or that they're "practicing reading aloud with really easy books," but in the noncompetitive culture of our school and in the manner reading is taught, books may be leveled in the teacher's mind, but *the children are not.* This distinction is a very important one. We most always ask ourselves about the message we are giving our struggling students. Teachers carefully select books when they are offering reading instruction and they carefully select books to place on the shelves of their classroom libraries. This does *not* mean that all books are leveled. Teachers work hard to create classroom libraries that contain books with a wide range of topics, formats, and levels of sophistication. Yes, teachers direct students to reading material that would be most valuable for students at any point in time, but students must also have occasional opportunities to learn how to select their own appropriate materials. When students browse unleveled classroom libraries, teachers can assess whether children can choose appropriate texts. This ability is essential if our students are to borrow appropriate books from the public library. In addition, especially as students move up in the grades and pursue content studies, they also need to learn to navigate more difficult texts, learning additional strategies for making meaning when material is more complex.

Word Study

If you were to visit any reading workshop (most particularly early-childhood ones, but upper-elementary ones as well), you would see small groups of children engaged in word study, at times on their own, at other times with a teacher, student teacher, trained volunteer, or family member. Children might be making words with letter cards, sorting words based on spelling features, and using word cards to build sentences. This word study does not, however, serve as an introduction of new vocabulary for a story to come. Nor is it based on an out-of-context set of workbook ideas. Instead, students first became familiar with the words they are working with through familiar songs, stories, poems, and so on. The word study comes after their reading, not before it. The children are playing with words in order to discover how what they have learned can lead to new learnings.

Recording Children's Needs, Interests, and Accomplishments

There are as many different record-keeping systems as there are classrooms in our school. Some teachers keep their notes in bound notebooks, others on loose-leaf paper attached to clipboards (to be filed after the workshop), yet others on index cards, filed alphabetically by child and kept in little metal cans. No matter the container, teachers keep notes on individual children. The contents include running records of children reading aloud, the strategies offered to each child, and comments on the child's success with each. Teachers might also include notes on each child's areas of interest, and distinguishing features about their tastes as readers (any series they prefer, genres of choice, favorite authors, etc.). Students, of course, have record-keeping responsibilities as well, usually being asked to fill out some sort of reading log. (See below as well as p. 244 for more information on these.)

Talking About Reading

Teachers often carve out time for children to share the news of their reading. Many provide log sheets for students to record comments about the books they are reading as well as discoveries about their own process of reading. Some teachers provide time for students to present their findings orally to the whole class or in small groups. When students do have opportunities to talk about their reading, the rewards are great. A student who can talk explicitly about strategic moves he made during reading is more likely to call upon those strategies on another occasion. In addition, other students hear about books they might want to read as well as reading strategies they might want to try. This time to swap stories about reading can be thought of as a parallel to the share meetings in the writing workshop.

Using Writing to Inform Reading

We trust that our students' participation in a daily writing workshop does more than just produce enviable pieces of writing. We know that our students grow as readers when they attempt to create their own literary works. They become insiders, paying heightened attention to the shape, language, and literary techniques of text in a wide range of genres. They become more committed and voracious readers because they are looking to establish mentor relationships with published writers who have accessible lessons to teach. If some frightening science fiction monster swooped down into our school, eliminating the writing workshop from our students' lives, we know their reading abilities would falter. Even those coveted high reading "scores" would decline if writing hours were curtailed! (See *Writing Through Childhood* for additional information on how writing regularly benefits readers.)

Modeling Literacy

If teachers are to serve as powerful literacy models for their students, they need to spend some time talking about their own literate acts. In addition to demonstrating reading strategies as described previously, teachers should also talk about their own reading tastes and habits. I think it is a very good sign when students can tell me what newspaper their teacher reads and who are some of his/her favorite authors. Our students, particularly as you move up in the grades, should also be aware of the teachers' book-talk group at school. They should be able to see the monthly title posted on the main office door, spot copies of the book around the building, and eavesdrop on teachers talking about the book before and even after the book group meets. (See *Going Public* for further information on teachers' book-talk groups; a bibliography of book-club titles is in Appendix 25 of *Going Public*.)

Planning for the Teaching of Reading

All of the above activities take place when children are in the classroom. This one, the setting of goals, planning of instruction, and preparing of materials, takes place when children are *not* in the room. Sometimes it is hard for teachers to resist working on their plans, when all the students are comfortably engaged in independent reading. Quiet instructional time is too precious, however, to give up. Teachers are expected to plan during their preparation periods. (Most of the teachers in our school also plan, prepare, and reflect on their teaching before and after school.) I expect to see teachers teaching every minute of their reading workshop. If you entered a classroom that was empty except for a teacher at work, you might find her reading over her notes on individual children, browsing books to make perfect matches, thinking through small-group instruction, preparing materials for word study activities, copying poems onto large charts for shared reading experiences, and so on.

As the principal of the school, I am expected to have literacy plans as well. Similar to the teachers, I don't create these plans while children are in the school. Instead, it takes a long quiet weekend, after I have had long conversations with staff members to fulfill my district obligations and write my yearly literacy goals and objectives. Just as teachers need to be well-informed to plan for their teaching, administrators can only write literacy goals and objectives if they are knowledgeable about literacy. (See "Well-Informed Teachers," p. 217.) One year, my literacy goals read in part as follows. (Note: The term *study groups* as used below refers to our grade-level meetings described on p. 223.)

> Our literacy goals for this current school year involve forming think tanks around significant grade-level interests. Early in the school year our K–2 study group will be looking closely at word study. We will be probing such related issues as the use of word walls, methods for teaching phonics as one of the cueing systems, thoughtful word building and word play activities and their appropriate use in the reading workshop, the role trained

volunteers can play in word study, ways to involve parents in effective at-home word study, and the teaching of spelling and its relationship to contextualized phonics instruction. Our plan for studying these issues will include weekly staff meetings, monthly grade-level meetings, classroom intervisitations, and response to such professional texts as Pinell and Fountas's *Word Matters,* Cunningham's *Making Words,* and Moustafa's *Beyond Traditional Phonics.*

Later in the school year, our K–2 discussions will move to such significant topics as the reading of nonfiction in the early-childhood classroom, the use of assessment checklists throughout the school year, the use of nonleveled books in the classroom library, ways to strengthen literacy learning through song and poetry, classroom management and record keeping that supports the careful matching of children and books, thoughtful selection of read-aloud material, and a careful look at an array of kindergarten reading practices.

Our 3–5 study group will be looking closely at the quality, content, and effectiveness of reading-workshop minilessons. In other words, we will be asking, "Is there a core group of strategy lessons that all children need to participate in? Is there a way to shift children from having a list of strategies that they can talk about to being confident strategic readers who know how and when to apply these strategies?" For too long in the teaching of writing, teachers were determined to fill the student's "toolbox" with such tools as adding details, sharpening leads, focusing, and so on. Very often students could apply these techniques when encouraged to do so. "Why don't you add details right here and slow this important scene down?" the teacher would say. Students got quite good at following such a helpful suggestion, but I rarely witnessed students moving to the next level and being able to make those decisions on their own. In other words, to become strategic writers, students need to be able to reread their own texts, spotting those scenes that need to be slowed down (among a zillion other possible weaknesses), and then dip into their toolbox of writing strategies to accomplish the goal they determine. On their own, students need to be able to know why and where to slow down and, equally important, how to do so. They need to know, for example, that adding details, descriptions, and dialogue can slow a scene down. The same holds true in the teaching of reading.

Readers must have a toolbox of strategies that they know when and how to employ. Students need to learn to monitor their own reading and detect moments when they are, for example, reading passively. Then they must be able to dip into their toolbox, searching for ways to become active. For some readers on some texts, stopping to predict what is going to happen next might help them to stay engaged and active as readers. It is not enough for readers to be able to make predictions about what is going to happen next whenever the teacher asks them to do so. Rather, on their own, readers must come to value that technique as a means of reading actively and aggressively.

In other words, readers must shift from having a list of reading strategies to becoming strategic readers who have internalized these strategies and use them independently without a teacher's prodding. Readers need to know when and how to apply the reading strategies they are learning. Otherwise, minilessons become trivial. This will be our year to probe reading-workshop minilessons in the upper grades. We will explore what should be taught and how these strategies should be taught so that they can be used independently by students when they come upon a problem in their reading. We will work toward creating a resource pack for each teacher, filled with strategy lessons that might be offered to the entire class as well as ones that might be shared in small groups and individual conferences. (In addition to recording the best practices of individual teachers, we will be culling from such professional texts as Rhodes and Dudley-Marling's *Readers and Writers with a Difference,* and Keene and Zimmerman's *Mosaic of Thought.*)

In addition to strengthening our upper-grade minilessons, we will also be studying those classroom practices that help the struggling reader in the upper-grade classroom. These will include reading conferences, guided-reading lessons, and effective upper-grade shared-reading experiences. (The overhead projector has become an essential teaching tool in the upper-grade reading workshop.) We will also be looking at such additional teaching practices as assisted reading (reading along with a fluent reader at your side who assists you as you read), reading along with books on tape, and providing students with opportunities to read along as teachers read aloud to the whole class.

During this school year, we will also be assessing the work of the Reading Recovery program that is new to our school, providing PTA presentations aimed at helping parents understand how to really support readers at home, discovering ways to communicate with non-English-speaking parents so that they can receive the same suggestions we make to English-speaking parents, adding to our collection of videotaped classroom sessions, scheduling team visits earlier and more frequently during the school year, using our grade-level checklists to continually monitor children's strengths and weaknesses, discussing appropriate reading-related artifacts to keep in children's cumulative portfolios, and making sure that teachers involved in extended-day and extended-year programs articulate with the students' full-time classroom teachers.

School Requirements for Raising Committed Readers

When my son Michael was an undergraduate, he informed me that he had a few daily non-negotiables. These included reading *The New York Times* and watching David Letterman. Everything else was negotiable. I've long thought school communities needed a few non-negotiables, especially if they are committed to helping children learn and choose to read. The following are our basic requirements for doing the best literacy work imaginable.

A Set of Beliefs About How Children Learn to Read

Our first non-negotiable, in which all the others are grounded, is that classroom practice must be based on richly understood and deeply held beliefs about how children learn to read. In other words, what teachers say and do and how they engage children in reading acts must have theoretical underpinnings. Their practice is not based on a publisher's set of teacher directions or a handbook filled with teaching tips, but on concepts they themselves have examined carefully. Of course, it takes a commitment to long-term quality professional development for teachers to be able to clearly state what they believe in in the teaching of reading. (See Chapter 7, "Professional Growth in the Teaching of Reading.") My colleagues would agree that the following beliefs about how children learn to read and how children are best supported in learning to read have helped them design their reading workshops and choose their teaching practices (see pp. 199–205).

In other words, if the following statements ring true for readers, there should be evidence of these beliefs in their classroom practice.

- **Learning to read requires an understanding that reading is a meaning-making process.** Teachers do not separate reading from making meaning. This belief helps them filter out any activities that rely on isolated or nonsense practice. We don't want children to simply learn how to read, we want them to *choose* to read. Children will only choose to read when reading makes human sense.

- **Learning to read is a problem-solving process.** Teachers want students to have many strategies for solving problems with respect to reading. They want students to use what they know about the meaning of words, the structure of language, the conventions of print, the formats of genre, and the elements of phonics to solve their reading problems.

- **Reflecting on the content of their reading enables children to grow as human beings.** Teachers who value reading as a humanizing tool will never bastardize literature in order to teach reading skills.

- **Reflecting on their reading process enables children to grow as readers.** Teachers want children to be able to talk about their growth and process as readers in order to reveal strategies that are most helpful as well as to discover their dysfunctional ones.

- **Children need demonstrations of fluent reading behavior.** Teachers model their own literacy in order to give students an image of where they are heading.

- **Children need big blocks of time to read lots of appropriate material.** Teachers know that appropriate material enables children to use a full range of reading strategies. They also know that nothing can replace lots of time to practice what you are learning. Doing isolated skill work is not reading. It wastes precious time and gives children the wrong image of what readers do.

- **The reading environment should support teachers' and students' efforts.** Teachers work hard to organize reading, response, and record-keeping materials as well as establish efficient routines and room arrangements in order to maximize reading and teaching time.

- **Students need to see the relationship between reading and writing.** Teachers help students see the connections between what they read and what they write and in fact try to use the same language when talking about both processes.

These beliefs have become so essential to the teaching of reading at the Manhattan New School that they have informed and influenced our ways of living and working alongside one another.

Beautiful Settings in Which to Read

A playground in Peter Stuyvesant Park, near my apartment building in Manhattan, had recently been renovated. Walking past it one day, I looked down upon the sidewalk bordering the park and was delighted to discover that the designer had added a surprising touch. There, carved into the concrete, were tributes to many of the beloved Peters in children's literature. They included Peter Rabbit, Peter Piper, Peter Pan, Peter Peter Pumpkin Eater, Peter Parker (Spiderman), as well as two historical New Yorkers—Peter Cooper and Peter Stuyvesant. I wished such sidewalk salutes would be used throughout the city, not just in front of playgrounds but in front of all the public libraries. Wouldn't that be a grand way to announce, "We expect children to visit here!" It would also be such a beautiful literary touch.

Chapter 1 of this book describes the attention we pay to designing a beautiful literary environment at school. Our teachers are free to carry in couches, throw pillows, book shelves, reading lamps, and area rugs, to create the kind of setting where you or I would feel comfortable pulling out the book we are currently reading. My colleagues are detail people, and it shows. They fret over furniture, fabric, folders, and flowers. They request that their rugs be shampooed and their windows washed. They back their bulletin boards with fadeless black paper, place interesting centerpieces in the middle of their tables, and are not afraid to bring their life passions into the classroom. They love the look and feel of books, and pay careful attention to the arrangement of texts in their classroom libraries. It's a lot easier to do beautiful work when you have a beautiful setting.

Real Reasons to Read

We don't ask students to do anything with their reading that you and I wouldn't consider doing with our own. This doesn't mean they don't sometimes *choose* to do rather unusual things with their reading (or their writing), but we don't assign these things (see explanatory note on p. 210). After I read Arundhati Roy's *The God of Small Things,* I wasn't about to make a mobile with my favorite passages dangling, or dress up as my favorite character and ask my colleagues to guess who I was. Instead, I desperately needed to talk to other folks who've read that book, to puzzle over the confusing parts, to read aloud the breathtaking ones, to record those I want to save and savor, and to talk about how that book has changed the way I think about the world. These are the same things I want all our students to be able to do.

An article appeared in *The New York Times* entitled "The Dangers of Letting a President Read." The article detailed a book President Clinton had chosen to read about the crisis in the Balkans and how that reading influenced his thinking and decision making regarding the conflict in Yugoslavia. Those of us who put our trust in literature and understand the importance of allowing children time to read and respond to books are not surprised that a president's reading could have an effect on foreign policy. We expect books to change the way we think about the world, and we expect nothing less for our children.

This only happens when we arrange authentic acts of literacy in our classrooms. (See *Going Public,* p. 125, "Valuing Literature as a Humanizing Tool.")

When my son returned from his freshmen year at Harvard, he told me that his roommates could not believe he had never read J. D. Salinger's *The Catcher in the Rye.* That summer he decided to fill in the gaps in his reading of "classic" books. He made a long list of books he had always intended to read. He began with Studs Terkel's *Hard Times.* As a summer job during the four years of his undergraduate studies, Michael worked as a school custodian, cleaning a local high school. One day he returned from work, announcing, "You won't believe what I found in the girl's locker room." (I dared not even guess.) It was a copy of *The Catcher in the Rye.* "So that's going to be my workbook," Michael added. It took me a minute to comprehend Michael's use of the word *workbook.* He planned to continue reading *Hard Times* at home and he would read *The Catcher in the Rye* on his breaks at work.

I bristled when Michael first used the word *workbook,* because of all the sorrowful memories I associate with this ultimate of behavior-management tools. Workbooks do keep students in line, but they also give them a false image of what reading is for. Students who have only been given watered-down texts, or who have been asked to read wonderful books but are then given boring, tedious workbook assignments to complete, will not feel at home in the world of real readers. When boredom or agony are attached to students' images of reading, they will never choose to fill their leisure moments curled up with a great book.

Once our children have learned *how* to read, we make sure they want to keep on reading. If experiences with literature *inside* of school provide solace, comfort, and nourishment, students are more likely to continue reading *outside* of school. If reading books is seen as a means of satisfying students' personal inquiry concerns, students are more likely to continue looking to books for answers and as a means of deepening their questions. If students take very personal delight in becoming totally absorbed in a book at school, they are more likely to carve out time to read at home. So too, if students are asked to do *in* school the things that committed readers choose to do *outside* of school, chances are they will continue to read on their own.

(Explanatory note: Readers might find it puzzling or contradictory when I say that we do not invite children to do things with their reading that grown-ups do not do with theirs. After all, I do suggest early on in this book (and continue the argument in *Writing Through Childhood*), that childhood is different from adulthood. Children love to make mud pies, skip down the street, and talk to imaginary playmates. They *are* different from grown-ups. Therefore, we should expect childhood readers (and writers) to engage in behaviors different from those of adult readers, particularly when they are beginning the adventure of learning to read (or write). And they do. Young readers want to hear the same story read over and over and over again. They "pretend read" their favorite stories, even before they know the difference between a number and a letter. They would sleep with their favorite books under their pillows if grown-ups would let them. Similarly, beginning writers put random strings of letters together and "read" aloud their story, pay attention to the feel of letters in their mouths before deciding how to spell words, and select topics only after they have drawn pretty pictures. Certainly, adults don't engage in such "childish" activities.

What I mean, however, when I say that we don't ask students to participate in activities inside of school that have no connection to adult behaviors outside of school refers more to eliminating those assignments that don't lead to passionate, literate ways of being. (Hearing your favorite story over and over again or sleeping with your favorite book under your pillow probably do.) I want to eliminate every reading activity that promotes a twisted or false image of reading, such as asking children to fill in the blanks with vocabulary words as a prereading activity. Doesn't reading involve figuring out the meaning of new words as a way to make sense of the story? Do books at Barnes and Noble come with preselected vocabulary words for grown-ups to study before they read the book? Of course not, or who would buy books? Mind you, I don't think having kids dress up as their favorite character is equivalent to having them fill in vocabulary worksheets, but unless the dressing up pushes the reader into a deeper understanding of the text, I'm not for taking up precious reading time to engage in such an activity. If we want children to choose to read on their own, we need to find more natural ways for them to delight in reading.

Big Blocks of Time

In *Going Public* as well as in earlier chapters of this book, I suggest that we challenge the use of time in our school. It is not surprising to see children at the Manhattan New School reading for a big block of time. We want students to experience the feeling of getting totally lost in a book. Mem Fox, the brilliant Australian writer, teacher, and storyteller, revealed that she had once been in a hotel room in the United States and was reading a wonderful novel that took place in England. She was startled when a copy of *USA Today* was slipped under her hotel room door. She was surprised to see an American newspaper, because she was so engaged in her reading, she thought for sure she was in England. *That's* getting totally lost in your reading. Classroom implications are clear. We must end the constant interruptions and allot bigger blocks of time to students, just for reading.

I recently read an essay by Rabbi Marc Gellman in *"Always Wear Clean Underwear!" and Other Ways Parents Say "I Love You,"* in which he points out that some children get caught up in "sort of" doing things as opposed to "really" doing things. There is, of course, a major difference between "sort of" reading and "really" reading. (See references to additional Gellman essays on p. 322.) When children are rushed, they can only sort of get the gist, sort of solve problems in their reading, sort of respond to text. We're after the real thing. Therefore, our students deserve and require big blocks of uninterrupted time to read.

We must keep in mind, however, that posting an hour-long reading workshop on an agenda board still doesn't guarantee that students will be really reading. Sometimes, the grown-ups get in the way. In some settings, even those calling themselves "literature-based," children spend their precious reading time taking practice reading tests even months before the scheduled exams or developing rubrics for various skills remotely connected to reading. In other classrooms, teachers who no longer have workbooks to accompany basal stories fill the chalkboards with teacher-made end-of-chapter questions that take the pleasure away from reading a good book. Perhaps we need to hang posters on every staff room wall reminding teachers that

- reading "extension" activities are not reading
- creating rubrics for your reading is not reading
- getting ready for reading tests is not reading
- talking and writing about your reading and your reading process may be important but they are not reading

In some classrooms, it is the children who do not take full advantage of their precious reading time. I've seen lots of pretend readers, children who look like readers, but if you followed them closely you would be disappointed to discover how few pages they actually read in any given reading workshop. Some children get quite good at browsing, flipping pages, selecting books, returning books, entering titles in logs, and talking about books or discussing their reading tastes and habits to anyone who will listen. They have learned to look like readers; they have not become committed readers. Perhaps we should hang another poster on classroom walls asking, "Are you *really* reading or *sort of* reading?" We must also keep asking ourselves, "Why? What keeps some students from really reading? Is it the student's lack of strategies, emotional state, the choice of reading materials, the culture of the classroom, or all of the above?" (More on this issue in Chapter 9, "Providing Safety Nets for Struggling Students.")

High Quality Books and Plenty of Them

I always look forward to browsing the *Levenger: Tools for Serious Readers* catalog whenever it appears in my mailbox. It's filled with beautiful bookstands, reading lamps, bookcase ladders for those fortunate enough to have floor-to-ceiling bookcases, and even some ingenious device called an "armapillo," which promises to make any sofa, bed, or loveseat into a comfortable place to read. The items are all appealing and no doubt people turn to the catalog for gifts for book lover friends. I still prefer, however, to buy the only tool my serious reader friends really need: plain old books. That's what serious readers need, be they five or fifty years old.

Our Central Board of Education ran an ad in *The New York Times* that showed a $250 leather belt with a tag reading, "For the price of this belt you could buy an entire library for a third-grade classroom." Although I loved the drama of the ad and the spirit behind it, as the administrator of a public elementary school, the words do not ring true. Two hundred and fifty dollars does not an entire library buy! The teachers I know best would be lucky to buy two dozen picture books, at discount, for that amount of money. They know that it takes a great many more books to meet the needs and interests of a full classroom of students. Our teachers don't want to order dozens of books, they want to order hundreds of books. I was pleased to see the *New York Post* headline after dismal fourth-grade standardized test scores were posted. The grim but honest headline read, "Our Worst Schools Have Fewest Books." Of course they do.

I once began a column for *The New Advocate* with a story about the library in my neighborhood in Staten Island. I wrote,

> My local library recently suffered an emergency closing. *The New York Times* reporter cover-ing the story wrote that "something out of a science fiction movie was found growing inside the walls and ventilation system; sprouting black wisps of toxic mold that has been linked to skin rashes, heart palpitations, respiratory problems, headaches and chronic fatigue." Neighborhood residents were interviewed about the loss of the library, calling it a treasured luxury. They talked more about not having books at their fingertips, than about having rashes and respiratory problems. Personally, this news story brought me an expected sadness but also quite a bit of civic pride. I didn't know my neighbors cared so much about their local library. They want books at their fingertips and so do the teachers I know best.

New Yorkers love their libraries as they love their bookstores. Another article appearing in *The New York Times* shared the frustration of the residents of Chelsea, an interesting neighborhood on Manhattan's West Side. It seems a new bookstore opened, Fox and Sons Books, complete with awning and windows filled with book displays. The neigh-bors were very upset when they discovered that the store was a sham. It was only a set for the Meg Ryan and Tom Hanks movie *You've Got Mail*.

Members of our faculty were sympathetic to the residents' plight. We would all love to see a bookshop on the corner of our block. Books are the tools of our trade and we delight when visitors are bowled over by the quantity of books in our classrooms. When the widow of Carter Burden donated an eight-million-dollar literary collection to the J. P. Morgan Library, she was quoted as saying that their eighteen room apartment was so crowded with these eighty thousand volumes that her "stepchildren had to walk side-ways down the hall to get to their bedrooms." We can never imagine students having to walk sideways down the corridor of our school, but we are determined that teachers have all the books they need to do the best job possible. Of course it is not sheer quan-tity of books that we are after. More importantly, we are after quality.

Last year our school's proposal for speaking at the NCTE convention was entitled, "Literature in the Lives of Students and Teachers: Being Fussy About the Books We Share." I can't stress enough the importance of carefully selecting books to place in the hands of young readers. We don't have a lot of money, but what little we have we spend on books. We don't have a centralized library. Instead, our books go directly into classrooms. Every classroom has a library feel and teachers are fussy about the books on their shelves.

My daughter went to Brown University. On the first day of their freshmen year, the students are asked to walk through the Van Wickle Gates. These are then locked, and the students don't walk through them again until their graduation day. Elementary educators can also serve as gatekeepers. The very first day our five-year-olds enter our school I want them to fall in love with books. From that first day up until graduation day, we need to surround children with fine books. Some students are lucky and their families have already seen to this. But we can't take any chances. First impressions count. Just as the lead to a novel helps us decide if we will bother to keep on reading, so too our students' first experiences with high-quality books can get them longing for more of the same and lusting to be able to read on their own. If we settle for mediocre books, no one will plead, "Read it again." Each September teachers think long and hard about the very first book they will share with their students. They know how important beginnings are. Teachers also know that middles and endings are important. Yes, our students do occasionally get hooked on some of the formulaic series books, but their main diet is filled with gourmet-quality texts, written by culturally diverse accomplished authors. (See more on series books on p. 313.)

One of the most important roles our teachers accept is that of matchmaker. (Just imagine every child singing the words of the *Fiddler on the Roof* matchmaker song. Children need to ask their teachers to look through their books to find the perfect match.) They work very hard to match children and books. They fill their classrooms with a wide range of quality texts in many genres. They don't want students spending their precious reading time on mediocre texts or on texts that don't support their growth as readers.

A Schoolwide Stance That Reading Is "Cool"

Pretty rooms filled with lots of books are not enough. If we are to offer lifetime guarantees to parents that their children will not just learn how to read and write but will choose to read and write, we must do more. We must spend as much time thinking about life-long personal reading habits as we do about making sure that our students will be at that coveted and lackluster place known as "on grade level." In fact, if we spent more time talking about what we used to call "recreational" reading, more children would probably be "on grade level." The most important September question I ask remains, "What did you read this summer?" We need to have lofty goals. It's simply not good enough for students to read because they need to pass a test or get a satisfactory report card grade. We need to provide students with deep roots, valuing reading as nourishment, the pastime of choice. In other words, students must consider reading to be cool.

Almost twenty years ago, I met my friend Hindy List, who was then the director of curriculum in the district in which I was teaching. She seemed to surround herself with the most interesting progressive teachers, people who traveled, went to the theater, and most of all, read books. The first time I went to lunch with this intellectual crowd, I knew I couldn't keep up. I traveled every summer, knew how to get affordable tickets to Broadway shows, but I could not talk about books the way these people could. I was a nonfiction reader and they were talking fiction. They seemed to know the names of so many writers, ones I had never heard of. They didn't just read for professional growth, they read for sheer pleasure. I aspired to be part of this cool crowd. I became a reader of fiction. Today, I remain a voracious reader of both fiction and nonfiction. In my social world, it is cool to be a reader. The same must hold true for our students.

Laura, a dedicated fifth-grade reader, looked at me one day and honestly asked, "How come you don't just stay in your office and read all day?" The culture of our school has demonstrated to Laura that it is cool to be a reader. In fact, the culture of reading sweeps our students in. Loving to read is almost taken for granted, making it unnecessary to talk to children about the value of reading. It just seems so obvious. Our kids may not think hand-me-down clothes from older brothers and sisters are cool but hand-me-down books are.

(We remain hopeful that students who haven't become committed readers during their school years will somehow become avid readers when they are grown. The success of Oprah's Book Club and the appearance of excerpts from Nora Roberts's romance novels on twelve-packs of Diet Coke lead us to believe that many more people—women, at least—than we expect are choosing reading as a pastime of choice. One wonders if there are any pop culture indicators that males are choosing to read. It still remains a more secure path to invite children to become committed readers when they are young. As most health studies find, children who learn at an early age about the benefits of eating right and staying fit are more likely to continue these habits when grown.)

The points I've been making are cumulative ones. Reading can only become socially acceptable, the in-thing to do, if we have wonderful books and plenty of opportunities to get lost in them. In addition, we must not add any painful activities to the reading of these books. It therefore becomes essential that we have well-informed teachers leading reading workshops. (See p. 217.)

Powerful Models

One important way that the culture of our school supports the teaching of reading and writing is the importance placed on teachers' efforts to maintain their own literate lives. One year Donald Graves visited and spent the day having writing conferences, not with the children but with the teachers. Every teacher who had a working draft or a plan to produce one met with Don to talk through her ideas. He also dropped in on a reader-response group; again it was an occasion for teachers to participate and talk about their own reading. (See *Going Public* for details on our regularly scheduled book club for teachers, in which we read good juicy novels.)

I grew up in a household that lived in the kitchen, ate with gusto, and appreciated cooking as an art form. My mother prided herself on preparing memorable homemade meals, the bigger the portions the better, the more guests the merrier. I carry her love of cooking around with me today and pride myself on being able to serve forty guests a worthy sit-down dinner. The community in which we grow up can have a lifelong influence on our cooking, eating, and entertaining habits. So too, the community in which we grow up can have a lifelong influence on our reading habits. It is therefore essential that all the adults in a school community take care of their own literacy, with gusto.

As suggested in *Going Public* and earlier in this text, when the adults in a school community lead literate lives, the potential for literacy demonstrations knows no bounds. Students need to realize, time and again, that the adults at school read not because they are teachers, but because they are human beings. It came as no surprise to us to learn that several fifth graders were reading Pete Hamill's adult book *Snow in August* because they heard their teachers talking so much about it. Likewise, when Paula Rogovin, first-grade teacher, was turning fifty, Ida Chaplin, our security guard, asked me to choose a Langston Hughes poem for the plaque the parents were planning to give her. Everyone in our community knows that Paula loves poetry, and everyone knows who her favorite poet is.

Last year I came down with hepatitis. When I returned to work, I explained to a group of fifth graders that it was so hard for me to miss school. "The only thought that cheered me," I told the students, "was that I would have time to catch up on my reading. Unfortunately," I continued, "I was so sick, so tired, that I couldn't read. To read a really good book takes work." We went on to have an honest and valuable conversation about trying to read *without* a mind at work. (See Chapter 9, "Providing Safety Nets for Struggling Students.")

Even seemingly small acts let children know we care about literacy, our own as well as theirs. Teachers treat all books with respect, always handling them with care. Some even inscribe their personal books with the names of the people who recommended them as well as the place where they were purchased. When they read aloud, they never forget to mention the names of authors and illustrators. They share the dedication and book jacket information about authors' lives. They always place books back on the shelf, right-side-up, with the spines facing forward. They fret over misplaced or misused books. They share their concerns with students when they hear of books being censored, exploited, or turned into basalized materials. They know it is just as powerful in a school building to fill a display cabinet with the books the adults are reading as it is to line our walls with alphabet books, picture books, or popular children's classics.

Teachers also refer to literature across the curriculum, not just during reading and writing times. They talk about books in their letters to families and they share books at parent meetings. They encourage students to ask for recommended reads when they meet new friends or correspond with their pen pals. They create literary adventures for students, filling student calendars with the time, date, and place poets will be reading their works and authors will be speaking and signing books at local bookstores. Students are never surprised to meet their teachers at these events; in fact, they count on it.

As a school, we never turn down a literary happening. We involve students in Reading Rainbow productions whenever we are asked, arrange field trips to the openings of new bookstores, and attend tributes and celebrations of new books. (New York does have its literary advantages.) Our students have toasted Virginia Hamilton on the publication of *Her Stories,* attended the American Librarian Association convention, where we listened to Kathryn Lasky talk about her book *A Journey to the New World:*

The Diary of Remember Patience Whipple, ridden an actual Magic School Bus, run around our playground with a band of Goosebumps skeletons, distributing minieditions of *Goosebumps,* and listened to famous actors at a midtown cathedral pay tribute to Anne Frank.

We have also welcomed many writers to our school. When children get to meet such literary heroes as Mem Fox, Paula Danziger, and Michael Rosen their excitement brings to mind Ted Williams's appearance at an All-Star game. They feel privileged to be in the company of such talented writers (and so do the grown-ups, of course).

We let parents know that Madeleine L'Engle and Tomie dePaola are appearing at Books of Wonder, a downtown children's bookstore. We inform them about the Great New York Read Aloud celebration, in which celebrities read aloud at many of our public libraries. We send home reminders about plans to turn Dr. Seuss's ninety-fifth birthday into a national reading event.

Our students and their families have also become some of the main characters in children's writer Ann Morris's photograph-rich picture books. You can meet our custodian James Smith and his daughters in *The Daddy Book* and get to know Carmen Colon and her kindergartners in *I Am Six.* One year, as part of the city's Principal for a Day program, the CEO of Marvel comics accompanied me on my rounds. Unannounced, he had an employee dressed as Spiderman run through our cafeteria at high noon. (Some New York perks are not so literary.)

Our fourth graders dance with Jacques d'Amboise and the National Dance Institute. The children who show a real talent and commitment to dance are invited to join his SWAT team, a special Saturday dance class. Jacques told me that usually 10 percent of the children in a school qualify for this special program. In our school 40 to 50 percent of the children are good enough to become members. Does our admissions policy require students to have dancing talent? Of course not. We don't have any admissions policy, other than proof of address. Our children dance well because they are used to having big blocks of time, to working hard, to giving it their all, and to helping one another. Our children don't compete to be the best dancer just as they don't compete to be the best reader. Our children also dance well because they are used to taking lessons from teachers who practice their craft. Tracy, their dance teacher, is a real dancer, just as our students' literacy teachers are real readers.

Well-Informed Teachers

Above all, the most essential factor in creating a school where children succeed as readers is to have well-informed teachers responsible for those children's literacy. Hallmark cards produced a pad embossed with the words "Life was so much easier when it was Dick, Jane, and Spot." And so it was. Easier, duller, and less effective. Using a literature-based approach to teaching and individualizing instruction based on continuous assessment is not easy. It is in fact incredibly hard work. But it is guaranteed to be interesting and effective if placed in the hands of knowledgeable teachers.

Last autumn, a neighbor slipped a flier under my front door announcing a neighborhood-wide garage sale. The flier contained three pages of detailed information about how to have a successful sale. She suggested, for example, that we set up quarter, fifty cent, and dollar boxes at the curbside, with items we would normally throw out, just to attract attention and encourage browsing. She noted that things are more easily sold in labeled collections rather than in unmarked piles. For example, she suggested that we create a Halloween costume box, tossing in old hats, gowns, and gloves. She also suggested that children sell homemade snacks to keep the shoppers energetic while walking from lawn to lawn and that we play soft music on a tape deck. She even suggested wrapping musty books in newspaper for a week or longer prior to the day of the sale to eliminate that up-in-the-attic, down-in-the-basement odor. Each suggestion was as sensible and well thought out as the next. And all of them were intended to sell the junk in our homes. The least we can do in the teaching of reading is to be as sensible and clear thinking.

The answer to the question about how to support teachers' efforts begins for me with thinking about the reading expertise in our schools. Could each of us come up with three pages of sensible teaching-of-reading strategies? Should we be invited to teach reading if we can't? Does each of us know where or who to turn to in order to become better teachers of reading?

We don't feel we've arrived even though our students' scores on those mandated standardized tests are worth writing home about. We don't believe the researcher's stance belongs exclusively to graduate students and university scholars. We know that you don't have to be enrolled in a course or pay tuition to be a student. Student teacher is not an oxymoron. School structures that support teachers' professional growth in the teaching of reading is the subject of the next chapter.

RELATED READINGS IN COMPANION VOLUMES

Going Public (Heinemann, 1999) is abbreviated as GP. *Writing Through Childhood* (Heinemann, forthcoming) is abbreviated as WC.

Running reading workshops in differing ways	**GP:** Ch. 3
Reading aloud	**GP:** Ch. 5; **WC:** Ch. 5
Creating beautiful settings	**GP:** Ch. 2
Having real reasons to read	**GP:** Ch. 4
Reading to improve writing	**WC:** Ch. 5
Having literacy goals	**WC:** Ch. 2, Ch. 7
Appreciating the uniqueness of childhood	**WC:** Ch. 1, Ch. 2
Carving out big blocks of time for reading	**GP:** Ch. 1, Ch. 6
Having powerful models	**GP:** Ch. 2; **WC:** Ch. 5, Ch. 7
Professional growth in literacy	**GP:** Ch 7; **WC:** Ch. 11

CHAPTER 7

PROFESSIONAL GROWTH IN THE TEACHING OF READING

Key Literacy Lessons

1. School structures enabling professional development must be in place to guarantee that all teachers remain students of literacy. These structures include:
   - accessible professional libraries
   - opportunities for teachers to visit colleagues' classrooms
   - possibilities for teachers to serve as consultants to colleagues
   - meaningful grade-level meetings
   - opportunities to review children's literature
   - lush classroom libraries
   - videotape libraries
   - formal teacher observations
   - opportunities to conduct research
   - occasions to take part in team visits
   - opportunities to study with a master teacher and attend study groups

2. Weekly staff meeting are central to the professional life of a school, affording teachers essential opportunities to engage in meaningful professional conversation. In our staff meetings, we swap reading stories, tell the story of puzzling readers, study children's literature, hold demonstrations with students, listen to in-house experts, respond to professional reading, respond to assessment reports, view professional videotapes, talk about new ideas, and use prompts to analyze specific teaching issues.

3. Teachers should have ample support from the school district with respect to their professional development.

4. Teachers must be aware of their responsibility as students of literacy.

Last summer I visited the town of Cognac, in France. I went on a tour of a cognac factory and was awed to discover just how complex the process of creating cognac was. The tour guide explained that the cognac taster, the man who mixes the various *eau-de-vies,* is required to put in fifteen years of training before being given the job. Mixing cognacs is an art, not a science. So is the teaching of reading, and many veteran teachers would probably agree that even after fifteen years of training, there is still much to be discovered.

This past school year I was invited to attend a meeting with Vice President Al Gore when he was visiting our city. The guests seated around the table in an elegant New York hotel included the leadership of the teachers' union, our superintendent, and ten teachers from our district, who represented various grade levels and parts of the city. The vice president wanted to know what made our district so successful. (Fifty-three percent of our students are eligible for free lunch, 12 percent are immigrants who arrived in our country during the last three years, and a little over 17 percent are limited in their ability to speak English, and still 75 percent of our students scored at or above grade level on recent standardized tests, making our district one of the highest ranking in New York City.)

Everyone present, bar none, spoke of the district's commitment to abundant and high-quality professional development. Elaine Fink, our superintendent, revealed that in the past school year, our one school district in Manhattan (forty-four schools, 1400 teachers, and 23,000 students) had spent $11 million on professional development, over 6 percent of its annual budget. Elaine suggested that if she had more, she would spend even more to ensure that teachers would have all the support they need to do the finest work imaginable. How many districts in this country have taken such a stance? Our students do well because our teachers know what they're doing. What are other school districts waiting for? (Our reputation for providing superior staff development makes our district a very attractive one for teachers seeking employment. Therefore, in addition to being able to offer ongoing professional development opportunities to all their teachers, our principals can be demanding and selective when choosing new staff members. All this leads to high-quality instruction and students who can more than pass those insufferable and seemingly endless tests.)

The vice president left that day with a new understanding of what it means to take the teaching of teachers seriously. We hope he carried our message back to all the other powers that be in the nation's capital. It does take money to do what is right for children. And what is right is to enable the development of expert teachers of reading.

Structures for Enabling Teacher Development

At the Manhattan New School we pride ourselves on the rich conversations we have about our children and their growth as readers, writers, mathematicians, and the like. We also pride ourselves on having colleagues who are eager to share their areas of expertise. Sharon Taberski is one such colleague who has made a steadfast professional commitment to understand what it takes to become an accomplished teacher of reading. In the foreword to Sharon's brilliant new book *On Solid Ground: Strategies for Teaching Reading K–3*, I thank Sharon in part by stating that she "eloquently reminds us that there is no room for automatic pilot in the teaching of reading. We can no longer blindly follow steps in a manual or dish out prescribed dialogue from a teacher's edition. Nor can we simply fill our classrooms with the best of children's literature and believe we will magically teach all children to read." I go on to say that Sharon's greatest gift to the Manhattan New School has been thoughtfulness. "She has taught us all to pause and think deeply about the teaching of reading and then proceed with clarity and expertise." We have used the structures described below to make sure that we regularly pause and think deeply about the literacy work we do.

(Note: Although our district spends a great deal of money on professional development, providing staff developers in schools and organizing summer institutes and year-round workshops, the structures described below are those that have been created within the confines of our own school. Most do not require additional money. A few require funds for professional literature or substitute coverage. For additional information on how our school makes staff development a top priority see *Going Public*, Chapter 6, "Talking Curriculum and Assessment," and Chapter 7, "Turning Schools into Centers for Professional Study.")

Accessible Professional Libraries

We try to update our professional library each year, adding titles that come highly recommended. When we are satisfied that a title can make a difference in the life of a school we are willing to buy multiple copies of the book. Most members of the staff at our school have read the books listed below on the teaching of reading:

> *Mosaic of Thought*, by Keene and Zimmermann
>
> *Readers and Writers with a Difference*, by Rhodes and Dudley-Marling
>
> *Guided Reading*, by Fountas and Pinnell
>
> *Beyond Traditional Phonics*, by Margaret Moustafa
>
> *Whole to Part Phonics: How Children Learn to Read and Spell*, by Henrietta Dombey, Margaret Moustafa, and the staff of the Centre for Language in Primary Education
>
> *Classrooms That Work: They Can All Read and Write*, by Patricia Cunningham and Richard Allington
>
> *Literacy at the Crossroads* and *Invitations: Changing as Teachers and Learners, K–12*, by Regie Routman
>
> *Growing Up Literate: Learning from Inner-City Families*, by Denny Taylor and Catherine Dorsey-Gaines
>
> *On Reading: A Common Sense Look at the Nature of Language and the Science of Reading*, by Ken Goodman

Of course it is not enough for teachers to merely sign out these books. We must set aside staff meeting time to discuss ideas as well as set aside time to try out new ideas together. Our professional talking must be connected to what we are doing. We can't just blah-blah-blah at staff meetings. We've got to roll up our sleeves and try out new ideas in the company of colleagues. It's too easy to read a professional text and watch nothing happen. All the information can wash over us if we don't have opportunities to interact with the ideas. Many structures for taking theory into practice follow in the remainder of this chapter.

Opportunities for Teachers to Visit Colleagues' Classrooms

I always try to arrange extra coverage for new members of our staff to visit the reading workshops of expert and experienced members of our staff. Even established faculty members benefit from watching colleagues, especially if they are exploring something new in their own teaching. All teachers deserve opportunities to view the intricacies of teaching reading when they are not the center of attention. Visiting another teacher's room allows you the luxury of driving in the slow lane, stopping to see the big picture as you take notes, jot questions, and think about children other than your own. Then too, intervisitations guarantee interesting follow-up conversations in staffrooms. Not only does the visitor learn but the host as well. Sometimes when I pass a big truck on the highway, I'm struck by the fairly common question hanging on the back of the vehicle. It says, "How's my driving?" followed by a toll free telephone number. I wonder if anyone ever calls to voice an opinion. Having colleagues visit your classroom is like hanging a sign, "How's my teaching?" but in this case lots of conversations will follow.

Possibilities for Teachers to Serve as Consultants to Colleagues

Teachers not only watch other colleagues at work they also solicit the help of colleagues within their own classrooms, much as a hired consultant would do. This past year, for example, Sharon Taberski gave up her preparation periods to help Pam Mayer study the teaching of reading in her kindergarten class. (Whenever possible, however, teachers who give up their own preparation time deserve coverage during the day to catch their breath and take care of their own professional needs.) In-house consultants have several advantages over experts who can only visit periodically. They are familiar with the student and parent body as well as the school schedule, resources, expectations, et cetera. In addition, teachers do not have to make phone calls to ask follow-up questions, they need only walk across the corridor. (Our district also provides expert *outside* consultant services in many curriculum areas. A great deal of money is spent to guarantee that every teacher has the support he or she needs. (See additional district opportunities on p. 249.)

Meaningful Grade-Level Meetings

Once a month, instead of our weekly whole-school staff meeting (see p. 231), teachers on the same grade level and occasionally teachers of contiguous grade levels meet to talk about common concerns. (See *Going Public,* Chapter 6, "Talking Curriculum and Assessment.")

The topics they discuss are wide-ranging but necessarily include reading issues. At our weekly schoolwide meetings, we tend to focus on one broad topic for most of a school year. One year, when we shifted our schoolwide focus away from the teaching of reading to the teaching of writing, I sent the following list to my colleagues in the hope that they would continue to study reading issues at their smaller grade-level meetings:

Issues to Continue Exploring

In Kindergarten and Grades 1 and 2

Use of word walls (rationale behind and appropriate uses of words)

Flexible groupings for guided reading (how and why ever changing groups are brought together so that no child feels labeled)

What guides your choice of read-aloud? (range of genres, topics, levels of sophistication)

What are children doing when you are working with a small reading group? (Productive work versus busy work)

How do we talk about vowels? (Is there such a thing as a long vowel? Are we giving mixed messages? How do spelling patterns fit in all this?)

How are we supporting parents' literacy work at home?

Do we offer "formal" or explicit reading instruction in our kindergartens? If not, should we?

Do we know for sure how volunteers are working with our students?

What reading artifacts are in early-childhood portfolios?

In Grades 3, 4, and 5

What are the essential reading-comprehension strategies you find yourself teaching large groups? Small groups?

What materials do you share on the overhead projector during reading workshop minilessons?

What professional books have helped you create effective minilessons? Should we be swapping our best ideas?

How are children using Post-it notes when they read? Are these being overused? Are they interfering with fluent reading?

Apart from the reading workshop, during what parts of the day do you find yourself teaching reading? If not, why not?

What makes sense to place in a reading portfolio? What are children learning from continuing to do so?

Are there simple ways to make newspaper reading part of everyday life? What kinds of articles do you choose to help you teach reading-comprehension strategies? Is it more advantageous to make copies of the articles for each child or to display a copy of the article on the overhead projector? Are there reasons to do both?

What about reader-response groups or book clubs? Does every one have this structure built in? What goals are attached to these? Are they started equally well in the fall as in the spring? How are group members organized? Do groups need guidelines, record-keeping systems, designated leaders, and strategies for deepening reading? How can we be learning from one another about them?

What about struggling readers? What additional school supports are needed? What kind of materials, instructional strategies, personnel help do you need? How do you keep parents especially up-to-date about your concerns?

When we work with struggling readers, do we use their writing to help us understand their reading needs?

Opportunities to Review Children's Literature

One way our staff learned to fine-tune our ability to purchase quality books for young readers was to write reviews of these books. Several years ago, we were fortunate enough to have been asked to review books for the children's literature journal, *The New Advocate*. Teachers need not write reviews for professional journals, they can also write for school newsletters, teacher network publications, local library bulletins, district publications, and their own school websites. No matter the forum their comments take, the benefits will be great. As is indicated in the following excerpts, our teachers became very demanding when choosing books that are supportive of young readers. (See additional information on p. 234.)

Layne Hudes, a first-grade teacher, promotes the kind of books that demand children to call out, "Read it again!" (See *The New Advocate,* spring 1996, for her book recommendations.)

> Imagine a pie cooling on the window sill, its aroma wafting through the air, exciting the taste buds of the hungry, creating an anticipation that mounts as the time to eat it nears. Imagine a book engendering the same kind of hungry desire in a young child. Eyes light up, backs straighten, a grin reminiscent of the Cheshire Cat appears, and fingers itch to open the book. Beginning readers need to have access to a large and varied collection of such high-interest "read-it-agains" which provide safe and friendly texts that support the acquisition of early reading strategies. Just as a "security blanket" eases social transitions, "read-it-agains" promote literary risk-taking by challenging young readers to build on existing language strengths.

Kevin Tallat-Kelpsa makes suggestions for struggling students who are anxious to read thicker books. (See *The New Advocate,* summer 1996, for his book recommendations.)

> What do we do when a student's reach overextends his grasp? "But I want to read those books," was all one struggling third grader had to say as he looked at a display of chapter books. His voice and eyes are familiar to every teacher who has struggled with a struggler. That child looks around at others knee deep in those books. Those thick and juicy books that give you the coveted right to whisper to a friend, "I'm on chapter six, what about you?" It's those books that are too "grown-up" for all those illustrations and can't be finished in a single day. You can "work on" those books. To be able to say that you're

reading one of those books is a rite of passage. It's the reader outgrowing a tricycle and getting to ride a real bike. But with text and concepts too difficult for these struggling readers we know that they are going to do more falling than reading. So what do we do when a student's reach overextends his grasp? The answer: find books with training wheels. Books that look and feel big but give plenty of support and stability. Books with words within reach and stories that feel familiar but still sound fresh. It's a tall order but luckily a few familiar voices fit the bill.

(For additional books carefully selected by Manhattan New School teachers for the teaching of reading, see also *The New Advocate* winter 1996, summer 1997, winter 1997, and spring 1997.)

Lush Classroom Libraries

Sections in every classroom library are devoted to multiple copies of books. In the younger grades, these books are often used for variations of what has been labeled "guided reading" (see p. 200). Sets of books are also used for reader-response groups and book clubs. In addition, the walls of our staff room are lined with six-copy sets of books intended to be borrowed by classroom teachers, resource room teachers, volunteers, early-intervention teachers, after-school tutors, and so on. The books range from titles appropriate for very beginning readers in the early grades (kindergarten and first), to more transitional readers in the middle elementary grades (second and third grade), to more sophisticated readers in the upper grades (fourth and fifth grades).

As is true of the poetry, fiction, and nonfiction rooms described previously, our system for borrowing books from the staff room is based on trust. Actually, teachers are supposed to sign the books out by listing the titles and their name in a folder. Eventually Dora Cruz, one of our school aides, looks to see if borrowed books have been returned. She also reshelves any books that have been returned to the room. It *is* a system of trust because the room is unattended.

Videotape Libraries

Some of our teachers ask student teachers or parent volunteers to videotape selected moments of their reading workshops. First and foremost they use these clips to study their own teaching. What can be more revealing than being able to watch your language, actions, and interactions over and over again? Teachers who are particularly proud of their teaching and/or those interested in honest feedback can then share these clips with others.

There never seems to be enough time to visit in one another's classrooms, and viewing these schoolhouse videotapes seems like the next best thing. I have had myself videotaped as I taught students as well as when I interviewed children from across the grades about various aspects of their schoolwork. It's always revealing for teachers to hear comments about their reading/writing workshops from a child's perspective. Our district also has videotapes available of staff development meetings, principals' conferences, and exemplary classroom practices. In addition, we own several worthwhile commercial videos. These include the NCTE teleconference *Reading Instruction: What's It All About?* and several others involving members of our staff. These include the following:

> *A Close Up Look at Teaching Reading: Focusing on Children and Our Goals,* by Sharon Taberski
>
> *The Classroom Interview in Action,* by Paula Rogovin
>
> *Inside Reading/Writing Classrooms; Reading Conferences, Reading Mini-lessons, Writing Conferences, Writing Mini-Lessons,* by Joanne Hindley Salch

These videos need to become part of an organized lending library so that all interested staff members can view them in the privacy of their own home. Student teachers or new teachers will want to review scenes that their more experienced colleagues may not feel the need to. Viewing any of these clips can also lead to lively discussions at staff meetings. (See pp. 231–249 for additional staff meeting activities).

Formal Teacher Observations

It would really make a difference in the lives of teachers if administrators saw formal teacher observations as opportunities for professional development. In other words, these periodic required reviews of teachers should be seen as a time for the "master teacher," (the instructional leader) to make some smart, specific comments that push the teacher's thinking about the teaching of reading (or whatever subject area is being observed). When the administrator takes detailed notes on a lesson and bases his/her comments on teaching expertise, clarity of thought, a mind at work, and an ability to write well, the teacher can expect the observation to be provocative, generative, and above all useful. (See a detailed observation of fourth-grade teacher David Besancon's reading workshop in Appendix 5.)

Then too, each time an administrator walks into a room, not just on these formal occasions but *every day,* there should exist the potential for learning on the part of both adults, the teacher and the administrator. Having professional company in lots of informal ways is perhaps the best way to guarantee professional growth.

(If this sounds like a tall order for administrators, it's intended. We can't have high standards for teachers without the same applying to principals. When members of a school community are responsible for choosing a new principal or a new teacher they should take it as seriously as buying a new mattress. If you make a mistake you *will* lose sleep.)

Opportunities to Conduct Research

Over the last several years, doctoral students as well as local professors have asked to conduct research in our school. We take their requests seriously, although we haven't been able to honor all of them. If topics are of interest, teachers are inclined to agree to the research because they know they will learn a great deal when someone looks at their teaching with fresh eyes and pushes them to regularly reflect on their practice. Mindy

Ochsner studied gender issues in Isabel's kindergarten classroom. Lori Wolf studied family participation in Paula's first-grade classroom. Then too, there are also the less formal but still rigorous school-based studies, the ones that colleagues can create for themselves or create collaboratively with one another.

Lisa Siegman and Regina Chiou have been studying the powers of observation of second-grade scientists. Layne Hudes and Debby Yellin have been studying first-grade inclusion models. Judy Davis and Sharon Hill have been studying how to improve the writing quality of fourth and fifth graders. These studies have been long-term ones, lasting several years. Some school research is quicker, providing just enough focused attention to get intellectual sparks flying.

For example, one day I asked Joanne to serve as researcher and record everything that took place when I read aloud to her third graders. My request resulted from my realization that read-aloud styles were incredibly different and depended on who held the books in their hands. The transcript of the read-aloud discussion as well as my reflections in response to this forty-five-minute teaching session appear in Appendix 6. Having a colleague record classroom talk and providing time to discuss the content can lead to big insights and topics for future study. (See p. A-17 in Appendix 6.)

Occasions to Take Part in Team Visits

Whenever teachers are worried about a student, they can ask for a team of colleagues to read with that child. The classroom teacher sits in on the team visit to provide background information on the child and to share his or her concerns. After doing a running record of the child reading aloud, retelling and responding to a carefully selected text, this volunteer crew of teachers meets *without* the child present to talk about their concerns and to help the concerned classroom teacher be strategic about the child's needs. (See discussion of the role of benchmark books on p. 342.) The principal's responsibility is to provide the coverage that enables teachers from the same and contiguous grades to be present. (If the principal is not needed to provide coverage, he or she should also be present.) It is very tempting to arrange team visits only at the end of a school year, in order to help teachers determine the most beneficial placement for the child in the upcoming year. Team visits, however, are probably more valuable when they are ongoing throughout the school year in order to help the teacher decide on instructional methods and materials. It probably would make sense to hire a cadre of substitute teachers for several days in November, March, as well as in June in order to allow teachers, in the company of their colleagues, to monitor a child's progress. (See *Going Public*, p. 257, for ways to cover teachers at a minimum of expense.)

Opportunities to Study with a Master Teacher

As valuable as it is to have teachers visit on occasion with their colleagues across the hall, nothing compares to more concentrated collegial study. I would love to be able to arrange for beginning teachers or any teachers looking to fine-tune their abilities to teach reading to have long-term opportunities to study alongside master teachers. It would be possible in our school to ask interested teachers to sit in on extended year (summer school) or extended day (after-school) tutorials taught by master teachers of reading. These sessions are limited to fifteen students per classroom and are designed to strengthen students' reading abilities. In these short blocks of time, away from the stress, pressures, and interruptions of the regular school day, observing teachers have the opportunity to study effective assessment and instruction of our neediest students. (See related district structures on p.249.)

Opportunities to Attend Study Groups

Everyone is tired at the end of a school day. Our minds are filled with teaching and learning stories, concerns about individual children, "to-do" lists, and if we're lucky, interesting plans for the evening. I've always thought it hard to do our very best thinking after school hours. An alternative for early-morning people is to meet before school. This past school year a small cluster of teachers and I met to discuss the teaching of reading in the third-, fourth-, and fifth-grade classroom. Our goal was to sort through all our teaching-of-reading reference material and create an organized three-ring binder filled with reading workshop minilessons to be shared with the rest of the staff. Each of us (there were only four in total), agreed to reread our favorite materials, lifting the raw material that was most generative in our classrooms. (Our favorite materials included the books listed on p. 222. We also took a look at Debra Goodman's *The Reading Detective Club: Solving the Mysteries of Reading,* Margaret Yatsevitch Phinney's *Reading with the Troubled Reader,* and dog-eared issues of *The Reading Teacher, Talking Points, Language Arts,* etc.) In other words, we were determined to answer the question, "What do minilessons in the teaching of reading look like in the upper-elementary classroom?" (We still consider third grade an early-childhood year, but interested teachers of grade three found the task intriguing.) We began by dividing three-ring binders into categories of needed lessons. Some of the categories for minilessons included those for inaccurate readers, passive readers, readers with poor attitudes, readers who disregard built-in clues, readers with limited background in genres, and readers with little familiarity with literary language. (See explanation of these on p. 247.)

We then designed a worksheet to help us translate theory into practice (see Appendix 7). That sheet contains ample space to credit our sources (the research that inspired us), describe the minilesson topic (what we were hoping to teach), provide our rationale for teaching (why we thought it worth teaching), record the actual words we might say (in order to make our teaching as explicit, clear, and powerful as possible, and to prevent colleagues from misinterpreting our intentions), list needed materials, and note possible follow-up sessions.

These sheets were not intended as scripts for mandatory reading lessons but rather as samples of the kinds of lessons that make sense in the upper-elementary reading classroom. There is so much written about what content to teach in the early-childhood reading workshop, but much less straightforward suggestions for the upper-elementary classroom. By duplicating these sheets and sharing them with colleagues we intend to receive feedback as well as additional teaching suggestions for each category. See Figure 7.1 for a sample worksheet of a lesson filed under "Readers Who Disregard Built-in Clues." (See Appendix 7 for blank worksheet.) Our work is still in progress (we intend to create dozens of prototype lessons), but forming such goal-oriented study groups seems essential if we are to grow as teachers of reading.

Reading Workshop Minilesson

Source of Information

"Teaching Skill Within Meaningful Contexts," by Sharon Kane, in The Reading Teacher *52, no. 2 (October 1998)*

Minilesson Topic

Helping students to notice structures within texts.

Rationale for Teaching

Students in the upper grades often have trouble making meaning when the structure of the text is not conventional. In other words, when texts do not follow traditional patterns of organization, some students get confused.

Words Spoken

Many books are more difficult to read because the author tells the story in ways that we are not used to. Not every book or story moves from the beginning to the middle to the end. For the next several days I'm going to begin each reading workshop by sharing a picture book that contains one of these surprising structures. Your job when I am finished reading the book aloud will be to jot down what you noticed about the shape, design, structure, or pattern of organization of the book. We will then share your observations and what you did to make sense of the book when you realized that the story was not told in the usual way.

Materials Needed

Sunflower Island, by Carol Greene

Possible Follow-up Lessons

Read aloud other books with unique patterns of organization including:

Cocoa Ice, by Diana Appelbaum
The Christmas House, by Ann Turner
Pawprints in Time, by Philippa Butler and George Smith
Motley the Cat, by Mary Fedden and Susannah Amoore
The Clay Ladies, by Michael Bedard

Figure 7.1

Our early-morning study group also spoke to the needs of fluent readers who needed bigger challenges. Our intention was to create a list of suggested projects for children who became complacent in their reading. These included making a commitment to read all the works of one author, reading about one topic in many genres, trying to answer questions that are inspired by your reading but not answered by your reading, challenging yourself to read genres you've never attempted, and researching the historical settings of novels and paying attention to how that knowledge informs your reading.

In addition, we began thinking about what strategies we could suggest to our fourth- and fifth-grade fluent readers that would help them have more thoughtful reader responses. These included jotting down notes when you read, making connections to other books you've read, rereading texts to discover things you hadn't noticed during the first read, recalling personal experiences that somehow connect to the text and lead you to read it differently. Note, although we were thinking of ways to promote richer responses to books read, we were not trying to make children sound like adults. Each strategy would be presented tentatively (with a, "Here's something you might try . . ."), and with an eye toward revision in teaching if the strategy did not prove helpful.

Judy Davis and colleagues also began a file of short texts that would challenge accomplished readers in big ways. These were primarily well-crafted personal essays from the local newspaper as well as poems that children might not comprehend on their first read, but could with necessary supports. These one-page potential handouts were duplicated, hole-punched, and slipped into binders to be continuously added to. We were sure our colleagues would eventually desire copies of all these loose-leaf collections.

The Essential Structure: Weekly Staff Meetings

The structure that is central to the professional life of our school takes place right in the middle of the week—every week.

Our staff gathers together every Wednesday afternoon from 3:30 to 5:00. As I reported in *Going Public: Priorities and Practice at the Manhattan New School,* our superintendent suggests that our staff meetings should be of such high quality, that they could be shown on cable TV. I think ours could actually be on prime time. We don't merely read aloud memos and deal with one administrative item after another. We come together to talk about teaching and learning. And we don't flit from one subject to another. We have devoted years to portfolio assessment, rethinking writing, and the subject of this chapter, our own professional growth in the teaching of reading. The following activities help us engage in meaningful professional conversations. (See additional thoughts on staff meetings in Chapters 6 and 7 of *Going Public.*) In our staff meetings, we:

- swap reading stories
- tell the story of puzzling readers

- study children's literature
- hold demonstrations with students
- listen to in-house experts
- respond to professional reading
- respond to assessment reports
- talk about new ideas
- view videos on the teaching of reading
- use prompts to analyze specific teaching issues

Swap Reading Stories

Teachers often entertain friends and family with school stories and anecdotes. These stories can also serve educational purposes inside of school when we appreciate that the memorable things children say to us often provide insight into their thinking about reading and about learning to read.

Imagine sharing the following stories at a staff meeting and then thinking through the teaching implications of each.

- Samantha, a kindergarten student, was listening to me read a picture book aloud to her class. The book included many children in the realistic illustrations. The text was at the bottom of the page. Samantha asked me, "If these children look down, can they see the words?"
- I was waiting my turn in a restroom while out of town. A little girl emerged from the stall, looked me straight in the eye, and quite politely announced, "I didn't flush!" When I asked her why, she answered, "There's a sign that says, 'Do not flush sanitary napkins.' I don't know what they are, so I didn't dare flush."
- When my daughter was about seven she was eating a bagel that had just been taken out of a cellophane bag. She asked me, "Why can't babies eat bagels?" "What makes you say that?" I asked. "It says right here," she responded, pointing to the cellophane bag, which read, "Do not give to babies. Danger of suffocation."
- When I explained to my third-grade reading group that the narrator in the story was omniscient, that he knew everything that was happening everywhere, Angel asked if the narrator knew we were sitting around reading this story.
- Sharon Taberski tells of the time she introduced Beverly Cleary's *Dear Mr. Henshaw* to her students. "This book is very special," Sharon suggested, "because it is filled with letters." One of Sharon's second graders interrupted, "Aren't all books filled with letters?"
- Pam Mayer was reading aloud Leo Lionni's *A Busy Year*. When she came to the word *manure,* Pam asked her kindergartners if they knew what the term meant. Milo volunteered, "It's what we light on Hanukkah." (He was thinking of *menorah,* of course.)

- One of our fathers explained that he was so proud of his daughter Julia at the end of first grade, because she was now a reader and was willing to read aloud to her younger brother. He then explained that he always plays the all-news radio station whenever the family is at home, even during the summer of 1998, when the reports were filled with stories of President Clinton's scandalous affair with Monica Lewinsky. One day, his daughter called to him from the bedroom, where she was reading aloud to her younger brother from a *Lion King* book, "Dad, what's semen?" Very alarmed, and wishing he wasn't in the habit of always keeping the news on, he entered the bedroom to ask her where she had heard such a word. Pointing to the book in her lap, little Julia responded, "See, it's right here!" She was pointing to the contraction *C'mon.*

- Pam was listening to kindergartner Karla read aloud. When she came to the word *bike,* she miscued and said "bicycle," but quickly self-corrected. Pam asked, "How did you know it was *bike* and not *bicycle*?" Jenna, an eavesdropping five-year-old who was looking at the picture in the book, answered before her friend Karla had a chance, "Because there are no training wheels!"

Tell the Story of Puzzling Readers

In our school it is not a problem to publicly discuss our concerns about children's growth as readers. Teachers need to feel that they are not alone. Just like two architects who can pore over blueprints together or two attorneys who can go over evidence together, so too teachers need to be able to turn to their colleagues with their concerns. In the early years of our school, teachers took turns telling the story of particular students and looked to their colleagues for wise counsel. More times than not, the child would be a struggling reader. Lorraine, for example, talks about struggling readers with the kind of energy and wonderment you would expect to hear from a world-class detective bent on solving an important mystery.

Teachers, no doubt, have concerns about "satisfactory" readers who seem to have no motivation to read, voracious readers who are obsessed with one genre, or successful readers who refuse to take part in discussions or write in response to their reading. These problems, however, don't compare with the problem of a child who finds learning how to read a really big challenge. These problems are the kind teachers chat about during lunch or when colleagues drop by their rooms after school.

Don't misunderstand. Classroom teachers do pay close attention to the sophisticated readers in their care and devise ways to challenge and stretch them as readers. But as a staff, we have spent more professional development time puzzling over the struggling children, the ones Don Holdoway calls the "extra-time" kids.

And so as a staff we have had to set priorities. When we do talk about reading at a whole-staff get-together we more often talk about the children who don't seem to be responding to our instruction than about the ones who are. We talk at length about the very young ones who can't seem to develop a sight vocabulary or employ strategies for figuring out a new word, as well as the ones who have somehow made it to fourth grade and are still not competent readers. We desperately want these children to acquire whatever skills it takes so that they too can one day feel confident about participating in the bookclubs they join. I know far too well that if they don't become confident and competent readers in school, they probably won't choose to read after they leave school.

When we work with a struggling third grader who can't retell a short passage because she reads so slowly that she can't hold onto the meaning of the text, we need to give instructional priority to the speed of her independent reading. Yes, we also want this eight-year-old to be a full participant in classroom book talk. We want her to make connections to other books she has read, to tell personal stories in response to text, to make insightful comments about the author's craft, but first we must figure out why she is reading so slowly. Of course, her teacher will make sure that this child is a full participant in the daily talk that surrounds the classroom read-aloud, but the heart of our individualized reading instruction for this child is in giving her the strategies she needs to become a fluent independent reader.

Study Children's Literature

Earlier I discussed ways for staffs to keep up with children's literature. Here I am specifically interested in ways for staffs to study literature using the lens of the teacher of reading. We learned many years ago that just because a book is published in big-book format doesn't mean that it's worthy of putting into our early-childhood classrooms. So too, just because a chapter book is thin and has a catchy title and cute cartoonlike characters on the cover doesn't mean it's worthy of handing to a young reader.

Scrutinize Texts   Sharon Taberski suggested a staff meeting ritual that required teachers to prepare on acetate sheets a few pages from a book they frequently use to teach reading. The staff would study the pages on the overhead projector and talk about the supports the text offers or any obstacles it presents to young readers. It's no surprise that Sharon suggested this ritual. She has been researching the teaching of reading in the primary grades for several years. Teachers talked about such variables as the familiarity of children with the topic, the chunking of phrases in natural line breaks, the repetition of key phrases, the helpfulness of illustrations, the choice of words, the placement of text on the page, and so on. This close study of texts across grade levels helps raise all teachers' consciousness to the variables on a page that can support readers or interfere with the reader's ability to make meaning.

For beginning readers, we looked at commercially published sets of books that come with the publisher's predetermined "leveling" attached, but we spent a great deal more of our time looking at the beautiful trade books that line our classroom walls, the ones that were *not* written with a particular teaching-of-reading intention or specified audience. For example, we pored over Simon James's picture book *Leon and Bob,* deciding that it would be a most supportive text for an early reader, since it contained all the positive aspects of the variables listed above.

We should never forget that beautiful books that are not written with any grade levels or reading supports in mind are a major resource in our reading workshops. We need to make sure that not everything beginning readers hold in their hands is part of a series or written with deliberate supports. Children need to attempt a wide range of texts and perhaps discover strategies we hadn't thought to teach. In addition, as previously noted, these are the books that they will probably be borrowing from the public library and sharing with their families at bedtime.

We also read books intended for "transitional" readers with a critical eye, focusing on many of the very popular series books. In an article they wrote for *The Trumpet Club* newsletter, Joanne Hindley and Sharon Taberski note, "As children read about Henry and his dog Mudge, Nate the Great, the Kids at the Polk Street School, and the Pee Wee Scouts, they anticipate certain behaviors and adventures from these characters; this facilitates their comprehension of related books in the set." (See pp. 313–318 for a longer discussion of series books). Despite the advantages of such series books, we wondered about editorial decisions they share. Why do so many of these books begin with so much dialogue, making it hard for the struggling reader to get an initial and essential grasp of the situation? Similarly, so many of these series books have so many quick and subtle scene changes, readers really must be quite competent, even though the words chosen and the sentence structures appear to be aimed at less fluent readers. We also wondered why so many authors insist on selecting names that are so difficult to pronounce or are proper nouns that often confuse the struggling reader. Similarly, we questioned the placement of illustrations in some of these short series chapter books. Many are marketed with the struggling reader in mind, yet the illustrations on the page don't necessarily give clues as to the meaning of the words on the page, as they consistently do in books for very young readers. One teacher put up a page in which the text dealt with getting ready for Christmas. The illustration on the same page showed one character feeding her dog while the other searched the refrigerator! We questioned as well the marketing decision to emblazon grade-level equivalents on the back of some series. (We cover ours with stickers so that children don't feel limited or threatened by these often poorly assigned reference points). (See p. 317 for questions to guide analysis of books in a series.)

Again, we need to make sure that not everything a student reads is part of a series or packaged with a specific grade level in mind. I would be most pleased to walk into third- and fourth-grade classrooms and see children reading such short, beautifully crafted chapter books as Jane Resh Thomas's *The Snoop,* Carol Carrick's *Upside Down Cake,* Betsy Byars's *Tornado,* Susan Shreve's *Warts,* and Natalie Kinsey-Warnock's *Sweet Memories Still.*

Sort Books   Another way we consolidated what we were learning about the variables that make a text easy or difficult to read was to spend time together sorting books. Sharon Taberski suggested that we create a multiple-copy lending library filled with books categorized for the "emergent," "early," "transitional," and "fluent" reader.

We gathered sets of multiple copies from all over the school and devoted several staff meetings to the nitty-gritty of placing books in the appropriate cases. There are times when such terms as *emergent, early, transitional,* and *fluent,* can seem quite complicated, especially when additional qualifiers as *beginning* and *advanced* are added to each category, but the terms helped us become familiar with what to look for in the texts that we were choosing for our students. The labels were not important; what we were learning about what supports readers and what gets in the way of readers was. Our confidence as teachers of reading grew as we found ourselves able to offer such explanations as the following:

> This book belongs in the "emergent" category because there is a close match between the pictures and the text, the language and structures match young children's oral experiences, the font is large and clear, the placement of print on the page is consistent, the subject is a familiar one to children, and there are just a few lines of text per page.

> This book might be a good match for an "early" reader since it has a bit more text per page, the picture still supports the text, the structure of the story is predictable, the line breaks support natural phrasing of language, and the topic is one young children can relate to.

> This book should be shelved with other "transitional" readers because it has very short chapters that stand on their own, only occasional picture supports, more characters and dialogue and sentence variety than "early reads," and it is still related to young children's interests.

> A student would have to be a "fluent" reader to make sense of this book because the chapters are much longer and they depend on one another. (Each chapter does not stand on its own as a self-contained story.) The sentence structures are more complex and varied. There are practically no picture clues, and there is some literary language. In addition, the dialogue is woven throughout and the characters are much more complex.

Hold Books in Your Hands   My daughter occasionally buys books for me by tapping the resources of Amazon.com. After typing in the titles of the books I've recently read and enjoyed she then orders a few from the Book Matcher list of suggested titles that quickly appears on her computer screen. (How can Amazon.com be so sure that I'll like Kate Atkinson's *Behind the Scenes at the Museum* or Bret Lott's *Jewel*?). The first time I heard of such a service I was amazed. Who would have thought that such a source of instant gratification would be so easily available to book lovers? Would we want such a service for teachers of very young readers? Just imagine, we could simply type in Eric Carle's *The Very Busy Spider,* Mercer Mayer's *There's a Nightmare in My Closet,* and Erik Hill's *Spot's Birthday* and be told that a child who can read these should also be able to read Jan Ormerod's *Story of Chicken Licken.* Perhaps this service already exists. I hope not. Such a computer service would take away one of the essential jobs of the reading teacher—to study texts closely in order to understand what makes a text easy or hard to read. Teachers don't need just titles and topics. They need to hold those books in their hands, to evaluate subject matter, to look at the placement of the lines of print on the page, to note how the illustrations support the text, to pay attention to the size of the font, and so on. Then they will be able to select just the right books for the child seated next to them, one based on his interests and filled with just the right amount of supports and challenges.

Write Books for Children   A more ambitious way for teachers to understand what makes a text supportive of young readers is to attempt to write a text with those young readers in mind. I've never asked my colleagues to spend time at a staff meeting trying to write the kind of books they love to put in their students' hands, but I think the "exercise" would be well worth the effort. (One text I wrote specifically for struggling readers in our school, *What's Cooking?* first appeared on brown paper bags with illustrations in marker by kindergarten children, and is now available from Mondo publishers, beautifully illustrated by Fiona Dunbar. You just never know where these school projects can lead.)

Study Texts for Older Readers   It also became important that we not neglect the teaching of reading in the upper-elementary classroom. I often wondered why my mother, who enjoys television mysteries, insists on watching reruns of very old programs instead of some of the new dramatic police stories. When I finally asked her, her answer had to do with the modern structure of most detective stories. She can't be bothered with so many tangled stories taking place at once. She prefers her mysteries to be straightforward and one at a time. My mother is eighty-one, and there's no need for me to push her to accept new challenges. But some of our upper-grade readers also choose the straight and narrow, never pushing themselves to solve new problems in their reading. Our job is to find the material that can invite them in, gently and supportively.

I shared with my colleagues the following challenging picture books and asked them to think about what reading comprehension minilessons they could design around them for their upper-grade reading workshop.

> Melvin J. Leavitt, *A Snow Story*
> Sheree Fitch, *There's a Mouse in My House*
> Wolf Erlbruch, *Mrs. Meyer the Bird*
> Mirra Ginsburg, *The Old Man and His Birds*
> Eve Bunting, *Fly Away Home*

These are the kind of books that students don't quite get the first time you read them aloud. There's a mysterious air about them, with things occurring that you're not quite sure could really occur. They're the kind of stories that push readers of all ages to honestly say, "Wait a minute. I'm not sure I got that. Does that mean . . . ?" These books invite readers to see the value in rereading, stopping to ask questions, identifying symbols, questioning motives, wondering about authenticity, and so on.

We also looked at short chapter books, the kind that we could easily use in upper-grade reading workshop minilessons. For example, at one staff meeting I shared how I used Mary Stolz's *A Ballad of the Civil War*. This is the story of two brothers who are on opposing sides in the Civil War, each not able to understand the other's position on slavery. I offered my colleagues the following information about the use of this book.

I chose to share the book with Cindy's fifth graders, not only because they were studying this time period but because when I read the text I was very conscious of what I was doing as a fluent reader to make sense of it. I wondered if fifth-grade readers used similar strategies. (I also chose the text because it is well-crafted and the brevity of the opening makes it suitable for the usual time constraints of a minilesson.)

I began by explaining to the students that when I read the book I was taken by surprise at how much work I had to do to fully understand the opening. It reads:

> On an evening in August 1862, Tom Rigby, lieutenant in the Sixth Union Cavalry, returning from reconnaissance, rode through a storm toward camp.
>
> Soldiers of both armies—Union and Confederate—struggled through mud, blood, and wind-tossed rain. The sound of distant cannon fire vied with thunder, and the dead lay in ditches, next to a rutted road lit now and then by flashes of lightning.
>
> Almost asleep in the saddle, Tom jerked upright as his horse, Pompety, stumbled.
>
> "Tired, are you?" he said, leaning to pat the drooping neck. "And hungry, too, I know. So am I hungry, and tired, and I haven't washed for days."
>
> Damp and drowsing. Horse and rider splashed on.
>
> Again Lieutenant Rigby leaned over and spoke in his horse's ear.
>
> "Pompety, this is the twenty-fourth of August, 1862. Today I am twenty-one years old, and a long, long way from home."
>
> The horse, accustomed to his rider's conversation, made a motion with his head.
>
> "I am thinking, Pompety," the young officer went on, wiping rain from his face. "I am thinking of Jack. My twin. We shared nineteen years, nineteen birthdays. Now I don't even know where he is, or how he is, or if even he is still alive. And he knows no more of me."
>
> He'd been keeping his eyes down. To avoid the nightmare around him, but now a figure at the roadside seized his attention. A soldier in a bloodied rebel uniform sat, arms folded around his knees, quietly crying.
>
> Dismounting, Lieutenant Rigby approached the huddled figure,
>
> "Jack?" he whispered. "Is it you, Jack?"

I gave the students copies of this two-page opening chapter to read silently. I then asked them to do some writing about their process of reading as well as their reaction to the text. In other words, I was after the story of their reading and some proof that their minds were at work while they read.

I provided the following questions to guide their reflections.

Did you bring any background information that helped you make sense of the text?

What are you sure of? What factual information is woven into the text?

What thoughts did you have because you were reading actively and aggressively?

Did you come across any problematic words and what did you do about them?

What questions do you now have?

Zara's reflection, shown in Figure 7.2, demonstrates a wide range of responses. Gaby responded quite differently (see Figure 7.3).

When the class finished sharing their reflections, I asked volunteers to role-play the conversation they imagined would probably take place when we turned the page. This impromptu drama really brought to life the children's varying interpretations of the text.

I like the way the author stated this: "mud, blood & wind-tossed rain."

I can really picture Lint. Rigby riding his horse in the middle of all that, because the author described it well. I wonder; when both sides of war are stumbling back to camp, do they shoot at each other

or just mind their own buisness? Do they grasp at the chance to ruin the enemy even more or just leave well enough alone?

I think Rigby talks to his horse because he is really lonely. I mean, you can't say to a friend, "Hey, I'm joining in the army wanna come?!" It's not like summer camp.

Also it was mentioned

that it was Lint. Rigby's birth day. Some great birthday, killing people and having people try to kill you.

I think the person on the road is Jack, but he's really hurt bad or something, be-cause it seems every thing is hurt in this story.

How do people decide which side they'll fight on? If the person is Jack, will they kill each other? Union ~
Confederate ~ Rebel

Figure 7.2

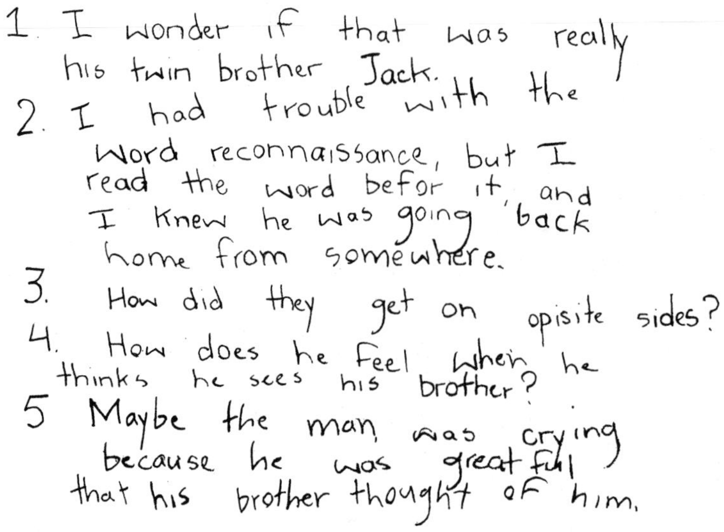

1. I wonder if that was really his twin brother Jack.
2. I had trouble with the word reconnaissance, but I read the word befor it, and I knew he was going back home from somewhere.
3. How did they get on opisite sides?
4. How does he feel when he thinks he sees his brother?
5 Maybe the man was crying because he was greatful that his brother thought of him.

Figure 7.3

I asked if they could ever imagine choosing to run scenes through their mind's eye as they read as a means of handling a puzzling text. In the days ahead, many children asked to complete this very short novel, as the activity had sparked great interest in the outcome of the story.

(I suggested to my colleagues that I could easily imagine devoting additional reading workshop minilessons to similarly guiding upper-grade students through the beginnings of other short, well-crafted novels. These might include Kevin Henkes's *Sun and Spoon*, Michael Morpurgo's *The Dancing Bear*, or Sara Harrell Banks's *Abraham's Battle*. No doubt, these too would become popular reads.)

Share Books That Pay Tribute to Literacy   Occasionally, I close staff meetings by sharing books that pay tribute to literacy. The predominant theme of each of the picture books listed below is becoming a reader. They are good reminders of how important our work is.

Running the Road to ABC, by Denize Lauture

Snowed In, by Barbara Lucas

Read to Your Bunny, by Rosemary Wells

The Old Woman Who Loved to Read, by John Winch

Read for Me, Mama, by Vashanti Rahaman

Edward and the Pirates, by David McPhail

Thank You, Mr. Falker, by Patricia Polacco

Wolf!, by Becky Bloom

Jeremiah Learns to Read, by Jo Ellen Bogart

Hold Demonstrations with Students

Several teachers on staff have volunteered to demonstrate various components of their reading workshop at our Wednesday after-school gatherings. (I've demonstrated the work I do at my third-grade tutorials as well. See p. 298 for details.) There is never an issue of demonstrations being "too early-childhood" for upper-grade teachers or too "upper grade" for primary teachers, when real children are present. Everyone remains totally engaged when children participate, and the children remind us that no matter our particular grade-level interest, our students have either come from this stage or are headed that way.

Components that are particularly worthy of live demonstrations include:

- individual reading conferences, including demonstrations of running records, retellings, and discussion of books read
- the shared reading of new as well as familiar texts
- small guided-reading sessions for specific purposes
- book club response groups either led by a teacher or without teacher leadership (Teachers watch a group of children meet for talk about a book with no adult intervention.)
- read-aloud session (A teacher reads aloud to a group of students.)
- upper-grade reading workshop minilessons (These could involve the presentation of texts on the overhead projector, the sharing of picture books with layered meanings, and teacher think-alouds (first-draft reading in front of students).

Listen to In-House Experts

In any school building there are staff members with particular areas of expertise. It makes sense to take full advantage of this local talent. Teachers can be encouraged to sign up to host a staff meeting addressing a particular issue in the teaching of reading. Meetings can actually be held in the room of the "guest speaker." For example teachers can:

- explain the organization of books in their class libraries
- walk colleagues through the components of their reading record-keeping system
- share files of parent correspondence related to literacy (letters, journal articles, questionnaires)
- narrate any videotape clips they've made of scenes from their reading workshop
- share important learnings from professional literacy books they've been reading
- prepare summary notes of reading conferences or workshops they've attended
- share content of workshops or speeches they've given

Respond to Professional Reading

As described in *Going Public,* we set aside regular staff time to respond to good, juicy novels. We must also include time to talk about professional books and articles. If selected titles apply to grade-specific interests, these response groups can take place at grade-level meetings; if not, these reader-response groups based on professional reading can take place at large-group staff meetings.

I have left many articles in teachers' mailboxes over the last few years, requesting that they be read before the next staff meeting. Teachers, of course, are just as likely to leave articles in colleagues' mailboxes. The best articles we read are ones that provoke strong opinions and lead to new insights. (See Appendix 8 for a sampling of articles read.)

Professional books dealing with literacy can also lead to very lively whole-staff response. The following are sure to ignite discussion:

> *The Literacy Crisis: False Claims, Real Solutions,* by Jeff McQuillan
> *Three Arguments Against Whole Language and Why They Are Wrong,* by Stephen Krashen
> *Misreading Reading: The Bad Science that Hurts Children,* by Gerald Coles

Well-written readers' memoirs or books on the history of reading also make for great professional book talk. The stories of passionate readers offer insights for how we want to live our own adult lives and impact the lives of the young people in our care. (Mind you, we don't expect young students to act like the adults in these books. As teachers, we simply look to them for inspiration about the important work we do.)

Suggestions for staff reading include:

Lynne Sharon Schwartz, *Ruined by Reading*

Michael Dorris and Emilie Buchwald, eds., *The Most Wonderful Books: Writers on Discovering the Pleasures of Reading*

Steven Gilbar, ed., *The Open Door: When Writers First Learned to Read*

Eric Burns, *The Joy of Books: Confessions of a Lifelong Reader*

Daniel Pennac, *Better Than Life*

Susan Allen Toth and John Coughlan, eds., *Reading Rooms: America's Foremost Writers Celebrate Our Public Libraries with Stories, Memoirs, Essays and Poems*

Anna Quindlen, *How Reading Changed My Life*

Jim Burke, *I Hear America Reading*

Albert Manguel, *A History of Reading*

Henri Petroski, *The Book on the Bookshelf*

(Reading the writing portfolios of struggling students is another helpful way to figure out how to help them grow as readers. This topic is discussed in Chapter 9, "Providing Safety Nets for Struggling Students."

Respond to Assessment Reports

Pat Werner spent her first year in our school providing small-group instruction to upper-grade students who needed extra support. Periodically she would write up the work she was doing. I can easily imagine using her detailed reports as conversation starters in our staff room. An excerpt from her report on Nadia, a fifth grader, follows:

I am constantly amazed and delighted to watch how Nadia taps into all her many resources to comprehend a text. One time, before we started our reading for the day, Nadia told me how she had come to an unknown word, *trophies,* in her independent reading. At first she thought the word referred to diapers, yet she knew this couldn't be right because the children in the story were too old. So she read it again. The words in the story had to do with sports, swimming and running. She told me that she tried to think of swimming and running in her own life, and she remembered an incident that had something to do with winning a trophy for a sporting event. "That's how I knew the word was *trophy.*" Our group now refers to thinking about your own experiences and applying it to unknown words in context as the "Nadia" strategy.

Even with all of her capabilities, Nadia continues to struggle with many texts because she doesn't know so much of the vocabulary contained in the reading. When reading a newspaper article together recently, the group brainstormed familiar words to meaningfully replace the more difficult ones in the text. The group stopped at a sentence that read, "she has been dealing with the exigencies of sponge baths and . . ." I fully expected that the children wouldn't know *exigencies,* but Nadia could not figure out *dealing* or *sponge* as well.

Just this small excerpt from a two-page report on Nadia could lead to valuable talk. I could imagine teachers asking, "How do children improve their vocabularies? Which newspapers are appropriate for struggling fifth graders? How do we help children understand text that is removed from their experiences?" And of course, "What does *exigency* mean, anyhow?"

Any teacher who is about to share a narrative report with parents can bring drafts to staff meetings. Feedback from colleagues will help teachers revise their content if necessary and anticipate parents' questions and concerns.

(See also Chapter 9, "Providing Safety Nets for Struggling Students," for information on how teachers can study student writing to evaluate their needs as readers.)

View Professional Videotapes

Earlier I suggested that teachers videotape themselves as a way to self-assess their literacy work. Here I encourage the viewing of commercially prepared videos at whole-school staff meetings. A member of the staff should be asked to preview the tape to ensure the contents are appropriate for the subject at hand. The previewer should also take a look at any written materials that accompany the tape for helpful suggestions for use. Additionally, the previewer and/or leader of the meeting might preface the first viewing by offering background on the setting and the educators involved. Most audiences want to view videos more than once, the first time without pen in hand. Later, audiences can choose to revisit the scenes that are most resonant with respect to their school community and most appropriate for their field of study. Staffs usually have a great deal to say in regard to video footage, therefore the leader can expect small amounts of tape to inspire long amounts of conversation. (Readers will find additional suggestions for using videotapes at professional development gatherings in Calkin's and Harwayne's *The Writing Workshop: A World of Difference: A Guide to Staff Development.*)

Talk About New Ideas

Imagine inviting staff members to run their wildest teaching-of-reading ideas by colleagues. These "throw caution to the wind" sessions would no doubt lead to interesting, honest, and—it is hoped—tactful conversations. Teachers could be encouraged to begin their sharing with such phrases as . . .

> "Something I've always wanted to try is . . ."
> "This may sound crazy, but . . ."
> "Help me think this through . . ."
> "Does this sound way off . . . ?"
> "I'm not sure this makes sense but . . ."

One idea I'd been toying with, for example, has its roots in a collection of quotes I received from my friend, children's writer Louise Borden. She sent me a four-page spread of hand-copied favorite lines from Anne Michaels's *Fugitive Pieces,* a novel she knew I had enjoyed. It was startling for me to see the lines that she had chosen, all poignant, powerful, and at the same time lyrical. I slipped Louise's jottings into my copy of the book, as a permanent reminder of the book and of our friendship, and no doubt as a bookmark when I reread. This idea of lifting lines from a beloved book and sharing them with a friend really appeals to me, but I'm not sure if it has implications for our older students. Would it make sense to ask them to do the same? Would it have instructional or long-lasting value? Is it too adult-like? Would children appreciate the effort? In a case like this, I need to turn to my colleagues and say, "Does this sound way off . . . ?"

These sessions could lead to solid teaching ideas, but more importantly they could remind teachers that being innovative and experimental (as opposed to cute or gimmicky) is part of the joy of teaching, as is running ideas by thoughtful and respectful colleagues. After all, there is no one way.

Use Prompts to Analyze Specific Teaching Issues

The teaching of reading is such a huge topic that it is helpful to not only target areas for discussion but to suggest starting points for these talks. I have found it particularly helpful to prompt these targeted talks by either asking participants to bring artifacts connected to the topic or to provide teachers with a "preparatory think sheet" or questionnaire prior to our meetings so that they can informally prepare for the talk. Scaffolding the talk in such a way also keeps us on-task. The following artifacts, surveys, and work sheets were used to focus our attention on specific aspects of teaching reading. (See also "Studying Students' Writing for Clues to Improving Their Reading" on pp. 318.)

Samples of Reading Logs   Teachers were asked to bring and display samples of their reading logs, forms used by the children to keep track of their reading. The logs ranged from simple sheets requiring students to list titles, authors, and pages read on a daily basis, to elaborate records with spaces for reader's comments, reflective letters to the teacher, and response from the teacher. (See Joanne Hindley's *In the Company of Children.*) Some had places for students to reflect on their weekly growth as readers as well as systems for keeping tabs on the genres chosen. (See Sharon Taberski's *On Solid Ground.*)

Looking at one another's reading-log formats and noting the great variety pushed teachers to ask themselves such questions as:

Do I have goals attached to my reading logs?

Do my forms help achieve my goals?

Do these records gather the information I need?

Do the logs reveal helpful information about individual children? About my class as a whole?

Should I be responding to the logs?

Do the children benefit from keeping logs?

Have log entries become rote?

Are there better ways I could hold children accountable for their reading?

Here are some other artifact requests intended to prompt literacy talk:

- Bring the professional book that has been the most helpful to you as a teacher of reading. Be prepared to talk about your choice and about professional reading in general. How can we make professional reading more powerful in our school?
- Bring samples of reading self-assessment tasks that you have asked your students to do. Be prepared to talk about how these fit within your entire assessment system as well as student and family response to these tasks.
- Bring one reading "game" that you think fits well with what we believe about how children learn to read. Be prepared to discuss what you think this game teaches and how you fit such activities into your reading workshop or school day.
- Bring samples of students' written response to their reading that you believe show the student grew as a reader. Be prepared to talk about the role of written response to text for children throughout the grades.
- Bring one poem that you think lends itself to choral reading and be prepared to discuss why you chose the poem and what such activities do for students' growth as readers.
- Bring a sample of your reading homework assignment. (Is it the same each night or does it vary through the school year?) Be prepared to talk about the role of homework in the teaching of reading.
- Bring a photograph of your word wall. Be prepared to talk about its purpose and use as well as any concerns you have.

(Of course, not every teacher will bring an artifact to each meeting. Teachers' lives are just too busy. The good news is that you only need a few to get rich conversation going. Simply displaying artifacts side by side will highlight their range and versatility. If many teachers want to talk about their individual contributions, the conversation can extend to several meetings. It's always preferable to stick with a relevant topic than to jump from one to another. Don't expect the conversation to remain attached to the original assignment. The power of seeing so many possibilities will lead the participants down new paths.)

Read-Aloud Questionnaire   The read-aloud questionnaire appearing in Appendix 9 was distributed prior to a staff meeting; teachers were asked to star those aspects of reading aloud which they felt deserved the whole group's attention. Teachers might want to cover *many* of the aspects of reading aloud generated by the questions, thereby making reading aloud the topic of study for several weeks.

Discussion of any one of the read-aloud issues listed in the questionnaire could fill an hour-and-a-half staff meeting and produce information that could make a difference in the lives of young readers. For example, teachers could decide that question number 13, "Have you ever spoken to family members about the importance of reading aloud? What suggestions did you make?" deserved the whole group's attention. One teacher could serve as secretary, compiling the group's reading-aloud suggestions for family members. These could then be included in a school newsletter. (See Chapter 8, "Informing Families About the Teaching of Reading," for suggestions.)

Clusters of teachers might be asked to develop survey questions on other topics. These can be distributed well in advance of staff meetings to generate important issues for discussion. Possibilities for survey areas include:

- use of word walls
- teaching of phonics
- minilessons in the reading workshop
- concerns about small-group instruction
- use of the overhead projector in reading workshop
- reading recovery implications for the classroom teacher
- informing families about the teaching of reading
- looking at student writing for clues to growth as readers
- catapulting the passive reader
- reading portfolios

The above topics would make sense in our community, but each school will have its own concerns. Staff members could create a year's curriculum for professional study in reading by selecting topics and having questionnaires prepared.

Readers' Needs Think-Sheet   Several years ago I compiled a list of dysfunctional reading strategies connected to different categories of struggling readers. Under each category I tried to think of the things the readers were doing or not doing that got in their way. Some of those categories and behaviors follow:

The inaccurate reader is one who misreads many words, becomes paralyzed by hard words, or reads so slowly that his phrasing is usually off. He also might ignore punctuation or get caught up in minutiae, giving equal attention to all parts of a text.

The passive reader is one who does not reflect on what he is reading, never pauses, never puts his book down, doesn't ask questions, and doesn't make predictions. He doesn't monitor his reading. In other words, he doesn't know when he is lost, or he realizes that he is lost but doesn't ask for help and doesn't have any strategies for getting back into the text on his own.

The reader with a poor attitude is one who gets no pleasure out of reading. He sees no reason to bother and therefore gives up rather easily. He doesn't trust his instincts and would never question a text. He never ponders or doubts. He therefore interprets everything literally. As this reader gets older, not making sense of a text becomes the norm.

The reader who disregards built-in clues is one who doesn't take notice of such things as repetitions, patterns, structures, or predictable designs. This reader probably also ignores all the visual suggestions the good writer includes, and thereby rarely forms images in his mind's eye.

The reader with unique issues is one who might not be used to literary language, or is totally unfamiliar with a certain genre, or is making a transition to reading in a new language. Of course, there are also readers with unique processing problems that require specialized supports.

When I shared these thoughts at a staff meeting, my colleagues and I brainstormed even more specific dysfunctional strategies that we saw in our elementary readers. I then incorporated their thoughts into the worksheet that appears in Appendix 10 in order to help us think about instructional plans for children needing extra support.

This worksheet was never intended to be filled out in its entirety. Its sole purpose was to get us thinking about what instructional techniques we could use to help students become strategic readers.

Guides to Issues That Span the Grades   Teachers from kindergarten through fifth grade attend our staff gatherings. This across-the-grades group appreciates an occasional across-the-grades topic for study. (Reading issues that are particularly appropriate for specific grades are frequently discussed at grade-level meetings. See p. 223.)

To launch conversation in this direction, I attempted to think through one teaching technique that appears throughout the grades. I chose author study, asking myself, "What does an author study involve as we move through the grades?" My quick jottings appear in Appendix 1. After sharing my initial response, teachers were quick to challenge, modify, revise, and otherwise use these ideas as a springboard for further talk.

At future meetings, staff members working in small clusters can be asked to think through other worthy issues that span the grades. This activity requires sheets of large chart paper, markers, some willing note takers, and an enthusiastic group of teachers. Staff members can be divided into grade-level groups and such topics as the following might be introduced:

- What reading strategies do you teach? What exact language do you use to explain strategies?
- What things do you do in your own reading life that you talk to students about?
- What reading-writing connections do you expect your students to make?
- How can newspaper reading be part of your work?
- How do you use multiple copies of books?
- How do you involve parents in students' reading?
- What does reading homework look like?
- How is your class library organized?
- What kinds of talk do you hope for in response to a read-aloud?

Teachers can fill charts, post them around the staff room, and then think about the following:

- What similarities are evident?
- What differences?
- Is there a continuum forming?
- Are there noticeable gaps?
- Is the language we use to talk about reading consistent throughout the grades? Should it be?
- Are there any surprises?
- What new areas of research do these findings suggest?

When Ethan entered Pam's first-grade class after spending a year in Tammy's kindergarten, he explained to his teacher that he was using the "power tools" from his toolbox as he read. He was referring to very specific reading strategies taught to him by Tammy. I expect that brilliant literacy teachers will invent fresh and effective ways to talk to their students about reading, but I also expect that members of scholarly communities will create occasions for familiarizing themselves with one another's metaphors and vocabulary. (Teachers need not adopt one another's language, but they must understand it, so that they can best support children's efforts to become literate.) Probing issues that span the grades is one such mechanism for close language study.

(Teaching-of-writing issues that span the grades can be studied in similar ways. See *Writing Through Childhood* for details.)

Quotation Think-Sheets   Prepare or ask colleagues to take turns preparing a quote sheet related to an important literacy issue. Teachers can read in advance and respond to the ideas at a staff meeting. For example, imagine distributing the think-sheet related to comprehension that appears in Appendix 11. Teachers can argue the merits of each and discuss the classroom implications they suggest. The quotes in this sheet were found in such collections as Otto Bettmann's *The Delights of Reading: Quotes, Notes and Anecdotes,* and *The Readers Quotation Book: A Literary Companion,* edited by Steven Gilbar. Of course, teachers need not rely on these preselected quotes. Instead, they can select thought-provoking and appropriate quotations from the professional books they are reading as well as insightful comments made by colleagues and students.

Support from the School District

Our school is located in a district that makes professional development a top priority. Each school is given an annual allotment to be spent on a wide range of professional development opportunities. Rather than hire any literacy staff developers, as many schools do, we have come to count on the many teachers on staff (as well as the principal!) who have had experience offering literacy staff development. We can then spend our money on professional literature as well as on substitute coverage to free teachers to visit in one another's classrooms and to have time to engage in professional discussions.

Substitute coverage also enables us to take advantage of district workshops, conference days, and visits to exemplary classrooms throughout our district. Some district courses and institutes require no substitute coverage because they are offered during after-school hours and during the summer months. (They do require money, however, as districts are contractually bound to pay New York City teachers to attend these sessions.) Teachers throughout our district can also take advantage of Reading Recovery training, leadership training, residencies with master teachers, and distinguished teacher mentoring opportunities.

On Viewing Teachers as Students of Literacy

Whenever a school in our district requests to retain a student in a grade, an application is filed with the district office. On it, we must list all the teachers this struggling student has had. The implication is clear. Our superintendent wants to know who has been teaching this child. Has he had a string of first-year teachers or his fair share of experienced ones? Is his inability to read well due to some unknown factor or to a lack of expert instruction? We are also asked to reveal who the child will be studying with in the next school year. Every which way you turn in our district, the main thing is always teacher expertise. New teachers, as well as experienced ones, are always expected to be students of literacy. (See p. 234.)

In a recent column in *The New York Times,* Sandra Feldman, the president of the American Federation of Teachers, spoke about the professional development in our district. She writes, "New York City's District 2 shows one way of helping students meet high standards that works. For about eight years, District 2 has implemented a successful literacy program that provides sustained, high-quality professional development for teachers and individualized help for kids who need it. It has gotten excellent results with all children but especially with those who were having big problems becoming proficient readers." (The extra help offered to students in our district includes Reading Recovery and other early-childhood interventions as well as extended-day and extended-year tutorials for older students. See details on pp. 291–292.) We realize, of course, that for individual help to really make a difference it must be aligned with "sustained, high-quality professional development for teachers." The two go hand in hand. You can't make a difference in a child's growth as a reader if you don't really understand how to teach reading.

Not too long ago, my husband noticed that two pillars on our back porch were water damaged. He called in contractors for estimates on repair. The prices quoted ranged from $800 to $5,000. "How could there be such a discrepancy?" I naively asked. "One would get at the problem, the other would just add some cosmetic touches," he explained. In the teaching of reading, we can't afford to settle for cosmetic touches. It's rather easy to make a room look like an enjoyable setting for reading. It's an entirely different matter to place an expert teacher at the helm of that reading classroom, one who knows how to help children solve the reading problems they come upon. And just like with back porch repairs, to get the job done well requires money, money for staff development.

RELATED READINGS IN COMPANION VOLUMES

Going Public (Heinemann, 1999) is abbreviated as GP. *Writing Through Childhood* (Heinemann, forthcoming) is abbreviated as WC.

Making staff development a priority	**GP:** Ch. 6, Ch. 7; **WC:** Ch. 11
Providing professional libraries	**GP:** Ch. 4, Ch. 7; **WC:** Ch. 11
Arranging for teachers to visit one another	**GP:** Ch. 4, Ch. 7
Supporting grade-level meetings	**GP:** Ch. 6; **WC:** Ch. 11
Studying children's literature	**WC:** Ch. 5
Providing worthwhile teacher observations	**GP:** Ch. 3, Ch. 4
Covering teachers	**GP:** Ch. 7
Providing worthwhile staff meetings	**GP:** Ch. 6, Ch. 7; **WC:** Ch. 11

CHAPTER 8

INFORMING FAMILIES ABOUT THE TEACHING OF READING

Key Literacy Lessons

1. Family members need to be given the big picture of how reading is taught early on in their child's school career.
2. Literature-based methods of teaching reading can best be explained to family members through parent education structures such as:
   - guided tours of reading workshops
   - parent field trips
   - literacy workshop series
   - evening curriculum sessions
   - parent book clubs and literacy courses
3. Parents benefit from worthwhile materials sent home, including:
   - content-rich newsletters
   - relevant announcements, articles, and form letters
4. Family members benefit from materials posted at school. These can include:
   - responses to inaccurate media portrayals of literature-based teaching
   - publications by members of the school community
   - information about literacy events
   - entertainment suggestions based on children's literature
5. Families can also be well-served by teachers who give serious thought to the crafting of classroom correspondence. Such correspondence includes:
   - literacy surveys
   - literacy news bulletins
   - literacy assessment documents
   - photograph albums
6. Teachers and administrators should invite parent involvement in and contributions to school bulletin board displays.
7. Schools must take a strong stance on parent education and involvement, acknowledging that well-informed parents are essential components of successful schools.

My son told me about a restaurant in the Soho neighborhood of New York that has transparent stalls in its restrooms. Michael went on to explain that as soon as you enter and close the door, the stall clouds over and becomes opaque, only to become transparent again once you open the door to leave. I imagine many people would be afraid to enter those stalls, because they haven't a clue as to how they work. Once you understand the workings of this unique restroom, however, you no doubt delight in the craftsmanship. Although the teaching of reading is a far cry from designing a restroom, I do think that parents are likewise afraid to enter literature-based classrooms, because they don't understand how they work. But we've found that once they do, they too delight in the craftsmanship.

Providing Families with the Big Picture of How We Teach Reading

Family members need to understand how reading is taught in our school. Most receive this information on their very first tour. At prospective parent meetings I usually begin by reflecting on the bottom-up approach to teaching reading, which most members of the audience can recall from their own school days. I share my own childhood memories of progressing from the letters and sounds of the alphabet to simple one-syllable words to very short sentences. Then I went on to short paragraphs and eventually a story based on all the sounds and words I had been taught. I often show the audience an example of a dismal story based on a controlled vocabulary, and then I contrast this approach with the meaning-based approach our lucky students take part in each day.

I describe how we at the Manhattan New School start with the whole. We surround children with engaging songs, chants, poems, and predictable picture books that make our youngest students pay attention to print and long to be readers. I demonstrate early-childhood teachers' techniques for reading and rereading texts, all the while inviting students to read along, memorize, and point out their observations about print. I talk about how expert teachers know which story and language structures, sight words, spelling features, and phonetic elements to highlight and call children's attention to. I comment on how kindergartners acquire knowledge of sound/symbol correspondences and extensive sight vocabularies as a result of the rich print environment and daily shared-reading experiences that fill their school days. All this is accomplished, I explain, without the help of any prescribed systematic phonics program.

Yes, we teach phonetic elements, I am quick to point out, but we never allow the teaching of phonics to become synonymous with the teaching of reading and thereby distort what reading is all about. We keep phonics teaching in perspective, along with many other reading strategies. We point out essential phonemic elements in wise ways and never assign children endless workbook drills that not only bore them but actually encourage them to rely too heavily on sounding out when they come across unknown words.

When I speak to parents who are very new to our approach to teaching reading, I always tell them a true story about my early teaching experiences. When I was a beginning teacher many, many years ago, I had a drawer filled with buttons covered with inspirational and amusing sayings. One day I wore one that read "Go Fly a Kite." I'll never forget the little boy passing me in the hall who read aloud, "Go Fly a Kitten," and kept on walking. That little boy relied exclusively on phonics. He didn't know what reading was all about. If he did, he would have stopped in his tracks and said, "That doesn't make any sense!" Family members seem to understand the kind of readers we are interested in raising.

Today, I suggest to parents, I am still struck by students entering our school who have been fed a steady diet of isolated phonics. When they read, they rely exclusively on "sounding out" words, letter by letter, from left to right, in tedious, time-consuming ways that rarely enable them to figure out the unknown word. These children have never learned that reading is a meaning-making activity. Otherwise, they would have used their knowledge of how the world and our language work to precede their use of the sounding-out strategy.

I continue explaining to parents how our teachers carefully match children with supportive texts, ones in which they can rely on *many* reading strategies. And family members need to know that we do teach strategies. The media would have them believe that literature-based teachers think children learn simply by being surrounded by books. I tell prospective parents that reading strategies for beginning readers include such basics as recalling background knowledge about topics, using picture clues, and skipping words. When children skip words, I explain to parents, they are encouraged to read to the end of the sentence (or paragraph), and then return to choose a word that makes sense, using their knowledge about how language works, what makes sense in the world, as well as familiarity with phonetic elements, to confirm or reject their choices. During this process, children can be seen looking at initial and final letters, familiar parts of words, and known words within words (not just struggling from left to right), as well as rereading the sentence to keep the meaning in mind.

I explain to parents that by the time our children are leaving third grade, most have become fluent readers and the ones who haven't receive lots of individualized help in learning additional strategies. (See Chapter 9, "Providing Safety Nets for Struggling Students.") I then demonstrate to family members how such strategies as paying attention to punctuation, drawing story maps to keep tabs on what is happening in stories, or making mental pictures can help an eight-year-old who still reads haltingly and reluctantly. Even fourth and fifth graders who have not become confident and competent readers receive instruction in such valuable reading strategies as monitoring their reading, adjusting their rate of reading, and recalling what they know about particular genres in order to make more sense of texts.

If my brief lecture to family members seems overly filled with talk of strategies, this decision is a deliberate one. I want parents to understand that even though their children will not receive a heavy hard-cover reader to lug home every night, they will be taught how to read. Parents need to fully understand that well-informed teachers do have a body of knowledge about the teaching of reading and that they do believe there are explicit things to teach children that will help them grow as readers.

Structures for Parent Education

Once family members become full-fledged members of our community, they continue to receive important information about the teaching of reading. In *Going Public*, Chapter 5, "Reaching Out to Families," I described the many ways we educate parents at the Manhattan New School. These are appropriate means of sharing information about the teaching of reading and children's growth as readers. (Many of these activities also apply to informing family members about the teaching of writing, a subject that will be addressed in more detail in *Writing Through Childhood*.)

Schools must take the education of parents seriously, lest parents' only source of information be what they read in the newspaper. When I read some of the misguided and misinformed reports that have appeared in the media, I'm surprised that anyone is willing to send their children to public schools. As Yetta Goodman, acclaimed literacy expert, writes, "I believe that at the heart of the phonics movement is an attack on public education. State departments and self-proclaimed experts are ignoring professional organizations, professionally educated reading specialists, and teachers and providing simple solutions to reading instruction. There is disinformation disseminated about reading scores and the literacy rates in the United States that undermines what teachers, administrators, curriculum developers, and reading specialists do in schools."

Teachers themselves must take the initiative to challenge false claims about the teaching of reading. Below is a discussion of structures that are specifically designed to inform parents about our practices and goals with respect to the teaching of reading.

Before-School Curriculum Workshops

Early-morning meetings led by classroom teachers are particularly effective because teachers can walk family members through the actual routines listed on the daily agenda, explaining the approximate amount of time allotted for each. Teachers can also demonstrate the materials and record-keeping system that they and the children will be using that day. Teachers can show family members what book they will be reading aloud, what texts will be used for shared-reading experiences, what strategies will be highlighted, what conferences or small-group meetings are scheduled, and so on. Teachers can also point out on the daily agenda times during the day when children will have opportunities to read. They can go over actual home-reading assignments and answer family members' questions about their role in their child's reading. If meetings like these are scheduled at set intervals throughout the school year, family members will appreciate how the teachers' changing goals for children inform the materials used and the strategies taught.

Observation of Classroom Practice

Occasionally parents express an interest in gaining a deeper understanding of our approach to teaching reading. Sometimes this interest comes from the parents' own background as a teacher or interest in pursuing a career in education, as a school volunteer, aide, paraprofessional, or teacher. Sometimes the parents request to learn more in order to be more helpful to their own children at home. Whatever the reason, one of the best ways to help parents understand our approach is for classroom teachers to set up a specified time for parents to sit in on a reading workshop. It helps to carve out a few minutes after the visit to answer any questions the parent may have. Taking parents' inquiries seriously goes a long way to eliminating all those, "How come you don't . . . ?" questions and instead turns family members into enthusiastic advocates who in turn can help other parents understand the work we do. Parents with flexible schedules have been known to visit and get so involved in the work that they have become regular volunteers.

Guided Tours of Reading Workshops

Imagine the principal escorting a group of interested parents on a walking tour of the school which focused on the teaching of reading. I might hand clipboards and pencils to the parents gathered, suggesting that they take notes as we weave in and out of classrooms, kindergarten through grade five. I might even pose a series of focusing questions: "What's the same about all the classrooms we visit? What language (terminology) do we hear over and over again? What is the teacher's role in all these classrooms? What do you notice about how books are organized in all these rooms? What do you think is being taught?" After the tour I would meet with parents to hear their concerns and answer their questions. Prospective parents benefit from taking a guided tour of our school, but parents of enrolled children have a vested interest in truly understanding the methodologies used by the teachers who educate their children.

Coffee Chats

Although these gatherings in our fourth-floor ballroom (an auditorium with the chairs removed), are formally built into our yearly school calendar, they are very informal. Whoever shows up pulls a folding chair into a circle and our coffee chat begins. (The first few times I actually served coffee, but it was such a hassle to fill the big pot, then clean it, that parents now know to bring their own if they'd like to. We still call it a coffee chat.) They are scheduled to begin at around 8:15 A.M., when family members start dropping off their children in the cafeteria for breakfast, and usually end about an hour later. (Parents know that they can get up and leave at any time.) Although these chats have no announced topic, I usually kick off the conversation with a story or two. Very frequently the stories are about some aspect of literacy, a memorable teaching/learning scene, an insightful comment made by a child, or noteworthy books. These five minutes of principal talk often generate the next hour of conversation. People have questions, issues, concerns, and suggestions. People frequently come with their own agendas, and that's okay too. Anything goes, except talking about individual children or teachers.

Language Forums

As briefly mentioned in *Going Public,* a group of Asian parents—one Chinese, one Korean, and two Japanese mothers—approached me and asked if I could hold periodic meetings with them so that they could keep up-to-date on school happenings and ask the questions that were on their minds. They explained that the talk at PTA meetings was too fast for them to keep up with and that they preferred not to speak their beginning English in front of such a big gathering. Of course I agreed to such an important request; I was only sorry that I hadn't thought of it myself.

At the meetings, the women spoke only in English. They didn't, in fact, know one another's languages, so English was our common denominator. At this intimate gathering in my office, I could tell in an instant when I was not being understood and needed to slow down, repeat, or choose different words to make my meaning clear. I could also turn to visual aids, much the way second-language teachers do, to charts, books, and photographs that pertained to the topic at hand. The parents asked many important questions, often writing them down before the meetings to rehearse for these English conversations. Issues of homework, standardized testing, and how to increase English vocabulary for their children seemed to be most on their minds.

In *Going Public* I shared my wish to have a full-time parent educator in the school, someone who could help parents understand why we do what we do. Although I learned a great deal from these small-group meetings, I knew that our Albanian, Portuguese, and Maltese families probably needed the same. And of course, the days are too short for one person to lead numerous groups. We probably will never be in a position to hire a parent educator, but certainly we can organize teachers or parents who would be willing to host these periodic small-group gatherings. Leaders need not speak the language of the assembled crowd, but just be willing to speak clearly, slowly, and with visual supports. If the assembled group speaks no English, bilingual parents or translators from the community might be asked to attend. (See *Going Public* for ways that Carmen Colon, our Spanish instructor, reached out to our Spanish-speaking parents.)

Parent Field Trips

I wonder how many parents would show up if I advertised an escorted field trip to the nearest public library. I'd have fun browsing the shelves with a group of parents, talking about how they and their children go about choosing books. I'd talk about what appeals to different-aged children, and point out all the areas of the library devoted to different genres and books in different languages. We'd spend time investigating available resources (storytelling hours, videos, bibliographies of recommended books, summer programs, etc.) and getting to know the local librarian. Similarly, each year when Fordham University holds its Parents and Reading Conference, I've always felt that I should attend with a group of interested and available parents. Wouldn't it make sense for every university to host such an annual event and for every school to send parent representatives? (I'd love opportunities to spend this kind of time with parents, but these trips away from school also sound like the perfect assignment for the parent educator I dream of.)

Presentations at PTA Meetings

We usually attract bigger turnouts at PTA meetings when the fliers sent home not only announce a meaty literacy topic but also suggest how that information will be shared. In other words, family members respond well when the flier includes such descriptors as *panel discussions* (because they get to meet several teachers), *classroom workshops* (because they get to look around a new classroom, not necessarily their child's), *videotape demonstrations* (because they get to view actual teaching moments), and *slide presentations* (because there is a hope of seeing their own child at work).

Those meaty literacy topics would include such issues as supporting the struggling child at home, choosing books for reading aloud at home, preparation for standardized reading tests, the difference between phonics workbooks and classroom context word study, or the keeping of a family literacy portfolio. (See *Going Public* for more details on the family literacy portfolio.)

(Over the years, we have also hosted meetings encouraging parents to become political about the teaching of reading. For example, Sharon Taberski and I along with the leaders of the PTA informed parents about the Reading Excellence Act, a bill that was at the time before the U.S. Senate. We described the contents of the bill, which among other things would require a panel of federal officials to approve methods used to teach children receiving the funding provided by the bill. We encouraged parents to let their legislators know their opinion of this legislation. At that meeting, the copresidents of the PTA also distributed sample letters to aid parents in writing their own, as well as the postal and e-mail addresses and telephone and fax numbers of our senators.)

Literacy Workshop Series

When PTA presentations run overtime, it's probably a sign that the topic warrants follow-up attention. One worthwhile way to accomplish longer study and conversation is to create a course of study or a series of parents' workshops related to the topic. These series (probably held in the early evening hours over the course of a few weeks) could be hosted by a group of staff members including the principal. Leaders could take turns running the workshops so that no one staff member feels overloaded as a result of the extra commitment. These workshops could be aimed at a very small number of parents. Even if only ten parents attend out of a school of five hundred, the rewards will be great. Good news travels and well-informed parents are eager to share what they are learning with other interested families. If dense syllabi, such as the ones sketched out below, are distributed before the series begins, many participants will probably attend.

Supporting the Struggling Reader at Home
Week 1-Tending to Issues of Self-Esteem
      Not Letting Homework Become Heartache

> Taking Teacher's Comments and Suggestions Seriously
>
> Suggestions for Reading Aloud

Week 2-Helping Parents Understand Why Some "Mistakes" Aren't Bad

> Gracious and Insightful Ways to Respond to a Child's Miscues
>
> The Value of Rereading "Easy Books"
>
> Engaging Children in Talk About Their Reading
>
> Creating Supportive Reading Rituals at Home

Week 3-Choosing Books and Books on Tapes

> Involving Older and Younger Siblings
>
> The Pros and Cons of Commercial Tutorials
>
> Literacy Materials and Computer Literacy Programs

Issues in Reading Aloud at Home

Week 1-Choosing the Setting, Creating Rituals

> Choosing the Book (Is There a Place for Easy-to-Read, "Just Right," and Difficult Texts?)
>
> Talking Naturally About Books (Inside of School and Out)
>
> Noting Authors and Illustrators (and Dedications, About-the-Author Pages, etc.)

Week 2-Reading Aloud (Pace, Tone, Expression)

> Handling Questions and Interruptions
>
> Lingering over Pictures
>
> Responding Honestly and Emotionally to Texts

Week 3-Reading Aloud to Children of Mixed Ages

> Reading Aloud to Older Children
>
> The Value of Rereading
>
> Reading More Than Picture Books and Chapter Books
>
> Feeling Too Tired to Read Aloud

Sessions should be as interactive as possible, with displays of actual materials, demonstrations of their use, role-plays, question-and-answer periods, as well as suggested activities for parents to try out in the week apart. In other words, in this course of study parents can be given homework.

Evening Curriculum Sessions

As described in *Going Public,* these annual get-togethers, led by classroom teachers in their own classrooms, are held in the early autumn of each school year. At these evening meetings, intended to provide a broad overview of all areas of curriculum, very little time can be devoted to literacy alone. It becomes essential therefore that teachers inform family members at these meetings about additional ways they can learn about literacy. These would include the previously described PTA meetings, parent workshops, and classroom observations. Teachers might also let parents know that they intend to send helpful information home throughout the year. (See "Sending Worthwhile Materials Home," below.)

In most classrooms, either the teacher or a parent volunteer types up a summary of the information shared at the curriculum get-togethers. These notes are then distributed to class parents who were unable to attend the meetings as well as any who would like the key points in written form. The summaries refer to all key components of literacy instruction as described on pp. 281–284.

Reading Get-Togethers

In *Going Public* I suggest that one of the most powerful ways for parents of older students to understand what takes place in an upper-grade reading workshop is for family members to take part in one themselves. (The same holds true for the teaching of writing. See a description of our parent writing workshop in *Going Public,* Chapter 5, "Reaching Out to Families.") Imagine family members and their children reading the same novel and then coming to class one evening to respond to the text. Family members will finally appreciate what it means to have reading strategies, to write in response to your reading, to make personal connections to text, or to be awed by someone else's interpretation of a story.

In the younger grades we might get comparably rich talk going by asking all interested families to read aloud the same wonderful chapter book during the same month of the year and then meet at school to celebrate that reading. Coming up with suggested titles would be a worthwhile staff activity. How many times do you think E. B. White's *Charlotte's Web* and Roald Dahl's *Charlie and the Chocolate Factory* would be suggested? Then too, if thick chapter books seem like too big a commitment for families to make, we could put out a call for interested families to read picture books written by one wonderful author each month. Families could simply go to their public libraries, take out books written by the selected author, and come to school in the evening to eat pizza and talk about the author's works. Imagine a school calendar that informs families of early-childhood students that in September there will be a get-together to talk about the writing of Bill Martin, Jr., in October, Mem Fox, in November, Leo Lionni, and so on. In addition to becoming familiar with wonderful writers and their bodies of work, parents would see firsthand how teachers get talk going in response to books. In addition, teachers could point out how pictures, predictable texts, repetition, and natural language structures support young readers.

Parent Book Clubs and Literacy Courses

Just as members of our staff get together to talk about their reading, so too family members can be encouraged to take time out for theirs. We are very pleased that parents in our school do periodically choose an adult novel to read and discuss together. These parents serve as powerful models for their children, who need repeated reminders that reading is not a school subject but a life pleasure. We would probably engage many more parents if different types of reading material were read (including romance novels, detective stories, how-to books, New York City studies, etc.) and if different language groups were formed.

What also lies ahead for our school community is the creation of structures to serve those parents who would like to improve their own basic skills as readers. New York City does offer some adult basic literacy courses, but there never seems to be enough of these. In addition, the courses offered are not in our community, nor do they offer baby-sitting services, as our own homegrown course would. (The same would apply to second-language courses for our parents who do not speak English. Unfortunately, there is a scarcity of classes available and no tuition-free ones in our local community.)

Sending Worthwhile Materials Home

In *Going Public* I stressed the value of sending worthwhile "stuff" home. All of the following artifacts come in handy in helping family members understand and support our approach to the teaching of reading and the growth of their children as readers. (For more on what gets sent home, see "Crafting Classroom Correspondence," below.)

Content-Rich Newsletters

One major way I have shared information about the teaching of reading has been through the content-rich letters I write for the school newsletter.

At the end of our first year at the Manhattan New School, I wrote the following letter to parents regarding standardized reading tests. Our school was so new that our scores did not yet appear in *The New York Times*. I always receive positive responses from parents when my letters are personal and chock-full of examples and newsworthy bits of information.

> *Dear Families,*
>
> *Several weeks ago I came across a timely and significant joke told by opera singer Thomas Hampson (Newsweek, March 16, 1992, p. 70): A worker digs a hole; after he finishes, his coworker fills it in. They walk a few feet and do it again, then again. A bewildered passerby finally asks, "What are you doing? It doesn't make any sense." The digger replies, "The guy who puts the trees in the holes is out sick."*
>
> *"That," says Hampson, "is what is wrong with opera today. People are interested in shovels and holes, not what holes are for."*
>
> *That joke could easily be told about the teaching of reading, if we're not careful. Some people are interested only in tests and scores. Some people are only interested in a student's ability to fill in blanks. Some people forget what reading is for.*

April and May are filled with required standardized tests for our older students. We help them get ready for these tests. But we also keep in mind that these tests tell us nothing about children's love of reading, or their familiarity with books and authors, or their ability to talk about a powerful piece of writing.

These test scores do not tell us about the second grader who wants to read all the Nancy Drew *books, or the third grader who has memorized dozens of Shel Silverstein poems, or those students who've lost sleep over the plight of Brian in Gary Paulsen's* Hatchet.

The New York State reading test, "Degrees of Reading Power," consists of short nonfiction passages with words deleted throughout. Children are asked to fill in the blanks from a short list of possible choices. The example below is written in this "cloze" manner to give you a feel for this reading test.

1. *In New York City, the results of standardized reading _____ are published in* The New York Times.

   a) passages   b) tests   c) booklets

2. *The schools are _____, all 621 elementary schools, all 179 junior high schools.*

   a) ranked   b) opened   c) visited

3. *Unfortunately, some people who read the newspaper seem to think those scores are an _____ judge of a school's worth.*

   a) unimportant   b) unnecessary   c) absolute

When parents of prospective students visit our school, they ask about our reading scores. I tell them we don't have any as yet. The newspaper publishes last year's scores, and our school did not exist last year. . . . I remind parents that those scores do not tell the whole story, anyway.

Ranking high in The New York Times *list does not guarantee that students see reading as a lifelong pleasure. Those scores do not guarantee that those children long to hang out in bookstores and libraries, sneak books into their beds at night to read by flashlight, or ask for books to be tucked into their camp trunks and vacation suitcases. Those scores do not guarantee that in the future those students will feel comfortable reading aloud in front of their colleagues, their congregations, or their tenants' associations. Those scores do not guarantee that those children will make use of their library cards, belong to book clubs, or read the daily newspaper. Those scores are a very tiny piece of the literacy puzzle.*

At the Manhattan New School we teach in ways that we believe will make lasting impressions on our children's literacy. We trust that they will do well filling in the blanks on reading tests. You get good at filling in the blanks by being a fluent reader, not by filling in blanks on practice tests. You know that print makes sense. You choose words that make sense. We provide some "test-sophistication" material, not to teach them how to read, but to demonstrate test-taking strategies—another responsibility we take seriously.

As a parent, I cared about my children's scores on standardized tests, particularly when they were middle-school students. I knew those scores played a role in entering fine high schools and quality universities. But I also knew that a school's worth was more than standardized scores.

I wanted my son and daughter to love going to school and to love learning. I wanted their passion for learning to spill over into weekends and summer vacations. I knew their schools were doing a fine job when my children asked hard questions about geography and geology when we drove cross-country, when they pitched in to figure out the tax and tip in restaurants, when they peered over my shoulder to read the newspaper—asking questions, commenting, and borrowing the newspaper when I was done.

Let's keep things in perspective. Let's educate children who do well not only on standardized tests, but also in life.

Sincerely,

Shelley

(The above letter was reprinted in *The Whole Idea,* summer 1992, by the Wright Group.) (See Appendix 4 for additional letters related to literacy.)

Relevant Announcements, Articles, and Form Letters

We try to minimize the amount of paper teachers have to distribute to children on their way out the door at three o'clock. First, we don't want to take up anyone's time unless the reading material is worthwhile. We also attempt to lead environmentally conscious lives at school, being fussy about our choice of material whizzing through those duplicating machines. When those little bright green numbers read 550 copies, it had better be worth it. Then too, we inevitably find fliers, announcements, letters, and articles on the cafeteria floor, dropped by children as they were whisked out the door. Or several weeks later, we notice the crumpled edge of a handout sticking out of a backpack that hasn't been emptied in a long time. We're not surprised when family members say, "What notice?" (We have begun putting our newsletters online, but know this will never replace the hard copies. We have too many families who do not receive electronic mail.)

I've been meaning to invest in brightly colored, sturdy plastic folders for every student, designated as the "Family Reading Matter" folder. This fuchsia, turquoise, or hot pink folder would clearly announce to families, "This is for you," and it would be a visible reminder to all children that reading matter for their families has a safe and predictable container that should be honored and handed over whenever filled. Besides the PTA-sponsored newsletters described above, there are a few items that are sent home schoolwide on a regular basis. These include PTA fund-raiser announcements, invitations to school celebrations and special events, and required materials for distribution from the central board of education (standardized testing schedules, results of tests, requests for parent involvement grants, etc.).

From time to time we might also consider distributing to the entire population such items as the following:

- Pamphlets, informative bookmarks, or reproducible handouts intended for parents from professional journals or professional organizations. These might include such articles as Miriam Marecek's, "Reading Partners: Parents and Children Discover the Joys of Sharing Books," in *The Dragon Lode,* published by the International Reading Association, such pamphlets as "Some ABC's for Raising a Reader" and the strategies bookmark, "When I Come to Something I Don't Know While I'm Reading, I Can . . . ," both published by the Illinois Reading Council, and such booklets as *Beginning Literacy and Your Child: A Guide to Helping Your Baby or Pre-Schooler Become a Reader* and *I Can Read and Write! How to Encourage Your School-Age Child's Literacy Development,* both published by the International Reading Association, as well as other selected materials produced by the National Center for Family Literacy.

- Articles intended for parents published in professional magazines, such as the "Parents and Reading," column in the IRA publication *Reading Today.*

- Any reference material pertaining to literacy, such as a listing of locations and hours of public libraries, bibliographies of recommended titles or authors (see Appendix 3), and listings of social organizations providing literacy supports for adults as well as children.

- Form letters composed by staff members related to such schoolwide literacy concerns as care of reading material, importance of continued reading aloud, and concerns about student progress.

The central board of education mandates that we inform families in writing of a child's struggles in reading. We have tried to write that difficult letter with as much humanity and caring as possible. One year we used the letter that appears below.

> *Dear families,*
>
> *We're writing to share an important concern. Your child _____ is working very hard in class and we have individualized and intensified his/her reading instruction. At this point, however, we are still concerned with the progress being made. _____ is moving ahead in the ability to read, but is taking very small steps.*
>
> *Keep in mind, we believe in _____. We believe your child will be a reader. We are not confident, however, that at the present time his/her reading abilities will satisfy the Board of Education's grade-level expectations.*
>
> *Please attend a parent-teacher conference on _____ so we can develop together a plan to support your child's continued progress in reading.*
>
> *Sincerely,*
>
> _____

(It would be a worthwhile staff activity to take all form letters and attempt to rewrite them with the same voice, kindness, and literary grace we teach our students about in their writing workshops.)

It is essential that all important correspondence be translated into the language of families. Unfortunately, this is a standard that we don't live up to often enough.

Some letters may be distributed to certain grade levels rather than schoolwide. For example, families of all five- and six-year-olds might be sent the following letter regarding shared reading, originally written by Elizabeth Servidio.

> *Dear families,*
>
> *We are all aware of the importance of shared-reading experiences. Beginning this week, we will be providing opportunities for your child to share his or her growing competence with reading. We will be sending books home for your child to share with you.*
>
> *Many of the children are just emerging as readers. You may find your child "reads" the book with little attention to the print or may attempt to point to each word, but does so inaccurately. It is important that you respond positively to your child's attempts, and focus on what he or she* can *do. Allow your child to show off his or her knowledge of the book. Keep these sharing times full of warmth and good feelings.*
>
> *Your child's book will be sent home in a zipped locked plastic bag. This is to help protect the book and to serve as a special place and reminder to return the book. You can help your child develop responsibility by finding a place at home to keep the book. Please help your child return it in the bag by the date written on the enclosed sheet and talk to your child about the importance of keeping all books in good condition and returning them to the classroom so that they may be enjoyed by others.*
>
> *If you have any questions please stop by. Have fun!*

Posting Important Papers at School

Sometimes we don't make hundreds of copies of an article, but we do all that we can, short of scrawling "Read This!" in the margins, to guarantee that many people will pay attention to posted information. We enlarge, highlight, label in big, bold letters, and mount the articles on brightly colored papers. Then we display them on the front door of our main office, for all to see. A few examples follow:

Responses to Inaccurate Media Portrayals of Literature-Based Teaching

I am especially on the lookout for those newspaper and magazine articles that report that literature-based teaching ignores the teaching of phonics, especially those printed in popular publications. These articles never give the full picture. They never offer parents any specifics as to the kind of phonics materials, systems, and activities that literature-based teachers are opposed to or the reasons for their opposition. Nor do they ever include information about how literature-based teachers encourage children to use their knowledge of phonics as one of many reading strategies, certainly not the only one or the most important one. When these articles do suggest that some literature-based teachers offer phonics instruction, they refer to those who "mix" the two approaches. It's clear that these reporters haven't done their homework or visited rigorous literature-based classrooms run by expert and professional teachers. We aren't mixing approaches. We are offering what we know is sound instruction and we always have been. We haven't suddenly decided to add phonics to our approach because we've been listening to some politicians or textbook publishers talk. We understand the role phonics plays in learning to read and because we do, we offer a sensible array of strategies to children as they read meaningful texts. The media just hasn't taken the time to understand what literature-based teaching is all about.

I have found it helpful to shrink these articles down and run them off on long sheets of paper, thereby leaving lots of wide margins in which I can correct and critique the contents. It is better to be proactive in dispelling the myths, errors, and exaggerations contained in these articles than to let parents read them on their own and begin to question our practice. (Please note, I don't mind questions; I just want them based on the truths of our teaching lives.)

Publications by Members of the School Community

Whenever a member of our community writes a letter to the editor, a newspaper column, a magazine article, or even a book, it is a very big deal. We all beamed with pride when Lorraine Shapiro's son Michael wrote an article for *Family Life* magazine, in its "Parent to Parent" feature, about how very special it is to have his daughter attend the same school where his mother, Lorraine, is a teacher. (We were equally as proud when her daughter-in-law Susan Chira published *A Mother's Place,* a book about working mothers, or when her son James, a Shakespeare expert, published another book or review of books.)

When the material written by a member of our community concerns *children's literacy,* it is an especially big deal. Last year, fourth graders in New York City were given a new language arts exam that made headlines for several weeks. (*The New York Times* headline read, "As Parents Sweat, 4th Graders Cram for New Test.") Children were shown on the front page of all our major newspapers preparing for the January exam in schools that were kept open over the Christmas holiday. Parents were frantically hiring tutors and fretting over their children's future because the new exams were said to be much more difficult than previous ones. Children would no longer be asked to simply darken in bubbles but to take notes and write essays in response to their reading. Unfortunately, and perhaps predictably, editorials were printed claiming whole language schools were not preparing students for these new exams, which required a great deal of writing ability. After all, they concluded, whole language educators don't teach children to punctuate, correct their grammar, spell, or have decent handwriting. Imagine how furious we were. Many of us *planned* to write letters to the editor to protest, and one parent, thankfully, actually did. Cynthia McCallister, a parent as well as an acclaimed literacy educator, wrote the following editorial that appeared in *The New York Times:*

To the editor:

According to a Jan. 11 news article, the new reading test is "at odds with much of the progressive-education theory and the whole language movement, which assume that students will eventually pick up the mechanics of writing at their own pace." This wrongly implies that progressive education discourages the explicit teaching of written-language conventions.

Most progressive theories acknowledge that children learn best when teachers harness intrinsic abilities and interests. These theories advocate teaching and testing that are aimed at developing literacy capabilities required in real-life situations. Putting other justified criticisms aside, the new test has more in common with whole language than the old tests do.

A copy of Cynthia's letter was enlarged and displayed on the door to our main office. Of course, in the margins someone wrote, "Go Fiona and Patrick's Mom!!"

Susan Cheever, one of our moms, writes a regular "Mothering" column for the newspaper *Newsday*. Whenever her articles mention our school, we proudly mount them on the board hanging on our main office door. If the article refers to literacy learning, we are particularly anxious for all members of our community to read it. In an article entitled "The Limitations of Dick and Jane," she writes about her concern for her young son's inability to learn to read through a phonics approach. She includes her own efforts to help. In part, the article states,

> Night after night, as I read bedtime stories and he fidgeted, I tried to show him how words are made up of letters. I demonstrated that each letter, if sounded, added up to a word. "Beeee-beee-bee!" I buzzed around his head. "Duh-duh-duh-dog!" I sang. "Wha-wha-wha-whale! He was less than entranced by these antics. "Finish the story, Mom," he said. . . .
>
> It took a wonderful first grade teacher to find the problem: My son doesn't think phonetically. These days my son reads me stories but he doesn't sound out the words. . . .

Susan had interviewed me to understand our approach to the teaching of writing, and her article continues,

> "Phonics is just one of many strategies," explains Shelley Harwayne . . . who heads this public school. "The most important thing for us is that kids realize they can get meaning from the text and that it's a joyful process." Instead of the traditional "bottom up" method, in which children progress from the alphabet to small words to reading, Harwayne and her teachers use a "top down" process. "We put gorgeous books in their hands so they can't resist learning what the words mean," she says.

She then speaks of all the controversies attached to the teaching of reading in the United States and concludes, "Someday I'd like to write a book about the history of teaching reading in postwar America. It would be a story with heroes and villains, exploitation and excellence. In the meantime my son has learned to read and I've learned to relax . . . a little." I hope Susan decides to write that book, sooner rather than later. The public needs to understand who has been setting literacy policy in this country and what the issues concerning children learning to read really are. Who better to tell that story than a wonderful writer who has been paying attention to the way her children have been taught to read and write? (See additional comments by Susan Cheever in *Going Public*, pp. 125–126 and 281–282.)

Articles written by members of our staff are posted prominently as well. We do distribute copies to all teachers but our authors are usually too humble to want these distributed to all families (perhaps only to the families of students in their class). Over the years these articles have included:

> Sharon Taberski's "Motivating Readers" column in *Instructor Magazine* (August 1997 through December 1997)
>
> Joan Backer, "Separation," in The Trumpet Club newsletter
>
> Joanne Hindley and Sharon Taberski, "Transitional Reading," in The Trumpet Club newsletter
>
> Karen Ruzzo's "Best Bets" column in *Instructor Magazine* (1998–1999)
>
> Karen Ruzzo's "Saving James," in *Instructor Magazine* (May/June 1999)
>
> Paula Rogovin's "The Classroom Interview," in *Instructor Magazine* (April 1999)

And of course I should mention our school column in *The New Advocate*, "Weaving Literature into the School Community" (winter 1996 through fall 1998).

Information About New Books

We frequently post such easy-to-write one-line questions as:

> Did you know that E. B. White's *Stuart Little* is now available in a special read-aloud edition in big, bold print?
>
> Did you know that *Harry Potter and the Sorcerer's Stone* by British writer J. K. Rowling is outselling even the best-selling titles for adults?
>
> Did you know that old familiar *I Can Read* books are now published in hard cover, (including Gene Zion's *Harry and the Lady Next Door,* Russell Hoban's *A Bargain for Frances*, Syd Hoff's *Danny and the Dinosaur*, and Esphyr Slobodkina's *Caps for Sale*.
>
> Did you know that the actress Jamie Lee Curtis has a new picture book out called *Today I Feel Silly and Other Moods That Make My Day*?

Then too, we might post reviews of new literacy books, ones that might appeal to teachers and parents alike. (These could include *The Mother-Daughter Book-Club* by Shireen Dodson and Teresa Barker, and the revised edition of Dorothy Butler's *Babies Need Books*.)

Information About Literacy Events

Family members appreciate hearing about local author appearances. We always post the Barnes and Noble bookstore's calendar of events, especially the monthly First Book

Storytime hours. These events benefit the national nonprofit First Book, an organization that gives new books to children who might not otherwise own any. The publishers of the authors who present at these functions donate money to First Book.

We also post reading celebrations. In New York these are especially plentiful, and they include our New York Is Book Country annual street fair and our annual read-aloud celebrations, with the "rich and famous" appearing at local schools and libraries with favorite picture books in hand. We also post news about our New York City public libraries' "LEOLine" a twenty-four-hour-a-day service that enables readers to renew borrowed titles, confirm items loaned, cancel reserved titles, and find out about any outstanding overdue fees by telephone or Internet.

Parents also appreciate knowing about things happening across the country. Our parents read an article about the Starbucks coffee shops that have opened within the confines of libraries in Oregon and Connecticut. They read a clipping about mother-daughter book clubs popping up in cities throughout our country. They were also interested to learn that every month Dolly Parton gives a handpicked children's book to all the fifty-two hundred children living in her native Sevier County, from birth until their fifth birthday. She even provides a bookcase to hold the sixty volumes. The more people hear about such possibilities the better. Hopefully, one good idea will inspire others.

We would also post international news if the topic appealed to members of our community. Children and parents were surprised to learn that a British parliamentarian was launching a campaign to have the original stuffed bear that inspired A. A. Milne to write *Winnie the Pooh* returned to England. The bear now sits behind a glass display cabinet in our very own Children's Room at the Donnell Library Center in New York City. You can be sure several parents decided to take their children to visit the bear just in case it gets repatriated.

Entertainment Suggestions Based on Children's Literature
You might find a posting for discount tickets to such Broadway productions as *The Secret Garden, Beauty and the Beast, Peter Pan,* or *Into the Woods.* Then too, we might clip and mount an advertisement when a movie such as *Babe, Madeline,* or *Matilda* is playing at a local movie house. (We probably wouldn't encourage our students to see the screen version of Ted Hughes's *Iron Giant.* Some adaptions are not intended for the very young.)

(When teachers think that the posted information is important enough, they might add it to their regular homework packets. A personal reminder or announcement from a teacher makes these happenings or publications all the more significant. And if teachers inform students that they plan to attend any of the weekend events listed, you can be sure some students and their families will do likewise. Kids can't seem to resist seeing their teachers outside of school.)

In addition to the bulletin board on the door to our main office, our PTA also maintains a board in the cafeteria filled with parent information. Since parents drop off and pick up their children at this street-level location, many family members see this board.

Announcements include those exclusively directed at parents, such as information about parent resource centers, publications, and meetings.

Crafting Classroom Correspondence

Individual teachers put much thought into preparing material to meet the needs of their particular parent body. A discussion of such material follows.

Letters to Families

In addition to the generic ones described on pages 264–265, which are sometimes sent to many classes at a time, teachers also craft many letters to parents that are geared specifically to their own classroom practices, needs, and interests. Over the years, I have found copies of letters, left near the copy machine, on a wide range of topics, including

explanations

- of how their reading workshop runs
- of their classroom library needs
- of student and teacher record-keeping in reading
- of standardized testing (preparation, interpretation of results, importance of keeping them in perspective)

and suggestions

- for providing appropriate times and places for reading at home
- for what to say when a child is stuck on a word
- for helping children select books to read
- for family reading rituals
- for caring for reading materials
- for organizing bedroom collections
- for inexpensive sources of books and magazines
- for demonstrating adult reading behaviors

Literacy Surveys

Surveys and questionnaires intended for families about their routines, tastes, and memories as readers may seem to serve only the teacher and students who collect the data and reflect on the results. But of course, the family members who respond to the surveys reap the rewards as well. They become aware of what the class values in literacy. They initiate conversations with their children about where the survey fits with the rest of their literacy work. They hear about the results of the survey and perhaps become inspired to take care of their own literacy. Over the years I have seen teachers send home surveys related to family newspaper reading, use of the public library, and kinds of nonfiction reading matter contained in homes. (See Joanne Hindley's *In the Company of Children* for additional family surveys about reading.)

Annotated Book Club Orders

Some things in schools thankfully never change. Students continue to delight in placing book club orders. (I wonder if this service is now online.) When teachers take a few minutes to attach a personal note to family members, providing information and suggestions about possible purchases, the acquisition of books through book clubs becomes an even bigger delight. Students count the days until the arrival of that big carton brimming with brand-new titles with glossy covers and fresh-smelling print. Students love to help teachers sort and distribute the orders on those red-letter days. Teachers who have made suggestions to families about which books to buy are especially happy to see those new books go home. When parents have followed the teachers' advice, students take home books that connect to content-area studies, are supportive of readers, have literary quality, are written by accomplished authors, and so on.

Teacher-Selected Reading Materials

Occasionally Joanne sends home a handpicked article with a personal note attached. For example, she once sent the following:

> *Dear families,*
>
> *Every once in a while I come across something in my reading and I say, "I wish I had written that . . ." Attached is an article by Anna Quindlen. She used to write the "Life in the 30's" column in* The New York Times.
>
> *I hope you enjoy it.*
>
> *Joanne*

That day, Joanne had selected an inspirational excerpt from the author's memories as a reader. She is just as likely to send home a jargon-free article about why *Hooked on Phonics* doesn't work or why reading aloud to children does.

Teachers also distribute copies of articles written with parents in mind. These might include particularly relevant topics contained in "The Parent Connection," a monthly reproducible page for parents in *Teaching Pre-K–8*, or suggestions to read parent chapters in professional text such as the late Garth Boomer's very straightforward and immensely practical chapter, "A Parents Guide to Literacy," in his *Fair Dinkum Teaching and Learning: Reflections on Literacy and Power* or suggestions to borrow or purchase books about the family's role in reading, such as Bee Cullinan's *Read to Me: Raising Kids Who Love to Read* and Janie Hydrick's *Parent's Guide to Literacy for the Twenty-first Century*. Teachers also note when professional journals devote whole issues to family information, as in the March/April 1997 edition of *The Horn Book,* which includes articles on such relevant family topics as how to shop in a children's bookstore and how to read aloud well. That important issue also includes a collection of vignettes by popular children's authors about sharing literature with their own children. Teachers might also send home copies of brochures published by local public libraries that are filled with special literacy events and highlighted books.

Literacy News Bulletins

Teachers who choose to send home a class newsletter to families often detail the literary happenings within their own classrooms. The following tidbits were lifted from Pam Mayer's kindergarten news bulletins:

> *We recently labeled a book basket "Counting Books," which was added next to our basket containing "Alphabet Books." We read several new Big Books—Brown Bear, Brown Bear, What Do You See? by Bill Martin, Jr., Look, Look, Look! by Tana Hoban, and Mrs. Wishy Washy by Joy Cowley. Griffin's mom Kathy donated an exciting pile of Big Books to our class. We're eagerly beginning to read them together. Thanks Kathy!*

> *The kindergarten newspaper, Let's Find Out, may be sent home several times a week until we catch up to date. (We're still reading September issues.)*

> *Suzannah and Elena taught us two songs. I printed them on large song cards, which the class reads and sings together. You can expect to see them in the poetry folders in the near future.*

> *After reading Lois Lenski's poem "In the City," which ends with a line about east and west, we talked about who lives east and who lives west in our city. Some of the children weren't sure, which is how that address homework came about. Once they knew their address and whether they lived east or west, we graphed the results using tally marks. We labeled columns "East Side" "West Side," and "People who don't live on the East or West Side." Most people live on the East Side. Three people live on the West Side. Two people don't live on either the East Side or the West Side.*

> *Stephanie suggested graphing our favorite books. We listed the class responses then chose four books that we all know from our read-alouds. Each person responded to the question "Which book do you prefer?" by placing his/her photo on a grid next to the preferred book. The books in our graph were: Chicka, Chicka Boom Boom, by Bill Martin, Jr., and John Archambault, The Tunnel, by Anthony Browne, The Napping House, by Audrey Wood (Did you know that her husband, Don Wood, illustrated the book?), and The Giving Tree, by Shel Silverstein. It was a hard decision to make.*

> *Elena's mom, Liz, visited during our book graph. She talked to the children about their feelings as they chose a book and as their friends chose a book. Some children were disappointed when a friend preferred a different book. Some children felt excited as the photos were being placed on the graph.*

> *Other visitors included J. J.'s mom, Isabel, who celebrated J. J.'s birthday with us. They donated two books to our class in honor of J. J.'s birthday. We added I Pretend to our book basket that contains Heidi Goennel Books. They also donated I Read Symbols, by Tana Hoban. We had been borrowing this one from the library up until now.*

> *Laura Profeta chose a book from the book fair for her birthday book. We look forward to reading Snowballs, by Lois Ehlert. Thank you to those of you who donated books from the book fair. We can't wait to read them.*

Many family members have stayed for book partners and some have joined us for morning meeting. Shayla's mom, Suzi, taught us how to sing "Hello, Everybody" in German (Guten morgen alle ja naturlich). We've had some lunchtime helpers stay for restful read in the afternoon. Visitors are always welcome.

We're continuing our author study of Tana Hoban as we add new books to our collection as well as reread old favorites. The children have noticed that Tana Hoban often "writes" books with no words and that the pictures in her books are photographs. They've also noticed that in several of her books she wants the reader to guess things.

We read Tana Hoban's book I Read Symbols. *The children eagerly offered their guesses about what the signs and symbols meant. Some were quite familiar and easy to figure out ("Walk," "No Smoking"). Others were more challenging (hiking trail, hospital). We talked about why signs were useful. Last week we went on a neighborhood walk, and we each carried a clipboard with a trip sheet on it. We focused on signs and symbols in the neighborhood. The children's conversations were so rich as we walked. They recorded what they saw. We then shared our findings.*

We continue to read Leo Lionni books and talk about his style of writing and illustrating. Annie Lionni, Sammy and Nicky's mom, came in to help us make collage mice. Annie shared information about the way her grandfather, Leo Lionni, makes mice for his books. Annie explained several techniques used to tear paper. The children's mice are hanging in our room. Come take a look! We didn't stop at mice. Some children experimented with a variety of collage animals . . .

The children have become very familiar with the big book Mrs. Wishy Washy. *We acted it out in school. Some of the children were cows, some were pigs, and some were ducks. Ariella made a dramatic* Mrs. Wishy Washy. *We plan to practice the skit several times. Some of the children suggested making costumes and inviting an audience.*

Shelley came to read some poems and chants from her book Jewels: Children's Play Rhymes. *The children had fun choosing games or hand-clapping chants. Others are songs that the children recognized. Shelley also explained the dedication in her book.*

We have several poets in our class. Luca wrote a poem, "Let's Bake a Cake," which was added to our poetry folders. Noah, Aaron, and Quad all wrote poems which we are learning. A few more are in the works. It's very exciting.

The listening center is now a choice at center time. The children can follow along with favorite books on tape. They love singing along with Chicka, Chicka Boom Boom *and* Chicken Soup with Rice.

Family members who receive such a collection of classroom happenings will not have trouble finding out about their child's day. These short bulletins serve as effective conversation starters. Instead of asking the traditional "What did you do at school today?" parents need only say, "Tell me more about . . ." These newsletter scenes offer a fairly accurate picture of what literacy is all about in a kindergarten classroom.

These short accounts also become inviting reading material for young students. They frequently attempt to read the news over their parents' shoulders in order to show off about school events and their own growth as readers. And young children are frequently successful at reading part, if not all, of the messages because they are so familiar with the content. They are able to figure out unknown words because they're so familiar with the meaning.

These classroom newsletters also push more families to get involved. They open up the possibilities for involvement by describing a wide range of parent presence in the classroom. In these short accounts, the parents took on the following tasks:

- reading aloud
- donating books
- demonstrating art techniques in response to books
- participating in book partner gatherings
- teaching songs and poems in other languages
- leading discussion groups

This kind of close reporting of classroom literacy need not apply only to early-childhood classrooms. Upper-grade teachers who want parents to keep on being involved in their children's growth as readers could create the same structure, only in this case children can become the roving reporters, responsible for different aspects of literacy. Older students can do as Pam has done. The following kinds of reports were all included in Pam's newsletters.

- listing of new books
- description of classroom projects inspired by reading
- listing of favorite books
- acknowledgment of donated books
- learning from author studies
- acknowledgment of guest readers
- description of organization of class library
- updates on newspaper reading
- comments on recent poetry reading
- surveys of favorite books
- literary birthday celebrations
- book fair news
- story partners accounts
- listening center acquisitions
- comments on dramatic interpretations of text
- report of children's writing being treated as children's literature

As I teased out the kinds of news Pam included in her kindergarten newsletter, I realized how many of these events seem to fade away as children move up in the grades. Wouldn't parents of nine-year-olds still like to read aloud books in honor of their child's birthday? Wouldn't fifth graders enjoy listening to guest readers? Wouldn't ten-year-olds still like to read along with novels on tape in the listening center? Let's not forget that elementary school children are still children.

In addition to the kinds of reports present in Pam's summaries, the following could be assigned to fourth and fifth graders as they cover the literacy beat:

- reviews of books
- recommended books, movies, or television programs based on familiar texts
- posting of current classroom book club choices
- announcements of books being read for parent book club
- local appearances of authors and other bookstore happenings
- requests for donations of specific titles
- titles of missing books; requests for at-home search
- writing in response to reading
- comments on controversial newspaper stories on literacy
- reminders of literacy assignment due dates
- reminders about reading strategies recently studied
- summaries of chapters from novels being read aloud
- titles of books desired for upcoming birthdays, holidays, or other celebrations
- invitations to read aloud to classes

Literacy Assessment Documents

In *Going Public* I present a calendar of how parents are informed about their students' progress through the course of a school year. That timeline refers to such tools as portfolios, self-assessments, and checklists.

In that earlier volume, I briefly explore how teachers and students use portfolios filled with student work as well as students' reflection on that work to inform parents about their children's growth across the disciplines. Some teachers send portfolios home prior to parent/teacher/ student conferences. Others arrange for parents and children to read the portfolios together in school a half-hour or so before the scheduled meeting with the teacher. Either way, most teachers write a cover letter to family members with suggestions for getting the most out of their reading of the material. These cover letters help parents understand that some pieces were chosen because the child feels the work represents their best effort; others were chosen because the work represents some sort of breakthrough (the student tried something new, the student stuck with their work for a long time, the student used the work to teach something to others, etc.), or the work creates a clear portrait of the student (a timeline of their growth, a photograph of the student at work, a list of their reading preferences). (See list below for other possible reading portfolio artifacts.)

Teachers also explain to parents how selections were made (most by students; some by teachers). They also remind parents that the child at their side should be offering a running commentary and that they need to be offering positive response to their children's efforts. In addition, they remind parents that these pieces represent a sample of all the work done. Otherwise family members may think that these pages represent an entire semester's work. Selections in a reading portfolio might include such items as:

- a page from a reading log kept by a child
- a written response to material read
- an artistic response to material read
- an audiotape of reading aloud
- a piece of published writing inspired by material read
- a list of questions posed by material read
- a reflective piece about participation in book club response group
- a review of material read
- a recommendation to a friend about a selected title
- a collection of favorite lines from material read
- a personal list of helpful reading strategies
- a photograph of the student at work in the reading workshop, with comments
- a personal timeline demonstrating growth in some aspect of reading
- a summary of genre preferences based on list of books read
- a report on book buddy get-togethers
- a list of self-selected reading goals
- a list of titles for future reading
- a photocopied page of text with a teacher's running record
- a photocopied page of text marked up by student as he/she read

Many teachers also provide a means for parents to reflect on the experience of having shared their child's portfolio. Some ask for an open-ended response; others ask specific questions. These might include:

> What did you learn from looking at a portfolio that you don't learn when you see your child's standardized test scores?
>
> If you had been asked to keep a portfolio in elementary school, what can you imagine having put in yours?

Do you keep a portfolio connected to your own work or have you ever seen a portfolio when you have shopped for someone else's services? How are these the same? Different?

Did anything surprise you about the portfolio or about your child's presentation of the contents?

Are there changes you'd like to see in how we organize or use student portfolios? Please describe.

Questions such as these not only provide helpful information for the teacher, they also help parents crystallize what they are learning about our approach to teaching, and as such stand as a legitimate form of parent involvement and education. (See *Going Public* for an additional use of portfolios, the assignment of schoolwide portfolio tasks.)

In addition to portfolios, parents also count on self-assessments periodically written by students as well as on teacher- and student-developed checklists, to keep informed about their children's growth in all areas of the curriculum. Self-assessments are open-ended, reflective passages written by children, who comment on themselves as scientists, mathematicians, readers, writers, historians, athletes, artists, musicians, and so on. These pieces of writing are likewise sent home to families before scheduled parent-teacher conferences. And just as with the use of portfolios, many teachers ask parents to comment on their children's self-assessments.

In *Going Public* I describe the history attached to our student-assessment checklists, popularly called "Our Hopes." In that earlier publication, I include brief excerpts from these documents and note how they remain flexible; they are frequently revised as teachers and children forge new ground, develop new areas of expertise, and rethink curriculum needs and priorities. (See grade-level checklists in Joanne Hindley's *In the Company of Children*).

Photograph Albums Devoted to Literacy

In *Going Public,* I describe how Joanne Hindley Salch uses a classroom photograph album to keep family members informed about classroom happenings. I can easily imagine devoting an album exclusively to the teaching of reading. Children would take turns carrying the album to and from school and each afternoon it would be passed to the next child in the class.

Joanne and her student teacher, student photographers, and parent volunteers would take snapshots of such scenes as the following:

- teacher reading aloud
- students writing in response to read-aloud
- students filling out reading logs
- students reading in book clubs

- teacher and students in small-group instruction
- teacher and child having one-on-one conferences
- students reading with book buddies
- students selecting books from the class library
- parents or school volunteers working with students
- students playing reading games
- students attending small-group tutorials
- students drawing in response to reading
- students writing self-assessments in reading

(It would also be interesting to snap photos of children at work taking standardized reading tests. Parents might be surprised by the anguished looks on children's faces. Of course, the flashes would be too disruptive and the photos would probably be a breach of some security measure or other.)

Family members would be instructed to ask such questions as:

- "What's happening here?"
- "Tell me why the teacher (the children) is (are) doing this . . ."
- "What are you doing while the other children are doing this?"
- "How does this help you become a better reader?"
- "What sounds can you hear in the room while this is happening?"
- "How do you feel about this time of day? Why?"

Parent Involvement in School Displays

I once received a sustained round of applause at a conference when I suggested to the audience that bulletin boards should be the responsibility of principals, not teachers. (Of course, the room was filled with overworked teachers. Principals, no doubt, also feel overworked, but very few were present at this particular workshop.) I explained that my obsession with decorating bulletin boards is connected to the realization that bulletin boards in a school building should be counted on for information and inspiration, not merely as decoration. My rule of thumb has always been: If I can pass by a bulletin board display without stopping to read it, look closer at it, study it, or drag others over to appreciate something hanging on it, the display is probably not worth the paper and tacks spent on presenting it. Bulletin boards should not serve as white noise in school buildings.

I suppose I really don't mean that principals should be totally responsible for bulletin boards. Most teachers do appreciate having places to display student work, but I don't think teachers need the pressure that exists in some settings when it is their "turn" to decorate a board. Principals should do all they can to reduce stress and unnecessary pressures in teachers' lives. Very often I help teachers come up with an idea for a display and then watch as the teacher carries out these plans with her students. Their finished work is always more brilliant than I had ever imagined.

Then too, I care about bulletin boards because they provide a very public way for principals to share *building-wide* interests, talents, priorities, and teaching strategies. My Johnny-Appleseed role of traveling about the building enables me to create bulletin boards that combine the work of many children across many grades.

And above all, bulletin boards, if designed carefully, provide a significant way for principals who are instructional leaders to help parents, visitors, student teachers, volunteers, and inexperienced staff members understand the power of the work we do and how and why we do it.

(In *Going Public* I describe the bulletin board display created from families' explanations of how and why they chose their child's name. In that volume, I also introduce the notion of honoring powerful bulletin board displays by taking them down after a while and slipping the contents into three-ring binders as permanent anthologies for the school community. In *Writing Through Childhood,* the follow-up volume to this text, I suggest other ways to turn displays into anthologies. Additionally in that book, I include bulletin board displays that help parents understand young children's strategies for inventing spelling, as well as ways to simplify publishing in a school through the use of such displays. I also suggest ways principals could cover classes by deliberately offering the kind of challenges to students that lead to fairly instant and significant bulletin board displays, ones that make you stop in your tracks and say, "Hey, look at this!")

Here, I will highlight bulletin board ideas that help members of the community reflect on different aspects of literacy learning. One such display, entitled "Read About Our Reading at Home," was launched with the following short letter to families:

> *Dear families:*
>
> *I'm interested in creating a wall of family photographs highlighting the importance of reading to or with your child. Won't you send in a photograph that captures such a scene and write a short paragraph explaining the scene? You might include information about where and when you are doing this reading together and of course what you are reading. Either you or your child can do the writing. Please label the photographs so more of us can get to know one another.*
>
> *Thanks in advance.*
>
>
>
> *Sincerely,*
>
> *Shelley*
>
>

This solicited a number of responses, some examples of which are included here.

Lauren's mother wrote the caption for the photo of Lauren and her grandmother poring over a workbook together (see Figure 8.1). We were not aware before this time that five-year-old Lauren was given workbook assignments at home. We had been

Lauren Javaly works with her "ajji", retired NYC kindergarten teacher Nalina Javaly (ajji means grandma in the Indian Kanada language). These workbooks are one way Lauren has learned to read. Her ajji spends the night once a week and always reads to Lauren and her brother, Matthew.

Figure 8.1

watching her learn to read through very different means in school. This contribution provided us with information we may not have received otherwise. Luca, a third grader, labeled a photograph of himself sprawled on a deck chair on a balcony overlooking a beautiful beach, with palm trees in the distance (see Figure 8.2). His contribution gave us further proof that the Harry Potter books are a truly global phenomenon.

Here I am reading Harry Potter and the Sourcers Stone in Belize, a very Quiet and Peaceful Place to read.

Figure 8.2

Both seven-year-old Sam and his mother, Abby, chose drawing over photographs. Sam's sketch and passage appear in Figure 8.3; his mother's thoughtful response is in Figure 8.4.

I received many more responses to the "Read About Our Reading" request, and each one was as wonderful and informing as the last. Viewing the photographs on the bulletin board was like making home visits without leaving the school. I learned that Stephanie and her mother were reading *"Rapunzel"* together in Portuguese. I learned that Jesse and her mom had begun reading to one another by flashlight. On commenting about reading to his children, Gerry, father of Fiona and Patrick, tenderly noted, "One of the most important gifts I can give them is to send them to sleep hearing the sound of my voice."

I can easily imagine making the following additional literacy requests of family members:

- Send in a favorite family poem with an explanation of how or why it became important to your family.
- Send in ancestral stories having to do with reading.

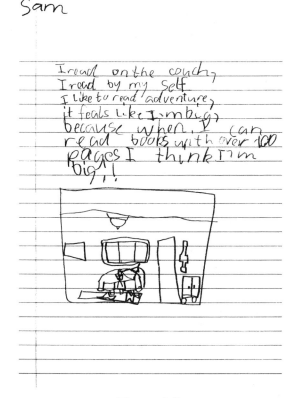

Figure 8.3

Sam reads on the couch. It is the best place to read because it's pretty much in the center of the entire apartment. I move around him, and back and forth doing chores, and I see him each time I pass. I go quietly so he is not disturbed. He looks very comfortable and very focussed. He is on an island. He takes himself to all sorts of places through his reading. Each book is full of adventures for my dear son. Arabian Nights, Treasure Island, Ramona Quimby, Otis Spofford, The Village of a Hundred Smiles. Watching him read is like watching him ride a magic carpet. I hope he'll always read with such abandon. Sometimes we read to each other.

My picture was inspired by Sam's drawing. I love how he drew the rug

Abby, Sam's mom 3/15/99

Figure 8.4

- Send in memories of children, parents, and grandparents learning to read, and comment on the materials read.
- Send in accounts of bedtime reading rituals.
- Send in a list of your top ten family read-alouds.
- Send in photos of family members and the titles of the books they are currently reading or the magazine or newspaper they regularly read.
- Send in a description of any household literary collections (including comic books, cookbooks, magazines, etc.).
- Send in newspaper pages written in other languages and the stories connected to how you keep up with reading materials in those languages.
- Send in descriptions of scenes of book browsing in bookstores, libraries, bedroom collections.

- Send in an account of your children's favorite book when they were very young. (Include book jacket or photocopy or drawing of jacket.)

When responses to any of my requests are slow to come in, I hang up the ones I do receive rather than waiting the amount of time it would take to receive materials to cover an entire bulletin board. People seem to enjoy the drama of the day-by-day ever expanding display. In fact, people check out the board each morning for new additions. They comment on the variety and diversity of the responses. I never hand out a form for response, since passersby appreciate the surprising mix of handwritings (and in some cases the fonts chosen), as well as the diversity in shapes, size, and color of papers. When parents and students stop to read the first contributions, they are inspired to send in their own. Teachers also send reminders in their homework packets for children who have misplaced, lost, or forgotten about the original request. When families realize that the display will be up for many months and then turned into a permanent three-ring-binder anthology that can always be added to, they realize that it's really never too late to respond. (For families without access to cameras, we sometimes use school funds to send home disposable cameras, or we encourage children to sketch, as Sam and his mother chose to do.)

It might be advisable to designate one large, centrally located bulletin board as the regular location of displays based upon family contributions. Naming such a spot in a school will motivate teachers and administrators to keep coming up with more and more invitations such as those above. (I wouldn't be surprised if parents eventually tossed out a few ideas of their own for literacy displays.) In addition, family members will grow accustomed to stopping by to read them and be inspired to contribute when asked. Our displays usually last for half the year before being turned into anthologies.

In addition to displays that depend on family contributions, we have also created boards designed for parent participation. These, similar to the story-lead guessing-game board described on page 13, also educate parents about what we value in literacy. All ask for some form of participation on the part of passersby. Several examples follow.

- Match the names of authors with titles of classic children's books.
- Fill in titles that would make appropriate gifts for people in the following categories: kindergartners, grandmothers, teenage baby-sitters, mothers, fathers, baby brothers, and so on. (Dangle pencils and leave white space for written responses.)
- List popular series of books and mount representative covers and pages from each. Ask the question, "What age range of students do you think usually prefers to read these books?" Under a hidden flap, mount the answer, complete with an explanation of how these different series offer different challenges to readers. (Parents will begin to appreciate how children's tastes and reading abilities

change with age. They will also begin to understand what makes reading materials easy or more difficult. See p. 313 for more thoughts on series books).

- Post a story on a topic of great interest to families (background about teachers, upcoming events, curriculum developments, school board elections, etc.). Prepare the text in cloze format, deleting certain words, leaving only the first letter of the omitted word in place followed by a dash. For example, "Did you know that Shelley is f_____-two years old and that her hair is n_____ curly?" Number the deletions, asking passersby to guess the missing words. Under a flap, mount the correct answers with an explanation of why readers are able to make such good and meaningful guesses without seeing whole words. No doubt, some students would be eager to take part in this fill-in-the blank news.

Taking a Stance on Parent Education and Involvement

Each year teachers stumble upon new and serendipitous ways to inform parents about literacy. When family members are invited to a readers' theater performance, one in which students are asked to talk about what it takes to read aloud well, parents are reminded that reading must be meaningful. When a parent notices a professional book on a teacher's shelf and asks to borrow it, we begin to rethink our reading suggestions for inquisitive parents. We realize that our professional reading library should be available to community members. When we browse the Internet looking for needed information and discover a treasure trove of good ideas for at-home reading, we realize that we need to publicly post these Web sites for family members who are technologically savvy.

I've always found it amazing that our city and our state mandate parental involvement in our schools. We are legally bound to form school leadership teams with ample parent representation, organize parent education components for all support services offered to students, and involve parents in selection committees when hiring teachers, principals, and superintendents. The day needs to come when these structures will not need to be mandated. Educators need to realize that we can't run successful schools without well-informed parents.

Our chancellor once challenged public school parents to volunteer in schools to support literacy learning. In fact, he once offered one-thousand-dollar awards to schools in which 50 percent of the parents volunteered twenty hours a year to fostering literacy. I don't think parents need monetary rewards for taking part in their children's literacy. Nor do I think the most helpful way for parents to take part in their children's literacy is to volunteer in schools. (See the limitations of asking volunteers to teach reading on pp. 294–295.) If parents are going to spend twenty hours a year at their children's school, I'd sooner have them attend PTA meetings, curriculum gatherings, and teacher workshops aimed at helping parents understand literacy learning. Parents who really understand how to help their child at home will spend twenty hours a month, not twenty hours a year. Their evenings will be filled with reading aloud to children and listening to children read aloud to them. As they read the evening newspaper, they will encourage their children to stay nearby so they can point out the sections, stories, and photographs that have childlike appeal. They will view together such literary delights as *Reading Rainbow* broadcasts, responding to the books shared. They will play Scrabble, Boggle, and Mad-Libs with their children, understanding that playing with words and language is also part of being a literate human being. They will escort their children to read-alouds and storytelling events at the public library and in local children's bookstores. They will make the giving of books a regular part of birthday and family celebrations.

Educators can't afford to think of parental involvement in literacy learning as a mandate, nor can parents. It must become a cherished given.

RELATED READINGS IN COMPANION VOLUMES

Going Public (Heinemann, 1999) is abbreviated as GP. *Writing Through Childhood* (Heinemann, forthcoming), is abbreviated as WC.

Helping family members understand our approach to teaching	**GP:** Ch. 5, Ch. 6; **WC:** Ch. 8
Keeping standardized tests in perspective	**GP:** Ch. 6
Offering a multitude of ways to reach out to parents	**GP:** Ch. 5; **WC:** Ch. 8
Creating informative hallway displays	**WC:** Ch. 8, Ch. 9
Suggesting a family literacy portfolio	**GP:** Ch. 5
Sending content-rich letters to families	**GP:** Ch. 5; **WC:** Ch. 8
Documenting student literacy growth	**GP:** Ch. 6

PROVIDING SAFETY NETS FOR STRUGGLING STUDENTS

Key Literacy Lessons

1. Teachers of reading must design their practice to suit the needs of individual children; they must take the teaching of reading one student at a time.

2. There are many classroom and schoolwide structures that support those children who find learning to read a particularly difficult task. These include reading buddies, the read-aloud as read-along, specialty teachers as informed literacy experts, staff developers, expert tutorials, intervention instruction, expert special education supports, well-trained and supervised volunteers, and respect for children.

3. Administrators who know how to teach reading, should teach reading; those who carve out regular time to teach learn about their students, their curriculum, and their materials.

4. Tutorials for struggling readers must be worthwhile and geared specifically to children's needs. The components of successful tutorials can include poetry reading, the reading of books, short stories, or magazine articles, and language games.

5. Educators can count on quality series books as effective tools in teaching struggling readers.

6. Educators can study students' writing for clues on how to improve reading instruction.

7. Educators become better teachers of reading when they examine student writing as a means of professional growth.

8. Test sophistication materials and activities should be kept in proper perspective.

9. There is no need for required reading lists in elementary schools; what's needed are informed recommendations.

10. There are benefits and detriments attached to the use of benchmark books.

11. Struggling readers as well as competent readers must receive our lifetime guarantee that they will not only learn *how* to read and write, they will *choose* to do so.

Two years ago Meggan Towell Friedman, a part-time teacher, sent me a letter after her first year at the Manhattan New School. She wrote,

> As much as MNS is a loving and nurturing place, it is also a learning place. That may seem rather obvious because it is a school, but I don't think that much learning actually takes place in many schools. I think a lot of instructing goes on, but that doesn't mean there's anything taken in.
>
> Prior to coming here, I had always adopted a somewhat hands-off, less directed, observer type role as a teacher. My belief was that children learn naturally on their own if we expose them to things, model, and allow them time to experiment. . . .
>
> But this year I started working with children who were exposed to print constantly, saturated in it, given model after model after model, and yet these kids still didn't get it?!? Not any of it?!? This did not fit into my theory of teaching reading. I had to discover for myself another way; a more directed, more purposeful, head-on approach to help these kids. I watched Layne, Sharon, Lorraine, Karen, and others work with struggling readers. I asked for help. I read lots of material that had been previously unappealing. I learned how very, very necessary it is to lay a solid foundation for these young readers so they can, after a time of learning, do things real readers do.
>
> But why was it here—in a place where teachers are trusted to teach as they see fit—that I learned (really took in) things I had been against, even fought, for years? Because MNS . . . in its warmth and support encourages you and provides space for you to learn and grow without fear. So I thank you for the most rewarding and informative year.
>
> *Meggan*

I include Meggan's gracious letter in this chapter because she so honestly and eloquently explains her growth as a teacher of reading. Meggan became startlingly aware of just how much attention and expertise is required to help children who struggle with reading. In order to understand what it is Meggan learned about such teaching-of-reading strategies as matching children and books, providing guided-reading instruction, and one-on-one conferring, the reader is referred to our use of these reading workshop components on pages 199–207. (Meggan's commitment to learning even more about the teaching of reading led her to take a leave of absence from our school to take part in our district's Reading Recovery training.)

One Student at a Time

Not long ago, I spotted what I thought was a kindhearted sign hanging on the door of a gas station minimart near Rochester, New York. It read, "One Student at a Time." A large mug filled with pencils decorated the lower half of the sign. I thought, "What civic pride in their schools, what a comment on sensible teaching practice to think of one student at a time." But then I got closer and read the fine print under the slogan. It read, in parenthesis, "Unless accompanied by an adult." It was disappointing to realize that clusters of kids were probably making too much noise in the local minimart and were therefore banned unless chaperoned by a grown-up. What a waste of a good slogan. Perhaps, teachers should use these words as a reminder to look individually at each student who finds learning to read a struggle. No two will be the same, of course. And no two will need exactly the same sort of safety net.

In addition to taking part in regular classroom reading workshops, our children in need of extra support gather on the rug for all the same read-alouds, minilessons, and share meetings as all the other children. They have as many opportunities and as wide a selection of appropriate and supportive reading materials during independent reading time as all the other children in the class. They have opportunities to confer with their classroom teacher as frequently as the other children. They are placed in small guided-reading, word-study, and reader-response groups as are all the other children in the class. There are, however, additional classroom-based and schoolwide supports for the children whose growth in reading is of particular concern.

Structures That Support Struggling Readers

Nancy Hope Wilson's short chapter book, *Old People, Frogs, and Albert* presents Mr. Spear, a school volunteer who suggests to Albert, a struggling reader, that one day he will read without even noticing the words. The following schoolwide structures have helped children learn to read so that they no longer notice the words. (See think-sheet on Questions to Promote Thinking About Struggling Readers in Appendix 14.)

Reading Buddies   Earlier in this book I described story partner or reading buddy arrangements. This structure needs to be included here because of the value it serves the struggling reader, be that child the older or younger member of the pair. As previously suggested, these shared-reading moments are wonderful opportunities for teachers to do bystander assessments of students. Kindergarten and first-grade teachers can take notes on their students' involvement in the experience, their participation in and response to the reading, the attention they pay to the illustrations, their attempts to read familiar words, and so on. Teachers of the older readers can listen for the fluency, accuracy, and expression the student brings to texts selected for the younger child in mind. These easier books are wonderful ways for older readers to receive valuable practice.

The Read-Aloud as Read-Along   Teachers spend a great deal of quality time reading aloud to students. Whenever possible and appropriate, teachers provide opportunities for students to follow along in the text. This requires that teachers are able to put their hands on multiple copies of the chosen title. In fact, every once in a while teachers choose a title to read aloud *because* they have several copies of the book. (This is not necessarily an expedient decision. If we have multiple copies of a book, it must be a quality read.) Teachers, without calling public attention to which children need extra support, distribute copies to a few children and ask them to read along. Most teachers avoid calling attention to the readers in need of extra support by always asking a couple of proficient readers, along with the strugglers, to read along. (Children don't see this invitation as embarrassing. In fact, many bring copies of the book from home or the public library so that they can always read along.) Some teachers ask two children to share a copy of the book, thereby adding more of a mix of readers to those reading along. Other teachers simply ask for volunteers to read along, trusting that children who realize the benefit of this activity will always raise their hands.

Specialty Teachers as Informed Literacy Experts All teachers in an elementary school must be expected to have expertise in the teaching of reading, particularly in ways their teaching of specialty subjects can support the struggling readers who attend their classes. When the art teacher reads aloud a picture book, she too can have multiple copies for children to read along. When the music teacher teaches a new song, she too can point to the clearly printed words as she reads along. When the science teacher invites students to research animals, she must be able to match readers with the books that they can read. Specialty teachers must therefore participate in all aspects of professional development so that when the opportunity arises, they will be well prepared to support students' reading throughout the day. In fact, it would make quite a worthwhile staff meeting to place a specialty subject center stage and have all teachers discuss the role reading plays during the music class, for example, and all the small yet significant ways the music teacher can support students' growth as readers. The same can be done with the science, second-language, art, and technology teacher.

Staff Developers When schools are fortunate enough to work with staff developers, be they in-house staff members or consultants, these experts must be counted on to address the needs of struggling children. It is never enough for the instruction to improve for most of the children; it must improve for all. It is up to principals as well as classroom teachers to make sure that staff developers keep on their front burners the needs of children who find learning to read difficult. (The same applies, of course, for staff developers who coach teachers working with children who struggle in writing or mathematics.)

Expert Tutorials Students who are in need of extra support in reading have opportunities to take part in small-group sessions during our extended-day programs (hour-long workshops after school hours) and extended-year programs (summer classes, mornings in July). These reading workshops provide the extra time that children need and deserve. They take place on school grounds and are taught by familiar teachers who use the kinds of materials and methods that children feel at home with. Literacy experts from our district office suggest best practice for these intense tutorial sessions, which are limited to twelve to fifteen students. That's half a class in New York City, and that makes all the difference in the world to teachers who can finally give children all the attention they need. (Of course summer programs are held in schools without air-conditioning, so the situation is not as perfect as it sounds, given the hot and humid New York summers.)

Intervention Instruction Each year we are given limited funds to provide small-group instruction during the school day for children in need of extra support. This money has been used in several ways. For many years we were able to hire a part-time person who would provide coverage to our first-grade teachers so that they could provide intense small-group instruction, within their own classrooms, for the children that did not seem to be making sufficient progress in learning to read. The coverage teacher would host read-alouds and shared-reading experiences for the remainder of the class, while the classroom teacher worked with her small group. Some teachers modified this plan and would actually leave the classroom with their small group or would invite the part-time teacher to conduct the tutorials. Last year we used these funds to bring Reading Recovery into our school for the first time.

We also try to allot money in our budget for the services of a part-time reading teacher who will work with small clusters of second-, fourth-, and fifth-grade children with reading needs. (I handle the third graders. See p. 298.) Meggan, the teacher whose letter opens this chapter, has provided that service in our school for several years. After individually assessing students' reading needs, she shares her findings with classroom teachers. Meggan then arranges convenient times to pull together small clusters of children who have similar reading needs. Just as in classrooms, these needs change and so might the members of the small group. Meggan works out a schedule with classroom teachers to minimize any disruption to the children. (See "The Nightmare of Scheduling Pullout Programs," p. 71 in *Going Public*.)

Meggan finds a quiet spot in our school, usually in a corner of our grand fourth-floor ballroom. (As much as we would like to, we don't have any spare rooms to offer her.) Her students gather round and Meggan first inspires them to want to read by offering the very best material. Her choices of course are based on the ages, needs, and interests of the students. One group may be reading a newspaper article about the fortieth birthday of the Crayola crayons box, another a short story from one of Paul Jenning's collections such as *Uncovered!: Weird, Weird Stories,* and yet another an article from *Cricket Magazine*. What remains crucial to Meggan's work, as with all building specialists, is that she continues to share what she is learning. Communication between teachers can't stop with initial assessments. Then too, Meggan's approach to teaching reading must be philosophically in tune with classroom teachers, so children never get mixed messages about what reading is for and how one becomes a better reader. Like that of classroom teachers, Meggan's main goal is to turn students into self-confident, strategic readers. Her eye is not on test taking or test-preparatory materials. When students become strategic readers, they will have no problem passing those tests.

Expert Special Education Supports

This service is provided for children who have been formally assessed through the city's special education division and were found to have varying degrees of learning disabilities. Roberta, our resource room teacher, meets with children throughout the day, offering push-in as well as pullout instruction. What has become crucial is that Roberta's beliefs about the teaching of reading, and this can't be said often enough, are a natural fit with the rest of the school's. Through the years we have had several resource room teachers, and this was not always the case.

During the first year of our school, I didn't realize the power of the principal's office and I allowed a resource room teacher to be assigned to our school without ever having interviewed her. (We were such a small school that we didn't warrant a full-time resource room teacher and so I was sent someone who was already teaching part-time in another school.) Special education at that time seemed mandated from above. The teacher assigned to our school was very hardworking but had a medical diagnostic-prescriptive approach to "curing" reading disabilities. Her little room was filled with worksheets, a stack for each isolated skill she wanted to drill into her students. Erika, then a third-grade student needing resource room support, sent me the letter that appears in Figure 9.1.

This letter has always meant a great deal to me. First, Erika helped me to see the glaring discrepancies between what was going on in her regular classroom with her wonderful teacher Joan, and what was gong on in this little room she was mandated to attend. It is clear form Erika's spelling that she is in need of some specialized strategies to make reading an easier task, but she needed to receive that extra attention in a setting

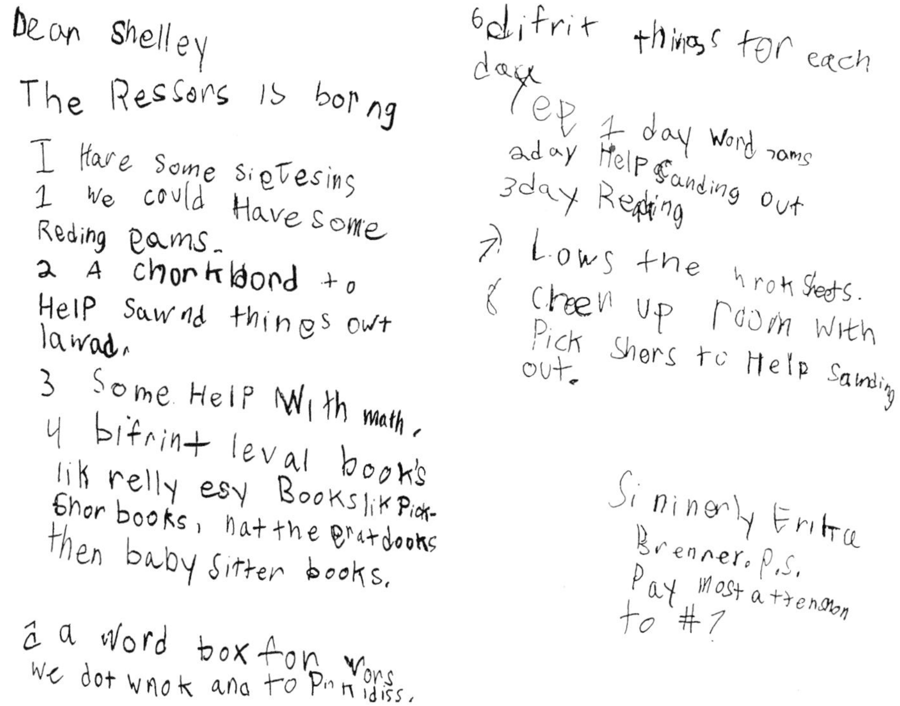
Dean Shelley
The Ressors is borng
I Have some sietesins
1 we could Have some Reding eams.
2 A chorkbord to Help Sawnd thines owt lawad.
3 Some Help With math.
4 bifrint leval book's lik relly esy Bookslik Pick-Shor books, nat the eratdooks then baby sitter books.
5 a word box fon wons we dot wnok ana to Pin tidiss.
6 difrit things for each day
ep 1 day Word gams
2 day Help Sanding out
3 day Reding
7 Lows the wrok Sheets.
8 Creen up room with Pick Shers to Help Sanding out.
Sininerly Erika Brenner. P.S. Pay most attenshon to #7

Figure 9.1

that was as sensible, whole, and nurturing as her regular classroom. If scheduling doesn't allow the learning disabilities teacher to push-in, then a child's experience outside of class had better be worthwhile.

Second, Erika's letter reminded me that we should never think of learning disabled children as being any less brilliant, creative, or productive than all our other students. Erika's suggestions indicate just how observant, clever, and thoughtful she is. All students receiving special education services must be full participants in the life of the school.

And finally, Erika's letter reminded me just how valuable it is to use children's writing to improve the life of the school (see Chapter 3). With her parents' permission, I forwarded a copy of Erika's letter to the powers that be. Thankfully, they understood why learning disabled children need to "lose the work sheets." (See poems written by Erika which were used at graduation, in Chapter 5, p. 181.)

Today we are very grateful to have a resource room teacher who understands the need for real literature and for the meaningful teaching of strategies. Miles Haas, a recent graduate, wrote the tribute to Roberta that appears in Figure 9.2.

Well-Trained and Supervised Volunteers New York City is rich in volunteers. There are many retired people who sign up with well-established organizations that provide screening, training, and regular assignments to schools. There are also high school students needing community service hours as well as students attending alternative high

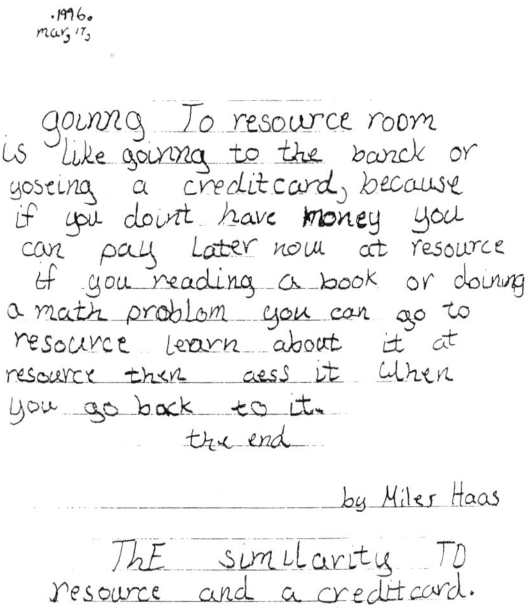
.1996.
mar, 17,

goinng To resource room
is like goinng to the bank or
yoseing a creditcard, because
if you dount have money you
can pay Later now at resource
if you reading a book or doing
a math problom you can go to
resource Learn about it at
resource then aess it When
you go back to it.
the end

by Miles Haas

ThE similarity TO
resource and a creditcard.

Figure 9.2

schools who are assigned to schools full-time for a semester as part of a work-study program. Schools also welcome parents and neighbors with time on their hands, as well as working people willing to give up their lunch hours to work with children in schools near their offices.

Schools that agree to have volunteers work with their struggling students need to work closely with those volunteers. Our beliefs about how children learn to read need to be understood and honored by anyone who works with the students in our care. After all, we don't want children taught in a hodgepodge of ways. We don't want children reading materials that don't meet our high standards. We don't want volunteers who decide that phonics workbooks have been missing from our children's lives.

Politicians who think that the easy solution to the reading problems in our schools is more volunteers have a lot to learn. Volunteers with a few days' training cannot possibly know what trained professionals know. Volunteers do provide a worthwhile service in our schools, but we must offer those volunteers school-based training in order that they understand in a broad way how reading is taught in any particular school. In addition, the teaching professionals must suggest those specific activities that are appropriate for volunteers who do not have extensive knowledge about reading development, children's literature, and ongoing assessment. When teachers send struggling children off with volunteers, they need to be very clear about what those volunteers will be doing to foster children's reading growth.

Respect for Children

I've been told that some posh New York City beauty parlors have a regularly scheduled tea and coffee service. A host arrives at set hours wheeling a beautiful silver cart filled with gourmet blends and delicate pastries. Judy Davis has teased me about arranging such a service for the hardworking teachers at our school. So too, the children who work incredibly hard to learn to read deserve such a break. Of course, I really don't plan to ever use food as a reward (my mother taught me well), but some days I do wish I had a cart filled with hot chocolate, slices of homemade bread, and luscious raspberry jam, just to boost the energy of all those hardworking children.

In addition to all the supports described in the previous pages (as well as the total involvement of family members, as described in Chapter 8), children who are working overtime to catch on to reading also deserve acknowledgment for all the subjects in which they excel as well as recognition for their social strengths and individual areas of expertise. They must never be excluded from participation in any school event. They must never be made to feel apart, different, or worthless. Years ago I heard Frank Smith criticize a popular literacy campaign poster. It was a picture of a dinosaur with a caption that read, "Don't be extinct. Read." What message is that spreading? We must always be conscious of issues of self-esteem when we work with our "extra-time" kids.

The Administrator as Reading Teacher

In *Going Public* I suggest, "Principals, heads of schools, can't be the kind of grand-parents who are only there for the birthday cupcakes and holiday celebrations. They also need to be the kind of grandparents who are willing to stay up all night with the feverish child." (In no way do I mean to imply that children who struggle with reading are suffering from some sort of illness. Rather, I mean that principals have to get involved in the hard work, in the nitty-gritty of teaching, especially the teaching of children who need extra support. We are all in this together.) My teaching-of-reading work begins by looking over the landscape, visiting reading workshops and trying to say smart things to teachers in response. In regard to the struggling child, I have told my colleagues that several things terrify me in the teaching of reading. I have summarized these fears below.

- I'm terrified of finding a child who is trying to learn to read with boring, deadly, watered-down texts that actually get in the way of learning to read. Fortunately, our school is now an "impoverished-print free zone." (In *Going Public* I mention that I frisk substitutes for worksheets!)
- I'm terrified of finding a child who thinks that he or she will never learn to read. Thankfully, we rarely meet a child like that, especially if the child has grown up as a reader in our school. But occasionally we do meet an older child who has transferred from another part of our city, another state, or another country, who has suffered painful experiences in learning to read. Unfortunately, it some-times requires more years than our time allotted with children to undo their negative feelings toward reading.
- I'm terrified of discovering a child who is struggling through a too-difficult book, or worse yet is *not* struggling through a too-difficult book. In other words, a child who doesn't even realize that he or she is not reading. Not getting mean-ing, but rather finding an occasional word or line that is recognizable has some-how become the given. I have seen children in our own school selecting big, thick volumes because the friends they admire are reading these kinds of texts. They sit very quietly playing the role of reader, but not growing as readers. The charade must end. Playing matchmaker and matching readers with appropriate texts is an essential task for all teachers of reading (see p. 202).
- I'm terrified of discovering the child who can't read for more than a few min-utes. These are the "pretend" readers I described earlier. Some of these children have gotten quite good at fooling us. They take on the air of reader, browsing the bookcases, picking up and putting down books, filling out logs, chatting about their reading, but not really reading. These children never experience the thrill of getting lost in a good book. (It would be interesting to ask a student teacher to keep tabs on a child such as this throughout the day, to document

exactly how much text that child actually reads. We'd probably be greatly disappointed.) We need to know why that child is not able to truly focus on text.

There are all kinds of struggling readers in a school, and our job is to make sure that we know who they are and how we can place safety nets under each one. Over the last few years I have become directly involved with the children who need extra support at the third-grade level. Some people have asked me if I chose this grade because it is the grade in which New York City children must take standardized tests for the first time. I do worry about children who are not ready to face such exams, but more than that, third grade is such a transitional grade. At some point early in the year, whole-group instruction stops feeling like early-childhood work. Most of our third graders are ready to read independently, establishing their tastes as readers, reading for information to satisfy their personal inquiries, even attempting to make sense of the daily newspapers. I worry especially about eight-year-olds who still need a great deal of shared-reading experiences and guided instruction as well as significant amounts of word study. Then too, these third graders no longer qualify for our early-intervention support services.

Of course it's true that there are children in every class at every grade level who need extra support, but it's also true that I have a limited number of hours to teach. It can be hoped that my work with third graders (alongside the hard work of their classroom teachers and reading specialists) will enable a few more children to become successful fourth graders. For those who continue to struggle, my year spent with the children allows me to follow their progress in fourth and fifth grade with a knowing eye and make sure they continue to receive other forms of support.

In Chapter 2 of *Going Public,* "Rethinking the Role of Principal," I describe the task of being a "devoted grandma" in working with struggling children. I briefly describe the benefits to administrators of carving out regular time to work with readers in need of extra support. These include:

- opportunities to assess the quality of instructional materials available in the school.
- a heightened awareness that interruptions must be kept to a minimum, or better yet, eliminated altogether.
- a reminder of just how crucial predictability of routines is. (As described below, our reading sessions include the same components each time.)
- a reminder of just how important it is to pay attention to the instructional language we use.
- a reminder of just how hard teachers must work with the easily distracted child. (Even in small-group settings there are children who can't stay focused.)
- a reminder of how crucial communication between staff members is. (When do I share with classroom teachers the work I am doing and the progress of the children?)

- a better understanding of teachers' grade-level expectations. (Which children do third-grade teachers consider to be struggling?)
- an additional means of professional development. (Colleagues are invited to drop in and observe these sessions.)
- a means of establishing closer and special relationships with an important cluster of students. (Getting to know these children well serves me through their remaining years in the school. They respond to me differently because they remember those intimate third-grade gatherings. They continue to think of me as a teacher).
- an appreciation on the part of teachers and parents that the principal is willing to roll up her sleeves. (No one person in a school should ever feel that the success—or failure—of any one child is totally on their shoulders. We are all in this together).

Tutorials for Struggling Readers

At the beginning of the year I ask our third-grade teachers for the names of any children who might need extra instruction. If there are many children recommended and I don't have enough time to read with each child individually, I make a tentative plan for instruction based on our teachers' careful assessments and recommendations. They know what their students need. I am always disappointed when a student who I didn't know was having difficulties is referred to me. (I wonder why I didn't hear about this child in second grade? Were they struggling then? How come they're struggling now? Do individual teachers have such different expectations? Would the same children be recommended if they were sitting in another teacher's room?)

Most years, each third-grade teacher recommends approximately six students. We have four third-grade classrooms, so in an "ideal" year I would have a dozen students in each of the two clusters described below. I send a letter to families announcing that their child will be going to the cafeteria ten minutes early a few times a week and unfortunately missing their recess as well, as they are being assigned to my lunchtime tutorial. Parents never seem to mind these arrangements, as they are always grateful when their children receive extra supports. Some children are upset at first by what they perceive to be a disruption in their daily schedule, but I work hard to win them over and I'm eventually successful. (I have heard older children tell their younger sisters and brothers that in third grade they might be in Shelley's reading club. It's become a rite of passage for some children.)

The notion of placing the children into two separate tutorial groups is perhaps a controversial one. Do I randomly divide the group into two equal clusters? Or do I think about their main areas of need and know that I will be able to provide more focused attention if students with similar needs are sitting alongside one another? Our classrooms are of course heterogeneously grouped, and so the question becomes, "Should our tutorial sessions be as well?" I have taken my cues from the best teachers of reading I know, who form groups based on students' felt needs for short periods of time. Struggling readers have urgent needs and I must figure out the most efficient ways to meet those needs. Grouping students according to needs is therefore beneficial, but bear in mind that these tutorial sessions are *not* full-time class assignments. They are *not* comprised of "bluebirds" and "robins," pitted against each other. They are *not* filled with students longing to make it to the thicker, harder books or materials. They are *not* viewed as punitive sessions for "at-risk" students. In fact, many children who attend ask if they can attend on all four days, and those who are not members ask if they can join my "club." So too, when students move on to fourth grade, some ask if they can continue their membership.

My reading tutorial groups are never even in the same room at the same time and I never discuss with children why I ask them to join a particular group. (I do discuss why they need to attend tutorials, but never why one tutorial is more appropriate than another.) If they pass by when the other group's tutorial is in session they are reassured to see that we appear to be engaged in the same activities on all days. And we are, although the strategies highlighted and the materials used are different. (I have, in fact, heard children ask one another, "Does Shelley play that word game with you when you go to her book club?")

I cluster children who lack fluency in one group. These children struggle with new words and make errors on words one would expect most children in third grade to be able to read on sight. They frequently ignore punctuation marks, not realizing how these can support their understanding of text. In their classrooms they are the *Nate the Great* type readers. My goals for this group are threefold: I want them to continue to see reading as a meaning-making process, using all the clues on the page (graphophonic, syntactic, semantic) as well as those they bring to the page (background knowledge of topic and genre) to construct meaning. I also want them to become strategic when they come across unknown words, and I want to keep them joyously engaged in becoming better readers. (Note: the "ideal" balance between groups (in numeric terms) is rarely achieved. Some years I have had only eight students in this group and about double that in the second group, described below.)

In the second group, usually, are students who can decode practically any text you might expect to find in a third-grade classroom. They can also recall the most literal of events in a story. They struggle, however, to do anything associated with the old cliché of "reading between the lines." They rarely make predictions, inferences, discuss character motivation, or get jokes woven into the texts. They don't even ask about the meaning of idioms or unusual words that sometimes appear in the stories we read. In reality, they are an assembled group of *passive* readers. My goal throughout the year during this twice-a-week lunchtime tutorial is to shift these children into *active* readers.

In the next several pages, I describe what I offer to these budding readers. The approximately fifty-minute reading session begins with time for poetry followed by time to read books or magazine articles together, and ends with a short reading game. More on each component follows.

Poetry Reading

I begin all our sessions with about ten minutes of poetry reading. I do so for the sheer joy attached to this activity and also to allow for the last lunchtime straggler to arrive at the tutorial, usually with a last bit of sandwich still in his mouth. In no way do I mean to imply that poetry is a "filler." It's just that the hour is marked by staggered arrivals and since we read, reread, and return to so many short familiar poems, latecomers do not feel at a disadvantage. More importantly, sharing wonderful poems reminds students why it is worth working so hard to become good readers.

For my Monday-Tuesday crew (also known to me as my "beginning-of-the-week readers") I select poems that are well-written and are of interest to children but ones that will also focus their attention on certain spelling features. I am always trying to prove to this group that if they know one word they can use it to read many words. (In other words, knowing *book* will help them to read *crook* and *shook*). The children follow along as I read the poems, and then they join me in subsequent readings.

The students have time to respond to the poems, perform, and choral read them before we look at the rhyming words and the spelling patterns contained in each. The poems in their binder include such pieces as "Chant" by David McCord, "Joan" by Eve Merriam, "Hard to Please" by Shel Silverstein, "The Diners in the Kitchen," by James Whitcomb Riley, "Snow Rhyme," by Christine Crow, "Parking Lot" by Marci Ridlon, and "Friends" by Alan Benjamin. Each of these poems is filled with many rhyming words containing common spelling features (e.g., ack, ay, ick, oke, est) as well as variant spellings of the same sounds, as in the words "Joan, Joan, answer the phone."

I've also added a few original poems. (See "School Rules" in *Going Public*.) For example, I wrote the following poem expressly for a struggling group of children who needed a lot of practice spotting familiar spelling patterns and using them to figure out new words.

You and Me
You snore, I roar.
You smoke, I choke.
You wiggle, I giggle.
You mop, I stop.
You bake, I take.
You win, I grin.
You fly, I cry.
You pay, I play.
You seed, I weed.
You drip, I slip.

You pick, I lick.
You bag, I drag.
You tear, I repair.
You say goodbye, I sigh!

They turned the poem into a picture book, illustrating each pair of words on a separate page. In the illustrations, the "you" always represented an older person, and the "I" a younger observer. The students became very engaged in trying to invent scenarios for each of the phrases. For example, the older person snored in his sleep and the younger person roared with laughter at the sound. The older person mopped the kitchen floor and the younger person stopped in his tracks so as not to make footprints on the wet surface. The older person bagged groceries and the younger one dragged the wagon home. The older person tore a piece of paper and the younger one applied cellophane tape. The older person dripped water and the younger person slipped in the puddle. (The children made these drawings on their own time, since our time together, being short, is used exclusively for reading.)

I also include songs in our poetry sharing, ones that serve the same purpose. These include popular hits like Simon and Garfunkel's "Hop Off the Bus Gus" and such classics as "Button Up Your Overcoat." (Remember the warnings against the dangers of crossing streets, "Ooh-Ooh," eating meats, and cutting out sweets). Once in a while I also share picture books that lend themselves to interesting word study, such as *In the Diner*, by Christine Loomis, in which the "bagels toast" and "turkeys roast," *Snow Dance*, by Lezlie Evans, in which the snowflakes are "drifting" and "sifting," and such rebus-filled rhyming books as those by Shirley Neitzel (*We're Making Breakfast for Mother*, *I'm Taking a Trip on My Train*, etc.). Children's gleeful response to such seemingly "juvenile" picture books convinces me, time and again, that eight-year-olds still need to be considered early-childhood students.

Children eventually bring their own contributions, including hand-clapping chants and jump-rope rhymes. We spend a few minutes brainstorming additional words that contain the patterns the children have discovered in the poems, songs, or picture books. We occasionally browse a set of rhyming dictionaries (such as *The Scholastic Rhyming Dictionary* by Sue Young) to make even more discoveries.

The poems I share with my Thursday-Friday group (also known to me as my "end-of-the-week readers") are markedly different. My goal for this group is to catapult them into being active readers. I therefore search for accessible poems in which the poet is very funny, opinionated, emotional, or controversial. I want these young readers to get used to having strong reactions to text. I want them to wonder, complain, sympathize, and laugh out loud. Poems have included Jack Prelutsky's "My Brother is a Doodler," about a mischievous little boy who draws on everything, Richard Edward's "Mary and Sarah," about two young girls with very opposite likes and dislikes (reprinted in *Going Public*), and Myra Cohn Livingston's "The Box," about the secret treasures a child hides in an old box. I read the poems to the children. I encourage them to ask any questions they have about words or ideas. They read the poems with me. I encourage a great deal of response to the poems. Children inevitably ask to read the poems aloud individually. They know that poems are meant to be performed.

During the year, I throw in an occasional twist to our ten-minute poetry share. Innovations include:

- reading aloud word play books such as Cathi Hepworth's *Antics!*, which is filled with words containing the word *ant*, or Polly Cameron's *I Can't Said the Ant,* which has dozens of pairs of words with common spelling patterns.

- playing commercial word games such as Think-it, Link-It (whereby a cycle climb is a "bike-hike," an intelligent Valentine is a "smart heart," and a hefty rodent is a "fat rat").

- writing additional lyrics for some of the songs sung in our kindergarten class-rooms. Third graders enjoy composing stanzas with a specific audience and purpose in mind. They often recall these songs from their own days in kinder-garten and relish the opportunities to be brought back to those "good old days" For example, Gary Renville, a visiting educator, taught Pam's students a won-derfully rhythmic, reggae-inspired song, filled with hand gestures, that began, "Put a pizza in my hand and I will be a pizza man" (pronounced "mon."). The many verses that followed each concerned a different item put into the singer's hands, which would lead to a new persona. (Put a book into my hand, I will be a librarian. Put a carrot in my hand, I will be a vegetarian). All of the personas listed rhymed with "mon." My reading crew loved inventing their own lines. They wrote, "Put a lightbulb in my hand, I will be an electri-ci-<u>an</u>!" "Put a puppy in my hand, I will be a veterinari<u>an</u>!" "Put a calculator in my hand, I will be a mathematici<u>an</u>!"

- writing original rhyming texts with students in order to study certain rimes. For example, one day I began a list of catchy phrases with students, all requiring a rhyming word that had the spelling feature "each" or "eech." Our text grew into the following poem:

To Each His Own, A Peach of a Poem!

I'm not a fruit store owner, I've never sold a peach.
I'm not a professor, I can't teach.
I'm not a minister, I can't preach.
I'm not a laundry man , I can't bleach.
I'm not a lifeguard, I don't work at the beach.
I'm not an astronaut, the moon I can't reach.
I'm not a politician, I've never made a speech.
I'm not a New York City taxi driver, my tires don't screech!

After composing this poem, students enjoyed reading, reciting, and (outside of the tutorial) illustrating these lines, placing each one on a separate page in a blank book.

Reading Books, Short Stories, or Magazine Articles

After enjoying poetry together and marveling at how words work, we read a carefully selected book, short story, or magazine article for approximately twenty-five minutes. This component is as close as I get to what is described as guided reading. (See p. 200 for description).

Earlier in the year, for my "beginning-of-the-week-readers," I prepare texts for viewing on the overhead projector. I want to be sure that these "on-the-road-to-becoming-fluent" readers are engaged and on-task every minute. I have a better sense of what children are doing when all eyes are focused on the same screen and I can reveal portions of text as needed. As soon as I am confident that readers understand the importance of paying undivided attention to the tasks at hand, I distribute personal copies of the chosen text.

We read a great deal of folktales. I deliberately choose this genre because these tales seem to resonate with all students, including those recently arrived from other countries. In addition, most of the children are attempting to read short chapter books in their classrooms, books from popular series filled with young children in semirealistic settings who are always getting into trouble, trying to solve a mystery, or having funny adventures. I realize that these children don't need to be reading more of the same kind of stories in these tutorials. Besides, many of the children I work with also attend resource room and extended-day tutorials. How many plot lines about little children and their adventures can any one reader keep clear in their heads?

Folktales are a breath of fresh air, and if chosen carefully can be very supportive of struggling readers. Most folktales have predictable story structures, a limited number of characters with easy-to-understand personality traits (it's fairly obvious who represents good, who evil), and repetitive language and situations. Then too, the problems to be solved are universal ones, in which the main characters will try a limited number of ways to achieve resolution, and/or some magical or mystical intervention will let the good guys, or good animals, live happily ever after. In addition, the stories, if well written, are usually worth reading again and again, a benefit to all struggling readers. Perhaps I also choose folktales because they give me such pleasure. C. S. Lewis once said, "Some day you will be old enough to start reading fairy tales again." I feel the same way about folktales.

Last year's beginning-of-the-week group read many of the books in the Beechtree Books series: *Favorite Fairy Tales Told in Poland* as well as those told in Russia, Scotland, Germany, England, and the Czech Republic.

During this part of the tutorial I also introduce many works of nonfiction to my beginning-of-the-week readers. This too is a welcome change of pace from the realistic fiction they often choose to read in their classrooms. And as noted in Chapter 4, "Paving the Way for Nonfiction Study," young children are particularly eager to figure out how this planet and everything on it works. We read some books from designated easy-to-read series, ones on such inviting topics as gargoyles, knights, and mummies. We also read carefully selected picture books, chosen for their topics and supports for young readers (see pp. 234–235 for specific supports), books like *Our Puppies Are Growing* by Carolyn Otto and *Who Lives Here?* by Maggie Silver. We often read articles about such things as beetles, kites, and circus clowns from *Cricket* magazine.

I also select "how-to" materials so that children get real-world payoff. For example, we read *Let's Play Cards: A First Book of Card Games* by Elizabeth Silbaugh. The children got to teach these card games to their friends during the next rainy day recess. They also took the directions home to share with family members. Similarly, we read *Hopscotch Around the World* by Mary Lankford, and the children took pastel chalk to the play yard to draw the new game boards they had learned.

My reading work with this group involves introducing each day's book by reading several pages aloud to the children as they follow along on the overhead projector or in a copy of the text in their hands. Children who lack fluency in their reading can never have enough models of good reading behavior.

I then call the children's attention to a particular strategy they need to learn and practice. Strategies might include figuring out an unknown word by reading to the end of the sentence or the paragraph and thinking about what would make sense, making meaning by pausing and searching for clues in pictures, charts, graphs, or other graphic aids, or making meaning by reading aloud difficult parts and paying close attention to punctuation marks. (As noted earlier, I determine the needs of these students based upon informal observations as well as upon classroom teacher assessments and recommendations. If these were my own full-time students, my work would be informed by essential and individual reading conferences in which students read aloud, retell, and otherwise discuss the content of the books they are reading.)

I then provide time for students to silently read the material, using the highlighted strategy. Afterwards, we discuss the text as well as their use of reading strategies. We always end these reading-together sessions by answering the same question, "What did you do today that you can do *on your own* when you are reading back in your own classrooms, so that you will get more out of your reading?" All students must understand why it is important to become strategic readers and how to go about doing so. They must know that *they* are responsible for knowing when they' re not making meaning and that there are strategies for solving these problems.

My work with my "end-of-the-week readers," the children who can say the words but don't necessarily construct meaning, also involves reading books and articles together. My emphasis with these "on-the-road-to-becoming-active" readers is to call their attention to the importance of being wide awake and aggressive when they read. I try to use metaphors to describe active reading that resonate with children. We engage in discussions such as the following.

- We talk about not being "zoned-out" when we read. (We can't be like viewers who watch mysteries and don't pay attention to clues or guess who the criminal is. We can't be "sort of reading.")

- We talk about not being "couch potatoes" when we read. (We can't be like people who get so glazed over or lazy that they can't get up to answer the door or the telephone when they are watching television. Readers have to pay attention and respond to everything that is happening in their books.)

- We talk about trying to "stay tuned to the right station" when we read. (Readers must not let their minds wander in ways that make them lose track of the story. Some students admit to getting easily distracted by a friend's new hair cut, a scuff mark on their sneakers, or the design on their teacher's shirt.)

- We talk about how reading is like braiding strands of hair, that readers are always holding strands of information in their hands. (For example, I reminded students that when we read Anne Rockwell's retelling of the folktale "Owl Feathers," we had to keep the title in our mind, as well as the fact that this story was in a collection of folktales, as well as all the background information we had about owls.)

- We talk about being like Curious George when we read. "Be curious," I tell the students. "Stick your nose in everything, ask questions all the time."

- We talk about how reading is a bit like being a gambler. "You are always betting," I tell the students. "You're betting that this is going to happen or that that word means such and such."

- We talk about playing the card game "go fish" poorly, without paying attention to the cards that our opponents have asked for. "That's playing without any strategies," I tell them. "That's no way to play cards and it's no way to read."

- We talk about how reading is not like doing a word search puzzle, where you're just trying to find words you recognize. "When you read," I continually tell students, "You are using the print to build meaning. Spotting words you can read doesn't make you a reader."

- We talk about how reading is not like calling words off a cue card. "Sometimes," I tell students, "I wonder about the news reporters we see on television. I wonder if they are paying attention to the words they are saying or if they're just reading the words off cue cards and not really listening to the meaning of the words. When we read we have to be thinking thoughts, otherwise we are not really reading."

All the ways I try to engage these passive readers involve putting them into the driver's seat on a busy city street. They can't act like they're on a desolate country road using their cruise control. They have to be totally alert. I want to give them experiences that require interacting with the text, never letting the words simply wash over them. I therefore guide students through their reading of such texts as Anne Rockwell's *The Acorn Tree,* George Shannon's *Stories to Solve: Folktales from Around the World,* and *Folktales Around the World* and *Nursery Tales Around the World* selected and retold by Judy Sierra.

After introducing each story I demonstrate a specific reading strategy and then ask students to do likewise. For example, I might ask students to take any of the following active stances as they read (or if necessary as they reread):

- highlight the really significant lines
- separate the background from the foreground information
- predict upcoming moments before turning each page
- imagine the story as a Saturday morning cartoon and try to visualize each scene and the scene changes
- stop whenever a character reminds you of someone you know in real life
- jot down questions you have in the margins of duplicated copies of the story
- stop after each of the main scenes to plan how you might retell the key events to members of your family

I also prepare texts on the overhead or opaque projector for this group of readers. Many of these picture books are folktales or fairy tales, including *The Fence* by Jan Balet, *A Spoon for Every Bite* by Joe Hayes, *The King's Fountain* by Lloyd Alexander, and *The Baker's Dozen: A Saint Nicholas Tale* retold by Aaron Shepard. (I keep the acetate pages of these stories in folders so that I can use them time and again on the overhead projector. I also purchase multiple copies whenever possible so that children can borrow the books to read on their own. They always ask to do so and it's no surprise. These are very good stories.)

My work with these texts has its roots in an afternoon I spent many years ago, watching Don Holdoway, the brilliant literacy educator, masterfully provide a shared-reading experience for a group of older elementary students. I have since attempted to replicate the way Don led students through a very good story. This criteria is key. Without a very good story in your hands, it is pointless to spend a great deal of time reading and thinking about narrative. That afternoon Don demonstrated his captivating read-aloud of the first few pages of a story and his use of oral cloze procedures (deleting certain words and inviting the listeners to make sensible guesses). The children were delighted when they could predict the words. Don would stop and give students the first letter if they were struggling. Every child seemed mesmerized by Don's enthusiasm for the story and for them as readers. Even if they predicted a word that was not on the page, Don made them feel brilliant if their predictions made sense, and most of the predictions did.

He continued by placing the next few pages of the text on the overhead projector, pages he had prepared as written cloze (again deleting particular words). Children now read the pages to themselves and called out the missing words. Don was certainly proving to them that reading is a process of making meaning. He also demonstrated progressive exposure of text, slowly revealing lines as the children read aloud, again proving to them that they were anticipating what was coming up on the page even before they saw the words *because they were constructing meaning*. Don also had children read entire pages to themselves to keep the pace of the story up; at times he asked them to call out the significant lines on a page. Throughout, Don got students to interact with the story. It was as if they were cowriting it as they were reading. That's how invested they seemed in the reading.

I didn't just learn teaching techniques from watching Don Holdoway on that one afternoon. I learned what it means to teach with voice, to love children and quality literature. In addition, I realized how important it was for teachers to attend conferences in order to learn from the masters. I also learned that teachers need to read professional books written by these experts in order to enrich the understandings they gather at professional conference presentations.

On some occasions, I do a bit of first-draft reading in front of the students using material I have not read before. (I usually choose brand-new picture books, preferably ones with bold print and large illustrations, so that the children gathered can see what I see.) One day students watched as I read Janet Stevens's *Cook-A Doodle-Doo*. All the way through I asked myself questions, reread, made predictions, changed my mind, laughed out loud, and jotted notes. In other words, I metaphorically cut off the top of my head and let my aspiring readers look inside as I demonstrated strategies that fluent readers use in order to make sense of texts.

I also ask children to read realistic fictional picture books, ones with appropriately challenging text on each page. Many are those containing one- or two-page chapters, such as Crescent Dragonwagon's *Brass Button,* Rosemary Wells' *Night Sounds, Morning Colors* and *Lucy Comes to Stay,* and Ann Turner's *The Christmas House.* (See how these same books are used in the teaching of writing in *Writing Through Childhood.*) I also share carefully selected nonfiction trade books, ones with appropriate supports and challenges. One year, students read Dick King-Smith's entire collection *Animal Friends: Thirty-One True to Life Stories.*

I also share how-to books with these readers, ones with a bit more complicated text, like *Crazy Eights and Other Card Games* and *Fun on the Run: Travel Games and Songs,* both by Joanna Cole and Stephanie Calmenson. These children eagerly share the songs and paper-and-pencil and card games they learn in tutorials with their friends and families.

I want students to view books such as those listed above as viable choices when they return to their classrooms. Not everything third graders read should be part of a series. (See discussion of series reading below.)

Language Games

I always try to leave the last ten to fifteen minutes of our time together for playing some sort of reading game. (The students miss recess while in the tutorial and delight in some relaxed, fun time together.)

Figure 9.3

For example, the children love to play a word game that involves some quick sketching. I might draw three jars, sacks, baskets, or boxes. I might label one "chocolate sauce," another "butterscotch sauce," and the third one, the one on the left, would be tucked behind the others so that only the first three letters, "str," are visible (see sketch in Figure 9.3).

Children love figuring out the incomplete words based on the semantic clues, (they know that the word must refer to another kind of sweet sauce, because of the two words given). They also rely on the graphophonic cues (they know the word begins with "str"). Of course, *strawberry* satisfies both. Similarly, I've presented the challenges shown in Figure 9.4. The second-language-learning children in the group are especially eager to learn these new words. I also invite students to attempt the complete spelling of the hidden word when they figure it out. Children eventually offer to present their own hidden-item sketches. They work hard to think of categories, appropriate words, as well as the initial sounds of hidden words. A few children's creations appear in Figure 9.5. Perhaps my favorite was *"Coffee, expresso, and ca—."* (What a sophisticated child to think about cappuccino!)

I've also brought along some commercial parlor games that require students to bring all that they know about reading to the table. These include such games as Mad Libs.

Figure 9.4

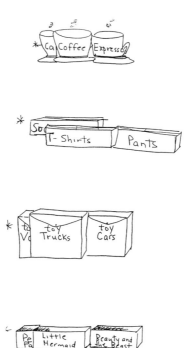

Figure 9.5

The game that has become the most popular with students is one created by Ann K. Hall and described in detail in the September 1995 issue of *The Reading Teacher,* in the article "Sentencing: The Psycholinguistic Guessing Game." (The subtitle brings to mind Ken Goodman's important research about the process of reading.) The game reminds readers to use all the strategies available to them as they attempt to figure out a hidden sentence using syntactic, semantic, and graphophonic cues. In other words, students must rely on their knowledge of the world, how our language works, as well as what they know about how letters are used to form words in order to figure out a meaningful sentence.

I follow Ann Hall's directions and begin by dividing the cluster of children into two teams, selecting a captain for each. (This itself is a novelty in our school, as we downplay competition. I continually remind students that this is just a game, aimed at improving all students' reading abilities; it is not to be seen as evidence of any group of students' superiority over another.)

I then show them a previously prepared sentence, usually written on a large chart and placed on an easel. The schematic represents a sentence in which all the words but one are initially missing.

I offer each team three "free letter" cards, to be used at their discretion. (I draw three happy faces under each captain's name and cross them off as the free-letter cards are used.) To play the game, teams alternate guessing the correct words. Each team huddles with the captain as they decide their strategies and make their guesses. The team captain speaks for the team.

(I've revised the author's original directions a bit, as I deliberately match the length of the blanks to the length of the missing word, in order to remind students that they always have the length of the word as a clue when they come across an unknown word in their reading. I've also added ten points to the score of the team that guesses the entire sentence, so that teams unsuccessful in guessing individual words can still win the round. I've also added a third free-letter card to the author's suggested two, because students seem to need this extra support.)

I begin the game by engaging students in a conversation about the one word revealed at the beginning of each round. I always select a high-content word to reveal, so that children can guess topics and related words that might be hidden. For example, I might say, "We know that this sentence has the word *rains* in it. What other words might you expect to find in this sentence?" Students might then offer such possibilities as *wet, umbrella, puddles,* and *showers.* I remind students that this type of activity is what we can do whenever we begin a new book. I might say, "If you took a book from the library with the word *rain* in the title, you might also begin by imagining the possibilities inside, the ideas and the words. Then you might be better able to understand the meaning of the book and to attack new words." (Of course, their guessing doesn't always pay off, as seen below, but it is a good strategy to build in to the beginning of each session.)

When it is their turn, a team begins by selecting the number corresponding to the word they would like revealed. They are only entitled to have one word revealed on each turn. (Choosing which word to have revealed is a strategic decision. I learn a lot by listening in on the students' decision making. I pay attention to who is rereading the sentence, who understands how the English language works, and who is making sensible predictions.) Teams can also get letters revealed if they decide to use their free-letter cards. (This part of the game brings to mind the television show *Wheel of Fortune.*) After I reveal the one requested word at the beginning of a turn, I remind players of their three choices:

1. You can guess at a missing word ("We think number one is *If.*)
2. You can use a free-letter card ("We want to use a free-letter card for number two.")
3. You can pass ("We're not sure what to guess, so we want to pass our turn.")

Teams keep going until they guess incorrectly or they pass. Each time they guess a word correctly they get points. As per the originator's instructions, I give two points for words guessed without the help of any letters, and one point if a free-letter card has given them a hint. I keep score on the bottom of the chart page, and I also cross off the happy faces representing free-letter cards as they are used.

The game moves quickly because with each turn a complete word is revealed, offering significant clues to the players. I always encourage rereading as the main strategy for making good predictions. The children know that they have to continually read for meaning.

Our example sentence may result in the following scenario. The first team asks for word number one to be revealed, so the board now looks as follows:

If		rains									
1	2	3	4	5	6	7	8	9	10	11	12

Most students will now be able to guess that the word in the number-two spot is *it*. Some might suggest *the*, and other children will argue with them that we wouldn't say "the rains." If they guess correctly they will score two points and the board will look as follows:

If	it	rains									
1	2	3	4	5	6	7	8	9	10	11	12

Strategic players might now suggest using a free-letter card to get a hint at word number four. Supplied with a *w*, they will probably guess *we*, scoring one additional point.

If	it	rains	we								
1	2	3	4	5	6	7	8	9	10	11	12

The team continues their guessing until they miss. If they guess that number five is *will* and they're told they're incorrect, the second team has a chance to play.

Perhaps the second team will ask for word number twelve. There is no requirement to go in order. Many children, in fact, think that the longest words will be the hardest to guess and therefore ask for the long blanks to be revealed first. Some learn that it is often the smallest words that are the hardest to figure out. The board now looks like this:

If	it	rains	we								playground.
1	2	3	4	5	6	7	8	9	10	11	12

The game continues until the entire sentence is complete and the captain of the winning team reads the entire sentence back—If it rains we won't be able to go the playground. (Note: students need to know that if only one missing word remains in the sentence, this word is never revealed. That would take the fun and value out of the game.)

As the year goes on and students grow as readers I make the sentences more complex and the content richer. Students learn to pay attention to the punctuation marks and get especially good at realizing that whenever there are a lot of commas, there is probably a series of items in the sentence, as in some of the examples below.

Children like to play in lots of places including parks, playgrounds, beaches, pools, and gymnasiums.

There are many kinds of dances including ballet, tap, ballroom, and country western.

When spring arrives, flowers start to bloom, children fly kites, and people put away their heavy winter coats.

If you play in an orchestra you might play a violin, a flute, a clarinet, or a saxophone.

George Washington and Abraham Lincoln were both presidents of the United States and we celebrate their birthdays in February.

At the restaurant I ordered a hamburger, but my brother had a salad because he doesn't eat meat.

After elementary school, children go to middle school, then high school, then on to college.

At some point in the year, I encourage students to suggest sentences themselves, either original ones or ones lifted from the books they are reading.

(I am grateful to Ann Hall for inventing this game and publishing it in a professional journal so that others can learn from her. The activity has gotten many Manhattan New School students interested in words and in understanding how the English language works. As a principal I have shared this game with many students needing extra supports as well as with whole classes in spur-of-the-moment coverages. It can be similarly used by reading support teachers in small-group tutorials or by classroom teachers as a whole-group activity (dividing the class into two big teams), whenever their students need a pleasurable break.)

Dismissal Rituals

When our reading session is over, no student dashes out the door. I have begun a rather formal "saying goodbye" ritual. I took my cues from our National Dance Institute instructor, Tracy Straus, who closes each dance lesson with a very theatrical and musical way of saying thank you. She and the children in unison thank the piano player. Then she thanks the students and the students in turn thank her. Each week they perform this same ritual, with interesting modifications. Sometimes they use a British accent, pretend to be sipping teas as they very formally say "thank you" and "cheerio." Some weeks they take on a French persona, saying *merci* and bidding one another *au revoir*. I don't go to such elaborate extremes, but I do insist that each child shakes my hand and we exchange common courtesies. As I shake their hands, I might say such kind words as, "Thank you, Brian, for being the team captain." "Thank you, Valerie, for sharing the book with Olivia." "Thank you, Driton, for helping me clean up the papers." "Thank you, Kousoke, for finding the dry erase markers." "Thank you, Angel, for trying so hard." "Thank you, Aaron, for teaching us what you know about dolphins." "Thank you, Pierre, for helping your friends understand that story." "Thank you, Luan, for coming on time." (In this way, children know that I am paying attention to each and every one of them. They look forward to hearing what I am going to say about them each day.) In return, the children have to say something nice to me. (That's only fair.) As they shake my hand, I hear comments like "Thank you for teaching me, Shelley." "I liked the story." "I learned a lot today." "Have a good afternoon." "I'll see you tomorrow." Some even give me compliments, like, "I like your earrings!" It doesn't really matter what they say to me; I began the ritual in order to add a gracious closure to our time together and also as another way to become personally connected to the children in my care.

Counting on Series Books

I would be remiss not to address the issue of series books in this chapter, as our less fluent readers do spend a great deal of time with these collections. In *Writing Through Childhood* I suggest that we take advantage of all childhood interests as we design reading and writing workshops. Being a collector, or wanting to be one, seems to come naturally to most children. Young people seem to delight in counting, organizing, and swapping their collections. This holds true for series books.

Below I list the series that fill many of our classroom shelves, particularly in the second and third grade, although some appear in fourth grade as well. Most are purchased with school funds; some are introduced through a child's bedroom collection. Once a few are brought in, the rest follow. Also refer to Appendix 12, "Reading Series Worksheet."

(I have chosen not to separate series books from the newer ones in these lists. Students get hooked on the latest series, but they outgrow them much the way they do their school clothes. But just as those jeans that have grown too short are passed on to younger brothers and sisters, many series books are rediscovered by up-and-coming readers. With respect to the violent, stereotypical, or otherwise insulting-to-our-intelligence series books, we are, in fact, glad when the pages grow ragged or the content becomes dated. Over the years, some students have borrowed my own children's *Hardy Boys* and *Nancy Drew* collections, and several issues of bias and stereotyping arose, as should be expected in a scholarly setting.)

The following are popular series books in our first-grade classrooms:

Else Minarik's *Little Bear* books

Peggy Parish's *Amelia Bedelia* books

Patricia Reilly Giff's *Ronald Morgan* Series

James Marshall's *Fox* books

Arnold Lobel's *Frog and Toad* books

Jean Van Leeuwen's *Oliver and Amanda Pig* books

First graders also enjoy hearing their teachers read aloud such classic series stars as Ludwig Bemelmans' *Madeline*, H. A. Rey's *Curious George,* and Judith Viorst's books about Alexander. These books were *not* of course written with deliberate reading supports as many of the books listed. They were written thankfully to simply be enjoyed, period.

The following are very popular in our second-grade classrooms. Most children seem to spend some time reading these as they move through the year. (Of course, you would still find some of the books listed above in our second-grade collections. Teachers match children with appropriate books so the range of texts *must* be great.)

> Marjorie Weinman Sharmat's *Nate the Great* books
>
> Cynthia Rylant's *Henry and Mudge, Poppleton, Mr. Putter and Tabby* and *Cobble Street Cousins* books
>
> David Adler's *Cam Jansen* and *Young Cam Jansen* books
>
> Suzy Kline's *Horrible Harry* and *Mary Maroney* books
>
> James Howe's *Pinky and Rex* books
>
> Laura Ingalls Wilder's *Little House* beginner books
>
> Pat Ross's *M&M* books
>
> Ellen Conford's *Jenny Archer* books
>
> Patricia Reilly Giff's *The Kids of the Polk Street School* books
>
> Debbie Dadey and Marcia Thornton Jones' *Adventures of the Bailey School Kids* books
>
> Stephen Krensky's *Lionel* books
>
> Judy Delton's *The Pee Wee Scouts* books

Second graders who still require a great deal of support are particularly eager to read such books as the *Young Cam Jansen* series and the beginner *Little House* books, because as second-grade teacher Karen Ruzzo suggests, they feel included in the conversations with classmates who are reading about the same characters in the more sophisticated and related series.

Of course, some of the above titles will also be found in our third-grade classrooms. There you will also find the additional series that follow. Children who are not yet fluent readers often spend time with these.

> Dan Greenburg's *The Zack Files* books
>
> Dorothy Haas's *Peanut Butter and Jelly* books
>
> Janice Lee Smith's *Adam Joshua* books
>
> Mary Pope Osborne's *Magic Tree House* books
>
> Louis Sachar's *Marvin Redpost* and *Wayside School* books
>
> Dick King-Smith's *Sophie* books
>
> Donald Sobol's *Encyclopedia Brown* books

Barbara Park's *Junie B. Jones* books

Elizabeth Levy's *Something Queer . . .* books

Ann Martin's *Baby-Sitter's Club Little Sister* books

Books in the *American Girl* series written by different authors

Students who are well on their way to becoming accomplished readers often delight in reading such series as Beverly Cleary's *Ramona* and Paula Danziger's *Amber Brown.*

Series books in the fourth-grade classroom are no longer *that* popular. A few students who lack confidence in their reading will look to a few series. Some girls still delight in Ann Martin's *Baby-Sitter's Club* books and some continue reading Paula Danziger's *Amber Brown* series, anxious to read these stories that continue from one book to the next. Some fourth graders, mostly boys, might still be caught reading R. L. Stine's *Goosebumps.* I say "caught" because these violent books are never the teacher's choice for inclusion in the classroom library. More recently, K. A. Applegate's *Animorphs* series has become the "underground" literature of choice. Again, I say underground because I've never seen teachers use school funds to order any of these series. Students bring these "thrillers" into school having taken them out of the public library or purchased them as collectibles. By the time this book is published, no doubt, some other series with flashy, irresistible covers will be the new must-reads.

(Popular series that are *not* thought of as being directed toward struggling readers include Lois Lowry's *Anastasia* books. These full-size chapter books appeal to some of our most sophisticated readers in third and fourth grade).

By the fifth grade, most of our students stay clear of the easier-to-read, trendy series books. Instead, they get hooked on such newer and lengthier series as J. K. Rowling's *Harry Potter* books.

For a complete listing of series possibilities, the reader is directed to *Reading in Series: A Selection Guide to Books for Children,* edited by Catherine Barr with a wonderful foreword by Barbara Barstow, children's literature expert and chair of the 1999 Randolph Caldecott Award Committee. Barstow, in commenting on the popularity of series books today, refers to the Stratemeyer syndicate, publishers of many series including the *Hardy Boys* and *Nancy Drew.* She concludes her foreword as follows:

> In the thirty years since I began working in public libraries, the changes have been tremendous. We no longer wear hats and gloves and are relaxed enough to be on first-name terms. We have also moved from stigmatizing "popular" series books to recognizing that they naturally fit into the lives of children, that the Stratemeyer syndicate titles can exist and be read alongside the very best of children's literature. It is no longer a case of "either/or" but "both"; a recognition of a child's need, as well as an adult's, to have a great variety of literature in his or her life. May this book help children to have access to both the best and the popular, the sustaining and the diverting, as they make their way toward adulthood.

Making Judicious Selections

I have heard teachers complain about various aspects of series reading. Some series books do not provide enough supports for the readers for whom they were intended. Some don't have enough illustrations, or the illustrations are not appropriate. (See staff meeting discussion on pp. 234–235.) Some children get so hooked on them that they refuse to read anything else. Some series books are too formulaic. Some of the characters do not represent the same respectful ways of life that we are trying to teach our students. All these issues may be true, but none are insurmountable for the teacher willing to tackle them. A few suggestions follow:

- We need *not* clear shelf space or label a basket for every series that comes along. We must remain as fussy about the series books we order as about any other literature we bring into our classrooms. (See list of questions below when making decisions about adding series to classroom libraries.)

- We can talk to children honestly about why we don't like the one-dimensional characters or actions in some series. (Teachers let students know that they are concerned with all the violence in the *Goosebumps* books, and they wisely warn students not to expect so much rapid-fire action in all their reading.) We can also display our abhorrence of racism, classism, or gender stereotyping in any of these books.

- We can openly discuss the literary limitations of books written in formulaic fashion. Teachers demonstrate such limitations by continuously reading aloud the very finest literature available, so students never think that series books are "as good as it gets."

- We can discuss our response to the pictures on the covers of books in a series. Are the main characters diverse in background or appearance? Are the covers (or titles), too frightening, violent, and commercial for teachers' tastes? Are the covers the main attraction for young readers? (We might also talk to older students about the moneymaking issues attached to such rapidly produced best-sellers.)

- We can crack open the "how-to" of writing books by formula, giving students behind-the-scenes information on the writing of stories in a series. Teachers can explain, for example, how Donald Sobol collects what he calls "indisputable facts" and uses these as solutions to all those *Encyclopedia Brown* mysteries.

- We can discuss how reading these books might help students who are determined to become better readers. (Teachers can let children in on their teaching-of-reading information. They can inform students that it's easier to read a book that is predictable, one in which the characters and setting are familiar, etc.)

- We can work hard to match readers with books, not being afraid to direct children to the kind of books that will help them grow as readers, postponing some series for a later date or having some books read aloud to or with students. (See discussion of matching books with readers on p. 202 and shared reading on p. 200.)

- We can require students to branch out, reading nonfiction, poetry, and non-series books on our library shelves. We can have honest talks with children about the need to *not* be exclusive in their reading. We can tell students about our fears that they will get so used to one kind of reading that they will expect all books to sound like the ones that they have become immersed in and they will not have a chance to practice the new reading strategies they are learning.

Despite all the concerns listed, we must acknowledge that series do claim a significant role in the life of most elementary school readers, especially the ones who find learning to read the biggest challenge of their school career. Many of the series welcome aspiring readers into the world of chapter books, giving them a leg up on reading longer texts. Readers benefit from the predictability and familiarity of the characters and settings, and on the usually very straightforward plots. Many readers finally get the feel of having a good read, of getting totally lost in a book, because they truly understand what is happening in these very accessible stories. Reluctant readers who get hooked on a series probably read more books because of their mild "addictions." They no longer have to scrounge around or stall when they finish a book, because they know just where to find the rest of the set. For the first time in their lives, perhaps, readers are making connections between books. How can they not? Familiar characters reappear in all of them. And readers begin to finally understand characters' motives. How can they not? They are meeting up with the same personalities again and again and again.

Having established that series books are important to some readers, it is important to stress the role that the teacher plays in deciding which of these series are worth ordering in multiple copies, which are just too boring and bland to deserve serious attention, and which demand having honest and critical conversations with students and even with parents.

Criteria for Selecting Series Books

I have used the list of questions below when thinking about selecting series books for use with our less fluent readers. Some refer to the quality of the books in general. Most question the series' ability to support struggling readers.

1. Are the situations true to the life experiences or background knowledge of our students? (Or are the situations of such interest that with a little support, students will be able to enter the unfamiliar world of the story?)
2. Will the language of the stories sound natural and familiar to our students?
3. Are the leads to chapters ones that support the struggling reader (are they fairly easy to get into?) or ones that quickly disenfranchise the less fluent reader?

4. Do the stories contain too many abrupt shifts in scene, narrator, style, setting, time, without providing adequate reader preparation?

5. Do the books have illustrations that are helpful to the reader?

6. Are the grade levels printed on the cover in a way that is so obvious as to cause embarrassment to the less-than-fluent reader?

7. Are there so many main characters that they are hard to keep track of? Is there any diversity in the representation of characters?

8. Are the proper names of the characters unnecessarily hard to pronounce?

9. Are the chapters short enough and the pace quick enough to engage hitherto reluctant readers?

10. Is the dialogue easily woven into the narration with proper wording, so that the reader has no difficulty in deciding who is speaking? (See pp. 331–332.)

11. Are there enough elements of predictability within each book and continuity between books to make these particularly well-suited for our "extra-time" kids?

12. Do the stories contain those literary elements that enable children to see themselves or see the world in new ways after having read this book?

13. Do the books encourage the kind of relationships and caring that match with classroom expectations? (In other words, do the characters show empathy and the situations provide hope for young readers? Or does it appear that violent acts dominate?)

14. Should the books in the series be read in a set order? How much reading between the lines do readers have to do if they read the books out of sequence?

Studying Students' Writing for Clues to Improving Their Reading

Another major way teachers have to think about improving instruction for students who experience difficulties in learning to read is to study these students' writing. One Friday afternoon, I asked all the children who attend my reading tutorials (Shelley's book club) to lend me their writer's notebooks for the weekend. I spent several hours reading and rereading their pages, looking for clues as to why these children might be finding learning to read such an arduous task. There were of course no magic answers, nor any absolutes. Many of my struggling readers showed great needs as writers. The scarcity and paucity of some children's writing perhaps indicated that they didn't believe they had anything interesting to say. Some no doubt struggled with the mechanics of getting their thoughts on paper. Some were such breathtaking writers that unknowing colleagues would be stunned to discover that these children had any reading difficulties. Some, like

Elena, remind us that struggling readers must always be viewed as children with important things to say despite any weaknesses they may have in spelling, grammar, or punctuation. See Figure 9.6 for this third graders incredible tribute to writing.

Students who exhibited weaknesses as writers had a wide range of weaknesses. In other words, very few areas of weakness showed up in *all* students' writing. Some areas of concern were unique to just a handful of students, or perhaps just to one. There simply were no absolutes.

After studying these students' writing, I listed the following questions as a guide for colleagues who joined me in looking at the writing of struggling readers in order to tease out teaching-of-reading implications.

1. Do writers reveal areas of interest? Would it support their growth as readers if they were invited to read about these topics?

2. Do writers have genres of strength? Would it support their growth as readers if they were asked to read these genres?

3. Do writers have major weaknesses as spellers? Does this interfere in any way with their growth as readers?

4. Does their writing lack clarity? Would it support their growth as readers if they were held accountable to clarify their meaning each time they wrote?

5. Does their writing lack punctuation? Does this mean that they might not be paying attention to punctuation when they read? Would tending to punctuation more in their writing support their growth as readers?

6. Does their writing reveal weaknesses in grammar? If we strengthen their grammatical understandings will they be better able to read more complex text?

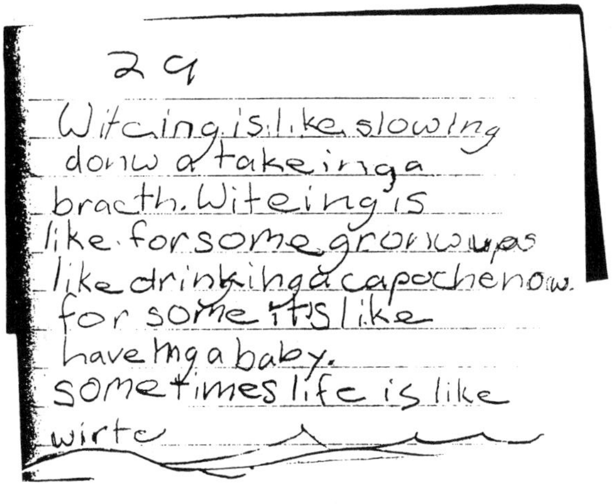

Figure 9.6

7. Does their writing improve when literature is used as a scaffold? What are the implications of this for the teaching of reading?

8. Will deliberate writing challenges that require students to use the techniques that confuse them when they read benefit the struggling reader?

9. Does it take some children a very long time to write very short amounts? If so, is their reading pace likewise so slow that it interferes with comprehension?

10. Do children write about themselves as struggling students? If so, how do we respond? Does what they say give us windows into their areas of difficulty? Do we think about self-esteem issues often enough when working with the struggling student?

(See Appendix 13 for a reproducible handout of these questions.)

As previously noted, these questions were designed to help colleagues realize the potential of continuous exploration of student writing in order to gain insights into the teaching of reading. They also served as an impetus in the designing of teaching practices that take advantage of writers' strengths and pay attention to their weaknesses.

The questions lead teachers to develop their practice with respect to the teaching of reading. Please note: the teaching suggestions that follow are not meant to burden an already busy teacher. The ideas can simply shape how the regular classroom teacher responds to students' reading and writing during regularly scheduled workshops. Teachers who regularly respond to students' writing realize that to be a good teacher of writing is really to be a good teacher of reading. Every time we respond to students' writing can be seen as a means of improving their reading. We teach children to read their own writing. We teach children what readers expect. We teach children to note the conventions of genre as they read so that they can navigate these on their own when they write. Here, however, I am suggesting that for the students about whom we have the most academic concerns, we can make the teaching of reading, through response to their writing, more explicit. We in fact need to find more opportunities to view their writing as an assessment window into their reading as well as an instructional tool to strengthen their reading.

Some of the suggestions that follow the observations below may be better suited to small-group and one-on-one instruction than to whole-class teaching. Most can be shared with trained and supervised student teachers, school volunteers, or paraprofessionals. They are particularly well suited for the teacher who provides reading intervention tutorials or conducts small-group work with learning disabilities students.

Writers Reveal Areas of Interest

As I read through each student's notebook, I jotted down their areas of interest, subjects that appeared more than once or were written about with gusto. Kristina showed an interest in how chocolate is made. On one page of her notebook is the entry that appears in Figure 9.7.

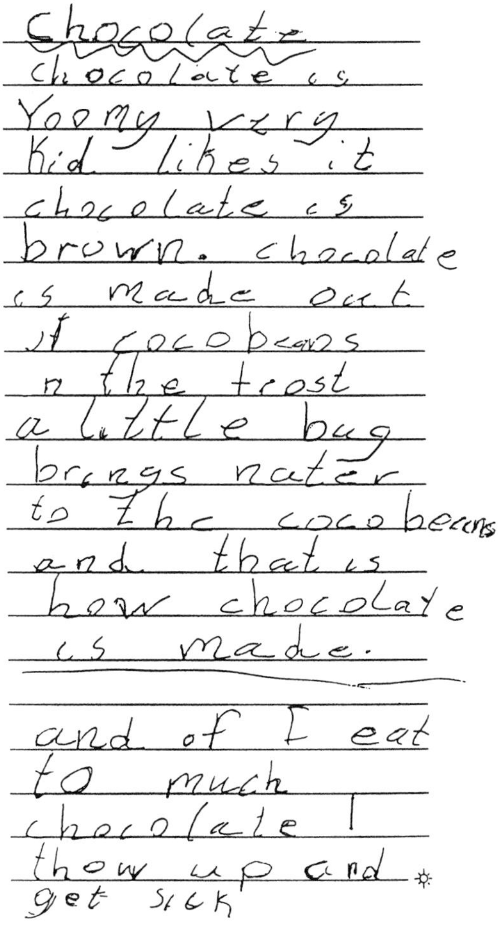

> Chocolate
> Chocolate is
> Yoomy very
> Kid likes it
> chocolate is
> brown. chocolate
> is made out
> of coco beans
> n the trost
> a little bug
> brings nater
> to the coco beans
> and that is
> how chocolate
> is made.
>
> and of I eat
> to much
> chocolate I
> thow up and
> get sick

Figure 9.7

Accordingly, I set out to find a related nonfiction text with appropriate supports and challenges for Kristina. Having read her notebook, I knew that she would be eager to learn in detail how chocolate is derived from cocoa beans. Her background knowledge would give her a leg up in the reading of new material on this topic. Her enthusiasm would no doubt encourage other students to be likewise interested in this topic. Students can be asked to reread their writer's notebooks looking for topics they would like to read about. They can hand their lists to a librarian who understands their reading needs or to any other well-informed teacher of reading.

Writers Have Genres of Strength

Reading through a third grader's entire writer's notebook made it easier for me to spot his or her preferences with respect to writing genres. Some wrote pages and pages of short poems; others wrote many passages of informational text. I wondered how many of those struggling readers were being asked to read the genres that so obviously appealed to them. Patrick is a case in point. His interesting notebook entries appear in Figures 9.8 and 9.9.

Patrick's charming writing strikes me as the beginnings of essays titled "Why Legos Are Great," "Why My Dad Is the Best." I imagined that since he tends to make bold statements and then support them with specific bits of information, he would have success reading other writers who did the same. The question arose, "Are there short essays for Patrick to read that would be supportive of him as a reader and be on topics he would be interested in reading?" Of course there are. We just have to search for them. I matched Patrick and a group of like-minded readers with passages from Marc Gellman's collection *"Always Wear Clean Underwear!" and Other Ways Parents Say "I Love You."* We read short essays together with such intriguing titles as "Don't Pee in the Pool" and "Don't Talk with Your Mouth Full." (Note, some of Gellman's essays have religious references and I necessarily avoided these. See also p. 211 for reference to another Gellman essay.) I also selected several pieces from Jean Little's classic collection, *Hey World, Here I Am!* Even though this is described as a poetry collection, there are several pieces that look and sound like short prose and have an essay-like quality (they include "Five Dollars," "My Journals," and "About Old People"). It's important that we tell students like Patrick what we see in them as writers and why we are asking them to read specific kinds of texts. If

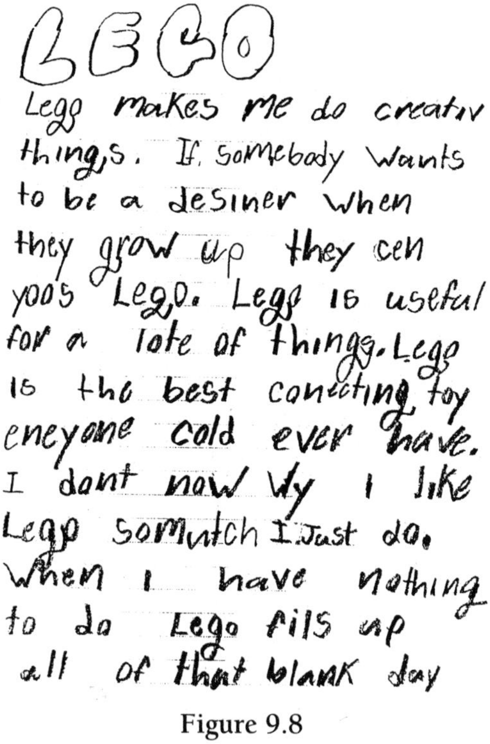
LEGO
Lego makes me do creativ things,s. If somebody wants to be a desiner when they grow up they cen yoos Lego. Lego is useful for a lote of things. Lego is the best conecting toy eneyone cold ever have. I dont now wy I like Lego somutch I just do. When I have nothing to do Lego fils up all of that blank day

Figure 9.8

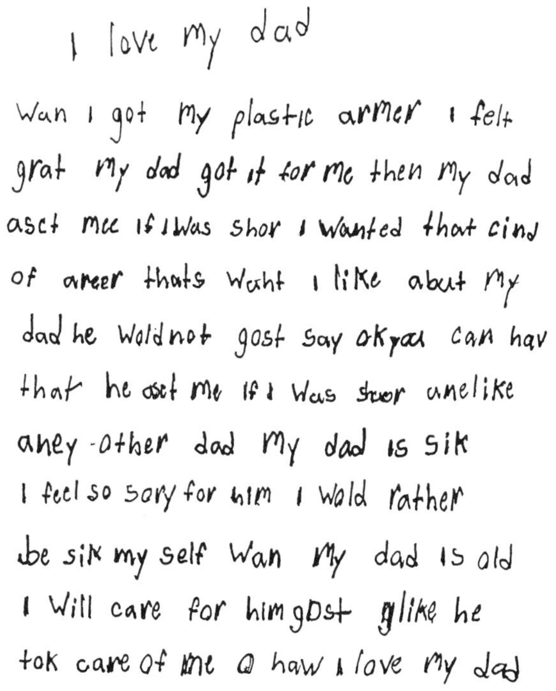

I love my dad

Wan I got my plastic armer I felt
grat my dad got it for me then my dad
asct mee if I was shor I wanted that cind
of areer thats waht I like about my
dad he woldnot gost say okya can hav
that he oset me if I was stor anelike
aney other dad my dad is sik
I feel so sory for him I wold rather
be sik my self Wan my dad is old
I will care for him gDst glike he
tok care of me a haw I love my dad

Figure 9.9

someone told me I had the makings of a great essayist, I am sure I would read essays with pleasure and I would keep trying to write better and better ones.

Writers Can Demonstrate Spelling Needs

It's important to take a look at struggling readers' spelling, if only to remind ourselves that some of these students are competent spellers and some are weak spellers. We all, of course, know fluent adult readers who remain poor spellers. So being a poor speller doesn't mean that one will be a struggling reader and being a good speller doesn't guarantee being a good reader. (We must also remember that some children only tend to their spelling when writing for publication. In other words, they simply don't bother to apply what they know about spelling unless it is absolutely necessary. They choose to write fast and furiously without stopping to think about the conventions of print. These children would probably benefit from being reminded to always apply what they know.)

It was helpful however to look at each child's work individually and wonder if poor spelling and the supposed poor visual memory attached to it could get in the way of some children's fluency when they read. In other words, does a child's inability to spell the word *again* have anything to do with his inability to recognize the word instantly when he sees it in print? I doubt it does, but I certainly couldn't tell that from reading their writer's notebooks. (I would have to be listening to them read aloud a text that contained words they misspell.)

We can also wonder if some of the teaching-of-reading strategies we offer are less helpful to children who are having great difficulties with spelling. Does it help the poor speller, when confronted with an unknown word during reading, to be asked to look for familiar parts of words or small words inside of big words? Can this student use known words to figure out a new word? Should children who have difficulty reading what they wrote be called upon to read their responses to material read? Of course, the bottom line is, we must help children become better spellers so that they can participate fully in all aspects of classroom life.

Reading their writing closely certainly reminds us how crucial it is to provide sound and explicit instruction in spelling. Of course, noting the patterns of error in their spelling enables us to begin figuring out what children need to know to become better spellers. (I always turn to Faye Bolton and Diane Snowball's *Teaching Spelling, Ideas for Spelling*, and *Spelling K–8: Planning and Teaching* for their expertise in this matter.)

Then too, I wonder if struggling readers would benefit from seeing their writing written in standard form fairly soon after having written it. In other words, when Patrick shows me the notebook entry in Figure 9.10, would it be helpful, after empathizing with him about his painful cut, to ask him if he'd like to see his writing in standard spelling, the way most grown-ups would spell it? (I'd prefer rewriting his words fairly soon after he first wrote them, when he is most likely to remember what he wrote and poor spelling is not apt to interfere with his recall.) He could be shown the following:

> I have a cut on my hand. It stings so badly
> I could yell out loud, "Pick on somebody your
> own size and don't come back!" It feels so bad.

It would be interesting for me to hear Patrick talk about what surprises him when he sees the standard spelling. Of course, I would also point out those spelling patterns which he seems to have down pat, like -and, -out, -ad, -ick, and -ing. I would also like to hear his response to the rewritten passage with respect to the conventions of print. Seeing the correct version might raise his consciousness to standard punctuation.

With respect to the lyrical piece in Figure 9.11, written by Aaron, we don't need a standard English spelling version to be able to read it. Aaron's attempts at spelling bring to mind those younger children who are quite good at invented spelling. He does have a few words written in standard spelling, but he has many more written in the kind of invented spelling we would proudly show off if he were five- or six-years-old. It does surprise us that Aaron, with all the printed text he has no doubt seen in the last four years, still spells the word *use* as "eoos" and the word *done* as "dun."

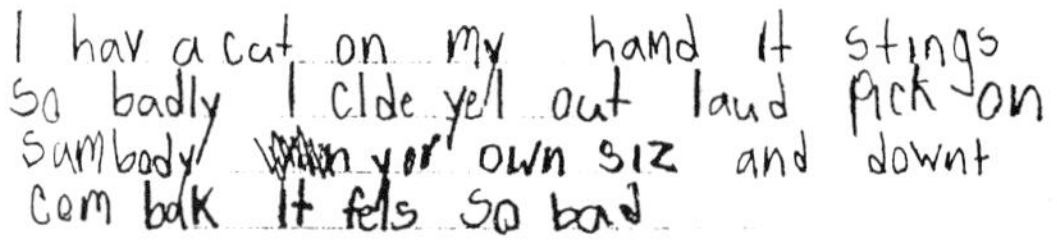

I hav a cat on my hand It stings
So badly I Clde yell out laud Pick on
Sumbody With yor own siz and downt
Com bak It fels So bad

Figure 9.10

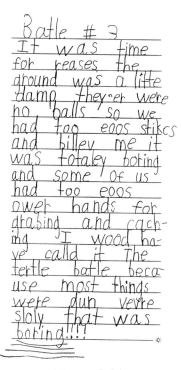

Figure 9.11

One of the big revelations I had as I reread the notebooks of our struggling readers is that so much of what they write is not responded to. After all, we usually only respond to the entries that children select as potentials for publication. Many entries never lead to formal writing projects (pieces that are revised and then edited for publication). I began to see their unused writing as potential teaching material. I could easily imagine using some of Patrick's or Aaron's unused entries as the basis of direct and explicit spelling instruction. (Or I could train a student teacher, literacy volunteer, tutorial teacher, or special needs teacher to do likewise.) Imagine if once a day, a fluent speller shows them their own writing in standard spelling and suggests the spelling features they each need to learn and how to learn them. The boys would not only grow as spellers but as readers of their own writing. (See *Writing Through Childhood* for additional thoughts on the teaching of spelling.)

Writers Can Demonstrate a Lack of Clarity

Some of our struggling students wrote in ways that can best be described as skimpy, lacking clarity, fluency, and specificity. They have not as yet learned that writers must answer their readers' questions. The entry in Figure 9.12, written by Jorge, represents this kind of writing.

As stated previously, many of the entries in student's notebooks never get responded to. Here again, I wonder if we aren't missing out on some important teaching

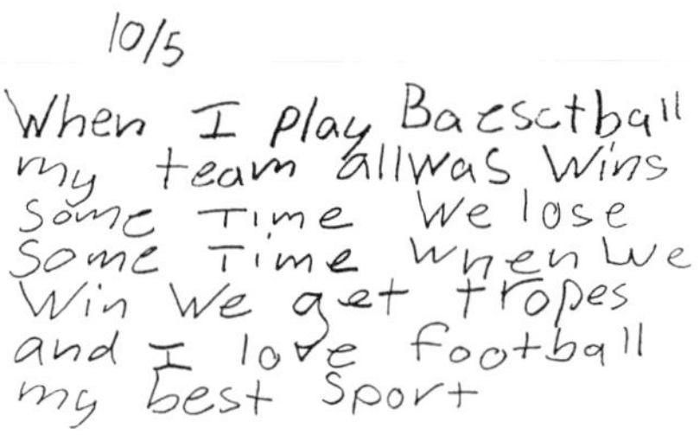

10/5

When I play Baesctball
my team allwas Wins
Some Time We lose
Some Time When We
Win We get tropes
and I love football
my best Sport

Figure 9.12

opportunities. Perhaps if we put away our teacher-of-writing hat for a time and don our teacher-of-reading one, we might use these brief entries as points of departure for reading instruction. Certainly children who understand the importance of clarity of thought when they write will expect the same in their reading and will then be able to monitor their own lack of comprehension when they read.

I have the urge to put two hands on Jorge's shoulder, even though he might not choose to revise his piece toward publication, and say, in my kindest, most nurturing voice, "Jorge, I am the reader of your words and I don't understand what you're saying. How can you *always* win and yet *sometimes* lose? What are you really trying to say? How can you make your meaning clear?" Not only will I be demonstrating that readers expect texts to make sense, I will be offering Jorge strategies for making his meaning clear (modify language, add examples, reorder sentences, etc.).

Similarly, when Jorge writes the short entry in Figure 9.13, he should be pushed to become a better reader and writer. Jorge needs the teacher who is willing to say, "Do you mean 'when' or 'then' in the second part of the sentence?" If he means "when," he needs to finish his thought. If he meant to write "then," the piece is very skimpy. He needs to be asked, "What are you thinking about here? Do you want your readers to understand something? If yes, what is it you want the readers to appreciate about your day?" Jorge needs to expect text to make sense, whether it's the text he reads or the text he writes.

So too, when I read the entry written by Jessica, in Figure 9.14, I don't want to simply pass it by. I want to let Jessica know why her meaning is not as clear as it could be for her reader. I want her to learn to reread her work, looking for missing words and incomplete or skimpy thoughts.

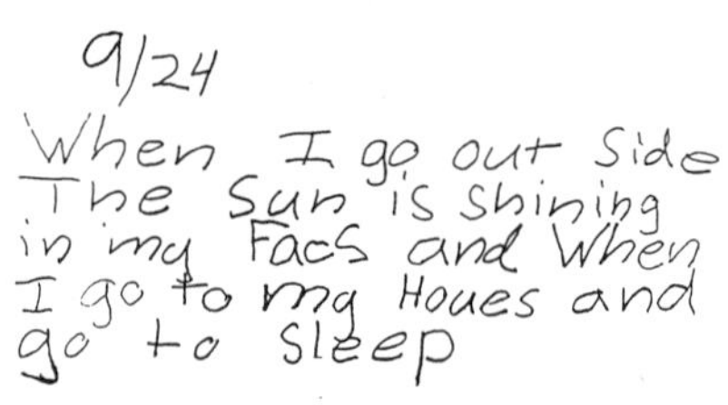

9/24

When I go out Side
The Sun is Shining
in my Facs and When
I go to my Houes and
go to sleep

Figure 9.13

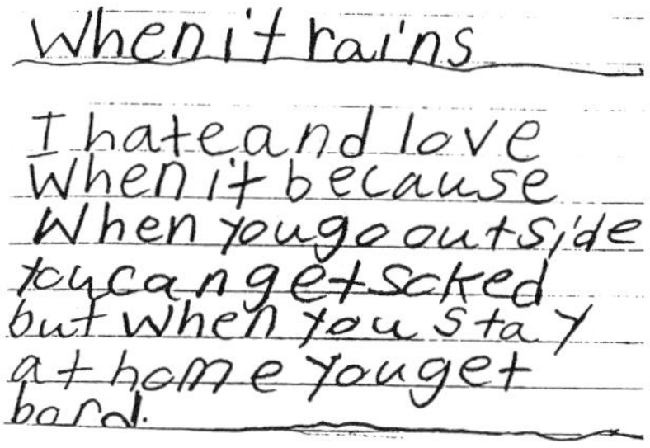
When it rains

I hate and love
When it because
When you go outside
You can get sceked
but when you stay
at home you get
bord.

Figure 9.14

These children have a lot of hard work ahead of them in becoming fluent readers and writers. Teachers need not be afraid to kindly offer the kind of advice and assignment that will send them off in the right direction.

Writers Can Demonstrate Unfamiliarity with Conventions

There is, of course, no guarantee that a lack of punctuation in students' writing means that students don't pay attention to punctuation when they read. We can only get a sense of students' attention to punctuation by once again listening to them read aloud. We learn that some students who omit punctuation in their writing do pay attention to it when they read. And some who usually punctuate their own writing don't always pay attention to punctuation when they read published texts. And then there are those who don't punctuate their own writing and don't pay attention to these important cues to meaning that the author provides. Once again there are no absolutes. But I'm fairly confident that for children who need to pay attention to punctuation when they read, it makes sense to begin by making sure they are punctuating their own writing.

I know that many teachers don't fret too much when children don't pay attention to their handwriting, spelling, or punctuation when they write in their writer's notebooks. But I think they should. I don't mean that teachers should correct student's entries in these pages filled with raw material, but I do think that students should be encouraged to always do their best. How else will students ever have enough occasions to practice the skills they are learning? Children should always be encouraged to reread their work, correcting words that don't look right, filling in words that they omitted, using legible handwriting, and adding the punctuation that makes their work meaningful. I know that I have often explained to students that punctuation is for the reader, that without it, the reader can't appreciate your ideas. But I also think that punctuation in writer's notebooks is for the teacher as reader, peer as reader, and self as reader. Students who struggle with reading and writing often can't reread an old entry because in addition to poor spelling, it lacks any punctuation. There's really no need to include a sample of writing without punctuation here. Unfortunately, most teachers already have ample examples of these.

Writers Can Reveal Weaknesses in Grammar

In some circles, the word *grammar* is treated like a four-letter word. Not so when peo-ple care deeply about language, communication, and literary grace. What's abhorrent to most writing instructors I know is when the teaching of grammar comprises the entire content of language arts instruction or when grammar is taught in isolated skill-and-drill fashion or when children are made to memorize dozens of rules without ever being asked to write.

Sharon Hill shared with me the page from Phil's writer's notebook that appears in Figure 9.15. This fourth grader took notes on the grammatical errors he was hearing in the conversations (and songs) around him. His work is evidence that children can actu-ally enjoy learning grammar.

One day Meggan, our part-time reading teacher, sent me a note attached to the opening page of one of Paula Danziger's popular *Amber Brown* books. The note read,

> Shelley,
>
> *An excerpt which demonstrates the importance of knowing how to read punctuation and more complex sentence structure.*
>
> *This stuff is hard for some kids.*
>
> Meggan

Complex sentence structure is particularly hard for some of our students, because they are learning English as a second language. Our English-speaking children bring their intuitions about English grammar to the task of reading, and therefore are more prepared to handle complex sentence structures. After all, they have been hearing such structures

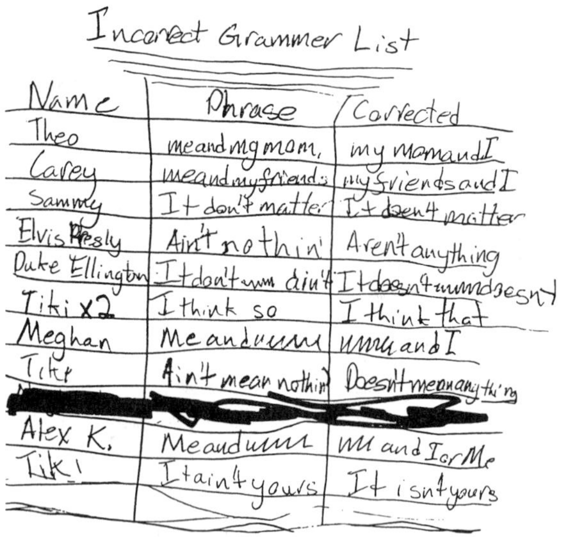

Figure 9.15

and making sense of them all their lives. That doesn't mean that only our second-language learners make grammatical errors when they write. Of course not. All of our English-speaking children make grammatical errors, when they write and when they speak. Of course, some make more than others. (Many of the children listed on Phil's chart are English speaking.) In fact, most of the adults I know make occasional grammatical errors when they speak and when they write. (That's why authors are ever in debt to their editors.)

When reading the notebook pages of my struggling readers, I do discover students whose writing is filled with significant grammatical errors. See, for example, Jessica's entry in Figure 9.16. Granted, this is a first-draft notebook entry, not a revised, edited, and polished work, but the grammatical errors contained in this piece are not ones Jessica would notice or be able to correct on her own had she been preparing this piece for publication.

The question again becomes, "Does having so many grammatical gaps in their writing interfere with their ability to read more complex material? And if so, are there particular ways to be working with children that will provide them with a richer storehouse of grammar learning so that they will be able to tap into that knowledge as they become strategic readers?" Certainly the teachers I know best are not afraid to study students' writing closely and use grammatical assessments to inform their minilessons, influence their choice of literature to read aloud, and suggest topics for individual conferences with students.

For example, I deliberately chose to share Nancy Price Graff's picture book, *In the Hush of the Evening*. First, I read this book aloud to my cluster of third graders to simply enjoy this poetic glimpse of a young boy watching and listening to the arrival of nightfall. Children had ample opportunities to respond to the text as well as the beautiful

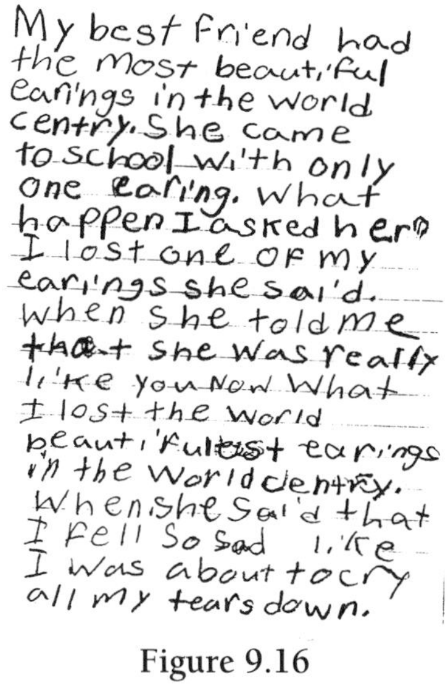

My best friend had the most beautiful earings in the world centry. She came to school with only one earing. What happen I asked her I lost one of my earings she said. When she told me that she was really like you Now What I lost the world beautifulest earings in the World centry. When she said that I fell so sad like I was about to cry all my tears down.

Figure 9.16

illustrations by G. Brian Karas. Later, I displayed several pages on the overhead projector, pointing out that the writer had made it easy for us to read this book, because each group of words (prepositional phrases) is on a separate line, making it easier for us to chunk our words together in the way the author intended. The first page reads,

> In the hush of the evening
> in the last of the light
> at the close of the day
> into the night
> the whippoorwill sings
> his song.
> "Whip-poor-will," he calls
> from the old pine tree,
> "whip-poor-will."

We read the pages aloud together several times and then rewrote a few pages on chart paper, imagining what the text would look like if it hadn't been placed in such poetic form. The students easily understood why commas help the reader. We then pored through the pages of their writer's notebook looking for places where they might have used similar constructions. Students were then on the lookout for more as they read.

(Readers are directed to Connie Weaver's important book *Teaching Grammar in Context* for expert guidelines on the teaching of grammar.)

Writers Can Demonstrate the Power of Literacy Scaffolding

Every once in a while, students discover ways to scaffold their writing. On their own, students choose to write a version of a book they have read, borrow a favorite writer's technique, or lift a pattern from a book or poem they have enjoyed. Sometimes, of course, teachers suggest these kinds of scaffolds in order to strengthen students' language learning and writing abilities. (See the use of templates in Chapter 10, "Loving and Learning Language," and in *Writing Through Childhood*.)

One of the best pieces I discovered in Jorge's writer's notebook was a takeoff on Marjorie Weinman Sharmat's *Nate the Great* books. Jorge's title appears in Figure 9.17.

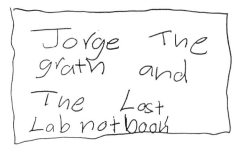

Figure 9.17

Throughout the writing of this short chapter book, Jorge's writing sounded more literary than his usual work because he borrowed such techniques as the classic introductory line, "I, Jorge the Great, am a detective," added a few clues, used dialogue, and had an ending that sounded like an ending.

When children care about a series of books, an author who writes with distinguishing features, or even one book with a distinct pattern, these resources can be considered tools for young readers and writers. (See also *Lasting Impressions,* Chapter 9, "When Mentors Really Matter.") When Jorge tried to write in the style of *Nate the Great,* his writing improved. No doubt, if he is encouraged to continue, his desire to imitate will change and strengthen his future readings of that series. He will be reading closely, looking for more techniques to borrow. He will need to become familiar with conventions of genre as well as conventional language structures. Instead of considering student parodies and takeoffs as copying, I think we need to reconsider their value for children needing safety nets in their reading and writing.

Writers Can Demonstrate the Power of Explicit Challenges

Occasionally when I am reading a stack of notebooks, I come across an entry that sounds vaguely familiar. For example, in one child's notebook I found the words, "The front stoop of my house," followed by a list of some memorable moments. In the next notebook I found the words, "My grandma's house in the Dominican Republic," followed by a series of brief memories. And then in a third, "My dad's shoemaker shop," also followed by a list of some significant gatherings. It became clear to me that the teacher had invited children to write in response to a particular prompt. As is usually the case in our school, the prompt was a piece of children's literature. (In this case it was *In My Momma's Kitchen* by Jerdine Nolen. Details of this minilesson appear in *Writing Through Childhood.*) The teacher had asked the children to do what the author had done, select a place that was important to them and share a few stories connected to that place. Students love the occasional prompt. It gets them thinking about things they had never planned to write about. It gets the juices flowing. And of course, it provides a bit of a scaffolding for some reluctant writers. (See more on prompts in *Writing Through Childhood.*)

I wondered if other prompts, or deliberate challenges (not connected to topics, but techniques), could be used to support children who face particular obstacles when they read. For example, I have seen the following elements cause struggling readers in grades three through five to feel out of control:

- dialogue with frequent interruptions of description or reflection. An example of this is in the opening scene of Louise Fitzhugh's classic book *Harriet the Spy,* which begins:

  Harriet was trying to explain to Sport how to play Town. "See first you make up the name of the town. Then you write down the names of all the people who live in it. You can't have too many or it gets too hard. I usually have twenty-five."

"Ummmm." Sport was tossing a football in the air. They were in the courtyard of Harriet's house on East Eighty-seventh Street in Manhattan.

"Then when you know who lives there, you make up what they do. For instance, Mr. Charles Hanley runs the filling station on the corner." Harriet spoke thoughtfully as she squatted next to the big tree, bending so low over her notebook that her long straight hair touched the edges.

Some of the struggling readers I work with seem to have a hard time holding onto conversations when so much information about the setting and characters are interspersed between the remarks.

- dialogue without any "he said" or "she said" added. (This can also be illustrated using a passage from *Harriet the Spy:*

> You keep a notebook?"
> "A notebook?"
> Well, don't you?"
> "Why?"
> "Answer me, Harriet." It was serious.
> "Yes."
> "What did you put in it?"
> "Everything."
> "Well, what kind of thing?"
> "Just . . . things."

Some students have difficulty following conversations when no names are attached to the speakers.

- out of the ordinary flows of time, including flashbacks and quick jumps ahead. Some students expect the stories they read to be just like the stories they write, with straightforward beginnings, middles, and endings all moving along at the same pace. In other words, no parts get speeded up or slowed down, and certainly nothing appears out of chronological order.
- stories that seem to start in the middle of the action (the ones that take you a while to get a handle on what's happening). An example of this is the opening of Ben M. Baglio's *Animal Ark:*

"How exciting!" said Mandy's mom, Emily Hope. "They're going to make a film at Bleakfell Hall."

Dr. Emily was busily reading the morning's mail over breakfast. She stuffed the letter back in its envelope. Breakfast at the Hopes' busy veterinary practice, Animal Ark, was always a hurried affair. Fruit, juice, cereal, low-fat yogurt as Dr. Adam was on a diet . . . toast if you were lucky. All eaten at a huge old pine table in their oak-beamed cottage kitchen.

Mandy dragged her eyes away from her last minute studying for a biology test that morning.

Texts like this one are difficult for many struggling readers because the reader has to be willing to read on without being sure of exactly what is happening. The reader has to be asking, "What is Bleakfell Hall? Who sent the letter and why? Are the mother and father both veterinarians? Why is it a hurried place? Is Mandy a teenager (since she is studying for a biology test)?" and so on.

How much easier this book would become (and necessarily more bland), if the students were given a few straightforward introductory sentences. For example, "Mandy lives with her parents Emily and Adam Hope, who are both busy veterinarians. Some filmmakers want to use an old house in their town to make a movie." If these remarks preceded the opener "How exciting!" said Mandy's mom," children who are not as yet accomplished readers might have a way in to the text. Mind you, I am not advocating that books start this way. I'm only offering these examples as a way to illustrate one reason struggling readers meet a brick wall. Our job of course is to figure out ways to help them become active readers with strategies for making sense of cloudy texts.

- use of italics or other font changes to indicate exaggeration, emphasis, or sarcasm. An example is in this bit of dialogue, also from *Harriet the Spy*:

  "*You* will make a *wonderful* stalk of celery."
  "What? Said Pinky stupidly.
  "And *you*"—she pointed to Harriet—"are an ONION."

  Students who don't understand or pay attention to these clues often miss the humor or subtleties of a situation.
- very long, winding sentences with lots of commas. Our example, again, is from *Harriet the Spy*:

  Now, also at this very moment, on the other side of town, over here past the gas station, almost to the mountain, the robbers have stopped at a farmhouse which belongs to Ole Farmer Dodge.

  Similar to the issue raised in the grammar section above, some students seem to get lost in these mazelike sentences.

I have begun to help students become familiar with the above elements by engaging them in written exercises. (I make it very clear to the children that I am asking them to take part in these exercises in order to help them become strategic readers. I want to be sure the children don't think of these assignments as mere busywork.) After showing a few examples of these elements from appropriate books (ones the students *can* read), I challenge the children to do as these writers have done. For example, I have asked students to create dialogue without using "he said," or "she said" phrases. (Of course, I attempt to create one of my own as well.) We then place the conversations on the overhead projector and talk about the strategies we use to figure out who was talking. These include paying attention to the indenting, rereading to catch the alternating pattern of speakers, understanding characters well enough to realize who would say what, and so on. I can similarly ask children to think of a reason to use italics in their writing, create long, winding sentences, interrupt dialogue with descriptive sentences, and so on. Students seem to feel less threatened by these "more sophisticated" writing techniques in the books they read because they have attempted to use them in their own writing. (See test sophistication section for additional writing exercises directed toward test taking.)

Writers Can Demonstrate Labored Efforts

It is surprising to see the disparity among the quantity of writing done by children who are in the same class and offered the same amounts of time to write. Are some children *not* attempting to write during these times, for one reason or another, or are they *on-task*, but their process of coming up with words and thoughts, spelling those words or forming those letters is a painfully slow one? It would be particularly helpful if all students were required to date their writing, even when they continue an entry over several days. In that way, teachers could see how much text is actually produced within each writing workshop. Of course, there is no contest to produce large quantities of writing, but it is important to note which children are working in particularly slow ways. We then need to wonder about the pace of their reading. Are they reading too slowly to hold onto meaning? Is the text too difficult and therefore the reading necessarily labored and slow?

Writers Can Reveal Low Self-Esteem

Then too, as we read children's writing we need to be aware of any affective issues that arise and we need to address them. Here, I am particularly concerned with issues of self-esteem attached to their struggles as a reader. For example, we need to be sure that children are not being teased because they need to work extra hard on their reading. In fact, in a classroom with no labeling of children, no public announcements with respect to which children are reading from which basket of books, and absolutely no homogeneous grouping, students shouldn't be particularly aware of different children's reading abilities. (Children always seem to know who the good spellers are because they learn who to go to for help, but I've rarely heard our students talk about who the good readers are.) If a school downplays competition, other students' reading abilities should not be a topic of conversation.

In our school, I'm more concerned about children who are beating *themselves* up because they are finding learning to read such hard work. We must be ever on the lookout for student's negative thoughts about themselves as readers and we must respond to them.

Seven-year-old Hallie made great strides as a reader in second grade, but as shown in Figure 9.18 still had concerns about herself as a speller, and necessarily as a reader of her own writing. We need to be sure to talk to Hallie, building her confidence that she will become a better speller in time. We must also pay tribute to all the wonderful writ-

Figure 9.18

ing that she does and share our hope that writing will always make her feel special. We must also compliment her because she has learned to use writing to share her honest feelings.

Using Student Writing as a Means of Professional Growth

In Chapter 7, "Professional Growth in the Teaching of Reading," I explore many ways for teachers to become better teachers of reading. The one I saved for this chapter is the opportunity for teachers to pull together and study student writing as a means of gathering insights into students as readers and designing teaching strategies accordingly.

Teachers can be asked to bring to staff meetings, grade-level meetings, or small study groups the writing of children who struggle as readers. As they tell the stories of these youngsters, they can share selected pieces from the students' folders, portfolios, or writer's notebooks. Colleagues can be asked to look for clues as to what might be getting in the way of children's progress as readers. The questions outlined on page 319 can serve as a starting points for teacher discussions, as can the questions that follow. All are intended for teachers who are determined to think through wise ways to learn from and employ student writing to strengthen students' reading abilities, as well as their own abilities as teachers. (Teachers, of course, will develop their own insights, make their own discoveries, and follow their own lines of inquiry).

1. Does reading student writing teach us some of what we need to know about our students' background knowledge, ease with English vocabulary, and familiarity with literary language ("Once upon a time," "Happily ever after," and all the "stuff" in between)?

2. Does reading our student writing provide evidence that our students reread their own writing? Does this have any connection to rereading the writing of others?

3. What forms of shared writing (teachers and children writing together) would make sense in the early-childhood classroom? (In addition to writing a version of a predictable text together, with teacher as scribe, what other forms might shared writing take? How do these benefit beginning readers?)

4. What forms of shared writing would make sense in an upper-grade classroom? (Does the teacher have to be in on the writing or can clusters of students collaborate on their own? What would they be asked to produce? How would these benefit readers?

5. How might dialogue journals be used to support the struggling reader? (See Chapter 1, "Designing the Literary Landscape.") What other kinds of interactive writing can we design? (Note: I am using the term *interactive writing* here not as a form of shared writing in the early-childhood classroom, but to refer to ways that two people can interact with one another through the written word, such as through dialogue journals, as opposed to collaborating together on a piece of shared writing.) How might these interactions support readers?

6. Are there powerful ways to use students' writing as reading material for other students? (In guided as well as shared reading? In reading-strategy mini-lessons?)

7. Are there ways we could use the old "language experience charts" (in which teacher records students' comments about a shared experience) to promote more student growth as readers?

8. Are there strategies that would be particularly advantageous for a student who is reading material off the computer screen ? (For example, would the flexibility of being able to physically separate texts into chunks be of help to some readers?)

9. Is there ever an occasion in which scribing for children would support their growth as readers? (For example, would it help to scribe very reluctant writers' stories and use them as reading material, or record older students' responses to text and give them the notes to analyze?)

10. What sorts of writing do fluent readers do to make sense of texts that upper-grade teachers could demonstrate (writing in the margins, recording questions, copying critical lines, etc.)?

The Place of Test-Sophistication Materials in the Elementary Classroom

The Manhattan New School is a regular New York City public school and as such our students must take all required standardized tests. As suggested in the letter to families included on pp. 261–263 and in Chapter 6 of *Going Public,* we try to keep these tests in perspective. There was a time, in fact, when we had absolutely no test-sophistication materials in our school. My colleagues convinced me that we really must have some, as children deserved a chance to become familiar with the format before taking the standardized reading tests. Once we ordered some and our children did well on the tests, it was perceived that those materials were essential to their success. Teachers took comfort in knowing that they had shown students samples of what the tests look like and had shared well-thought-out tips for taking the tests. (Upper-grade teachers periodically brainstorm the test-taking tips they offer students.)

Teachers continue to prepare children for test taking, but they do so at reasonable times of the year. Booklets are stowed away until the not-so-merry month of May rolls around. (Tests in New York City have recently been spread out between January and June, so now *several* months aren't so merry. Children do not think of test-preparation reading as real reading. And this is as it should be.)

I have come to understand the need for test-preparation booklets, but I still wince when I have to sign purchase orders for them. There are so many more important ways to spend our limited dollars. But when I realize how much taxpayer money is spent on the production, distribution, grading, and analysis of those standardized tests, I realize that my discomfort is misplaced. It's the tests, of course, that cause me pain, not so much the practice booklets. Still, to this day I can't bring myself to use commercially produced test-sophistication materials with my third-grade readers. Instead, I write my own.

I have looked at those little passages and the often inane questions that accompany them and, as if I were studying a new genre, I attempt to do what the writers of those materials are doing. In essence, I crawl inside those texts to figure out how they are constructed. So a few weeks before the reading test, the children in my tutorial group work on some of the materials that follow. (I highly recommend that teachers attempt to write their own test samples, as it will help them realize what children need to do to select the right answers. Teachers will become well-versed in effective test-taking strategies.)

The following passage was inspired by the line "Bullies and big dogs have a lot in common," from a Richard Margolis poem that appears in *Writing Through Childhood.*

Bullies and Big Dogs

Alex was the schoolyard bully. Whenever Jesse walked by, Alex called out bad words. Jesse was scared, but he tried not to show it. He thought, "If Alex knows I'm scared, he'll really give me a hard time." Jesse was afraid of Alex in the same way that he was afraid of big dogs. Whenever he walked by a big dog, he also tried to look brave. "Bullies and big dogs have a lot in common," thought Jesse. "If you look scared, they will probably attack.

Sample test questions related to this passage appear below.

  1. Another good title for this story would be
     A. Bad Words at School
     B. Schoolyard Games
     C. Alex and Jesse
     D. Looking Brave
  2. Jesse pretends to be brave in order to
     A. be a bully
     B. scare Alex
     C. stay safe
     D. call out bad words
  3. What Jesse will probably do next is
     A. attack a big dog
     B. play in the schoolyard
     C. keep acting brave
     D. tell on Alex
  4. In this story, Alex
     A. attacks
     B. walks dogs
     C. bullies
     D. acts brave

I read about eggcup ice-cream sundaes in Rosemary Wells's picture book *Night Sounds, Morning Colors*. I have no idea where the image of a mother bribing her children to eat their dinner comes from, certainly not any family history that I can recall. But this idea informed the following sample passage.

A Just Dessert

The children didn't finish their dinner. Margaret left over her spinach. Jonathan left over a slice of meatloaf. Their mom was very disappointed. "I don't like to throw out food," she scolded. "And I worry that you two don't eat healthy meals."

"Please finish your dinner," she continued. Margaret and Jonathan tried to eat a little more, but their mother wasn't satisfied. "Just a little more," she began to tempt them," "and I'll give each of you an ice-cream sundae for dessert!"

Margaret and Jonathan each swallowed one more bite. Then their mother walked in with two tiny eggcup sundaes. Now it was the children's turn to be disappointed.

The test questions for this passage follow.

1. Mom offers the children ice-cream sundaes to
   A. disappoint them
   B. encourage them to eat more
   C. use up her eggcups
   D. help them gain weight
2. Another good title for this story would be
   A. Ice-Cream Treats
   B. Dinner Disappointments
   C. Staying Healthy
   D. Throwing Out Food
3. What will Margaret and Jonathan probably do next?
   A. eat their sundaes
   B. throw out their sundaes
   C. wash the dishes
   D. eat more meat and vegetables
4. In this story, who did the scolding?
   A. Margaret
   B. the mother
   C. Jonathan
   D. the children

Although this passage may in some ways be distasteful (we don't want to highlight parents who bribe their children to eat and then trick them), it did lead to lots of class discussion. Not only did it add spice to a dreary test-taking session (one child thought that as a choice for number three I should have included "vomit"), the discussion helped me to see that sometimes children select the wrong answer because they choose what they personally would do, not necessarily what the characters in the passage would do.

In addition to crafting passages and composing test-like questions to accompany them, there are other ways teachers can use writing to improve students' abilities to take tests. We can pay attention to the kind of questions that seem to throw our most struggling readers and then design writing tasks that help students figure out how those often tricky questions work. For example, many of my third-grade readers have difficulty selecting the one big idea in a passage, the main message intended. (These questions often begin with "What the author is trying to say here is . . ." or "The main idea of this story is . . ." or "Another title for this story could be . . .") In order to strengthen their ability to see that the details, events, or anecdotes in a story should add up to this one overall idea, I begin with big ideas and ask students to imagine what a well-written story might sound like if the writer wanted you to get this one big idea. I selected a few one-liners from H. Jackson Brown, Jr.'s *Wit and Wisdom from the Peanut Butter Gang: A*

Collection of Wise Words from Young Hearts. For example, one line reads, "Being a good friend is a twenty-four-hour job." I asked the children, if this were the big idea in a story (the message the author intended to prove; the right answer when you have to select a choice on a test), what kinds of information would you expect to find in the story? We began playing with these ideas orally. It took a lot of talking for these struggling readers to realize that the story would most likely show a situation in which people had to call upon friends for lots of reasons throughout the day.

We did the same with other words of wisdom from the collection, such as, "When you are sick, friends can sometimes be a better medicine than the kind the doctor gives you," and "You should never tell your friends your parents' nickname for you or you'll never hear the end of it." Eventually I offered a one-liner and asked students to write the story that would precede it. This assignment was difficult for many children. They didn't seem at home making small moments add up to big ideas. Their struggles helped me to understand why they were circling the wrong bubble on the answer documents. Some were selecting the wrong answers because the choices were too similar, with only a very slight difference in meaning, and the children were not used to dealing with such nuances of language. Others had never realized that when you write you expect the reader to walk away with one big thought. The idea seemed rather abstract for many of the students in my tutorial and reminded me to keep asking such questions as the following whenever children show me their writing: "What's the one thing you want your reader to really understand? What's the one thing you want the reader to remember long after they read your piece? What's the one thing you want the reader to hold onto when they walk away from reading your writing?" These questions are good for both writers *and* readers.

It would probably be beneficial for teachers to look at other kinds of test questions that prove difficult for students and try to figure out what kinds of thinking are required by students. They then can create writing challenges that promote these kinds of thinking (e.g., instead of merely guessing what the characters would do next, would students be better at deciding if they had to write a continued passage to the story?) This kind of test preparation is more challenging, but a whole lot less expensive and probably more effective than taking one more sample test.

Reading Requirements, or Informed Recommendations?

Our district is deeply involved in the New Standards work emanating from the University of Pittsburgh and the National Center on Education and the Economy. Lauren Resnick, the lead researcher, and her colleagues have been working toward standards-based reform in our school district as well as standards-based curriculum in our classrooms. Such concepts as "effort-based education," "academic rigor," "accountable talk," and "learning by apprenticeship" have become fairly common in academic discussions in the district. (See *Going Public* for our school's response to this work.) Teachers are expected to teach to the New Standards English Language Arts standards, and our students are expected to participate in the New Standards assessments.

One of the first language arts standards to receive attention was the requirement that fourth graders read twenty-five books a year. The standard didn't seem very high to us, although we have never got into the business of counting the number of books our students read. The standard made me wonder if *I* read twenty-five books a year. I also wondered if the people who created the standard read twenty-five books a year. At any rate, from informally observing the children in our school and talking to my colleagues, I guessed that most of our students were already meeting this standard. Talk flowed naturally to the question, "What books?" I don't think that there should be required reading lists in elementary schools. I don't think teachers should be able to say to a colleague, "You can't have that book in fifth grade; I use it in fourth!" There are just too many great books around to quibble, and besides, rereading is a grand way to grow as a reader.

My district did ask me to chair a literature committee, in the hopes of creating a recommended reading list. I have nothing against recommended reading lists. I love to get recommendations from friends for books that are "too good to miss." *Recommended* does not mean *required.* To that end, the committee met several times and gathered recommendations from many sources (see Chapter 1, "Designing the Literary Landscape.") In the end we produced a bibliography entitled, "Does your library have books by . . . ?" which contained a list of essential authors, rather than titles, for kindergartners and first graders, second and third graders, fourth and fifth graders, and sixth, seventh, and eighth graders. (See Appendix 14.) I am still working on an additional one entitled, "Books that are too good to miss," which would contain specific titles as well as additional bibliographies for poets and nonfiction writers. The first bibliography that was distributed had an explanatory letter attached. In part it read,

Dear colleagues,

We've all seen the buttons that read, "So many books, so little time." Adults who take their own reading seriously never think they have enough time to do all the reading they want to do. That's why so many of us tuck novels into our airline carry-ons, tote paperbacks when we visit doctors with particularly crowded waiting rooms, and make sure that in the event of an unexpected "snow day" we have a great book sitting on our night table. We don't want to spend time on a mediocre read. We want surefire winners. We often count on friends whose tastes in reading we admire. I'm forever asking, "So what have you read recently?" and I'm forever shoving little slips of paper covered with titles and authors into my bag, hoping I'll have these suggestions with me the next time I'm browsing a bookstore or library. (Cyberspace custom-tailored book recommendations make the choices even more daunting.) There are so many books and there is so little time.

I want to fill my reading life with "sweep-me-off-my-feet" books, ones whose story and shape and language remain with me long after I have turned the last page. I long for books that not only make me think about my own life, but ones that make me look at the rest of the world just a little bit differently because of having read them.

And what does all of this have to do with the students we teach, in kindergarten through the high school years? All of the above seems to hold true, whether the reader is five, fifteen, or fifty. There are so many books for children, and there never seems to be enough time during the school day devoted to uninterrupted "just reading." The message seems clear. First, we must carve out as much time as possible for students to read, enough time so that we can guarantee that our students have the experience of getting lost in a really fine book. Secondly, we must surround our students with the best literature available. Students should not be spending precious reading time on mediocre texts. They too deserve surefire winners. Whether we are reading aloud to children, gathering small clusters for guided-reading experiences, providing shared reading material for the entire class, or above all inviting children to choose their own titles during independent reading time, we have to be fussy about the books in our classrooms. When we fill our classroom libraries with books that are too-good-to-miss and we create big blocks of time in calm, comfortable settings, we will be doing our part to raise the kind of students who read when we don't ask them to. We will be educating students who read for pleasure, solace, and nourishment, on weekends, holidays, and summer vacations.

Our literacy goals need to be far-reaching ones. We can't only be interested in our students' scores on standardized reading tests. We can't only be interested in counting the numbers of books students read per year. If we really turn children on to reading and give them the supports described above, the elementary language arts standard of twenty-five books a year will not seem like a lofty goal. There will be no stopping children who see reading as a pastime of choice and value reading as one of life's pleasures. We need to imagine that the students who gather around us on the rug today will be the kind of adults who make regular visits to the public library, join adult book clubs, and who are as envious of their friends who seem to read all the latest books as they might be of the ones who catch the latest movies. We need to graduate students who turn into the kind of adults who tuck books into their carry-ons, and regularly ask their coworkers, "So, what have you been reading?"

Let the attached lists serve as those little scraps of paper covered with friends' recommendations. They are not meant to be required grade-level books. Instead, they are filled with the names of authors who have been well received by many young readers. These writers have written the kind of books you'd like to have on your classroom shelves, so that your students have a rich array from which to choose. These writers have written the kind of books you might like to have a few copies of so that clusters of children might get together to read and form a response group. These writers have written the kind of books you might suggest to family members who accompany children to the public library or the local bookstore. These are the kind of lists you might pass on to students when they ask about summertime reading. . . .

(See bibliography in Appendix 3).

The Use of Benchmark Books: Pros and Cons

When we opened our school I never imagined that we would have to consider such complicated and often controversial notions as promotional policy, national standards, grade-level assessments, benchmark books, and retention. If I had realized that public schools have to deal with so many layers of accountability, I probably never would have unpacked my bags. Be that as it may, I am gainfully employed by the New York City Board of Education and as such have to ensure that our school meets all the regulations.

While there are no required books in our school, we do of course have expectations for the kind of books children should be able to read as they move through the grades.

In fact, for many years small groups of teachers have been making team visits in late May and early June to help their colleagues assess a child's readiness to move on to the next grade. Reading is just one of the factors we consider, but we have never had any formal "benchmark" books in mind. (A benchmark book refers to a book that serves as the bottom line, the bare minimum at which one could consider promotion. If a child cannot independently read an appropriately leveled *unfamiliar* book with 90 percent accuracy, fluency, and comprehension, chances are the child needs more instructional time on the same level.) In the past, a teacher who was puzzled by a particular child's lack of progress would ask for a team visit. The teachers gathered would listen to the child read whatever book felt appropriate, talk to the teacher about such related issues as the child's age, attendance, health issues, work habits, disability concerns, and performance in other school subjects. We would also meet with parents to hear their concerns and then we would decide whether or not this child would benefit from another year at the same grade, usually with the same teacher. We didn't think in terms of failure, we thought in terms of progress.

In order to succeed as a reader, we thought the classroom teacher and the child deserved another year to keep the momentum going. After all, we understood what Holdoway meant when he called struggling readers the "extra-time" kids. Over the years, when we have asked for exemptions from our district's promotional policy (and we did so quite frequently), we did so with our eyes wide open, with optimism in our hearts and minds. And the children who have remained with us for an extra year have been most successful. They left well prepared for the rigors of middle school, their self-esteem intact. (We are not a school culture in which children are made to feel inadequate when they need extra time. It is out of respect for our students that we believe we are doing a disservice if we promote children who are not ready for bigger challenges. I would worry about the self-esteem of children who enter middle school unable to read all the material they will be expected to read. Once our district restructured, and our sixth graders were moved to middle school, we really felt the shortage of time.)

I can't stress enough that *many* factors go into our decision about promotion. We are not bent on labeling children "holdovers." It would probably be more sensible and less stressful, in fact, if it became common knowledge that in our school there is an early literacy block, from kindergarten through grade two. Some children take the three-year path and some take the four-year path. We are currently rethinking the information we share with parents early on, so that they know such a possibility exists and that there is no stigma attached to children who take the longer route. (It's always interesting to me that children who have attended posh private nursery and kindergartens and then transfer to our school enter at a later age. In other words, if a child attends private school they are usually six years old in kindergarten and seven years old in first grade. No one thinks anything is wrong with these children. They have been in preschool programs for several years, just taking a longer route.)

This past year, with our district's involvement in the New Standards movement, coupled with our chancellor's recent stand against social promotion, we were called upon to actually choose benchmark books to share at an upcoming principal's meeting. The process was a long and arduous one, and led to quite heated professional conversations. If the district hadn't asked, it would never have occurred to us that we should pick specific titles to be used to determine if a child is ready to move to the next grade. The process had definite pros and cons.

The Benefits of Benchmark Books

We always believed that we had shared expectations in reading as children moved up the grades. Selecting benchmark books helped us to "put our money where our mouth is." We realized we had in fact different grade-level expectations among staff members, within grades, and between grades. Although we agonized over choices, trying to discover benchmark books in the long run has worked toward building consensus. Everyone is clear about what we are hoping to accomplish by the time a child leaves this elementary setting.

The process of choosing the benchmark books in a school community is quite a conversation starter. Be prepared to go off on lots of tangents. The notion of having benchmarks led to talk about such big and controversial issues as the assumption that all children should read by the end of first grade, the need for lower class size, intervention possibilities, the assumption that all children will be fluent readers by the end of third grade, standardized testing, promotional policy, as well as the need to disagree graciously with your colleagues. In fact, after one particularly spirited meeting I sent a letter to my colleagues which in part read,

> *Our last staff meeting was a most difficult one and we will no doubt come up against many more controversial issues. My hope is that we can approach difficult issues with the same generosity of spirit as when we talk about a family in crisis, kvell over a child's piece of writing, celebrate a colleagues' publication, marriage, or new baby, or swap schoolhouse stories. We must ask of ourselves what we demand of our students. I have a framed quote hanging on my wall. It reads, "Separately, we are as fragile as reeds and as easily broken. But together we are as strong as reeds tied in a bundle." We need to remain strong as a school community.*

The actual choice of texts to be used as benchmark books can also make for lively staff discussions. To prepare for our first meeting I left a form in the staff room asking for possible benchmark titles. It read

Benchmark Possibilities

At the end of grade 1, in order to move onto grade 2, children should be able to read . . .

TITLE   SUGGESTED BY

_____   _____

_____   _____

_____   _____

_____   _____

The same request was made for each grade as follows:

At the end of grade 2, in order to move to grade 3, . . .
At the end of grade 3, in order to move to grade 4, . . .
At the end of grade 4, in order to move to grade 5, . . .

We then made overheads of sample pages from each of the books that were suggested and discussed them at our meeting. Each time we discussed a title, we talked about such readability factors as word choice, sentence length, amount of text, genre, sentence structure, the presence of picture clues, accessibility of topic, cultural bias, and the quality of the writing. We discussed the advantage of using books that had a contained episode within each short chapter so the child could read aloud an entire meaningful text. We talked about the difficulty of choosing a text set in a different time period, such as *The Boxcar Children,* due to possibilities of outdated language. We talked about books that would be too dependent on familiarity with middle-class lifestyles such as the *Amber Brown* books. We talked about the pros and cons of using a book from a series as a benchmark book. Are children too familiar with them, or would they provide a helpful instructional suggestion for next year's teachers?

If I had to initiate this conversation again I would ask every teacher in grades one through five, to answer the following *two* questions:

1. What is the bare minimum kind of book you would like students to able to read when they *enter* your grade? (All teachers except grade one could answer this, since many of our children first learn to read books in grade one.)
2. What's the bare minimum kind of book you would like students to be able to read when they *leave* your grade?

I think asking each teacher to have bare minimums on both ends of the grade would help us see the world of possibilities for the children we are most worried about.

We also acknowledged that during each year, the steps children take are not equal ones. In other words, children may take baby steps in first grade, medium steps in second grade, and giant steps in third. Therefore when you look at a timeline of possible benchmark books through the grades, one should *not* expect the books chosen for each consecutive grade level to be equal in increments of sophistication. The benchmark book at the end of first grade may appear fairly easy, the one chosen for the end of second grade may appear to be a bit more than a year's growth in difficulty, and the book chosen for the end of third grade may indicate an even greater amount of growth. Once children catch on to reading, there is often a great growth spurt. Most of our students have internalized reading fluency by the end of grade three, and so they grow by leaps and bounds toward the end of that year and continue to do so in grades four and five.

The use of benchmark books within our familiar structure of team visits also increased the number of children who were assessed by a group of colleagues. In fact, team members now read with *every* child who was recommended to attend our district's extended-year literacy program (summer school). We no longer just read with children about whom teachers had promotional questions. A team of familiar faces, the teachers in our own school, evaluated every child who was struggling in reading. I took part in these team visits, and as principal it was reassuring to know that I was now personally aware of all the children who needed extra support. If schools are to meet the needs of all their students, there should be no surprise strugglers in the community.

The use of benchmark books eliminates the possibility of retention being random, idiosyncratic, or whimsical. The decision is a serious one and has implications for all teachers, parents, and classmates. Of course, the classroom teacher plays the major role in describing the circumstances having to do with a child's growth as a reader, and the reading of one book will never be the sole deciding factor, but it does promote equity to know that we have a consistent lens and a consistent procedure for thinking through expectations and promotional policy in our school. (We of course promote struggling children whose life story indicates that promotion is the judicial thing to do, but those children enter the next grade with our safety nets well extended, the parents well informed, and the instructional plan clearly mapped out.)

The team visits were wonderful vehicles for staff development. How rare it is in a school community for four or five teachers to take the time to read with one child and talk about the child's needs. In retrospect, these visits, the child's reading aloud as well as the discussion that followed, should have been videotaped. This worthwhile footage could be shared at staff meetings and lead to great professional conversations about the literacy instructional needs of the children in our community.

Thinking about benchmark books pushed teachers to rethink the range of books in their classroom libraries. Joanne Hindley Salch sent me the following list of series that are considered easy to read. It was labeled, "Books I'd love to *not* need and I'd be happy to donate."

Mr. Putter and Tabby
Henry and Mudge
Lionel series

M&M

Nate the Great

Pinky and Rex

I Can Read

Joanne explained to her colleagues that if *too* many third graders were at such beginning-reading levels as these books indicate, she would have to rethink her whole-class instruction. She would need to spend more time on shared-reading experiences, bring back the Big Books, and rethink the reference materials she has gathered for her student's social studies inquiry projects. She can tend to the needs of reasonable numbers of struggling readers within the time she has allotted for small-group instruction and individual conferences. She can additionally provide for small groups of children through the wise use of student teachers, volunteers, and schoolwide support services. Her colleagues agreed and the conversation turned toward placing reasonable numbers of struggling children within any one class, knowing that classroom registers can move toward thirty at any point in the school year.

When all was said and done, the books listed below (two books for each grade, to improve our chances that children would be unfamiliar with one of the titles) became a starting place for team visits at the end of the 1998 school year. Unfortunately *Nate the Great,* one of the books Joanne would have been happy not to need, became the benchmark book for children leaving second grade and entering third grade. Therefore, Joanne probably needed to keep a few around, since after a two-month summer break children who read this series at only 90 percent accuracy in June (that's still ten errors per one hundred words in a running record), will probably need to begin the year reading similar books. The questions remain for us, "How many children who are reading these bare-minimum benchmark books can we teach wisely and well in any one class?" and "How many children can any one school retain at any one grade level?" The notion of having benchmark books opens up many controversial issues.

Benchmark Choices for June 1998

For first graders entering second grade

Town Mouse and Country Mouse, by Val Biro

Morris Goes to School, by B. Wiseman

For second graders entering third

Nate the Great, by Marjorie Weinman Sharmat

The Growing Up Feet, by Beverly Cleary

For third graders entering fourth

Busybody Nora, by Johanna Hurwitz

Teddy Bear's Scrapbook, by Deborah and James Howe

For fourth graders entering fifth

The Trumpet of the Swan, by E. B. White

Absolutely Normal Chaos, by Sharon Creech

We didn't select any benchmarks for fifth grade, since our district frowns upon retaining any children in their graduation year.

Detrimental Aspects of Benchmark Books

Perhaps the greatest danger attached to benchmark books is that they will be misused. Every child has a rich history, and it would be neglectful to rely *solely* on the reading of one book to assess any child as a reader or as a potential candidate for promotion. We used these books to bring one strand of consistency to the manner in which we assessed our struggling readers and to the manner in which we made promotional decisions. They were particularly helpful in assessing children about whom teachers were undecided.

We were quite flexible at team meetings, more than willing to try alternative books and consider the child's attitude and eagerness to learn to read as well as their emotional state. We did not retain every child who could not successfully read a benchmark book, and we did not promote every child that could. (Additionally, children who attended extended-year programs were reassessed at the end of the summer. Therefore, final promotional decisions were sometimes postponed.)

Another worry connected to benchmark books involves parents' concern over them. I recall visiting children's bookstores in England and seeing titles posted with reading levels alongside so that parents could help their children meet national curriculum goals. We know that whatever books we use in our team visits will not be posted nor used again next year. We do not want well-intentioned family members priming children to read a particular title for a fifteen-minute assessment. I have shown a sequence of texts at parent meetings, demonstrating what makes a text more challenging and suggesting where on the continuum of difficulty we hope most readers will be at different grade levels. Parents need to understand where we are headed and to appreciate that no one book is the be-all and end-all of our literacy work.

I am also concerned that benchmark books will lead to an overreliance on and a glaring presence of leveled books. I appreciate a teacher's need to have a clear sense in mind about what makes a book easy or hard to read. That kind of information is essential for any literacy professional. I appreciate that experts in the field have leveled many books that appear in early-childhood libraries. This too is helpful for the teacher who is determined to get good at matching children with books. (A note of caution however, as a staff we have often disagreed with some published lists of leveled books. Teachers need to use these lists as a starting point and move toward an internalized sense of what makes a book supportive or challenging. See additional information on matching children with books on p. 202.)

My worry is that *students* will become overly concerned with levels of books if this "background information" is publicly displayed. In other words, when books have been assigned a level to support a teacher's ability to match reader and text, that information should be for the teacher's eyes only. Yes, teachers will suggest that children select books from "that basket over there," but the basket need not be labeled level "J" books. As noted previously, my colleagues are disappointed when they spot books with preprinted levels in big bright colors on their front or back covers, and they regularly hide these markings with colorful stickers of their own. I remember the days when students worried that their friends had made it to the purple-edged cards in the SRA kit and they were still on the orange ones. Let's not bring back those days. Let's make sure leveling talk takes place in staff rooms, not in classrooms.

My final concern, perhaps the hardest issue to deal with, involves benchmark books on a grand scale. I am responsible for just one school. The teachers in our school are expert teachers of reading and we pretty much agree on grade-level hopes and expectations. We have a manageable number of children who struggle with reading, and using benchmark books with individual children and having conversations surrounding these assessments is very possible. I can't help but think about settings in which a majority of the children struggle with reading and/or settings in which the majority of teachers are new to the profession.

Does the movement toward benchmark books and national standards mean that the books we selected could be used in schools across our district, throughout our city, or across the country? *Should* they be used in such a way? (Our school's choices for benchmark books were, in fact, distributed to schools throughout the district. Had I realized that the choices I presented at that principal's conference might be used districtwide, I would have spoken more that day about my ambivalence about them and my concerns about their widescale use.) Are schools prepared to retain great numbers of children who don't meet these standards? Can principals across this nation guarantee that if children repeat a grade they will receive effective interventions that will help them grow as readers?

When I think of the use of benchmark books on a very small scale, in regard to the one school I know best, I can understand the challenges before us. No one from the outside gave our professional community the titles to use. We selected those ourselves. No one told us how our team visits should take place. We decided that ourselves. No one told us that Adrianne, who couldn't read with 90 percent accuracy, *must* repeat second grade. After all, those from the outside were not there to see her energy, inquisitiveness, and desire to become a great reader. No one told us that Peter, who couldn't read with 20 percent accuracy, *must* repeat second grade. After all, those from the outside hadn't spoken to his teacher, his parents, and his therapist.

Benchmark books and the notion of having consistent ways to make decisions about children works for us because we are trusted by our district to be knowledgeable and to do the right thing. Benchmark books works for us because their use was not carved in granite, but placed in the hands of artists who knew how to work the clay.

When I think of benchmark books on a larger scale, my head spins.

Extending the Lifetime Guarantee to All

This book opens with an explanation of the title *Lifetime Guarantees*. I included my promise to parents that their children will not just know how to read and write, they will choose to read and write. This promise must apply to *all* children. This chapter has addressed the needs of our least experienced readers, those needing all the supports we can wisely provide. It is not enough that these aspiring readers pass the standardized reading test. It is not enough that they read "on grade level." The students themselves— *all* the students—must be part of our dream to graduate children who will choose to read and write, now and forever. Mark Twain is often quoted as having said, "The man who hasn't read good books has no advantage over the man who can't read them." We can likewise say, "The children who don't choose to read good books have no advantage over the children who can't read them." We want it all. We want them to know how to read and we want them to choose to read. We can't settle for anything less.

RELATED READINGS IN COMPANION VOLUMES

Going Public (Heinemann, 1999) is abbreviated as GP. *Writing Through Childhood* (Heinemann, forthcoming) is abbreviated as WC.

Expanding the notion of administrators as master teachers	**GP:** Ch. 2; **WC:** Ch. 4, Ch. 8
Scheduling interventions	**GP:** Ch. 2
Keeping test taking in perspective	**GP:** Ch. 6
Writing original poems	**GP:** Ch. 4, Ch. 5, Ch. 7
Studying student writing	**WC:** Ch. 11
Teaching spelling	**WC:** Ch. 10
Responding to standards	**GP:** Ch. 6
Writing in response to deliberate challenges	**WC:** Ch. 2, Ch. 7
Making professional development a priority	**WC:** Ch. 11

CHAPTER 10

ON LOVING AND LEARNING LANGUAGE

Key Literacy Lessons

1. Our ways of teaching and learning require a commitment to and a fascination with language, all languages.
2. Bilingualism is cause for celebration.
3. We must appreciate that newly arrived immigrants are learning a new way of life, not just a new language.
4. Literature-based, language-rich process classrooms are particularly well-suited to the English-language learner.
5. There are specific structures that support English-language learners including
   - writing workshops
   - read-alouds
   - community service
   - reading workshops
   - hands-on opportunities
   - dialogue journals
6. Environmental print in schools can support the English-language learner.
7. Opportunities to delve deeply into topics of study are beneficial to second-language learners.
8. Some teaching techniques specifically support second-language learners.
9. English-language learners deserve excellent specialized second-language instruction.
10. Emphasis must be placed on all students' understanding the language-learner's experience.
11. All teachers need continued professional study of second-language learning.
12. Schools must commit to celebrating language and language learning.

I spent one winter break in Mexico City, teaching at a private school. When I returned home, my colleagues asked me about the experience. I eagerly shared what I had learned about the wonderful people, history, culture, and food of Mexico. I then shared two learnings that stood out for me above all the others.

The first took my breath away, quite literally. At this lovely school, there was a high-tech machine located on the roof that measured pollution levels. Each day at lunchtime, the custodian read a computer printout and then hung a flag in the court-yard. If memory serves correctly, a green flag meant that the children could eat and enjoy themselves out of doors. It was okay to play soccer or tag. A yellow flag meant that they could eat and do some moderate activities but no competitive sports. A red flag meant that they could eat outside but nothing more. A black flag meant that the pollution levels were so high, the children had to eat indoors. Folks were always glancing upward to see if the custodian had changed the color of the flag. I learned a great deal about not taking the air we breathe for granted. I also learned not to complain when inclement weather made it necessary to have indoor recesses back home. New York City has many problems, but at least we don't have to remain indoors because of dangerous pollutants in the air.

The second of my big learnings took place away from the school. I was staying with a wonderful family from Texas. Andy, then a fifth grader, attended the school I was working at, studying in English in the morning and in Spanish in the afternoon. One day I asked Andy, "Who is your Spanish teacher?" "Mari," he answered. "Mari?" I asked, not remembering having met any teacher named Mari. "Yes, Marisol, you know, the woman who helps my mom." Andy was talking about the young woman who worked as a domestic worker in his home. "Sure," he continued, "she's the one who has taught me the most Spanish."

In school, Andy received formal lessons in Spanish, conjugating verbs and memo-rizing nouns, but he believed he had learned more Spanish from Marisol. In my week's stay, I began to understand why. I watched as Andy and Marisol baked a dinosaur cake together for a younger child's birthday. I watched them play cards together after dinner. I watched them sort the family laundry, all the while talking and interacting in Spanish. Mari didn't know it, but she was a fine second-language teacher.

She was teaching Andy to speak Spanish without following any set sequence of skills or language lessons. Instead, Andy and Mari spent big blocks of safe, secure, plea-surable time together, doing things with real-world payoff. He gets to eat the cake, win an occasional card game, and wear matching socks. Andy did not appear afraid to take risks or make mistakes.

My visit to Mexico had a profound influence on my thinking about language and language learning at the Manhattan New School. First, it reawakened my love of lan-guage. I've often thought that my trust in whole language teaching stems from my com-mitment to and fascination with language, all languages. Whole language appeals to me because it so respects the integrity of language.

Secondly, my visit reminded me that being bilingual is cause for celebration. Even though my Spanish is far from perfect, my experience in Mexico was so much richer because I understood the language. Second-language learning has to be a priority for all our students. Speaking a second language has to be viewed as a strength, never a weakness.

Third, I was reminded how hard it can be to feel truly at home in a second language. Attempting to teach in Spanish was a rather humbling experience for me. I majored in Spanish literature as an undergraduate and yet I still felt inadequate. I knew I could not say things exactly as I meant them. I couldn't make jokes, play with language, or use any of the nuances that come to us so easily in our first languages. I found myself settling for expressions I knew rather than saying exactly what I wanted to. My meanings were never quite crystal clear. I thought about all the second-language learners in our school as well as their families in a more respectful light.

Then too, I thought about how we teach our English as a second language students. I thought about why our approach to teaching seems such a perfect fit for children learning a new language, but I also thought about how we could improve our instruction. The instructional implications for all of these realizations follow.

A Fascination with Language and Languages

The minute you walk into our school there are indications that the adults are language lovers. Some of these signs are visual ones, including the posters, crossword puzzles, and cartoons we hang. When I was trying to write the poem for Pam's class that appears on page 103, the one with the refrain, "Two-0-Si̲x, What a Mi̲x!," Neil Donovan, our custodian, borrowed a dictionary and tried to help me come up with additional rhyming phrases. He left a long list of possibilities on my desk. Some were rather difficult to weave into an early-childhood ode, to say the least. They included such words as *appendix, dominatrix, electronics, geriatrics, limericks, lunatics, mystics, metaphysics, obstetrics,* and *plastics*. When loving language is contagious in a school community, everyone joins in on the fun.

Some of the indications that the community loves language can be heard, not just seen. Beginning in kindergarten, children are taught to greet one another in the languages spoken by members of the class. Songs are sung in many languages. Multilingual poems are recited. Teachers choose to read aloud such word-loving books as Monalisa DeGross's *Donavan's Word Jar*. (See *Lasting Impressions* and *Writing Through Childhood* for additional ways to invite children to delight in language.)

Teachers also tell language stories. Some of these stories make us laugh, but most make us marvel. When Fikret, a young child from Albania, announced to Sharon Taberski that his aunt "was going to lay a baby," we didn't laugh. Instead, we were in awe of how aggressive Fikret was as a language learner. He doesn't hesitate. He figures out his own hypothesis about how language works and then he tries out his hunches, eager to learn to speak English well. Similarly, when Jameelah referred to our security guard as a "life guard," we didn't laugh. We appreciated that her misuse of this term was actually quite clever. One summer Elaine Daugherty, a teacher from Kentucky, told me that when she asked her students if they knew the four seasons, one young boy responded, "Squirrel, rabbit, dove, and deer." We may smile when we hear his answer, but that young boy is reminding us that every student views the school experience through his own unique lens. (See *Going Public* for additional language stories.)

We also tell stories about surprising uses of language outside of school. My daughter told me that her professor served raspberry *tort* at the last class in her law school course. I ate in a restaurant in St. Paul, Minnesota, named Table of Contents. I drank coffee in a gourmet shop in Denver and left a tip for the waiter in a cup labeled "Thanks a latte." I shared an article about the high-tech dictionary meanings now attached to such familiar words as *web, mouse,* and *scroll*. I also shared an article from *The New Yorker* magazine by Daniel Radosh in which he outlines how the *Harry Potter* books were edited for American English-speaking audiences. Students were surprised that English children read "barking mad," when American children read "complete lunatic." One of my all-time favorite language stories is about Yogi Berra, who once visited the Yoo-Hoo chocolate drink factory. He answered the phone in an office at the factory, and when the woman on the other end asked, "Is Yoo-Hoo hyphenated?" the baseball great responded, "No, ma'am, it's not even carbonated."

Teachers always share wonderful language stories they discover in the Metropolitan Diary section of *The New York Times*. There, city dwellers send in telling vignettes of life in the Big Apple. One resident brought placemats to the dry cleaner, explaining to the clerk that they needed to be dry-cleaned because they were wool and came from Wales. The clerk expressed surprise upon learning that wool came from *whales*! Another writes of sitting in an airplane on the runway at La Guardia airport for several hours due to inclement weather. Refugees from Kosovo were also onboard but unfortunately couldn't understand the explanation that had been given for the long delay. Flight attendants asked if anyone onboard spoke the language of the distressed family. The writer then used her cell phone to call her own apartment building in Manhattan, remembering that several ethnic Albanians were working there. She explained the situation to the workers, handed the phone to the mother from Kosovo, and there lies the happy ending.

When I worked in Durango, Colorado, I bought a set of blocks that paid tribute to Roy Rogers. The blocks spelled out, "Happy Trails." I keep them on a ledge in my kitchen. Whenever my grown children visit they can't resist rearranging them. One day the blocks read, "Al's hip party," another time, "L papaya shirt." I heard about a restaurant named Pharmacy, that lost a lawsuit regarding its name brought by the pharmaceutical industry. The restaurant could no longer be called Pharmacy, and so the owners regularly rearrange the letters over the front door. The first week it was called Achy Ramp. Many years ago, one of my students gave me a gag gift of bottled water. It had a long coiled metal spring inside and of course brought new meaning to the term *spring water*. I've eaten in Chinese restaurants with friends who insist on adding the refrain "in bed" to the end of all our fortune cookie messages. There's an anonymously written poem entitled "The Budding Bronx," in which the poet pokes fun at the New York accent. It reads,

> Der spring is sprung
> Der grass is riz
> I wonder where dem boidies is?
>
> Der little boids is on der wing
> Ain't dat absoid?
> Der little wings is on der boid!

There are all kinds of ways to play with language.

Literacy educators need to find all aspects of language and language learning interesting and to invite children and parents in on the fun. Several years ago, I sent the following letter home.

Dear families,

Part of what it means to be a "whole language" school is to demonstrate a commitment to language, all languages, and a fascination with language, all languages.

It is no surprise, therefore, that Carmen is teaching Spanish as a second language, Dawn has displayed poetry from many of the countries our children call their first homes, and our second-floor stairwell is home to our language board, enabling all of us to get to know the fortunate bilingual students in our school.

It is also no surprise that our students and teachers in their reading and writing workshops spend so much time reading aloud and performing the lines, poems, and passages they love. We love the sounds of words and their arrangements.

Our love of language also makes it easier to teach and learn vocabulary, spelling, and grammar. When you love language, these areas do not become drudgery but delight. When you are fascinated with the story of language, you want to know why mortgage *is spelled with a silent* t. *(The root is from the French* mort, *meaning death.) You want to know why we call the boroughs Manhattan, Staten Island, Brooklyn, and Queens, but add a "the" to the Bronx. (This borough is named after the Bronx family.) You want to know how to choose the most precise word when you're writing. Your character can live in an apartment, a mansion, a cottage, a hut, a hovel, a bungalow, a ranch, a duplex, a townhouse, a brownstone, a high-rise, a cabin, and so on . . .*

Then too, lovers of language delight in unusual words, their meaning, spelling and origins. In school you will see us sharing palindromes—words that read the same forward and backward. You've probably heard about "A man, a plan, a canal, Panama." Now read it backwards. We even have a teacher on staff whose name is a palindrome. That's right—Eve.

We also compile lists of acronyms. You've heard the word snafu. *It stems from "Situation normal, all fouled up." I've been told that* tips *has its root in "To insure prompt service."*

You'll also see us figuring out the meanings and origins of idiomatic expressions and figures of speech. Why do we say that grandma has "a green thumb," and grandpa has "an Adam's apple?"

We also devour new books like A Chartreuse Leotard in a Magenta Limousine, *by Lynda Graham-Barber. Did you realize that all of the long words in this unusual title are eponyms or toponyms, words that derive from the names of people or places?*

You could also ask our seniors to give you some "portmanteau" words, two words that have been squeezed together to form a new one. They'll probably explain how the words brunch, smog, *and* spork *were created.*

All this adds up to a strong plug for playing with language, not only at school but at home.

(This letter continued with a passage about language play that appears in Chapter 1, p. 26.)

I ended the letter about language play by inviting family members to read a rebus sent to us by a wonderful visiting principal from California, David Cooper. His joyful tribute to language play appears in Figure 10.1.

When children are surrounded with rich language experiences and are offered endless opportunities to join in, the rewards are great. Just as we don't offer children watered-down texts to read, so too we don't water down our conversations. I'm quite certain that when I was in elementary school I never even heard the words *manipulatives, revisions,* and *portfolios,* let alone was able to discuss their meaning and utilize the tools and strategies connected to each.

When adults demonstrate a fascination for language, children catch the spirit. They too become interested in the history of words. I wouldn't be surprised to hear our students ask about the curious title *M*A*S*H* if they were watching reruns of the show on television. And when we tell them it's an acronym, they will understand that term and be eager to guess what word each initial stands for. Similarly, I wasn't surprised when Jameelah sent me the note shown in Figure 10.2.

Then too, our students pay attention to lyrical lines. I wouldn't be surprised to hear them delight at discovering that their new crayons are labeled "candy-apple red," "leap-frog green," and "sunshine yellow."

All members of our community find English interesting, and we make sure that this love of language applies to *all* languages. When I travel I always look forward to making language discoveries. How many American tourists have taken photographs of the "Schmuck" signs in Vienna? (The word means jeweler.) I've spent several summers working in Sweden. My friend Anne Boglind, a Swedish author and staff developer, told me that when McDonald's first arrived, the teenagers wrote about "handburgers" in their journals. I was also struck by some very small differences in language. When Swedish children get hurt, they don't scream, "Ow!" they call out, "I-I-I." When some Swedes want to agree with you, they don't merely nod their heads and murmur, "Uh-huh." Instead, they suck in their breath, making a sort of gasping noise. (It's most disconcerting the first

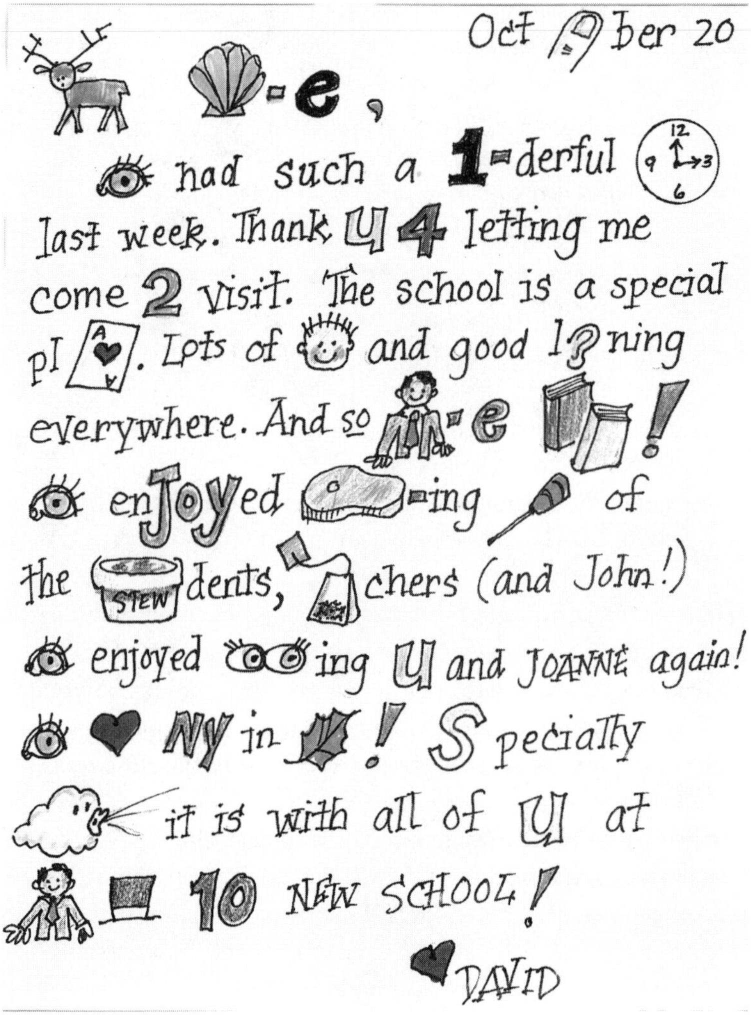

Figure 10.1

time you speak publicly and the audience gasps. You think you've offended people, when in actuality they are showing support.)

Fortunately, I don't have to travel to make language discoveries. I was delighted when a Bulgarian father corrected the spelling of the family name on our language board. "It's Tegov for my son Alexander," he explained, "But Tegova for my daughter Iliana." When the cover of a children's news magazine showed a close-up of an insect with the caption "Bicho feo?" Carmen, our Spanish teacher, complained that the word *bicho* was culturally insulting to some Caribbean cultures. *Bicho* may be defined in some Spanish dictionaries as an insect, but to Puerto Ricans, for example, the word refers to a part of the male anatomy. The caption on the cover, in essence, is asking if the male organ is ugly! Carmen suggested that the word *insecto* was preferable.

Figure 10.2

Albi, an Albanian speaker, wrote down, "A moony me shcooa in vetse," trying to teach me to say, "May I go to the bathroom?" in his language. I can also marvel at the Macedonian alphabet, view "Hansel and Gretel" in Maltese, and practice all those silent g's in Turkish words. Being surrounded by so many bilingual children reminds us what a gift it is to be bilingual and to continually advocate for second-language teaching and learning.

In January of 1996, fifteen of our students appeared on the cover of the periodical *Scholastic News*. The children were shown offering greetings from Turkey, Mexico, Korea, Macedonia, France, Pakistan, Serbia, Croatia, Benin, Myanmar, Albania, Bulgaria, Hungary, Malta, and the Netherlands. They were being interviewed about the English-only debate that was raging at the time. All our students do learn English, but they know how much we care about their first languages. Maureen Barbieri, writing about our school in *Voices in the Middle* (September 1996), pays us a very big compliment when she says that we are living up to Walt Whitman's notion that our "nation is a teeming nation of nations."

In Figure 10.3 are notes from Tugba (pronounced "Tu-ba," as the g is silent in this Turkish name), who wrote a Turkish translation of her English message, because she knew I'd be interested in both. Figure 10.4 shows a third grader's attempts to write all her classmates' names in Hebrew letters in order for her new classmate Matan to make friends quicker.

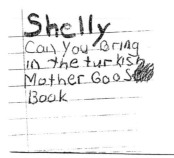

Figure 10.3

English	Hebrew	English	Hebrew
Alexandra		Rose	
Albi		Chelsea	
Alexei		Mina	
Aslan		Sari	
Avram		Lindsay	
Carmen		Millicent	
Chanetta		Joanne	
Gina		Valerie	
Jasmina		Gary	
Kathy			
Lez Lorere			
Mahmet			
Natalie			
Peter			
Ricardo			
Sarah			
Tugba			
Rosa			
Matan			
Billy			

Figure 10.4

Bilingualism as a Cause for Celebration

As previously noted, a language board prominently displayed in our school boasts all the languages spoken as well as the names of the students who speak those languages and the classrooms they are assigned to, just in case a translator or a welcoming committee is needed for a new student.

One day I noticed a ragged-edged slip of paper had been added to the board. There written in marker was the word *Tana* and the name Daniella Hill. This precocious second grader had taken it upon herself to add to the language board the language she had created for her own imaginary world. (Daniella can offer a complete description of the people and customs in the land of Tana. She can even let you hear what the Tana language sounds like.) No doubt Daniella added her own second language because she has learned that in our community, being bilingual is something to be proud of.

Constance Foland, our English as a second language teacher who is also a Reading Recovery teacher and author of *A Song for Jeffrey,* occasionally allows students to invite friends to her small-group sessions. One day Brendan, a monolingual kindergartner, attended and suggested, "I know how to say *bucket* in Irish." "How?" asked Constance. "Pail," Brendan answered. When he discovered that his teacher Pam lived in New Jersey, five-year-old Alexander asked, "Do they speak English there? All our children have a keen awareness of the multitude of languages spoken in the world. The student-made language sign shown in Figure 10.5 was proudly displayed on Julie's door.

Figure 10.5

Our students have come to expect that people will speak several languages. They aren't surprised to see a man of Japanese ancestry introduced on the evening news as the president of Peru or to find out that the leader of Ecuador is of Lebanese ancestry. I don't know how many languages these leaders speak, but our students would guess they are multilingual. Everywhere our students turn in New York City they meet people who speak more than one language. When a cat was missing, in addition to a sign in English, our children spotted "Gato Perdido," and "Chat Perdu." They hear family members talk about the advantages of knowing more than one language. They sense that their teachers are in awe of students who know several languages. They know that we think having speakers of so many languages is a privilege not a problem in a school. They hear their classmates talking in mysterious and exotic ways, and they long to understand what they are saying. In the early years of our school, monolingual parents requested that I hire a second-language teacher. They thought that their monolingual children were at a disadvantage. I couldn't ask for a better reversal in thinking.

Not Just a New Language but a New Way of Life

All teachers who work with second-language learners would benefit from an annual reading of Eva Hoffman's *Lost in Translation,* a memoir written by a Polish émigré to Canada. The author reminds us that many relocated students are learning a new culture along with a new language. As she points out in her poignant and often painful tale, even the milk tastes different to a child in a new land.

After reading *Lost in Translation* I couldn't resist asking my mother to share her own immigration memories. She spoke of the New York City public school she attended in the late 1920s. She remembered being ushered into a room filled with other newcomers and given a bit of broken mirror. The teacher would direct the students to practice sounds, all the while looking into the slivers of mirror to make sure that their lips, teeth, and tongue were in the correct position. When all the sounds were mastered, the children were assigned to classrooms, not based on their age but on their ability to speak English. At age ten, my mother towered over her first-grade classmates.

In my daughter's circle of high school girlfriends, she was practically the only one who had been born in the United States. Hers was a high school filled with immigrant children. Vicky, a close friend from Russia, recalls hearing many questions she didn't understand and her own refusal to admit her lack of comprehension. She clearly recalls interpreting "Are you hungry?" as "Are you a hundred?" and "Are you thirsty?" as "Are you thirty?" Of course her answers were always "No!"

Isabel Beaton, one of our devoted kindergarten teachers, shares the roots of her compassion for second-language learners in the following piece of personal writing.

> It is Graziele's first day of school. Her brother Guiseppi, a year younger, is starting school too. They are wearing their church clothes, their Sunday go-to-mass clothes. Mama points to a group of children walking down the street and says, "Those children are going to

school. Follow those children." The nun at the door speaks but Graziele and Guiseppi don't understand what she says. The nun points back toward the sidewalk and closes the door, leaving the two children outside. Graziele and Guiseppi walk back home and tell their mother that they were not allowed into the school. The next day Graziele and Guiseppi put on their Sunday go-to-mass clothes again. Mama points to a different group of children and says, "Those children are going a different way to school. Follow those children." Graziele and Guiseppi follow the children to school. Again at the door they are met by a woman who speaks words they cannot understand but this time they are permitted to enter. They go to a room, each to a different room. The woman in Graziele's room speaks. Graziele doesn't understand the words. All she can think is, "Where's Guiseppi? How will I find him?" The woman keeps saying crayons, crayons, crayons. Graziele doesn't know what the word means but she knows it must be important. Finally, the bell rings and Graziele goes to the gate. She finds Guiseppi and they walk home. Graziele tells Mama about the word *crayons*. Mama doesn't know what the word means. Papa doesn't know either. The next day the woman in school yells at Graziele. She yells about crayons.

Graziele is my mother. Every first day of school I look at my class of non-English-speaking children and I remember Graziele.

Last summer I began the new school year by sharing an excerpt from Alan Sherman's memoir *A Gift of Laughter*. As a child, he mistook his Yiddish grandmother's mispronunciation of the words "fruit bowl" and thought she wanted a "football." In the end, the story reminds adults that "From a child is beautiful, anything." (The excerpt appears in *Leaving Home,* a collection of stories about personal journeys selected by Hazel Rochman and Darlene Z. McCampbell.) I also made "Must Be the Language Thief," by Stephen Carey in the *Journal of Intercultural Literacy,* required reading. The author suggests in no uncertain terms that "all kids, barring rare physical trauma, enter school with language and plenty of it." I topped off this return-to-school sharing with Kitty Tsui's "Don't Let Them Chip Away at Our Language," from Neil Philip's anthology *Singing America: Poems That Define A Nation.* In this poem the poet shares her grandmother's mispronunciations in English as she lyrically and eloquently lists many of the contributions Chinese Americans have made to this country.

Language-Rich Teaching and Second-Language Learners

Many years ago, Janet Emig, in the *Encyclopedia of Educational Reform,* listed several descriptors about teaching writing as a process. She noted the following:

> *Writing is a process to be experienced.*
> *Writers learn best from attempting whole texts.*
> *Writing is essentially social and collaborative.*

We could easily substitute the word *reading* and the phrase *language learning* for *writing* here. Whether you are talking about first-, second-, or third-language learning, we can state that language learning is a process to be experienced. We can also state that language learners learn best from attempting whole tasks and that language learning is essentially social and collaborative. That's why Andy identified Marisol as his Spanish teacher.

Literature-based, language-rich process classrooms are especially well suited to the second-language learner because there are so many occasions to eavesdrop on and participate in rich natural talk, not the "question-answer, question-answer" banter that was so characteristic of the schools I attended. All day long, in pairs, small groups, and in front of the entire class, children are invited to voice opinions, ask questions, seek clarification, offer criticism, tell stories, and so on. So too, there are many more opportunities to eavesdrop on adult conversations.

In addition, settings like ours are particularly supportive of immigrant children as we are so totally committed to bringing people's stories into the classrooms. As described in earlier chapters, knowing people's stories changes relationships. In a story in *The New York Times* entitled "When War Visits the Classroom in Stories and Pictures" (June 12, 1998), reporter Nicole Christina interviewed our students and their parents who come from what was once Yugoslavia. Upon seeing and hearing all the children's responses to war in their home countries, the reporter wrote, "At many schools, such powerful accounts might be left at the front door. But at the red brick school on East 82nd Street, a wide range of cultures and experiences cross and collide daily. The evidence is everywhere: in the drawing and stories taped on nearly every wall, on a bulletin board displaying more than 30 languages spoken and on the bookshelves, where textbooks have been replaced by popular children's stories written in a host of languages." It's no surprise that a father of two of our students is quoted in the article as saying, "God bless the people at that school. They teach my boys how to grow up normal, not afraid somebody is going to beat them or kill them. I don't want them to know what I know."

In the following section involving best practice, it will become obvious that many of the classroom ways of life that are commonly found in whole language classrooms are well suited to the second-language learner. This should come as no surprise. After all, these teachers know how valuable it is for *all* children to have big blocks of time to engage in safe, pleasurable, and meaningful activities, ones with real-world payoff. Teachers may need to offer the second-language learner a few additional structures, activities, or supports, but a well-organized workshop approach is a fine place to begin.

Structures and Strategies for the Second-Language Learner

Writing Workshop

The writing workshop approach works well for the child learning English. The instruction is individualized. Students are free to choose their own topics and work at their own pace. Writing and illustrating provides students with a means of holding onto memories of their home countries. Children can use drawings to make their meaning clear and are encouraged to share their work in progress. People aren't expected to get it right the first time. Revision is a way of life.

Looking at any one second-language learner's writing can provide helpful insights for working with all second-language learners. Mehmet, for example, was a third grader in Joanne Hindley Salch's classroom. His family emigrated from Turkey and this was his second year in the United States. He worked with our ESL teacher for one mandated period a day and the rest of the time he was a full participant in the life of his class. Figure 10.6 shows several entries from his writer's notebook, a blank journal all the children in his class were expected to keep. (See *Writing Through Childhood* for detailed information on writer's notebooks.) These entries were written in his regular classroom during a daily writing workshop or at home in the evening as part of his regular homework assignment. Most were accompanied by illustrations. His teacher never assigned any topics. The translations below are intended as an aid to meaning.

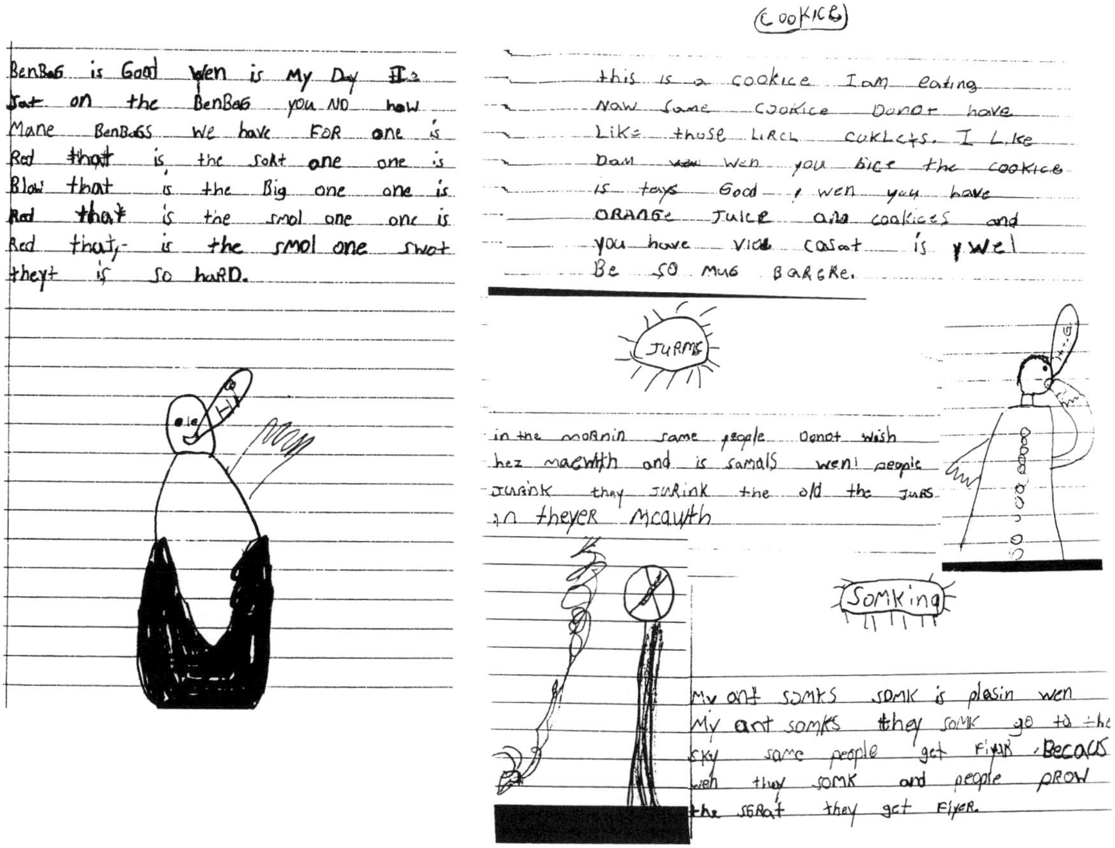

Figure 10.6

coklets = chocolates

mug = much

plaisin = pollution

sgrat = cigarette

viod casaat = video cassette

barere = better

maewth = mouth

samals = smells

benbag = beanbag

jurink = drink

somk = smoke

swot = shoot

prow = throw

It's obvious from reading the pages in Mehmet's notebook that he has many language strengths. We need to begin by marveling at those strengths. (For the full range of examples of Mehmet's writing discussed below, see Appendix 16).

- He has many strategies for coming up with topics. For example, he uses objects in the environment to get himself writing (glue, glasses, beanbag chairs, cookies, etc.). He writes as things are happening in front of him ("I am eating some cookies" "My cat is sleeping"). He taps into old memories (Turkey of long ago). He writes about recent events (the channel-changer breaking; his mom baking cookies).
- He uses illustration to enhance his meaning.
- He uses a wide variety of sentence structures. For example, he asks questions and includes quotations as well as compound sentences.
- He uses a wide variety of writing modes, including poems, narratives, and short expository pieces.
- He includes specific details. For example, there are many descriptors for kinds of noses in his poem. He adds orange juice and watching videos to the pleasures of eating cookies.
- He is reflective, offering opinions and surprising comments about a wide range of topics.
- He picks up on casual conversation. ("Let's say . . . ," "Hey, stop that!")
- He is willing to reveal his emotions. (He wants to be a strong boy. He loves his hands. He feels sad about people dying).

We need to celebrate Mehmet's writing by helping him to have authentic audiences and real responses. For example, we can help him turn his money jottings into word problems to be used by younger students. We can help him turn his comments about behavior into the school discipline code. We can challenge him to turn his Turkish memories into captions for the family photograph album. We can use the conversation about Africa to launch a dialogue journal between Mehmet and a classmate, parent, or staff member.

Then too, we can use his writing to guide us in providing appropriate instruction. In other words, his writing can teach us what he needs to know. We can study his patterns of error and try to understand if they are caused by gaps in spelling, grammar, vocabulary, pronunciation, or unfamiliarity with uniquely American concepts. The writing that second-language learners do must be made available as well to the ESL teacher in order to inform her work.

(Three years later, when Mehmet was a student in Judy Davis's sixth-grade class, he joined me at a principal's conference in which I publicly conferred with students. I was still marveling at what he could do and I was still celebrating his writing and helping him have authentic audiences. A transcript of that conference appears in *Writing Through Childhood*).

Read-Alouds

In every classroom, every day, our second-language-learning students are present when their teachers read aloud. If they are upper-grade students with very little English, they might be listening to a totally incomprehensible chapter book. Periodically, the teacher will ask classmates to retell the story or write up short summaries so that at least the newcomers can participate to some extent in the conversations that surround the texts. Classroom teachers as well will occasionally read aloud the kinds of books that have more entrance ramps for the second-language learner. These would include nonfiction books with lots of visual supports as well as age-appropriate picture books.

Even with the use of well-illustrated picture books, I've realized that some second-language learners don't always participate fully in the group discussions that surround texts. Unless they are particularly gutsy and aggressive language learners, they usually do not raise their hands whenever they need to ask a question or seek clarification. (Just as some of our Asian parents felt ill at ease at our PTA meetings.) Perhaps we need to institute the "Swedish pause," a technique used in Sweden when English presenters are asked to stop talking briefly. This pause enables speakers of the same language to chat in their home language in order to clarify meaning. When a cluster of same-language speakers does not exist within a classroom, we need to create alternate structures to help these students to enjoy the literature along with their classmates.

One day, I asked Joanne what she was planning to read aloud to her third graders that day. Her choice was *Full Worm Moon,* by Margo Lemieux. This picture book is a Native American tale about the earthworms that announce the coming of spring. During her reading workshop time I asked if her second-language learners could come to my office to hear the book read aloud as a preview to Joanne's afternoon reading. I gathered the children and read aloud the text, inviting lots of questions and close study of the illustrations. The small group of children, five in total, was able to touch the pages, pointing to things they wanted to ask about. I wrote any new words on a wipe-off board and additional words that came up in our conversations. That day I learned about springtime, backyard gardens, and animal life in Bulgaria, Turkey, Santo Domingo, Albania, and Korea. I also answered many questions about the history and life of Native Americans. I know the children spoke a great deal more because they were in a very small group and had fewer concerns about their limited English. That afternoon I watched as Joanne read the story to her whole class.

For the small second-language group, her reading was a rereading. They knew the story. In fact, they owned the story. They were at a real advantage. They could participate fully and even answer other children's questions. That evening I suggested that each child borrow the book in turn and share it with a family member. At the end of the week we would meet to talk about what it was like to share an English book with their families. I also suggested that each child begin a read-aloud journal to record the new words and ideas they heard in classroom read-alouds. The idea to preview books and create ways for children learning English to fully inhabit those texts seemed instructionally sound and sensible. Of course, the idea was *not* practical. I didn't have time to preview books with all our second-language learners throughout the school. Unfortunately, I wouldn't even have time to do it with just one class every day. What I needed to do was give the idea away. As I've said before, good ideas are a dime a dozen, the question is, "Who will parent those ideas?" I couldn't do a special read-aloud each day, nor could the classroom or ESL teacher. I could however train parents, volunteers, student teachers, or older students to do as I had done. Children don't just need a list of good ideas, they need and deserve a plan to carry out those ideas. (See Appendix 14.)

Community Service

It is essential to give all members of a school community work that is real, including English as a second language students. These young people benefit enormously from work that is meaningful. When Matan, an Israeli child who seemed to understand but was reluctant to speak English, was in third grade, I led him into the corridor and asked him to help me back a new bulletin board with construction paper. He was eager to help and therefore willing to ask for assistance as best he could. He needed to borrow scissors, a ruler, stapler, paper, and a step stool. He needed to talk to his friends, his teacher, the secretary, the custodian, and to me. Matan got the job done, felt great about his contribution, and practiced his English along the way. Over the years, I have called upon ESL students to help with such chores as organizing the lost and found, preparing snacks for the kindergartners, and stamping and categorizing new books.

Reading Workshop

Reading activities in a literature-based, whole language classroom are supportive of the second-language learner. There are no embarrassing round-robin read-aloud moments. There is no privileging of often hard to discern phonemic elements. There is no battery of preprepared questions at the end of each chapter. Instead, the focus is on making meaning and responding to text, emphases that are just right for the child trying to make sense of a new language.

Additional workshop supports for the second-language learner include:

- paired reading with fluent English-speaking classmates
- viewing of videotapes and follow-up reading of story presented on film
- reading of great quantities of visually rich nonfiction texts
- reading of bilingual material, if available (We have many Spanish-English texts, but far fewer texts in other languages.)
- selecting universal stories that are available in both languages

My work in other countries has taught me just how difficult it is to spend an entire day working hard in a new language. Swedish teachers who listen to me present in English all day have admitted that they are exhausted at the end of each day. They need a break. So too, when I've attempted to keep up with Spanish-speaking teachers in Mexico or Ecuador, I sensed I was working harder than usual. I too needed a break. We need to consider as well the children who enter our school and are immersed in English for six hours a day. (Our school offers no bilingual classroom. How could we? There are so many different languages represented.) Of course, our children can cut loose in the playground, relax at lunchtime, and feel more at home in the art, dance, chess, and physical education classrooms. But within the reading/writing hours, our students need to be able to turn to fairly easy material when they are feeling overloaded. It helps to have a special shelf set aside for the second-language learner. I'm speaking here of reference books—picture dictionaries, alphabet books, atlases, nonfiction pictorial guides to plants and animals, visually rich tourist guidebooks, subway maps, simple English texts about their home countries, even albums filled with labeled class photos. Reading such materials does not qualify as busywork, but as an activity that can be undertaken independently and that serves to build English vocabulary.

Of course, students can relax with a book or a newspaper in their first language if these are available. Robert brought a Maltese version of "Hansel and Gretel" to school. It made sense to offer him the same in English. The texts, of course, were not exact translations, but the Maltese version gave him enough of a leg up that he was able to understand and learn from the English version.

We do have students who come to us not reading the Roman alphabet, but rather the Modern Cyrillic, Japanese, Chinese, Korean, Greek, Indian, Arabic, and Hebrew alphabets. These children require an English buddy or volunteer assigned to begin at the beginning, teaching them to speak English, become familiar with our alphabet, and then to read English. Similarly, when very young children who are not yet literate in their first language arrive at the Manhattan New School, they learn to speak English, become familiar with how print operates, learn about the letters of the alphabet, and then how to read English.

Hands-On Opportunities

Many years ago, my daughter's junior high school Spanish teacher was in danger of losing his job because the school couldn't offer him a full teaching load. The school had uncovered art classes but no additional Spanish classes. Her teacher agreed to teach an art class, but he chose to teach it in Spanish. It was a wonderful experience for my daughter and her classmates, who learned a great deal of Spanish that semester because their learning was whole, hands-on, visual, nonthreatening, and purposeful.

So too, our newcomers learn to speak English as they work on a clay sculpture in art class, play basketball in the gym, play the recorder with our music teacher, and weave, build with blocks, and do woodworking during center time in their regular classrooms. Moreover, any experiences involving the preparation and sharing of snacks always promotes rich language uses (as well as healthy social relationships).

Perhaps some of the richest language I hear during the school day surrounds science learning. All children are eager to describe their observations, ask questions, and put forth hunches. Therefore, our science workshop needs to be included as a major hands-on setting for language learning. Lisa, our science teacher, is not just lecturing about animal life cycles, simple machines, and properties of water. Instead, all children have opportunities to dissect squid, design original machines, and conduct experiments like dropping objects into a pail to see if they sink or float. (Sometimes I think the messier the work, the more language is learned.)

Dialogue Journals

Over the years I have kept dialogue journals with select students. Dialogue journals can also be kept with the second-language learner. Imagine each child being paired with a staff member, neighborhood volunteer, or older student who agrees to write back to the language learner on a regular basis. A short training session can be held to remind journal keepers how to respond in ways that subtly improve the student's use of English. Journal partners can be encouraged to write short notes in a bound book that gets passed back and forth.

Environmental Print That Supports English-Language Learners

It would probably be worthwhile for teachers to periodically walk through the school reminding themselves that children who don't speak English live here. We need to ask ourselves, "How can these windows, walls, hallways, and bulletin boards offer more to the child attempting to learn English?" (We can ask the same question of course, if we want our English-language students to learn more Spanish.) Possible responses to this question follow.

- We can hang more environmental print, much the way early-childhood teachers do, in an attempt to teach sight vocabulary.

- We can be sure that every work of art has a title and every photograph a caption.
- We can hang multilingual signs when appropriate.
- We can require all plants and flowers to be labeled.
- We can hang helpful common phrases in key locations. (Students can think through what phrases their new friends would most need in the cafeteria, nurse's office, or at the copy machine.)
- We can create interactive bulletin boards.

Examples of this last item, interactive bulletin boards, are numerous. We can hang a wide roll of butcher block paper, with categories listed across the top and columns for passersby to complete. The categories might include such groupings as articles of girl's clothing, baby needs, writing instruments, playground equipment, desserts, kinds of houses, footwear, and so on. A bucket of markers can be placed nearby and all members of the community encouraged to draw and label appropriate items in English. When columns are complete, a new sheet listing additional categories can be hung atop the old. Eventually pages can be turned into an unusual picture "dictionary" for the school. Grown-ups as well as children enjoy thinking of as many words as possible and second-language learners benefit from the words and pictures.

Similarly, we can hang a sheet of paper listing languages across the top and key English phrases down the first left-hand column. Members of the community can be invited to fill in the grid, translating phrases and sentences into their first languages. Phrases might include such basics as "Hello," "Good Morning," "Where are you going?" "Do you need any help?" "See you later," and so on. When complete, classes can study the display, noting similarities between languages as well as any surprising discoveries about different alphabetic systems. Children delight in learning familiar expressions in their friends' languages.

Universal songs can also be hung, leaving space for members of the community to add their versions. These might include "Everybody Loves Saturday Night" and "Happy Birthday to You."

Various lift-the-flap boards can be created (see Carmen's chess board on p. 11). For example, on the outside of the flap, brief situations may be listed and illustrated. Lift the flap and find an appropriate response. One might read, "Someone sneezes." Lift the flap and find, "You might say God bless you," or "Salud" or "Gezhundeit," or all three. Students can create this entire board, posting such situations as, "Someone gets hurt," "Someone has a birthday," "Someone does you a favor," "Someone says thank you." Situations and responses can become more complicated and in fact quite humorous, depending on the age of the students preparing the board. This type of display must be hung low enough for students to be able to reach the flaps.

Children can also paint large murals filled with people in common neighborhood scenes. Cartoon bubbles can then be drawn for each person and appropriate dialogue added. Students might create scenes of people in a supermarket, on a school bus, in the playground, in the subway, on line at the movies, at a shoe store. If students understand that they are preparing these murals to teach English to their classmates, they will appreciate the need to have their spelling and grammar corrected as well as use their best handwriting.

The Importance of Delving Deeply

Children learning a new language benefit from studying one subject deeply. The child who is watching the chick incubator (turning the eggs, checking the thermometer, and listening to peeps) in his second-grade classroom, and simultaneously learning about the needs of chicks with his science teacher, researching chicks with his computer teacher, and writing and reading about chicks in his reading/writing workshop is likely to learn more English than if he were studying a different topic in each setting. The talk overlaps in all the classrooms. The child has the opportunity to extend his language, because he becomes familiar with key concepts. He develops a working knowledge of the topic and can take language risks. Vocabulary and language structures are reinforced throughout the day. In addition, when teachers deliberately choose teaching techniques that support the English-language learner, students learn not only how incubators work, they also learn how English works.

Teaching Techniques That Promote Language Learning

Aida Walqui, a professor from the University of California, spoke about meeting the needs of English-language learners at a principal's conference in our district. Her presentation was particularly well-received because she not only offered practical teaching suggestions for the English-language learner in our schools, she utilized these very same techniques as she spoke to the assembled heads of school. For example, Aida presented a diagram, what she called an anticipatory guide, that supported members of the audience as they took notes on her lecture. The page contained "fill-in-the-blank" lines strategically placed so as to alert the audience to the number of key points to follow as well as to the number of concepts attached to each. Her teaching was filled with many deliberate ways to help the non-fluent English speaker understand her presentation. The following are a few teaching techniques that all students learning English would appreciate:

- Abundant use of visual aids. Children learning English will get more out of their subject studies if their reading of content information and their listening to content presentations are accompanied by drawings, photographs, calendars, charts, and timelines.
- Graphic organizers. No doubt, my Swedish teacher friends, for example, will appreciate the reader's guides that precede each chapter in this book. These lists of key literacy lessons will scaffold their reading of the denser chapters. Other graphic organizers would include such tools as semantic maps, content webs, and the anticipatory guides mentioned previously.

- The explicit teaching of helpful classroom phrases. I have become more comfortable speaking Spanish because I know how to say, "Que significa . . . ? (What does . . . mean?) and "Como se dice . . . ?" (How do you say . . . ?). Teachers can give second-language learners a leg up by teaching such phrases as well as thinking about additional phrases that will provide support to language learners in their classrooms. Aida Walqui, for example, suggested the direct teaching of "prefaces," such introductory remarks as "The main thing I'd like to say is . . ." So too our young language learners would benefit from knowing such phrases as, "Excuse me, may I ask a question?" "I'm not sure I understand what you mean by . . . ," and "Can you repeat what you said about . . . ?"

- The use of templates or patterns for written products. Earlier in this book, when discussing the writing of the struggling reader (see p. 318), I noted the benefits of using carefully selected literature to scaffold the struggling writer. Students learning a new language also benefit from having patterns to follow. After reading James Berry's poem "Childhood Tracks," which appears on page 374, Vaidehi, a fifth grader, used it as a pattern for her own writing about India (see Figure 10.7). When students like Vaidehi share such finished work, we not only take pride in

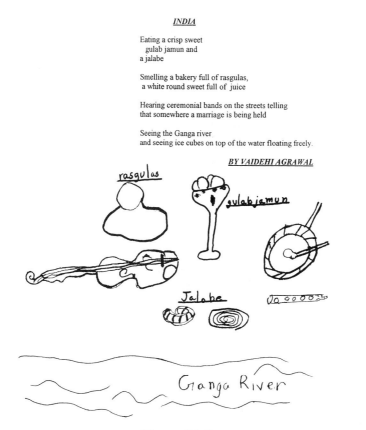

INDIA

Eating a crisp sweet
  gulab jamun and
a jalabe

Smelling a bakery full of rasgulas,
  a white round sweet full of juice

Hearing ceremonial bands on the streets telling
that somewhere a marriage is being held

Seeing the Ganga river
and seeing ice cubes on top of the water floating freely.

BY VAIDEHI AGRAWAL

Figure 10.7

their literary accomplishments, we also proudly note how their classmates are coming to know and appreciate one another's home countries. (See also *Writing Through Childhood* for a discussion of the use of templates with second-grade writers).

Childhood Tracks

Eating crisp fried fish with plain bread.
Eating sheared ice made into "snowball"
with syrup in a glass.
Eating young jelly-coconut, mixed
with village-made wet sugar.
Drinking cool water from a calabash gourd,
on worked land in the hills.

Smelling a patch of fermenting pineapple
in stillness of hot sunlight.
Smelling mixed whiffs of fish, mango, coffee,
mint, hanging in a market.
Smelling sweaty padding lifted off a donkey's back.

Hearing a nightingale in song
in moonlight and sea-sound.
Hearing dawn-crowing of cocks, in answer
to others around the village.
Hearing the laughter
of barefeet children carrying water.
Hearing a distant braying of a donkey
in silent hot afternoon.
Hearing palm trees' leaves rattle
on and on at Christmastime.

Seeing a woman walking in loose floral frock.
Seeing a village workman with bag and machete
under a tree, resting, sweat-washed.
Seeing a tangled land-piece of banana trees
with goats in shade cud-chewing.
Seeing a coil of plaited tobacco
like rope, sold, going in bits.
Seeing children toy-making in a yard
while slants of evening sunlight slowly disappear.
Seeing an evening's dusky hour lit up
by dotted lamplight.
Seeing fishing nets repaired between canoes.

- Opportunities for students to rehearse oral presentations. Danling Fu, author of *My Trouble Is My English,* has been spending time in our district. She continues to offer sage advice for teachers working with English-language learners. For example, she pointed out that students just learning a new language may be reluctant to speak in front of classmates and are more likely to do so if they are able to prepare for such presentations. Providing students with rehearsal opportunities is a simple yet powerful idea.

(Many more teaching suggestions are offered in the second-language-learning books listed in the bibliography on p. 381.)

Specialized Second-Language Instruction

Students who do not pass a standardized language assessment are required to receive a set amount of English as a second language instruction taught by a licensed ESL teacher. Constance Foland, our ESL teacher, is effective in our school for the following reasons:

- She has genuine compassion and respect for children learning English, as well as for their families.
- She understands our ways of working with children, both academically and socially, and uses similar techniques, strategies, and language.
- She is professionally and specially trained to work with English-language learners.
- She appreciates that attending to talk alone, without reading and writing attached, is time well spent.
- She engages the regular classroom teachers, offering suggestions for making every minute count for the English-language learner.
- She offers flexible scheduling. For example, Constance works with our older students before the regular school day begins, so that they do not miss any class subjects, and rather than pulling our youngest students out of their classrooms, she pushes in to their regular classrooms, bringing her reading background into her ESL work. She is also willing to accompany early-childhood children on field trips.
- She understands the value of work that is real. For example, one year her oldest students prepared a videotape tour of our school for newcomers.

Our teachers always prefer when specialists' schedules permit them to push in to their classrooms rather than remove children for extra supports. If an English as a second language teacher can work alongside children within regular classrooms, teachers are particularly delighted to see language instructors during content-rich moments. Over the years, I have seen ESL teachers in kindergartens talk with children as they cook chicken soup, turn blocks into skyscrapers, paint murals about class trips, and act out restaurant scenes in the dramatic play area. So too, how helpful it would be to have a language specialist on hand to help newcomers discuss the lima beans they are planting, the model of New Amsterdam they are building, or the snails they are observing. After all, you can't talk about nothing.

Similarly, when ESL teachers are able to push in with older students, I can't imagine a better time than during science or social studies classes. Imagine a cluster of non-English-speaking students working alongside a coach who can help them learn the language they need to describe the squid they are dissecting, the Revolutionary War skit they are preparing, or the election results they are discussing.

It is particularly crucial that when the ESL teacher pulls children out of class for instruction, the time away is well spent. I am only interested in work that is real. I'd like all ESL teachers to do as Andy's "teacher" Marisol has done and provide safe, pleasurable, and meaningful activities that have real-world payoff. For example, helping newcomers understand and be able to talk about baseball, understand the words to popular school songs, and learn the language of such card games as go fish, rummy, and war, seem like worthwhile activities. Children can root for the Yankees with their friends, join the chorus, and play cards on indoor recess days. Then too, I am interested in ESL students engaging in projects that result in meaningful products. Think how much English the children learned when they prepared that narrated video of the school for other newcomers. Similarly, we can invite ESL students, working closely with their language teacher, to research and prepare:

- booklets of handy phrases in their own languages so that teachers can understand students in their first weeks in class
- explanatory notes to accompany the monthly cafeteria menu so that newcomers become familiar with American foods
- introductory guides to American sports and playground activities so that newcomers can quickly take part in recess
- interviews with new families accompanied by photographs of family members so that the community recognizes new arrivals and welcomes them
- brochures about their home country to distribute to classmates, including maps, travel routes, customs, and traditional foods

My criteria for designing such projects are simple. I am looking for work that is interpersonal, relevant to the students' lives, allows for feedback from the community, and makes the students feel part of the school community rather than separated from it.

English-language teachers can also help children pursue individual areas of inquiry, set up interviews with people of interest to students, arrange pen-pal correspondences with fluent English speakers, read aloud carefully selected books that have natural language structures, work with students to create any of the interactive boards described previously, pore over students' writing folders to determine students' strengths and weaknesses, and provide scaffolded writing experiences that enable the second-language learner to take new risks in their writing.

Helping Students Understand the Language-Learner's Experience

It's not too difficult to make sure colleagues appreciate the English-language learner's experiences, especially when you hire teachers with compassionate and humane spirits. Our job, though, is to make sure that all our young people are as caring as the grown-ups.

Our third graders are particularly well informed about the experience of newcomers to America, as they study immigration as a major topic in social studies. Many students, however, probably need extra help to fully understand how challenging it is to learn a new language and get used to a new country. They need to realize that studying Spanish at school for sheer pleasure is quite different than being totally surrounded by a new language and feeling pressure to speak that new language. Teachers can help students develop a deep appreciation in any of the following ways:

- Interviewing family members about what it is like not to speak the language of a country you are living in.
- Role-playing situations of day-to-day life when you don't fully understand the language. (See Paula Rogovin's book *The Classroom Interview: A World of Learning* for suggestions about interviewing and role-playing.)
- Responding to realistic scenarios. These teacher-prepared written scenarios are similar to role-playing, in that they require students to respond to specific situations. In *Going Public,* I include two such scenarios, both involving a fictional brother and sister, Joseph and Hannah. The first presents the family on their airplane flight from New York to Budapest and asks students to jot down the kind of questions young children would probably ask their parents if they were about to move to a new country. The second presents the same family landing at the Budapest airport and asks students to list the first steps a family must take when they begin a life in a new country. Teachers can also create scenarios specifically designed to help students understand the challenges of learning a new language in a new country. In the ones below I continue with my invented characters, Joseph and Hannah.

Joseph and Hannah and their parents have just moved to Budapest from New York City. Right now, they speak very little Hungarian. The children are beginning to learn the language at school and their parents are reading several books so they too can learn the new language. Their mother has a job with an American company in Budapest and so can work without being fluent in the new language. Their father does not have such a job. What kind of work do you think their father can do if he does not speak the language? List these below.

Joseph and Hannah are attending Hungarian school. Joseph is in the third grade and Hannah is in the second. One day in the playground, Joseph notices that some children are teasing his little sister and she's starting to cry. What can Joseph do to help? List your ideas below:

> Children can be asked to jot down their ideas and then meet in small groups to share. The whole class can reconvene to share and record their ideas and understandings.

• Encouraging bilingual students to share their early language-learning memories. When Kristina writes the notebook entry shown in Figure 10.8, we need to invite her to share it with her classmates and receive response. A collection of these from students throughout the school would make a powerful anthology. (See publishing ideas in *Writing Through Childhood*.)

• Sharing carefully selected pieces of literature. Aliki's picture book *Marianthe's Story: Painted Words* and *Spoken Words* can help children walk a mile in the non-English-speaker's shoes. This two-part tale reveals what it was like for a young child to enter an English-speaking school. Aliki effectively describes what all that English sounds like at first to the young student. Her mother reminds her to look and listen and use body language to make her meaning clear. The young girl also uses her paintings to communicate. In the second part of the book, Marianthe has learned enough English to share her immigration story with her class.

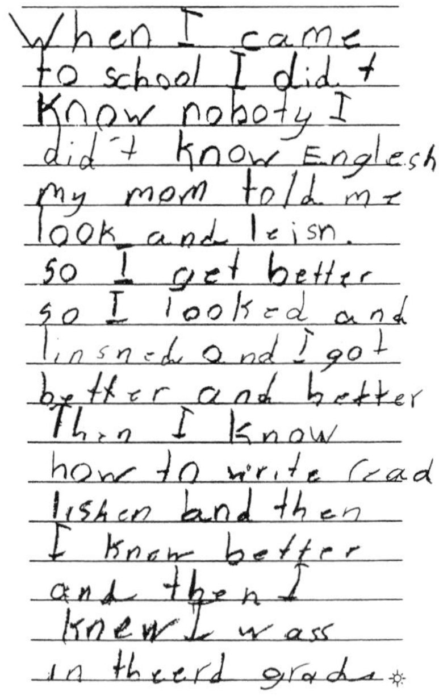

When I came
to school I did t
know noboty I
did t know Englesh
my mom told me
look and leisn.
so I get better
so I looked and
linsned and I got
better and better
Then I know
how to write read
lishen and then
I know better
and then I
knew I was
in theerd grade.

Figure 10.8

Other picture books related to learning a new language include *I Hate English!* by Ellen Levine, *Molly's Pilgrim* by Barbara Cohen, *My First American Friend* by Sarunna Jin, and *Love as Strong as Ginger* by Lenore Look.

When teachers share such carefully selected pieces of literature they can also turn students' conversations toward possibilities for making non-English-speaking children feel welcome. For example, the simple poem "A Different Language" by Edith Segal suggests one way for students to communicate with children who as yet do not understand English.

In addition, teachers need to be on the lookout for literature that will help students understand and respect their new classmates' home countries. These books will also serve to keep the newcomers' memories alive. It is therefore worth all the effort to build classroom collections dealing with students' home countries.

One year I asked students to suggest ways for us to do a better job with our students learning English. Alexei, then a third grader, sent me the definitive list that appears in Figure 10.9. This eight-year-old's suggestions let me know that our students understand what having to learn a new language is all about. Although unfortunately we can't always comply with the second item on Alexei's list, I think we are succeeding with Alexei's other suggestions. Along the way, we are always looking for members of the community, representing all the languages in our school, to serve as translators and teach us what we need to know about these young people, who face big challenges.

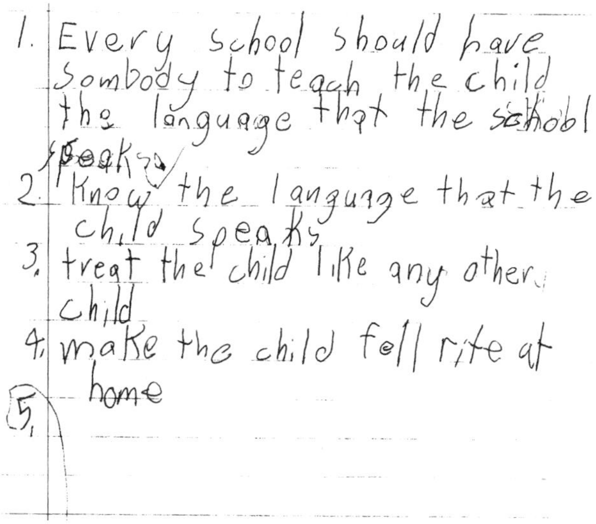

Figure 10.9

Continually Improving Instruction for the Second-Language Learner

All New York City teachers are required to receive ten hours of special instruction in working with children who are learning English as a second language. One summer, I devoted my professional reading time to issues surrounding the second-language learner. I wrote the following note to staff members when they returned to school in the fall.

Dear friends,

During the summer I read several texts that explored the issue of the second-language learner in English-speaking classrooms. In response to those readings I compiled the following list of questions to scaffold our professional conversations:

1. *How can we find out more about the children's literacy in their first language, their history with learning English, and any current first-language learning outside of school?(Are children attending Turkish school, Burmese school, Hebrew school? How are those languages being taught?)*

2. *Are there additional ways to make the children feel welcome?*

3. *How can we gather and make better use of additional books, newspapers, and games in their first language?*

4. *Are we providing them with language that will help them when they are studying as well as when they are playing?*

5. *Do our classroom libraries have material that is particularly helpful for our work with second-language learners? For example, do we have enough nonfiction texts, rich with visuals, for students to explore?*

6. *How can volunteers support our efforts with second-language learners?*

7. *Are there more community service projects the children could be involved with that would provide significant opportunities to learn language?*

8. *How can we work closer with parents, including supporting their own efforts to learn English?*

9. *What ways can we devise so that children get to meet the other students in the school who speak their first language?*

10. *Would dialogue journals benefit the second-language learner? Who else besides classroom teachers can parent these?*

11. *Are our second-language learners being left out of any areas of school life? How can we make amends?*

12. *How can we make everyday classroom structures more beneficial to the second-language learner (read-aloud, book buddies, meeting time, etc.)?*

13. *Are we working closely enough with our ESL teacher?*

14. *Do we need additional classroom strategies and techniques in order to meet the needs of second-language learners throughout all areas of curriculum? (Are the children ever "just sitting there?")*

15. *Are we conscious of our own talk as models (speed, clarity, diction, pronunciation, etc.)?*

16. *Have we helped the monolingual English-speaking students understand the challenge before their second-language-learning classmates?*

17. *Does our use of environmental print support the second-language learner?*

18. *Do we provide occasions for second-language learners to teach us about their first languages?*

It's clear from the preceding pages that several of the questions posed in the above letter have since been addressed in our school.

Principals, as well as teachers, parents, and students need occasions to continually pose their questions about second-language learning. Then, in order to begin to answer these questions, we need a full range of staff development opportunities. These would include:

- **Professional conversations.** No matter the topic we study at our staff meetings or grade-level gatherings, we must remember to include issues related to the second-language learner.

- **Observations.** Teachers need opportunities to visit accomplished ESL teachers as well as classroom teachers with expertise in this area.

- **Research studies.** Teachers with questions related to second-language learning need to be encouraged to pursue these inquiries, in formal or informal ways.

- **Professional reference materials.** We need to make sure that our process for choosing our professional library does *not* neglect the second-language learner. I can't imagine a professional library without such books as:

  "My Trouble Is My English": Asian Students and the American Dream, by DanLing Fu (Heinemann)

  Learning to Learn in a Second Language, by Pauline Gibbons (Heinemann, PETA)

  Kids Come in all Languages: Reading Instruction for ESL Students, edited by Kearen Spangenberg-Urbschat and Robert Pritchard (IRA)

  Your Land, My Land: Children in the Process of Acculturation, by Jacklyn Blake Clayton (Heinemann)

  When They Don't All Speak English: Integrating the ESL Student into the Regular Classroom, edited by Pat Rigg and Virginia G. Allen (NCTE)

  ESL/EFL Teaching: Principles for Success, by Yvonne S. Freeman and David E. Freeman (Heinemann)

  Between Worlds: Access to Second Language Acquisition, by David E. Freeman and Yvonne S. Freeman (Heinemann)

  And Then There Were Two: Children and Second Language Learning, by Terry Piper (The Pippin Teacher's Library)

  The First Step on the Longer Path: Becoming an ESL Teacher, by Mary Ashworth (The Pippin Teacher's Library)

  Teaching the World's Children: ESL for Ages Three to Seven, by Mary Ashford and H. Patricia Wakefield (The Pippin Teacher's Library)

Condemned Without a Trial: Bogus Arguments Against Bilingual Education, by Stephen Krashen (Heinemann)

Myths and Realities: Best Practice for Language Minority Students, by Katharine Davis Samway and Denise McKeon (Heinemann)

Of course, teachers need opportunities to meet, discuss, and try out new ideas learned from or inspired by these texts.

A Commitment to Celebrate Language and Language Learning

One summer, I attended an educators' conference in Bordeaux, France. One of the speakers, Regis Ritz, made the audience laugh when he suggested that a person who speaks three languages is called trilingual, a person who speaks two languages is called bilingual, and a person who speaks one language is called an American. Lack of language learning is, of course, no laughing matter. All children deserve the opportunity to become bilingual or, better yet, trilingual. At the Manhattan New School, celebrating and learning new languages is a quality-of-life issue. We know our lives right now are richer because we have made a commitment to language learning. We know our students' lives will be richer in the future because they have the tools and perspectives to mingle with the world.

RELATED READINGS IN COMPANION VOLUMES

Going Public (Heinemann, 1999) is abbreviated as GP. *Writing Through Childhood* (Heinemann, forthcoming), is abbreviated as WC.

Honoring language	**GP:** Ch. 4
Delighting in language	**WC:** Ch. 5
Designing content studies	**GP:** Ch. 6
Understanding the writer's notebook	**WC:** Ch. 3
Following Mehmet's growth	**WC:** Ch. 4
Providing professional development	**GP:** Ch. 7; **WC:** Ch. 11
Publishing student writing	**WC:** Ch. 9

CONCLUSION

Each year the New York City Board of Education arranges for business executives, politicians, and celebrities from various fields to spend time in our public schools. This "Principal for a Day" event often brings fresh insights to educators who rarely have time to get real distance on their work. One year Bob Sillerman, an entertainment executive, was assigned to our school and eagerly and eloquently spoke to our fifth graders. He shared an important lesson he had learned from his father, who advised, "Find a job in which you can learn something new every day." When I heard this thought I was doubly sure that I had chosen the right career. We must live our school lives so that all educators feel the same way.

When I leave school, tired after each long workday, I need to continue to ask myself, "So what literacy lesson have you learned today?" If I begin to struggle for answers, I need to rethink the way I spend those long hours at work. And so do all educators who care about the teaching of reading and writing. Our schools will only be as good as the hard thinking we continue to do. Everyone in a school who takes responsibility for children's growth as readers and writers, including principals, teachers, staff developers, student teachers, and volunteers, needs to continually ask themselves, "What have I learned today about the teaching of reading and writing?" Reflecting on what we have learned is considerably more significant than reflecting on what we have taught. Educators need to give themselves the lifetime guarantees they bravely pledge to their students. We too deserve the gift of scholarship, to have jobs in which we learn something new every day.

APPENDICES

Across-the-Grades Guide to Author Study

Kindergarten

Children should be aware of the meaning of *author* and *illustrator*.

Children should begin to talk about their favorite authors.

Collections of favorite authors should be housed together, labeled and displayed.

Children can begin to notice things that their favorite authors tend to do over and over again. (This is done orally and informally. You can expect children to say such things as, "He always writes about animals!" "Her books are always funny!")

Children should know that grown-ups have favorite authors.

Children should begin to inquire about how one becomes an author and how a book is made.

First Grade

Continuation of all of the above plus:

Children should begin to have favorite authors they can read, in addition to those read to them.

Children and teacher choose one of the favorite authors for closer study.

Children compose list of distinguishing features of this favorite author. (Teacher compiles list.)

Children are asked to share chosen author's works with family members. Additional features and qualities noticed are added to class list.

Children engage in a whole-class author project; e.g., creating a mural in response to author's body of work, preparing a booklet about their author to share with other first graders, hanging an annotated timeline of author's work using book jackets.

Second Grade

Continuation of all of the above plus:

Children can begin to be known as authorities on favorite authors. (Other children can be heard to say, "Show that book to _____, he loves that author!")

Whole-class author studies can be used the way genre studies are used in the writing workshop. Teachers select authors who offer accessible lessons for young writers.

If a child attempts to do what the author being studied has done, the child's work is highlighted at sharing time.

Authors studied should extend to additional genres (including poetry and non-fiction).

Third Grade

Continuation of all of the above plus:

Children can add breath and depth to author studies by reading background materials (biographical information, reviews, interviews, etc.).

Children can do an individual author's study to challenge themselves as readers.

Children can do individual author's study to challenge themselves as writers. (The choice of author would most likely be different from a reading challenge. A third grader might be able to read a stack of books by Beverly Cleary, but might choose to study the works of Cynthia Rylant as a writing challenge.)

Children should easily be able to answer such questions as, "Who would you consider for a poetry author study?" "A nonfiction author study?"

Children should delight in discovering new books by studied authors.

Children might be asked to present individual or small-group author studies to their classmates.

Grades Four and Five

Continuation of all of the above plus:

Children, in their writer's notebooks, can be asked to have a go at imitating an author studied.

As part of any genre study, children should be asked to closely study a favorite author.

Reader-response groups can be formed around selected authors.

Children can do an independent author study that includes:

- a biographical sketch of the author
- a bibliography of recommended readings
- a packet of related reference material about the author
- samples of original writing that demonstrate any lessons learned.
- a reflective piece about undertaking an author study

These studies can be added to classroom library for permanent reference.

APPENDIX 2

Children's Literature Survey

Dear colleagues,

As a district we are interested in spreading the wealth, guaranteeing that all the students in our schools are surrounded by the finest books written by the finest authors. To that end, we are planning to compile a K–12 list of books "too good to miss." Won't you please take a few minutes to fill out the attached survey? If you have additional thoughts, bibliographies, related resources, or suggestions, feel free to attach them or contact us in the fall.

Thanks in advance.

Children's Literature Survey

Name _____ School _____ Grade Level _____

Favorite picture books

Favorite poetry anthologies

Favorite chapter books for reading aloud

Favorite nonfiction books related to science

Favorite nonfiction books related to social studies

Favorite picture books containing concepts in mathematics

Are there authors that you're willing to say, "Read anything by _____?"

What books are falling apart in your room from overuse?

What whole-class sets of novels do you have, if any?

What multiple-copy sets of books do you have, if any?

Would you be interested in another bibliography more geared to specific purposes in the teaching of reading? (i.e., useful with struggling emergent readers, useful for upper-grade students who are just learning English, etc.)

Would you be interested in another bibliography more geared to the teaching of writing? (i.e., useful for minilessons in poetry, filled with authentic dialogue, etc.)

APPENDIX 3

Results of Children's Literature Survey

Does Your Classroom Library Have Books By . . . ?

These are lists of sure-fire authors that you might want every student to have the opportunity to become familiar with. These authors are, for the most part, very prolific and their titles are therefore readily available.

Kindergarten/Grade One

Tana Hoban	Heidi Goennel	Sid Hoff
Brian Wildsmith	John Birmingham	Eric Hill
Tomie dePaola	William Steig	Mercer Mayer
Else Minarik	Helen Oxenbury	Lillian Hoban
Kevin Henkes	Lois Ehlert	Mem Fox
Ezra Jack Keats	Susan Meddaugh	Ann Jonas
Leo Lionni	Marisabina Russo	Dr. Seuss
Arnold Lobel	Norman Bridwell	Bill Martin
Robert Munsch	Eileen Christelow	Shirley Hughes
Maurice Sendak	Leah Komaiko	Frank Asch
Bernard Waber	Amy Ehrlich	Lucy Cousins
Rosemary Wells	James Marshall	Jeanne Titherington
Donald Crews	Nancy White Carlstrom	Anita Lobel
Peggy Parish	Eric Carle	Janet Ahlberg
Charlotte Zolotow	Martha Alexander	Judith Caseley
Mary Ann Hoberman	Rachel Isadora	Diane Goode
Byron Barton	Jan Ormerod	Emily Arnold McCully
Vera B. Williams	Charlotte Pomerantz	Molly Bang
Anthony Brown	Anne Rockwell	Holly Keller
Don and Audrey Wood	Gail Gibbons	Bernard Most
Margaret Wise Brown	Nancy Tafuri	Russell Hoban
Pat Hutchins	Laura Numeroff	Robert Kraus
Marc Brown	Judith Viorst	Mitsumasa Anno

Does Your Classroom Library Have Books By . . . ?

These are lists of sure-fire authors that you might want every student to have the opportunity to become familiar with. These authors are, for the most part, very prolific and their titles are therefore readily available.

Grades Two and Three

Cynthia Rylant	Amy Schwartz	Harriet Ziefert
Robert Kimmel Smith	Amy Hest	Marjorie Sharmat
Barbara Cooney	Paul Fleischman	Kathryn Lasky
Chris van Allsburg	Jan Brett	Judy Delton
Eve Bunting	Suzy Kline	David Adler
Jon Scieszka	Marcia Brown	Pat Ross
Joanna Hurwitz	Joanna Cole	Ellen Conford
Beverly Cleary	Eloise Greenfield	Ann Cameron
Patricia Polacco	William Joyce	Patricia MacLachlan
James Howe	Trina Schart Hyman	Debbie Dadey
Jane Yolen	Ed Young	Barbara Park
Elizabeth Levy	Jerry Pinkney	Margaret Mahy
Patricia Reilly Giff	James Ransome	Arthur Dorros
Bruce Coville	Emily Arnold McCully	Richard Egielski
Miriam Cohen	Simon James	Arthur Yorinks
Betsy Byars	Eric Kimmel	Ted Lewin
Steven Kellogg	Alvin Schwartz	Ann Turner
Roald Dahl	Laura Ingalls Wilder	Byrd Baylor
E. B. White	Astrid Lingren	Aliki
Louis Sachar	James Stevenson	Eve Bunting
Matt Christopher	Judy Blume	Daniel Pinkwater
Dick King Smith	Paula Danziger	Janice Lee Smith
Donald Sobol	Lois Lowry	Gertrude Chandler Warner

Does Your Classroom Library Have Books By . . . ?

These are lists of sure-fire authors that you might want every student to have the opportunity to become familiar with. These authors are, for the most part, very prolific and their titles are therefore readily available.

Grades Four and Five

Mary Stolz	Walter Dean Myers	Lynne Reid Banks
Natalie Babbitt	Esther Hautzig	Joan Blos
C. S. Lewis	Katherine Cushman	Louise Fitzhugh
Lloyd Alexander	Jean Little	Betsy Byars
Avi	Chris Crutcher	Natalie Babbitt
Sid Fleischman	Carolyn Coman	Carolyn Reeder
Karen Hesse	William Sleator	Barbara Robinson
Madeline L'Engle	Lois Duncan	Will Hobbs
E. L. Konigsburg	Paul Fleischman	Sydney Taylor
Gary Paulsen	Sonia Levitan	Paul Jennings
Richard Peck	Patricia Hermes	Jan Marino
Ellen Raskin	Virginia Hamilton	John Bellairs
Mildren Taylor	Judy Blume	Ellen Raskin
Jerry Spinelli	Lois Lowry	Willo Davis Robert
Marilyn Sachs	Patricia MacLachlan	Constance Greene
Susan Shreve	Paula Danziger	Clyde Robert Bulla
Katherine Paterson	Roald Dahl	Walter Farley
Laurence Yep	Scott O'Dell	Janet Taylor Lisle
Paula Fox	Irene Hunt	Elizabeth George Speare
Cynthia DeFelice	C. S. Lewis	Frances Hodgson Burnett
Jean Craighead George	Oiuda Sebestyen	Norton Juster
Pam Conrad	Joan Lowery Nixon	L. M. Montgomery
Phyllis Reynolds Naylor	Bill Brittain	Eleanor Cameron

Does Your Classroom Library Have Books By . . . ?

These are lists of sure-fire authors that you might want every student to have the opportunity to become familiar with. These authors are, for the most part, very prolific and their titles are therefore readily available.

Grades Six, Seven and Eight

Bruce Brooks	Gary Soto	Anne McCaffrey
Robert Cormier	Francesca Lia Block	John Marsden
S. E. Hinton	Nicholasa Mohr	Theodore Taylor
Wilson Rawls	Brock Cole	Virginia Euwer Wolff
Robert Newton Peck	Felice Holman	Cynthia Voigt
Paul Zindel	Pam Conrad	Michelle Magorian
Susan Cooper	Michael Dorris	Vivian Vande Velde
Chris Crutcher	Jamake Highwater	Janni Howker
Bette Greene	Jane Breskin Zalben	Jan Slepian
Gordon Korman	Todd Strasser	Sarah Ellis
Donna Jo Napoli	Robin Brancato	Jeanne Dixon
Sue Ellen Bridges	Alden Carter	Barbara Ann Porte
Ann Rinaldi	Colby Rodowsky	Jill Paton Walsh
Margaret Rostkowski	Isabelle Holland	Marion Dane Bauer
Robin McKinley	Diana Wynne Jones	Barbara Joosse
Norma Fox Mazer	Zibby Oneal	Gillian Cross
Susan Beth Pfeffer	Rosemary Sutcliff	Ursula Le Guin
Sylvia Waugh	Robert Westall	Brenda Seabrooke
William Armstrong	Caroline Cooney	Judie Angell
Robert Lipsyte	Douglas Adams	Will Hobbs
Farley Mowat	Rita Williams-Garcia	Ben Mikaelson
Bette Greene	Joan Aiken	
Yoshiko Uchida	Philip Pullman	

APPENDIX 4

Content-Rich Newsletters

In April of 1993, still the formative years of our school, I sent the following letter, touching upon the issue of phonics as well as the need for abundant libraries and continued donations.

Dear families,

Each time I hear the radio advertisement calling for children to become hooked on phonics, I close my eyes, shake my head, and grit my teeth. The point is for children to become hooked on books, not hooked on phonics. The point is for children to become hooked on favorite authors, to become avid readers of such writers as Cynthia Rylant, Gary Paulsen, Katherine Paterson, and Walter Dean Myers. The point is for children to become hooked on poetry, fairy tales, science fiction or mysteries.

Prospective parents ask if we teach phonics at the Manhattan New School. Of course we do, but we think of phonic familiarity as one of the many clues children might use as they make their way through a good book, poem, play, or letter from a friend. When a teacher stops to confer with a child struggling with an unknown word, the teacher reminds the child that the word must make sense. Drawing on his vast knowledge and understanding of the story, the child makes an informed prediction. (What word would make sense here?) The teacher suggests that the child use their knowledge of phonics to confirm or reject their prediction. ("Could that word be ———?")

Teachers also highlight phonics elements at whole-class meetings. After children have read and responded to a wonderful picture book, poem, or non-fiction text, their teacher might point out a phonic element that appears frequently and naturally in that text. The children might begin to compile a class list, attending closely to that element. The children would then add their own discoveries, searching for example, for additional words that have silent letters, are compounds, or have distinctive spelling features. The classroom talk is rich and joyful and does not require three pages of workbook reinforcement.

Each day as well, the children take part in a writing workshop. That's an hour a day of children engaged in applying their understanding of how words are spelled. I recently met the superintendent of the Fairfax, Virginia schools. In his presentation he reminded the principals gathered that "the main thing was to keep the main thing the main thing." When it comes to reading, our main thing is to help children become hooked on books, not hooked on short vowels, consonant sounds, and endless rules that rarely apply.

To this end, we are forever gathering books. Robert Frost has suggested, "Surround youngsters with so many books they stumble over them." We want every classroom to feel as if it could be a library. We want a wide range of books, magazines and newspapers in every classroom. We agree with Bill Martin, Jr., who suggests, "The most important skill in reading is believing you can read." Therefore, we need a wide range of texts so that we can match each child with a book that says, "Bravo!"

We also want to satisfy children's different interests. We want to be able to say "yes" when a child asks if we have a book on quilting, cowboys, dinosaurs, or space travel. We also want to challenge growing readers, moving them towards books with layers of meaning. So far, we have been lucky. Publishers, commercial book clubs, professors, parents and friends have been donating shopping bags, cartons, and even station wagons filled with books, A private school about to close one of its duplicate libraries has recently offered us their upper school collection. And we're delighted. We will never turn down a donation of books.

We have big dreams for the Manhattan New School .W   e one day to not only have rich classroom libraries, but to also have small libraries throughout the building. We want to create easy access reading rooms that will support our efforts to do deep studies in the arts and sciences. I imagine a tiny room filled with poetry alone, a nonfiction reading room, and a small nook and cranny devoted to books in other languages that will honor all the language speakers who attend our school.

This all adds up to a big thank you—to those of you who have sent in bags of "outgrown" collections from the bedrooms of your nieces and nephews, to those of you who made classroom purchases at our recent book fair, to those of you who offer to box, transport and deliver books, to those of you who are ever on the prowl for much needed library pockets, bookcases and bookends, and of course to those of you who have sent in a book in honor of your child's birthday.

Thank you for helping us keep the main thing the main thing. We want our children to love school, learning, and books, real books.

With respect,

Shelley

This next newsletter was written in October of 1995 as I was attempting to entice more parents to attend PTA meetings and curriculum workshops on literacy.
I wrote:

Dear families,

As many of you know, I've recently been interviewed on some radio talk shows. The reporters began by asking me about my role as a spokesperson for the National Council Teachers of English and why this professional organization feels the need to redefine literacy as we move towards the 21st century.

I responded by suggesting that literacy needs to be long lasting. I shared our Manhattan New School belief in "lifetime guarantees." Your children will not only know how to read and write, but more importantly they will choose to read and write.

I went on to explain how this heartfelt promise—your children will choose to read and write—has implications for classroom practice. It is no longer enough in the reading classroom for students to be able to answer questions at the end of a chapter or fill in the blanks on a worksheet. In fact, those practices are no longer desirable. Instead, we have much higher expectations. Students throughout the grades are being asked to read a wide range of beautifully crafted authentic materials and to read them deeply and critically, discovering new meanings, making personal interpretations, connecting one text with another, and even reading as a writer intent on borrowing techniques for their own writing.

And that writing classroom, does not look like the one you or I attended, if indeed we ever attended a writing class. Writing no longer means simply following a teacher's specific instructions. We are no longer asking for 250 words on "Your summer vacation." Instead, students throughout the grades are working much harder and learning a great deal more. Students are filling journals, discovering important and original ideas, shaping and revising those ideas into appropriate forms, and editing those drafts into publishable finished works that do real work in the real world. Students are sending letters, crafting picture books for younger students, performing original plays for their peers, publishing non-fiction texts for their class libraries, etc. The news folks went on to ask me important questions about assessment, professional development, and the role technology plays in literacy development as we move toward the 21st century.

Thinking back on those interviews, and those reporters' broad-based questions I realized how much more fun it is to answer parents' questions about literacy development. The following are some of the most frequently asked literacy questions at our school:

1. *Why does everyone think reading aloud is so important?*
2. *My child wants me to read aloud the same book over and over again. Is that O.K. ?*
3. *What should I do when my child asks me to spell words for him?*
4. *What if my child complains, "I have nothing to write about?"*
5. *So what is really wrong with, "Hooked on Phonics?"*
6. *When my child is reading and gets stuck on a hard word what should I do?*
7. *How do I help my child get ready for those dreaded reading tests?*
8. *Whatever happened to those workbooks I used to have at school?*
9. *All my child reads are Goosebumps books. Should I be worried?*
10. *How come you don't ask for book reports?*

Rather than attempt to answer these important questions in this limited space I invite you to make this school year one in which you really learn about literacy. Attend PTA meetings, borrow our professional books and articles, ask for parent workshops, form adult reading and writing groups, pay attention to your child's growth as a reader. Share your questions and concerns.

Sincerely,

Shelley

(This list of questions could get quite good talk going if teachers were asked to answer them at a staff meeting. The session would serve as a real clearinghouse, allowing the staff to see if our literacy beliefs are consistent and providing background for new staff members who will no doubt be asked some of these questions by parents. Teachers could brainstorm additional literacy questions they are frequently asked and then pool their colleagues for solid answers.)

In this last newsletter I address the issue of summer reading and quote from a lead I wrote for our column in *The New Advocate*, summer 1996.

Dear families,

Traditionally, I use this last column of the school year to offer summer reading suggestions. I began writing some thoughts about pleasure reading in our months apart, but then real-ized I had recently written about my own summer reading habits for our school's column in The New Advocate, *a children's literature journal. I have therefore decided to quote some introductory paragraphs to give you a feel for our colu····* 's well as to offer some inspira-*tion for summer reading. The column begins,*

When I was a child, all my close friends spent their summers at sleep-away camp. I was the only member of the gang left to entertain herself on the steamy Brooklyn sidewalks, As soon as June arrived and our school days dwindled, I would start planning my summer months. While my friends, no doubt, were dreaming of lanyards, color war, and swimming holes, I would sign-up for Vacation-Day Camp at P.S. 179 and I would hustle a few babysitting jobs in nearby apartment buildings. But my dreams had nothing to do with weaving colored loops into potholders in the school cafeteria or playing games of peekaboo, no matter how cute the baby. No, my dreams all took place in the Kensington branch of the New York Public Library.

And summer months didn't mean leisure reading to me, no browsing the shelves and randomly selecting titles. No, to my youthful, yet ambitious way of thinking, summer months required thinking strategic thoughts. I needed to feel accomplished at summer's end. One summer I attempted reading the entire shelf of the Berlitz self-teaching language books. Another summer I attempted to read all the mystery books, alphabetically by author. I even recall filling one summer with nothing but cookbook reading. On each library visit, I would borrow as many cookbooks as I could carry, intent not only on reading them but preparing recipes as well. Of course our kitchen in summer was always too hot to bother.

When friends returned at the end of August and shared their summer victories, I did-n't boast of all I had read. Somehow I sensed that to this gang of giggling preteens, reading books took a backseat to short-sheeting beds in the boys' bunk. But deep down, I knew I had a summer worth remembering.

Today, I still plan my summer reading early on. Occasionally, I still intend to sweep through an entire shelf. What could be more pleasurable than spending a summer with all the books by Anne Tyler, Isabel Allende, or Wallace Stegner? Imagine how delightful it would be to spend a whole summer reading poetry or memoir. Then too, there are still all those cookbooks.

Of course, summers are especially dear to educators who finally have time to immerse themselves in a pressing professional issue. Will this be my summer to curl up with a stack of books on working with English language learners or to reread all my resources on wel-coming parents into the school community? Big blocks of time invite in-depth reading, filled with connected thoughts and overlapping ideas.

But of course, I've also learned to look forward to summers filled with lots of seren-dipitous reads, with nothing more to accomplish then the pleasure of getting lost in a goc book . . .

The column continued with a list of children's books that deserved to be read this summer season, whether they are read on park benches, at the beach, or even tucked into camp trunks. No doubt, a few of the books will be read by children who also see their public library as a summer haven, a literary refuge.

Rather than include here our list of reviewed books, I thought it more helpful to suggest the names of some wonderful writers whose work could easily fill up a child's summer reading times. No doubt, works of these prolific writers can be easily found on the shelves of your nearest public library. Note, this is just a brief listing. Ask your librarian for additional recommendations.

For our youngest readers:

John Birmingham, Shirley Hughes, Arnold Lobel, Byron Barton, Heidi Goennel, Mem Fox, Anthony Browne, Rosemary Wells, Eric Carle, Charlotte Zolotow, Vera B. Williams, Bill Martin, Jr., Jeanne Titherington, Kevin Henkes, Donald Crews, Frank Asch, Peter Sis, Brian Wildsmith, Lois Ehlert, Tana Hoban, Leo Lionni, Robert Munsch, Marisabina Russo, Peggy Parish

For our more independent readers:

Patricia Polacco, James Howe, Eve Bunting, Cynthia Rylant, Nikki Giovanni, Eloise Greenfield, William Steig, Patricia Reilly Giff, Gail Gibbons, Joanna Hurwitz, Byrd Baylor, Barbara Cooney, Jane Yolen, Robert Kimmel Smith, Elizabeth Levy, Louis Sachar, Beverly Cleary, Patricia MacLachlan, Jon Scieszka, Lloyd Alexander, Kathryn Lasky, Paula Danziger.

For our more mature readers:

Lois Lowry, Gary Paulsen, Bruce Brooks, Gary Soto, Phyllis Reynolds Naylor, Bette Bao Lord, Walter Dean Myers, Avi, Jerri Spinelli, Pat Hermes, Paula Fox, Lawrence Yep, Ann Grifalconi, Chris Crutcher, Katherine Paterson, Natalie Babbitt

Reading-Workshop Teacher Observation Report

Dear David,

It was joyful to observe your book talk conversations. Your fourth graders are certainly benefiting for your dedication to professional growth through the time you spend with your colleagues, your professional reading and your attendance ..t conferences and workshops. I applaud you for taking full advantage of all these opportunities.

On the day I visited, the room was in its usual state: calm, orderly and attractive. You certainly are masterful at management, social tone, and interior design. It was clear that you have been reading aloud Katherine Paterson's The Great Gilly Hopkins *and were seriously studying how to have meaningful and accountable talk. (How sensible it is to teach children about good book talk by focusing on a book read aloud, thereby including all readers.)*

The children, for homework, had been asked to imagine what Gilly Hopkins would have been like if she had remained with her mother. In other words, they had prepared for the day's whole group and small group conversations to come. Rehearsal is certainly an important support to learning, one all teachers probably need to think about throughout the day.

You began the meeting by asking for children to invent a name for the act of taking another perspective because it would make talking about it easier. (How wise of you to tell the children why you are asking them to do what they do). When someone suggested "flip side of the coin," talk, you reminded them that they were not going to look at just two sides of the issue, rather they might even invent twenty-seven perspectives.

(I wondered if imagining if Gilly stayed with her mother is really taking another perspective. For me, taking another perspective would apply if you asked students to read this book, for example, through the eyes of their parents. How would their responses change? Or to think about any one event from a different character's perspective. Were you interested in getting children to read from another point of view or to view the events in the story from a different character's state of mind? Or were you really interested in more of an "Imagining the Possibilities," response to the text? Isn't it fascinating to study teaching so closely?) Nonetheless, the value of asking children to invent labels for the kinds of thinking they are being asked to do facilitates the children's ability to think metacognitively and as you explained to talk about their processes. I'd be interested to learn what other labels you and your students have come up with this year and what you finally agreed to call "taking another perspective." (Would you consider simply sticking with "taking another perspective" if no better childlike term arises?) In addition, your children were totally engaged, responsive and respectful of one another's ideas during this whole class gathering.

When you announced that it was time to get together in small groups and to figure out who the children had never worked with before, I was completely taken aback with how orderly, respectfully and efficiently the children checked the names on their book talk response sheets and then rearranged themselves into small clusters. I recall hearing Albina say to her group that was beginning to form, "We need a boy!" You announced that everyone should be working within two minutes. I believe it took even less time. It's clear that you trust your children and they in turn trust you. It's also clear that your instructions and routines are clear and consistent. The children know what is expected of them and they take their work seriously.

You circulated the room, clipboard in hand, and eavesdropped on these small group discussions. Before asking children to reconvene on the rug, you asked them to record their comments on the effectiveness of that day's small groups. It's clear that you will be using these sessions to establish more permanent book talk groups.

When children reconvened you shared your own observations. You began by respectfully acknowledging that the talk time was not enough. (I wondered if you were cutting it short to ensure that I would see how you bring closure to these sessions or if you wanted to complete this work before the children needed to go to music class.) You then proceeded to share some of the notes you had taken. For example, you noticed that Moises had picked up on Samantha's body language and at a pause in his group's conversation even asked, "Samantha, what was it you wanted to say?" You also commented on Moises' ability to seek clarification, by asking a member of his group, "Could you explain what you mean?" (I appreciated that Nick publicly and confidently asked, "What does clarification mean?") You reminded all students to look for signals that group members give and to seek clarification when necessary. With so much attention paid to this kind of preparatory work, no doubt, the book talk groups that form in your classroom when children read multiple copies of books of their own choosing, will be successful and support children's growth as readers. You then asked children to place their reading folders in a neat pile, to gather their music folders and to walk down the hall to music class.

I so appreciate your attention to detail. I love neat piles. Then too, David, I appreciate your attention to detail in regard to individual concerns about your children. You worry about _____'s health _____'s absences, _____'s self-esteem, _____'s state of mind, and so on. Thanks too for all the extra hours you spend making your classroom beautiful. It is clearly a place where children and teachers can do good work.

Sincerely,

Shelley

Read-Aloud Transcript and Discussion

The following transcript was recorded by Joanne Hindley Salch as Shelley read aloud Belinda Rochelle's picture book *When Jo Louis Won the Title* to Joanne's third-grade class. The book presents the story of a young girl fearful that when the children in her new school hear her name they will tease her. Her grandfather, named John Henry, calms her fears by telling her the rich family story attached to her name. He informs her that her grandparents met the night Joe Louis won the title and in fact met because Joe Louis won the title. There was celebrating in the streets of Harlem and her grandfather, then a newcomer from Mississippi, stopped a beautiful young woman on the street to ask about the commotion. That is how Jo Louis' grandparents met. Her father was named Joe Louis in honor of the great boxer and she had been named after her father. Larry Johnson's full-page realistic illustrations make the streets of Harlem come alive.

Shelley—*I picked this book especially for you guys, especially for the beginning of the year, and I was really surprised when I first saw the title,* When Jo Louis Won the Title, *because I know of a really famous person named Joe Louis.*

Michael-*(interrupts to tell about Joe Louis) He was a hero, a black hero. He was called the Brown Bomber. He was born in Montgomery, Alabama.*

Shelley—*Michael, you know so much about Joe Louis, please come right up here and address the whole class.*

Michael—*(comes up and offers details about how Joe Louis won the title)*

Shelley—*(to entire class) Do you understand what Michael means by "winning the title"?*

Joseph—*Yeah, like becoming the champion.*

Shelley—*Thanks Michael for sharing all that information (Michael returns to the rug).*

Shelley—*Let's look again at the cover of the book. This is a different kind of title, the title of the book.*

And we have some Joes in this class. Joe Taveras, how do you spell your name?

Joe—*J-O-E*

Shelley—*And if I were going to call Joanne by her nickname Jo, how do you think we should spell that?*

Jameelah—*J-O-, like the Jo in* Little Women.

Shelley—*Sure, so when we look at the title of this book, what do we probably know about this Jo Louis?*

Jameelah—*It's a girl.*

Shelley—*She sure is, but when I first read the title, I thought the author or publisher misspelled the name of the famous Joe Louis. This book was written by a woman named Belinda Rochelle and it was illustrated by a man named Larry Johnson.*

Paul—*That's a famous basketball player's name—Larry Johnson.*

Shelley—*You're kidding? I didn't think of that.*

(Reads the back flap about the author and illustrator.) It's a different Larry Johnson. (Reads the dedications for the author and the illustrator.) (Children look at photographs of author and illustrator, showing surprise that illustrator is a grandfather as he mentions in his dedication.)

Jameelah—*He's too young to be a grandfather.*

Michael—*But your grandmother looks young.*

Shelley—*Some grandparents do look young. (Begins reading the book aloud and pauses at the end of the second page.)*

Michael—*(Commenting on lines read) That's a lot of "around and around." I thought it was going to say, "He swung her around and around until they both got sick."*

Shelley—*(Rereads page two adding Michael's invented line, ". . . until they both got sick.")*

(Continues reading until the question in the text reads, "What's the real reason you don't want to go to school?")

Any guesses? Does anyone think they know why she doesn't want to go to school?

Ramy—*Yeah, new schools are scary.*

Shelley—*Yes, sometimes new things are scary.*

Who is new to our school in this class? Maia and Max? So this story may have even more meaning for them.

So the grandpa asks, "What's the real reason?" He's not buying that stuff about her being short or slow.

Michael—*(interrupts) There's a famous John Henry. I think he's a myth—a Southern myth.*

Shelley—*Michael you're a real historian. If you're not sure about the famous John Henry, I have a book about him somewhere in the school. We definitely have one in Carmen's Spanish class.*

Michael—*She'd have to translate it into English*

Shelley—*I'm sure she would do that. Let's get back to the story. Any more guesses? Does anyone have a hunch why she doesn't want to go to school?*

Maia—*She's scared of new people.*

Liliana—*She doesn't think she's smart.*

Amber—*She's afraid to be teased because she's short.*

Charlotte—*She'll miss her grandpa.*

Paul—*The teachers and kids won't like her.*

Shelley—*Great guesses. You're all such thoughtful listeners. Let's find out.*

(Continues reading until the part reads, "THE question.")

I know that I have to say "THE" in a special way because it is written in all capital letters. The writer is telling me it's a really important word.

(Reads the line, "She just wished she didn't have to tell anybody her name.")

Joseph—*I know why. Maybe it's a boy's name.*

Shelley—*I think you may be right. O.K. Let's keep going.*

(Continues reading through to the grandpa's story in which he mentions growing up in Mississippi and wanting to visit Harlem.)

Mississippi, that's down South. We live up North in New York. Do any of you live in Harlem?

Chris—*My grandpa was in Harlem Hospital.*

Shelley—*This part of town where our school is, is called Yorkville. Harlem is north of here. Lots of people live there and there is a big hospital there.*

Michael—*Lots of black people live there.*

Shelley—*That's right. (Continues reading)*

(Turns to the classroom teacher, to comment on some fidgeting)

It really feels like the <u>beginning</u> of the school year in here, lots of wiggling, tapping and turning. Paul and Joseph, you are breaking my heart. Put your notebooks and pencils where they won't make noise.

(Continues reading and stops to talk about a line of text)

"Everything I owned fit into a torn, tattered suitcase and a brown box wrapped in string."

What does that tell you about the grandfather when he was young?

Michael—*He was poor.*

Shelley—*Good for you. The writer didn't have to come right out and tell you but you know.*

Michael—*Yeah, cause everything he owned fit into an old suitcase and a box.*

Shelley—*(Continues reading) ". . . his words were like wings . . ."*

What a beautiful line! It makes me think that words are like wings because they can both take you places.

(Continues reading) "Streets did seem to be paved in gold." Does anyone know what that means?

Max—*The streets were shiny.*

Shelley—*What made them shine . . . made them seem like there was gold?*

Michael—*There's broken glass in the concrete.*

Shelley—*Paula's class made some concrete last year we can check with her or her students.*

Jameelah—*Where my grandma used to live, there was sparkles on the sidewalk that looked like diamonds.*

Shelley—*Uh, huh. So it looked like it was paved with gold.*

People from all over the world used to talk about New York. They thought of it as a rich city. They thought even our streets were paved with gold. They dreamed of coming to New York and getting rich.

(Continues reading and turns to colorful celebration scene on sidewalks of Harlem.)

You can tell something is happening on this page. The illustrator worked real hard here.

Why do you think people might have spilled out on to the streets to celebrate?

Charlotte—*It's New Year's Eve?*

Shelley—*Maybe. Let's keep reading. Just one hint, always remember the title. (Continues reading.)*

Joe Louis won the title that night, but the grandpa says it was special for another reason. Any guesses? This is a great place to stop and guess.

(Students have no guesses.)
This part is real romantic.
(Shelley rereads the page before when the little girl's grandmother introduces herself to her grandfather for the very first time.)
(Continues reading)
Here we go now—She's going into the new class like Maia and Max had to do. She braced herself. Does anyone know what that means?
(Ramy demonstrates how he braces himself.)

Shelley—*Why do you think Jo Louis braced herself?*

Charlotte—*She thought the boy would tease her.*

(Book ends and children applaud.)

Shelley—*I just loved the line, "Every name has a special story. In fact, that's why I thought this would be a great book for the beginning of the school year. I thought it would get us thinking about the stories attached to our names.*

Liliana—*(Starts retelling a Gilbert Grape movie her mother told her about.)*

Shelley—*(To Liliana) Can you tell us what made you think of that movie right now?*

Liliana—*Because the people in the movie were poor and the people in the book were poor.*

Joey—*They weren't poor. They have a house.*

Shelley—*Let's talk about that. Do you think the people in the book were poor?*

Charlotte—*No, she went to school, so she's not so poor.*

Shelley—*Don't poor children go to school? Does our school cost your family money?*

Chloe—*No but she went to public school, otherwise she'd wear a uniform.*

Maia—*At UNIS (The United Nations International School) you don't wear a uniform and it's a private school. It costs money.*

Shelley—*Does anyone else want to add to this discussion—rich or poor family?*

Sarah—*She had on a nice blue dress—probably rich.*

Amber—*My family is not rich and I have nice clothes.*

Jameelah—*(Changing the subject, returning to Shelley's earlier comment.)*
I know about my name. (Proceeds to tell about the meaning of her name in the Koran.)

Shelley—*Jameelah, your story is just the kind I thought we'd begin to share after reading this book. We can learn a lot about each other when we tell the stories attached to our names. Does anyone else have a name story to share?*

Maia—*Maia means a goddess and a star.*

Adar—*Adar means the sixth month in Hebrew and I was born in June.*

Max—*Max from Maximillian the chef on TV.*

Joanne—*(Their teacher volunteers her story)* *My parents were thinking about Joan or Anne so they combined the two names.*

Charlotte—*My mom wanted Zoe but my brother was Zane. Too many Z's*

Michael—*Dad was a Jehovah's Witness. Michael means gift of God.*

Liliana—*I was born in Costa Rica. My birth mother named me Lily. My mother calls me Liliana, but my nickname is Lily.*

Ramy—*I named myself . . .*

Shelley—*(Room is buzzing with stories now)*

You know guys, these stories are so interesting, some of you might want to save them in your writer's notebooks. Some of you might want to talk to your parents to find out more.

The valuable part in having a transcript like this is that it leads to very targeted conversation. Joanne and I spoke at length about the children, their group participation or lack of it, their life stories, their reading interests, their knowledge about the world, as well as about the choices a teacher makes as she reads aloud. In addition, having the transcript in my hands to reread several times helped me to concretize what I value in these classroom occasions as well as to ponder several big issues.

What I Value in Classroom Read-Alouds

- The coming together around a book and the conversation that follows can build classroom community.
- The conversation during a read aloud demonstrates what is meant by, "A good book is one you must put down."
- The conversation that surrounds read-alouds can serve as a model for what can happen when small groups get together for reader response. The teacher can point out the essential elements of quality conversations.
- The conversation that surrounds read-alouds can demonstrate that each member of the community may have different areas of expertise.
- The illustrations in a read-aloud can be as evocative as the text.
- Teachers can use the occasion to share their own their own literary tastes and habits.
- Teachers can use the occasion to naturally demonstrate specific reading strategies.
- Teachers can use the occasion to point out craftsmanship in writing.
- Teachers can use the occasion to set the rules for respectful listening.
- Teacher can use the occasion to help children see the potential for writing in response to literature. (See more on the Teaching of Writing in *Writing Through Childhood*).

Things Worth Pondering About Classroom Read Alouds

- What if chatty children like Michael don't have as interesting things to contribute? How do we politely curtail less valuable interruptions?

- When do we worry about children who don't participate in group discussions?

- Knowing there are many English learners in the group, should we be more conscious of idiomatic expressions (e.g., "He's not buying that stuff about . . .")?

- How much explanatory information need the teacher provide? How much is too much?

- Does stopping to ask children to predict, help them become active readers when they are on their own?

- Were the African-American children particularly active participants because this story honored their heritage?

- Why didn't I tell the story of my name, especially since I believe we shouldn't ask children to do anything we are not willing to do? (Thankfully, Joanne added her story).

- Should teachers reveal their take on meanings before inviting the children to share their thoughts? (Why did I tell students *my* take on "words as wings"? Should I have asked for the students to think that one through?)

- What informs the teacher's decision to offer information, open up conversations, table conversations, follow a child's line of thinking, etc.? Does the teacher have a teaching agenda or is the teacher just following her natural instincts to engage in a conversation about a book?

- Do teachers usually follow through on casual offers and suggestions? (Will I remember to find that book about John Henry? Will I ask Paula about concrete? Will I ask children if they found out more about the story of their names?

Reading Workshop Minilesson Worksheet

Source of Information:

Minilesson Topic:

Rationale for Teaching:

Words Spoken:

Materials Needed:

Possible Follow-up Lessons:

Staff Meeting Advance Reading

The following is a brief sampling of articles read to demonstrate the range of our subscriptions and areas of interest. I did not list here, however, any of the articles we read that infuriated us. There's no reason to encourage more educators to read uninformed bashing of public education or literature-based teaching.

"Guided Reading—The Reader in Control," by Margaret Mooney, in *Teaching Pre K-8 (February 1995)*

"Saying the 'p' Word: Nine Guidelines for Exemplary Phonics Instruction," by Steven Stahl, in *The Reading Teacher* 45, no. 8 (April 1992)

"Ramona and Her Neighbors: Why We Love Them," by Barbara Chatton, in *The Horn Book Magazine (May/June 1995)*

"The Aesthetics of Informational Reading," by J. Kevin Spink, in *The New Advocate* (spring 1996)

"Motivating Readers" column by Sharon Taberski in *Instructor* (September 1997 through August 1997)

"The Role of Trust In Reader-Response Groups," by Dixie Lee Spiegel, in *Language Arts* 73 (September 1996)

"What Reading Does for the Soul: A Girl and her Books," by Annie Dillard, in *American Teacher* (spring/summer 1998)

"Gender and Literacy: A Subtle Message to Boys," by Donald Pottorff, in *Talking Points 9, no. 1 (October-November 1997)*

"Complementary Contexts Support Peer Talk and Reading" by Linda Fielding, Jean Hammons, and Carrie Ziegelbein, in *Primary Voices K-6,* 7, no. 1 (August 1998)

"Voices from the Fringe," by Jacklyn Blake Clayton, in *Voices from the Middle* 3, no. 3 (September 1996)

Read-Aloud Questionnaire

1. How many times a day do you read aloud?
2. Are there rituals attached to your read-alouds?
3. Who selects texts for your read-alouds?
4. Do your students bring pad and paper to your read-alouds?
5. What are your all-time favorite read-alouds?
6. What happens to the texts you read aloud? How do they become part of the class community?
7. If you could design the ideal setting for classroom read-aloud, what would it look like?
8. Do you read aloud differently at school than you would if you were reading a bed-time story to a child at home? If so, talk about the difference.
9. Is there someone whose reading-aloud you admire? What makes that person so effective?
10. Do you like to be read aloud to? Why or why not?
11. Have you ever watched a colleague read aloud? A student teacher? A parent? Were there any surprises?
12. Do you ever have guest readers in class?
13. Have you ever spoken to your family members about the importance of reading aloud? What suggestions did you make?
14. Have you ever given up on a read aloud? Why?
15. Do you always read a book before reading it aloud? Do you ever read books cold? Any surprises?
16. Do you ever re-read your read-alouds?
17. Do you add personal comments as you read aloud? If so, what kind?
18. When reading a chapter book aloud over time, do you have additional rituals to enrich the cumulative experience?
19. Do you ever turn read-alouds into shared reading experiences? What kind of texts make this possible? What strategies do you use?
20. How do you handle "in-the-middle-of-the-text" responses? Do you encourage them? Do you ever discourage them? What kind of interruptions do you welcome, if any?
21. What kind of non-fiction texts have you read aloud lately? If none, why not? If yes, is it a different experience than reading-aloud fiction?
22. How often do you read poetry aloud? How do you choose the poems? What happens to the poems after you read them aloud?
23. What extra efforts are you making for the struggling readers during read-aloud time?
24. What extra efforts are you making for the English as a Second Language student during read-aloud time?
25. Would it be helpful to watch videotape of yourself reading aloud?
26. What are your read-aloud needs?
27. How do you list read-aloud time on your daily agenda? In other words, do you call it something other than "Read-aloud Time"?

Readers' Needs Think-Sheet

If their reading need happens to be:	An effective kind of text might be	An effective teaching strategy might be
Guesses at unknown words based on initial consonant sounds rather than on meaning		
Doesn't ask if text makes sense		
Doesn't ask if text sounds like familiar language		
Gets stuck on small basic words that need to be known on sight		
Seems unable to figure out a new word even though he knows other words with similar spelling patterns		
Appears paralyzed by unknown words		
Reads word by word—no attempt at phrasing		
Ignores punctuation as an aid to make meaning		
Unable or unwilling to read silently		
Reads too slowly		
Never stops to recall information		
Never uses knowledge of characters or familiarity with genre to make meaning		

If their reading need happens to be:	An effective kind of text might be	An effective teaching strategy might be
Disregards such clues as book flaps, titles, chapter headings, pictures, literary structures or conventions		
Never stops to interact, pose questions or predict		
Never forms visual images		
Seems confused by literary language		
Gives equal attention to all parts		
Lacks confidence		
Doesn't realize he/she is lost		
Doesn't use background knowledge		
Doesn't expect to make meaning		
Loses attention, unable to read for any length of time		
Literal interpretations only, doesn't see bigger meanings		
Difficulty in reading longer texts over time, can't hold onto plot		
Doesn't get sarcasm or other forms of humor or innuendo		

Quotations Think-Sheet—Reading Comprehension

"There exists a passion for comprehension, just as there exists a passion for music. That passion is rather common in children, but gets lost in most people later on."
—Albert Einstein

". . . the quality of having to stare, of not getting the point at once,"
—Flannery O'Connor

"The reason I don't read is that books are so damned locked up. To me, the little black words on a page are stiffer than steel forks, more closed than the stones in the Great Wall of China. When I'm reading, I don't like the idea that I can't stop the yarn spinning for a second to ask a couple of questions, to clear up a point or two. Sometimes I'd like to reach into the text and switch a couple of things around, throw the spotlight on a character I think should be getting more play, or shove the narrator off in a new direction."
—Narrator's comment in Bruce Brooks's *Midnight Hour Encores*

To me, detective stories are a great solace, a sort of mental knitting, where it doesn't matter if you drop a stitch.
—Rupert Hart-Davis

A truly good book teaches me better than to read it. I must soon lay it down, and commence living on its hint . . . What I began by reading, I must finish by acting.
—Henry David Thoreau

Reading Series Worksheet

Name of Series	Author	Distinguishing Features	Location in Building

APPENDIX 13

Questions to Guide Study of Student Writing of Struggling Readers

1. Do writers reveal areas of interest? Would it support their growth as readers if they were invited to read about these same topics?

2. Do writers have genres of strength? Would it support their growth as readers if they were asked to read these genres?

3. Do writers have major weaknesses as spellers? Does this interfere in any way with their growth as readers?

4. Does their writing lack clarity? Would it support their growth as readers if they were held accountable to clarify their meaning each time they wrote?

5. Does their writing lack punctuation? Does this mean that they might not be paying attention to punctuation when they read? Would tending to punctuation more in their writing support their growth as readers?

6. Does their writing reveal weaknesses in grammar? If we strengthen their grammatical understandings will they be better able to read more complex text?

7. Does their writing improve when literature is used as a scaffold? What are the implications for the teaching of writing *and* the teaching of reading?

8. Will deliberate writing challenges that require students to use the techniques that confuse them when they read, benefit the struggling reader?

9. Does it take some children a very long time to write very short amounts? If so, is their reading pace likewise so slow that it interferes with comprehension?

10. Do children write about themselves as struggling students? If so, how do we respond? Does what they say give us windows into their areas of difficulty? Do we think about self-esteem issues often enough when working with the struggling student?

Questions to Promote Thinking About Struggling Readers

Let the following list of questions remind those who are responsible for establishing buildingwide literacy goals that we must never forget our most struggling readers. Our commitment to these children must be apparent in all the decisions we make. The questions are intended to promote important thinking about how time, money, personnel, and school structures are used to support students who struggle with reading.

1. Are there ways for everyday school structures such as reading aloud to children or children reading with their book buddies, to be more supportive of the struggling reader?

2. What can specialist teachers (music, art, science, technology, etc.), be doing within their regular blocks of teaching, to bolster the literacy of children who are not as yet fluent readers?

3. How are staff developers helping classroom teachers provide the finest extra supports for children who struggle with learning to read?

4. How can we be sure that intervention teachers, (those who provide specialized reading help to individual students or small groups), within classrooms or outside of classrooms are prepared to offer the most effective instruction to students? How can we make sure that intervention instructors share what they are learning with classroom teachers and vice versa? How can we be sure students aren't getting mixed messages about the teaching of reading (incompatible teaching techniques, inconsistent terminology used by teachers, etc.)?

5. How can we insure that tutorial sessions, those that take place after school, (extended day) or after the school year, (extended year), are also meeting the needs of the students in attendance? How can we create structures so that classroom teachers are aware of the work that has been done over the summer months or is currently being done at these tutorials?

6. How can we ensure that the instruction students receive as part of their special education support (resource room, consultant teacher models) works in tandem with their regular classroom instruction? What structures need to be in place so that *all* children, including those in self contained special education programs are always receiving the highest quality instruction based on continuous teacher assessments?

7. How can we be sure that the work of school volunteers, who are *not* usually highly trained reading teachers, fits well with our beliefs about how children learn? How can we *always* be sure that the time children spend out of their classrooms is worth the loss of classroom instruction?

8. What structures can we create so that family members are supporting students' efforts to grow as readers in ways that are compatible with what we belief about literacy learning?

9. What are the possible ways for principals to stay personally connected to all readers needing extra supports thereby eliminating the possibility of any one "falling through the cracks?"

10. What are the professional development implications for any educator in a school, including the principal, who cannot provide effective teaching of reading instruction?

11. How do school expenditures demonstrate a commitment to children who need extra literacy supports?

12. How does the programming of teachers' schedules support their ability to provide needed instruction for struggling readers?

13. How can the work that students do in other content areas such as social studies and mathematics be supportive of their growth as readers?

14. How can preparation for standardized tests be consistent in what we believe about how children learn? What are realistic goals concerning the use of "test-prep" materials?

What you'd like them to understand about . . .

	Students	Colleagues	Families	Administrators
Phonics				
Selecting Books				
Handling Unknown Words				
Reading Tests				

Additional Samples of Mehmet's Notebook Writing

my mom

Same Days My mom mack cookiecs wen I eat them is taes Dalahes. afDer I eat the cookics I go to My Friends hase to play we play wit the tundels and I go home for Dinneer

King Kon

this SunDay I was waGen
KinG Kon He kill the Big DainasoR
you No how Do the GReLa kill
the DainaSoR the GReLa open the
DainaSoRS mawt and EDoinoSoR mawt
BLcD.

(grela/gorilla, mawt/mouth)

one cent-

why one cent in the word?
one centr is nating of you go
to the StoR the man wel Gav you
nating Like you bave to get FOR
Doller and you counn't Buy abretan
you want.

why I have tan cenets? money
is to Buy Samethin you' Like
Les Say I Like a Boll I Ger the
tan cente to the man I got the
Boll.

(abretan/everything, word/world)

Glases

Glases mack your eys BaReR
wen my couint have Glases she
cant see baReR. then My friends
Glases Mack youR eys Stav.

(couint/cousin, barer/better, sta/strong)

Pencils Pe.n.

pancil witin Like now I am writing
pen with Like Blak. I like
pen's I love Pencil's do you love Pencils
yes I do

Glue

wen I youse Glue it Rele helps
me and youn do pRicetme
the Glue help aBReyone in My
class

(Abreyone/everyone)

My cat is sleeping on My sisters
bad wen he mavs h's tale its Like
he DReeMS obawlt his Life wen
he gats up. he Rans to My bad
wen in BeakVeS My cat mas the
Room up.

hay stop thoyt

(beakves/breakfast)

(Nose)

Big Nose
opsayt Donw Nose
short Nose
smoll Nose
Skanes Nose
Fat Nose
smokey Nose
seRat Nose
Like Joannes
Nose.

curSh is not Good wen you
-aLL cuRsh to Sameone you weh
jeRt Sameone FeLinGh an your FeLlnoh
-o is not Good taing you aRe Doing
you aRe Doing Roncnh taing to the
vold.

Donuts is Good go for
pepl is Like candes I Love
Donubts its toes Good
cafe and DonuDet is so so
Good same times Donuts is
not Good for pepl

Flowers

← Loyte

Cafe

Foods

why do people have Books
Bekos is to Read not to play
of you play wet the Books
eyou wal gat in drabl
people Mack Books foR adeR
people Donot Rep BookJx and
the papeRs go to the Garbeg caleR
and the papeRs RePs

(jrabl/trouble)

Some ofRkan peoples eat banens.
uBriDay they eat in BRkves lune
and Dinme they Donot eat Like
we eat we eat eggs Donnats.
Bayals Meet Bait ofRkan
people couldn Do aBRtan
wet B-nens.

(bayels/bagels, abrtan/everything, brkves/breakfast)

(In response to this entry, I wrote the following note to Mehmet:

Dear Mehmet,

      Did you learn this from Teresa's
slide show? Why do you think people
would eat the same thing for breakfast,
lunch, a l dinner? Do you remember some
of the ways the people prepared the
bananas?
      Let's meet to talk.

                              Love,
                              Shelley

TURKEY

in turkey Lon time a go
people have to mack more money
to Buy house wen people
mack more money thy wel have
mas money to Buy hose is.

TURKey

in TURKey I fell saDe to ADeRpeople
somepeople get sick and Died
and I fell saDe oBetite.

(abetite/about it)

Putting Poetry to Many Uses

In the forthcoming *Writing Through Childhhod* I likewise depend on poetry to enrich the literacy work in our school.

In this book, *Lifetime Guarantees*, apart from the chapter on poetry, the reader will also find text describing the following uses of poetry:

BIBLIOGRAPHY

Books for Adults

Arundhati, Roy. 1998. *The God of Small Things*. New York, NY: HarperFlamingo.

Atkinson, Kate. 1996. *Behind the Scenes at the Museum*. New York, NY: St. Martins Press.

Barr, Catherine, ed. 1999. *Reading in Series: A Selection Guide to Books for Children*. New Providence, NJ: R. R. Bowker.

Bettmann, Otto, ed. 1987. *The Delights of Reading: Quotes, Notes and Anecdotes*. Boston, MA: D. R. Godine.

Bolton, Faye and Diane Snowball. 1993. *Ideas for Spelling*. Portsmouth, NH: Heinemann.

——. 1993. *Teaching Spelling*. Portsmouth, NH: Heinemann.

——. 1999. *Spelling K-8: Planning and Teaching*. York, ME: Stenhouse Publishers.

Boomer, Garth. 1985. *Fair Dinkum Teaching and Learning: Reflections on Literacy and Power*. Upper Montclair, NJ: Boynton/Cook Publishers.

Brown, H. Jackson Jr. 1994. *Wit and Wisdom from the Peanut Butter Gang: A Collection of Wise Words from Young Hearts*. Nashville, TN: Rutledge Hill Press.

Burke, Jim. 1999. *I Hear America Reading*. Portsmouth, NH: Heinemann.

Burns, Eric. 1995. *The Joy of Books: Confessions of a Lifelong Reader*. Amherst, NY: Prometheus.

Butler, Dorothy. 1998. *Babies Need Books*. Portsmouth, NH: Heinemann.

Chira, Susan. 1998. *A Mother's Place*. New York, NY: HarperCollins.

Clayton, Jacklyn Blake. 1996. *Your Land, My Land: Children in the Process of Acculturation*. Portsmouth, NH: Heinemann.

Coles, Gerald. 2000. *Misreading Reading: The Bad Science that Hurts Children*. Portsmouth, NH: Heinemann.

Cullinan, Bernice. 1992. *Read to Me: Raising Kids Who Love to Read*. New York, NY: Scholastic.

Cullinan, Bernice and Brod Bagert. 1993. *Helping Your Child Learn to Read*. Washington, DC: U. S. Dept. of Education.

Cunningham, Patricia. 1994. *Making Words*. Good Apple.

Cunningham, Patricia and Richard Allington. 1999. *Classrooms That Work: They Can All Read and Write*. New York, NY: Longman.

Dombey, Henrietta, Margaret Moustafa, and the Center for Language in Primary Education. 1998. *Whole to Part Phonics: How Children Learn to Read and Spell*. Portsmouth, NH: Heinemann.

Dorris, Michael and Emilie Buchwald, eds. 1997. *The Most Wonderful Books: Writers on Discovering the Pleasures of Reading*. Minneapolis, MN: Milkweed.

Edwards, Carolyn, Lella Gandini, and George Forman. 1993. *The Hundred Languages of Children: The Reggio Emilia Approach to Early Childhood Education*. Norwood, NJ: Ablex.

Fitzhugh, Louise. 1987. *Harriet the Spy*. Santa Barbara, CA: Cornerstone.

Fitzpatrick, Jean G. 1998. *Once Upon a Family: Read-Aloud Stories and Activities that Nurture Healthy Kids*. New York, NY: Viking.

Fountas, Irene C. and Gay S. Pinnell. 1996. *Guided Reading*. Portsmouth, NH: Heinemann.

Frazier, Charles. 1998. *Cold Mountain*. New York, NY: Vintage Books.

Freeman, David E. and Yvonne S. Freeman. 1994. *Between Worlds: Access to Second Language Acquisition*. Portsmouth, NH: Heinemann.

Freeman, Yvonne S. and David E. Freeman. 1998. *ESL/EFL Teaching: Principles for Success*. Portsmouth, NH: Heinemann.

Fu, Danling. 1995. *"My Trouble Is My English": Asian Students and the American Dream*. Portsmouth, NH: Heinemann.

Gibbons, Pauline. 1991. *Learning to Learn in a Second Language*. Portsmouth, NH: Heinemann.

Gilbar, Steven, ed. 1989. *The Open Door: When Writers First Learned to Read*. Boston, MA: D. R. Godine.

——. 1991. *The Readers Quotation Book: A Literary Companion*. New York, NY: Penguin Books.

Goodman, Deborah. 1999. *The Reading Detective Club: Solving the Mysteries of Reading*. Portsmouth, NH: Heinemann.

Goodman, Ken. 1996. *On Reading: A Common Sense Look at the Nature of Language and the Science of Reading*. Portsmouth, NH: Heinemann.

Greene, Bette. 1993. *Summer of My German Soldier*. New York, NY: Dell.

Hamill, Pete. 1997. *Snow in August*. Boston, MA: Little Brown.

Harwayne, Shelley. 1992. *Lasting Impressions: Weaving Literature Into the Writing Workshop*. Portsmouth, NH: Heinemann.

——. 1995. *Jewels: Children's Play Rhymes*. Greenvale, NY: Mondo Publishing.

——. 1996. *What's Cooking?* Greenvale, NY: Mondo Publishing.

——. 1999 *Going Public: Priorities and Practice at the Manhattan New School*. Portsmouth, NH: Heinemann.

Hindley, Joanne. 1996. *In the Company of Children*. York, Me.: Stenhouse Publishers.

Hoffman, Eva. 1989. *Lost in Translation*. New York, NY: E. P. Dutton.

Hydrick, Janie. 1996. *Parent's Guide to Literacy for the Twenty-first Century*. Urbana, Ill.: NCTE.

Kaye, Peggy. 1995. *Games for Writing: Playful Ways to Help Your Child Learn to Write*. New York, NY: Noonday Press.

Keene, Ellin O. and Susan Zimmerman. 1997. *Mosaic of Thought*. Portsmouth, NH: Heinemann.

Kelsh, Nick and Anna Quindlen. 1996. *Naked Babies*. New York, NY: Penguin Studio.

Krashen, Stephen. 1999. *Condemned Without a Trial: Bogus Arguments Against Bilingual Education*. Portsmouth, NH: Heinemann.

——. 1999. *Three Arguments Against Whole Language and Why They Are Wrong*. Portsmouth, NH: Heinemann.

Lamott, Anne. 1995. *Bird by Bird: Some Instructions on Writing and Life*. New York, NY: Anchor.

Lott, Brett. 1991. *Jewel*. New York, NY: Pocket Books.

Malouf, David. 1993. *The Great World*. New York, NY: Vintage International.

Manguel, Albert. 1996. *A History of Reading*. New York, NY: Viking.

McQuillan, Jeff. 1998. *The Literacy Crisis: False Claims, Real Solutions*. Portsmouth, NH: Heinemann.

Michaels, Anne. 1997. *Fugitive Pieces*. New York, NY: Alfred A. Knopf.

Moustafa, Margaret. 1997. *Beyond Traditional Phonics*. Portsmouth, NH: Heinemann.

Pennac, Daniel. 1999. *Better Than Life*. York, Me.: Stenhouse Publishers.

Petroski, Henri. 1999. *The Book on the Bookshelf*. New York, NY: Alfred A. Knopf.

Phinney, Margaret Y. 1988. *Reading with the Troubled Reader*. Portsmouth, NH: Heinemann.

Pinnell, Gay S. and Irene C. Fountas. 1998. *Word Matters*. Portsmouth, NH: Heinemann.

Piper, Terry. 1003. *And Then There Were Two: Children and Second Language Learning*. Markham, Ont.: Pippin Publishers.

Pipher, Mary. 1994. *Reviving Ophelia: Saving the Selves of Adolescent Girls*. New York, NY: Putnam.

Quindlen, Anna. 1998. *How Reading Changed My Life*. New York, NY: Ballantine Publishing Group.

Rhodes, Lynn K. and Curt Dudley-Marling. 1996. *Readers and Writers with a Difference*. Portsmouth, NH: Heinemann.

Rigg, Pat and Virginia G. Allen, eds. 1989. *When They Don't All Speak English: Integrating the ESL Student into the Regular Classroom*. Urbana, Ill.: NCTE.

Rochman, Hazel and Darlene Z. McCampbell, eds. 1997. *Leaving Home*. New York, NY: HarperCollins.

Rogovin, Paula. 1998. *Classroom Interviews: A World of Learning*. Portsmouth, NH: Heinemann.

Routman, Regie. 1994. *Invitations: Changing as Teachers and Learners, K-12*. Portsmouth, NH: Heinemann.

Routman, Regie. 1996. *Literacy at the Crossroads*. Portsmouth, NH: Heinemann.

Russo, Richard. 1994. *Nobody's Fool*. New York, NY: Vintage Books.

Samway, Davis and Denis McKeon. 1999. *Myths and Realities: Best Practice for Language Minority Students*. Portsmouth, NH: Heinemann.

Schwartz, Lynn S. 1996. *Ruined by Reading: A Life in Books*. Boston, MA: Beacon Press.

Shannon, David. 1994. *How Georgie Radbourn Saved Baseball*. New York, NY: Blue Sky Press.

Sherman, Alan. 1965. *A Gift of Laughter*. New York, NY: Atheneum Publishers.

Silberman, Arlene. 1989. *Growing Up Writing: Teaching Out Children to Write, Think and Learn*. New York, NY: Times Books.

Spangenberg-Urbschat, Kaeren and Robert Pritchard, eds. 1994. *Kids Come in All Languages: Reading Instruction for ESL Students*. Newark, Del.: International Reading Association.

Stillman, Peter. 1989. *Families Writing*. Cincinnati, OH: Writers Digest Books.

Stone, Elizabeth. 1988. *Black Sheep and Kissing Cousins: How Our Family Stories Shape Us*. New York, NY: Times Books.

Taberski, Sharon. 2000. *On Solid Ground: Strategies for Teaching Reading K-3*. Portsmouth, NH: Heinemann.

Taylor, Denny and Catherine Dorsey-Gaines. 1988. *Growing Up Literate: Learning from Inner-City Families*. Portsmouth, NH: Heinemann.

Toth, Susan Allen and John Coughlan, eds. 1990. *Reading Rooms: America's Foremost Writers Celebrate Our Public Libraries*. New York, NY: Doubleday.

Trelease, Jim. 1995. *New Read-Aloud Handbook*. New York, NY: Penguin Books.

Wakefield, H. Patricia. 1994. *Teaching the World's Children: ESL for Ages Three to Seven*. Markham, Ont.: Pippin Pub.

Weaver, Connie. 1996. *Teaching Grammar in Context*. Portsmouth, NH: Boynton/Cook Publishers.

White, T. H. 1958. *The Once and Future King*. London, England: Collins.

Books for Children

Agee, Jon. 1991. *Go Hang a Salami! I'm a Lasagna Hog!.* New York, NY: Farrar Straus Giroux.

Alexander, Lloyd. 1971. *The King's Fountain.* New York, NY: Dutton.

Alford, Jan. 1997. *I Can't Believe I Have to Do This.* New York, NY: Penguin Putnam Books for Young Readers.

Aliki. 1998. *Marianthe's Story: Painted Words, Spoken Memories.* New York, NY: Greenwillow Books.

Appelbaum, Diana. 1997. *Cocoa Ice.* New York, NY: Orchard Books.

Arnold, Tedd. 1992. *The Signmaker's Assistant.* New York, NY: Dial Books for Young Readers.

Arnosky, Jim. 1999. *Big Jim and the White-Legged Moose.* New York, NY: Lothrop, Lee & Shepard.

Axworthy, Anni. 1998. *Guess What I Am.* New York, NY: Candlewick Press.

——. 1998. *Guess What I'll Be.* New York, NY: Candlewick Press.

——. 1999. *Guess Where I Live.* Cambridge, MA: Candlewick Press.

Balat, Jan. 1969. *The Fence.* New York, NY: Delacorte Press.

Banks, Sara H. 1999. *Abraham's Battle.* New York, NY: Atheneum Books for Young Readers.

Barash, Lynne. 1998. *Old Friends.* New York, NY: Farrar, Strauss and Giroux.

Bedard, Michael. 1999. *The Clay Ladies.* Plattsburgh, NY: Tundra Books.

Bemelmans, Ludwig. 1959-1962. *Madeline* books. New York, NY: Viking.

Bloom, Becky. 1999. *Wolf!.* New York, NY: Grolier Books.

Blume, Judy. 1984. *The Pain and The Great One.* Scarsdale, NY: Bradbury Press.

Bogart, Ellen. 1999. *Jeremiah Learns to Read.* New York, NY: Orchard Books.

Bond, Michael. 1999. *Paddington Bear: My Scrapbook.* New York, NY: HarperFestival.

Bonners, Susan. 1997. *The Silver Balloon.* New York, NY: Farrar, Straus, Giroux.

Borden, Louise. 1999. *Good Luck Mrs. K.* New York, NY: Margaret K. McElderry Books.

Boyko, Carrie and Kimberly Colen. 1996. *Hold Fast Your Dreams: Twenty Commencement Speeches.* New York, NY: Scholastic.

Brooks, Bruce, ed. 1998. *The Red Wasteland: A Personal Selection of Writings About Nature for Young Readers.* New York, NY: Henry Holt.

Browne, Anthony. 1989. *The Tunnel.* New York, NY: Alfred A. Knopf.

Bunting, Eve. 1991. *Fly Away Home.* New York, NY: Clarion Books.

Butler, Philippa. 1998. *Pawprints in Time.* New York, NY: Viking.

Byars, Betsy. 1988. *The Summer of the Swans.* Santa Barbara, CA: ABC-Clio.

——. 1996. *The Tornado.* New York, NY: HarperCollins.

Cameron, Polly. 1961. *I Can't Said the Ant.* New York, NY: Coward-McCann. C

Carle, Eric. 1984. *The Very Busy Spider.* New York, NY: Philomel Books.

Carrick, Carol. 1999. *Upside Down Cake.* New York, NY: Clarion Books.

Charlip, Remy. 1969, 1980. *Arm in Arm.* New York, NY: Four Winds Press.

Chesworth, Michael. 1994. *This is the Story of Archibald Frisby.* New York, NY: Farrar, Straus, Giroux.

Cleary, Beverly. 1983. *Dear Mr. Henshaw.* New York, NY: Morrow.

——. 1987. *The Growing Up Feet.* New York, NY: Morrow.

Cohen, Barbara. 1998. *Molly's Pilgrim.* New York, NY: Lothrop, Lee & Shepard.

Cole, Joanna. 1998. *The New Baby at Your House.* New York, NY: Morrow Junior Books.

Cole, Joanna and Stephanie Calmenson. 1994. *Crazy Eights and Other Card Games.* New York, NY: Morrow Junior Books.

——. 1999. *Fun on the Run: Travel Games and Songs.* New York, NY: Morrow Junior Books.

Cole, Joanna and Wendy Saul. 1996. *On the Bus with Joanna Cole: A Creative Autobiography.* Portsmouth, NH: Heinemann.

Cowley, Joy. 1999. *Mrs. Wishy Washy.* New York, NY: Philomel Books.

Creech, Sharon. 1995. *Absolutely Normal Chaos.* New York, NY: HarperCollins.

Curtis, Jamie Lee. 1998. *Today I Feel Silly and Other Moods That Make My Day.* New York, NY: HarperCollins.

Dahl, Roald. 1961. *James and the Giant Peach.* New York, NY: Alfred A. Knopf.

Dalokay, Vedat. 1994. *Sister Shako and Kolo the Goat: Memories of My Childhood in Turkey.* New York, NY: Lothrop, Lee & Shepard.

DeGross, Monalisa. 1994. *Donavan's Word Jar.* New York, NY: HarperCollins.

Dodson, Shireen. 1997. *The Mother-Daughter Book Club.* New York, NY: HarperPerennial.

Dragonwagon, Crescent. 1997. *Brass Button.* New York, NY: Atheneum Books for Young Readers.

Ehlert, Lois. 1995. *Snowballs.* San Diego, CA: Harcourt Brace.

Erlbruch, Wolf. 1997. *Mrs. Meyer the Bird.* New York, NY: Orchard Books.

Estes, Eleanor. 1973. *The Hundred Dresses.* New York, NY: Scholastic.

Evans, Lezlie. 1997. *Snow Dance.* Boston, MA: Houghton Mifflin.

Fedden, Mary. 1997. *Motley the Cat.* New York, NY: Viking.

Feder, Jane. 1995. *Table, Chair, Bear: A Book in Many Languages.* New York, NY: Ticknor & Fields.

Filipovic, Zlata. 1994. *Zlata's Diary: A Child's Life in Sarajevo.* New York, NY: Viking.

Fisher, Aileen. 1968. *We Went Looking.* New York, NY: Crowell.

Fitch, Sheree. 1997. *There's a Mouse in My House.* Toronto, Canada:. Doubleday of Canada.

Fleischman, Paul. 1999. *Weslandia.* Cambridge, MA: Candlewick Press.

Foland, Constance. 1999. *A Song for Jeffrey.* Middleton, WI: American Girl.

Friedman, Ina R. 1984. *How My Parents Learned to Eat.* Boston, MA: Houghton Mifflin.

Gardiner, John Reynolds. 1980. *Stone Fox.* New York, NY: Crowell.

Gellman, Marc. 1997. *"Always Wear Clean Underwear!" and Other Ways Parents Say "I Love You".* New York, NY: Morrow Junior Books.

George, Jean Craighead. 1965. *Spring Comes to the Ocean.* New York, NY: Crowell.

Getz, David. 1998. *Frozen Girl.* New York, NY: Henry Holt.

Ginsburg, Mirra. 1994. *The Old Man and His Birds.* New York, NY: Greenwillow Books.

Goennel, Heidi. 1992. *It's My Birthday.* New York, NY: Tambourine Books.

———. 1995. *I Pretend.* New York, NY: Tambourine Books.

Goffstein, M. B. 1986. *School of Names.* New York, NY: Harper and Row.

Golenbach, Peter. 1990. *Teammates.* San Diego, CA: Harcourt Brace Jovanovich.

Graff, Nancy P. 1998. *In the Hush of the Evening.* New York, NY: HarperCollins.

Graham-Barber, Lynda. 1994. *A Chartreuse Leotard in a Magenta Limousine.* New York, NY: Hyperion Books for Children.

Greene, Carol. 1999. *Sunflower Island.* New York, NY: HarperCollins.

Hamilton, Virginia. 1995. *Her Stories: African American Folktales, Fairytales, and True Tales.* New York, NY: Blue Sky.

Haviland, Virginia. 1994. *Favorite Folktales Told in England.* New York, NY: Beech Tree.

———. 1994. *Favorite Folktales Told in Germany.* New York, NY: Beech Tree.

———. 1995. *Favorite Folktales Told in Czechoslovakia.* New York, NY: Beech Tree.

———. 1995. *Favorite Folktales Told in Poland.* New York, NY: Beech Tree.

———. 1995. *Favorite Folktales Told in Russia.* New York, NY: Beech Tree.

———. 1995. *Favorite Folktales Told in Scotland.* New York, NY: Beech Tree.

Hayes, Joe. 1996. *A Spoon for Every Bite.* New York, NY: Orchard Books.

Heide, Florence P. and Roxanne H. Pierce. 1998. *Tio Armando.* New York, NY: Lothrop, Lee & Shepard.

Henkes, Kevin. 1997. *Sun and Spoon.* New York, NY: Greenwillow Books.

Hest, Amy. 1993. *Nana's Birthday Party.* New York, NY: Morrow Junior Books.

———. 1996. *Jamaica Louise James.* Cambridge, MA: Candlewick Press.

Hepworth, Cathi. 1992. *Antics! An Alphabetical Anthology.* New York, NY: G. P. Putnam's Sons.

Hill, Eric. 1991. *Spot's Birthday.* New York, NY: G. P. Putnam's Sons.

Hines, Anna Grossnickle. 1996. *When We Married Gary.* New York, NY: Greenwillow Books.

Hoban, Russell. 199. *A Bargain for Frances.* New York, NY: HarperFestival.

Hoban, Tana. 1983. *I Read Symbols.* New York, NY: Greenwillow Books.

———. 1988. *Look, Look, Look!.* New York, NY: Greenwillow Books.

Hobbie, Holly. 1997. *Toot and Puddle.* Boston, MA: Little Brown.

Hoff, Syd. 1999. *Danny and the Dinosaur.* New York, NY: HarperFestival.

Hoose, Philip and Hannah Hoose. 1998. *Hey Little Ant.* Berkeley, CA.: Tricycle Press.

Howe, Deborah and James Howe. 1994. *Teddy Bear's Scrapbook.* New York, NY: Aladdin Books.

Howe, James. 1999. *Horace and Morris but Mostly Dolores.* New York, NY: Atheneum Books for Young Readers.

Hurwitz, Joanna, ed. 1995. *Birthday Surprises: Ten Great Stories to Unwrap.* New York, NY: Morrow Junior Books.

Hurwitz, Johanna. 1990. *Busybody Nora.* New York, NY: Morrow Junior Books.

Hutchins, Pat. 1999. *It's My Birthday!* New York, NY: Greenwillow Books.

Jakobsen, Kathy. 1993. *My New York.* Boston, MA: Little Brown.

James, Mary. 1990. *Shoebag.* New York, NY: Scholastic.

James, Simon. 1997. *Leon and Bob.* Cambridge, MA: Candlewick Press.

Jennings, Paul. 1996. *Uncovered! Weird, Weird Stores.* New York, NY: Viking.

Jin, Sarunna. 1991. *My First American Friend*. Milwaukee, WI: Raintree Publishers.

Johnston, Tony. 1993. *The Last Snow of Winter*. New York, NY: Tambourine Books.

Juster, Norman. 1989. *As Silly as Knees, as Busy as Bees: An Astounding Assortment of Similes*. New York, NY: Beech Tree.

Ketterman, Helen. 1998. *I Remember Papa*. New York, NY: Dial Books for Young Readers.

Khan, Rukhsana. 1998. *The Roses in My Carpet*. New York, NY: Holiday House.

King-Smith, Dick. 1996. *Animal Friends: Thirty-one True to Life Stories*. Cambridge, MA: Candlewick Press.

Kinsey-Warnock, Natalie. 1997. *Sweet Memories Still*. New York, NY: Cobblehill Books/Dutton.

Krasilovsky, Phyllis. 1993. *The Woman Who Saved Things*. New York, NY: Tambourine Books.

Krupinski, Loretta. 1995. *Bluewater Journal: the Voyage of the Sea Tiger*. New York, NY: HarperCollins.

Lachner, Dorothea. 1995. *Andrew's Angry Words*. New York, NY: North-South Books.

Langsen. Richard C. 1996. *When Someone in the Family Drinks Too Much*. New York, NY: Dial Books for Young Readers.

Lankford, Mary. 1992. *Hopscotch Around the World*. New York, NY: Morrow Junior Books.

Lasky, Kathryn. 1996. *A Journey to the New World: The Diary of Remember Patience Whipple*. New York, NY: Scholastic.

Lauture, Denize. 1996. *Running the Road to ABC*. New York, NY: Simon & Schuster Books for Young Readers.

Leavitt, Melvin J. 1995. *A Snow Story*. New York, NY: Simon & Schuster Books for Young Readers.

Leighton, Maxine Rhea. 1992. *An Ellis Island Christmas*. New York, NY: Viking.

Lember, Barbara Hirsh. 1997. *The Shell Book*. Boston, MA: Houghton Mifflin.

Lemieux, Margo. 1994. *Full Worm Moon*. New York, NY: Tambourine Books.

Lerman, Rory. 1997. *Charlie's Checklist*. Orchard Books.

Levine, Ellen. 1989. *I Hate English!*. New York, NY: Simon & Schuster Books for Young Readers.

Lewis, Barbara. 1995. *The Kid's Guide to Service Projects*. Minneapolis, MN: Free Spirit Publishers.

——. 1997. *What Do You Stand For? A Kid's Guide to Building Character*. Minneapolis, MN: Free Spirit Publishers.

——. 1998. *The Kid's Guide to Social Action*. Minneapolis, MN: Free Spirit Publishers.

Lionni, Leo. 1992. *A Busy Year*. New York, NY: Alfred A. Knopf.

Little, Jean. 1987. *Little by Little: A Writer's Education*. Ontario, Canada: Viking.

LoMonaco, Palmyra. 1996. *Night Letters*. New York, NY: Dutton's Children's Books.

Look, Lenore. 1999. *Love as Strong as Ginger*. New York, NY: Atheneum Books for Young Readers.

Loomis, Christine. 1993. *In the Diner*. New York, NY: Scholastic.

Lorbiecki, Marybeth. 1997. *My Palace of Leaves in Sarajevo*. New York, NY: Dial Books for Young Readers.

Lowry, Lois. 1989. *Number the Stars*. Boston, MA: Houghton Mifflin.

——. 1993. *The Giver*. Boston, MA: Houghton Mifflin.

Lucas, Barbara. 1993. *Snowed In*. New York, NY: Bradbury Press.

Lyon, George Ella. 1998. *A Sign*. Orchard Books.

MacLachlan, Patricia. 1991. *Journey*. New York, NY: Delacorte Press.

Manning, Mick. 1994. *A Ruined House*. Cambridge, MA: Candlewick Press.

Manning, Mick and Brita Granstrom. 1996. *The World is Full of Babies*. New York, NY: Delacorte Press.

Martin, Bill Jr. 1992. *Brown Bear, Brown Bear, What Do You See?*. New York, NY: H. Holt.

Martin, Bill Jr. and John A. Archambault. 1989. *Chicka Chicka Boom Boom*. New York, NY: Simon & Schuster Books for Young Readers.

Mayer, Mercer. 1990. *There's a Nightmare in My Closet*. New York, NY: Dial Books for Young Readers.

McCully, Emily Arnold. 1998. *The Beautiful Warrior: The Legend of the Nun's Kung Fu*. New York, NY: Arthur A. Levine.

McPhail, David. 1997. *Edward and the Pirates*. Boston, MA: Little Brown.

Mennen, Ingrid and Niki Daly. *1992. Somewhere in Africa*. New York, NY: Dutton's Children's Books.

Meyer, Eleanor Walsh. 1998. *The Keeper of Ugly Sounds*. Bicester, Eng.: Winslow Press.

Michels, Tilde. 1990. *Rabbit Spring*. New York, NY: Alfred A. Knopf.

Milne, A. A. 1926. *Winnie the Pooh*. New York, NY: Dutton.

Mochizuki, Ken. 1993. *Baseball Saved Us*. New York, NY: Lee and Low Books.

Morpurgo, Michael. 1996. *The Dancing Bear*. Boston, MA: Houghton Mifflin.

Morris, Ann. 1995. *I Am Six*. Parsippany, NJ: Silver Press.

——. 1996. *The Daddy Book*. Parsippany, NJ: Silver Press.

Munro, Roxie. 1985. *The Inside-Outside Book of New York*. New York, NY: Dodd, Mead.

——. 1996. *The Inside-Outside Book of Libraries*. New York, NY: Dutton Children's Books.

Myers, Walter Dean. 1996. *Brown Angels*. New York, NY: HarperTrophy.

Naylor, Phyllis Reynold. 1991. _King of the Playground._ New York, NY: Atheneum.

Neitzel, Shirley. 1997. _I'm Taking a Trip on a Train._ New York, NY: Greenwillow Books.

——. Shirley. 1999. _We're Making Breakfast for Mother._ New York, NY: Greenwillow Books.

Nolen, Jerdine. 1999. _In My Momma's Kitchen._ New York, NY: Lothrop, Lee & Shepard.

Ormerod, Jan. 1986. _Story of Chicken Licken._ New York, NY: Lothrop, Lee & Shepard.

Otto, Carolyn. 1998. _Our Puppies Are Growing._ New York, NY: HarperCollins.

Paterson, Katherine. 1980. _Jacob Have I Known._ New York, NY: Crowell.

Polacco, Patricia. 1998. _Thank You, Mr. Falker._ New York, NY: Philomel Books.

Rahaman, Vashanti. 1997. _Read for Me, Mama._ Honesdale, PA: Boyds Mills.

Rockwell, Anne. 1995. _The Acorn Tree._ New York, NY: Greenwillow Books.

Rosa-Casanova, Sylvia. 1997. _Mama Provi and the Pot of Rice._ New York, NY: Atheneum Books for Young Readers.

Ryder, Joanne. _1991. Winter Whale._ New York, NY: Morrow Junior Books.

Schneider, R. M. 1995. _Add It, Dip It, Fix It._ Boston, MA: Houghton Mifflin.

Seuss, Dr. 1990. _Oh, the Places You'll Go._ New York, NY: Random House.

Shannon, George. 1985. _Stories to Solve_ series. New York, NY: Greenwillow Books.

——. 1988. _True Lies: 18 Tales for You to Judge._ New York, NY: Doherty Associates.

——. 1995. _Tomorrow's Alphabet._ New York, NY: Greenwillow Books.

Shepard, Aaron. 1994. _The Baker's Dozen: A Saint Nicholas Tale._ New York, NY: Atheneum Books for Young Readers.

Shreve, Susan. 1996. _Warts._ New York, NY: Tambourine Books.

Sierra, Judy. 1996. _Nursery Tales Around the World._ New York, NY: Clarion Books.

Silbaugh, Elizabeth. 1996. _Let's Play Cards: A First Book of Card Games._ New York, NY: Simon & Schuster Books for Young Readers.

Silver, Maggie. 1995. _Who Lives Here?_ San Francisco, CA: Sierra Club Books for Children.

Silverman, Erica. 1993. _Mrs. Peachtree and the Eighth Avenue Cat._ New York, NY: Macmillan.

Silverstein, Shel. 1964. _The Giving Tree._ New York, NY: Harper and Row.

Slobodkina, Esphyr. 1985. _Caps for Sale._ New York, NY: Harper and Row.

Soto, Gary. 1998. _Snapshots from the Wedding._ New York, NY: G. P. Putnam.

Steptoe, John. 1987. _Mufaro's Beautiful Daughter._ New York, NY: Lothrop, Lee & Shepard.

Stevens, Janet. 1999. _Cook-A-Doodle-Doo._ San Diego, CA: Harcourt Brace.

Stolz, Mary. 1997. _A Ballad of the Civil War._ New York, NY: HarperCollins.

Tamar, Erika. 1996. _The Garden of Happiness._ SanDiego, CA: Harcourt Brace.

Terban, Marvin. 1991. _Hey, Hay! A Wagonful of Homonym Riddles._ New York, NY: Clarion Books.

Thomas, Jane rush. 1999. _The Snoop._ New York, NY: Clarion Books.

Turner, Ann. 1994. _The Christmas House._ New York, NY: HarperCollins.

UNICEF Foundation. 1994. _I Dream of Peace: Images of War by Children of the Former Yugoslavia._ New York, NY: HarperCollins.

Varley, Susan. 1984. _Badger's Parting Gifts._ New York, NY: Lothrop, Lee & Shepard.

Waddell, Martin. 1990. _The Hidden House._ New York, NY: Philomel Books.

Watts, Jeri Hanel. 1997. _Keepers._ New York, NY: Lee and Low Books.

Weizmann, Daniel. 1996. _Take a Stand._ Los Angeles, Ca.: Price Stern & Sloan.

Wells, Rosemary. 1992. _Lucy Comes to Stay._ New York, NY: Dial Books for Young Readers.

——. 1994. _Night Sounds, Morning Colors._ New York, NY: Dial Books for Young Readers.

——. 1998. _Read to Your Bunny._ New York, NY: Scholastic.

White, E. B. 1943. _Stuart Little._ New York, NY: Harper and Row.

——. 1970. _The Trumpet of the Swan._ New York, NY: Harper and Row.

Willard, Nancy. 1995. _Gutenberg's Gift._ Baltimore, MD: Harcourt Brace.

Wilson, Nancy H. 1997. _Old People, Frogs, and Albert._ New York, NY: Farrar Straus Giroux.

Winch, John. 1997. _The Old Woman Who Loved to Read._ New York, NY: Holiday House.

Wing, Natasha. 1996. _Jalapeno Bagels._ New York, NY: Atheneum Books for Young Readers.

Winnick, Karen B. 1999. _Mr. Lincoln's Whiskers._ Honesdale, PA: Boyds Mills Press.

Wiseman, Bernard. 1970. _Morris Goes to School._ New York, NY: Harper and Row.

Wood, Audrey. 1984. _The Napping House._ San Diego, CA: Harcourt Brace Jovanovich.

Yee, Paul. 1998. _The Boy in the Attic._ Toronto, Canada: Douglas & McIntyre.

Young, Sue. 1994. _The Scholastic Rhyming Dictionary._ New York, NY: Scholastic Reference.

Zion, Gene. 1999. _Harry and the Lady Next Door._ New York, NY: HarperFestival.

Poetry Collections and Anthologies

Carlson, Susan Marie. 1997. *Getting Used to the Dark*. New York, NY: DK Publishing.

Cullinan, Bernice, ed. 1996. *A Jar of Tiny Stars; Poems by NCTE Award-winning Poets*. Honesdale, PA: Wordsong/Boyds Mill Press.

Dabcovich, Lydia. 1992. *The Keys to My Kingdom: A Poem in Three Languages*. New York, NY: Lothrop, Lee & Shepard.

Dakos, Kalli. 1990. *If You're Not Here, Please Raise Your Hand: Poems About School*. New York, NY: Four Winds Press.

——. 1993. *Don't Read This Books Whatever You Do: More Poems About School*. New York, NY: Four Winds Press.

——. 1995. *Mrs. Cole on an Onion Roll and Other School Poems*. New York, NY: Simon & Schuster Books for Young Readers.

——. 1996. *The Goof Who Invented Homework and Other School Poems*. New York, NY: Dial Books for Young Readers.

——. 1999. *The Bug in Teacher's Coffee and Other School Poems*. New York, NY: HarperCollins.

De Fina, Allan. 1997. *When a City Leans Against the Sky*. Honesdale, PA: Wordsong/Boyds Mill Press.

Dylan, Bob and Scott Menchin. 1999. *Man Gave Names to All the Animals*. San Diego, CA: Harcourt Brace.

Esbensen, Barbara. 1998. *Words With Wrinkled Knees*. Honesdale, PA: Wordsong/Boyds Mill Press.

Fisher, Aileen 1968. *We Went Looking*. New York, NY: Crowell.

——. 1991. *Always Wondering*. New York, NY: Harper-Collins.

Fleischman, Paul. 1988. *Joyful Noise: Poems for Two Voices*. New York, NY: HarperCollins.

Florian, Douglas. 1999. *Laugh-eteria*. San Diego, CA: Harcourt Brace.

Frazee, Marla. 1989. *Hush Little Baby: A Folk Song with Pictures*. San Diego, CA: Browndeer Press.

George, Kristine O. 1997. *The Great Frog Race and Other Poems*. New York, NY: Clarion Books.

Glenn, Mel. 1988. *Back to Class*. New York, NY: Clarion Books.

Goldstein, Bobbye. 1992. *Inner Chimes*. Honesdale, PA: Wordsong/Boyds Mill Press.

Harrison, David. 1993. *Somebody Catch My Homework*. Honesdale, PA: Wordsong/Boyds Mill Press.

Harwayne, Shelley, ed. 1995. *Jewels: Children's Play Rhymes*. Greenvale, NY: Mondo Publications.

Heard, Georgia. 1998. *The Words of True Poems (sound recording)*. Portsmouth, NH: Heinemann.

Hopkins, Lee Bennett, ed. 1990. *Good Books, Good Times*. New York, NY: Harper and Row.

——. 1994. *Hand in Hand: An American History Through Poetry*. New York, NY: Simon & Schuster Books for Young Readers.

——. 1996. *School Supplies: A Book of Poems*. New York, NY: Simon & Schuster Books for Young Readers.

——. 1999. *Extra Innings*. San Diego, CA: Harcourt Brace.

——. 1999. *Spectacular Science: A Book of Poems*. New York, NY: Simon & Schuster Books for Young Readers.

Janeczko, Paul. 1990. *The Place My Words Are Looking For*. New York, NY: Atheneum.

——. 1998. *That Sweet Diamond*. New York, NY: Atheneum Books for Young Readers.

Kuskin, Karla. 1975. *Near the Window Tree*. New York, NY: Harper and Row.

Little, Jean. 1989. *Hey World, Here I Am!*. New York, NY: Harper and Row.

Livingston, Myra C. 1995. *Call Down the Moon: Poems of Music*. New York, NY: Margaret K. McElderry Books.

Maestro, Marco. 1999. *Geese Find the Missing Piece: School Time Riddle Rhyme*. New York, NY: HarperCollins.

Margolis, Richard J. 1969. *Only the Moon and Me*. Philadelphia, PA: Lippincott.

McCord, David. 1977. *One at a Time*. Boston, MA: Little Brown.

Mora, Pat. 1998. *This Big Sky*. New York, NY: Scholastic.

Nye, Naomi. 1992. *This Same Sky: A Collection of Poems from Around the World*. New York, NY: Four Winds Press.

——. 1995. *The Tree is Older Than You Are*. New York, NY: Simon & Schuster Books for Younger Readers.

Nye, Naomi and Paul Janeczko, eds. 1996. *I Feel a Little Jumpy Around You*. New York, NY: Simon & Schuster Books for Young Readers.

O'Hara, Frank. 1971. *The Collected Poems of Frank O'Hara*. New York, NY: Alfred A. Knopf.

Panzer, Nora. 1994. *Celebrate America in Poetry and Art*. New York, NY: Hyperion Books for Children.

Philips, Neal, ed. 1995. *Singing America: Poems That Define a Nation*. New York, NY: Viking.

Ridlon, Marci. 1997. *Sun Through the Window*. Honesdale, PA: Wordsong/Boyds Mill Press.

Rosen, Michael. 1995. *The Best of Michael Rosen*. Berkeley, CA.: Wetlands Press.

Rosenberg, Liz. 1996. *The Invisible Ladder: An Anthology of Contemporary American Poems for Young Readers*. New York, NY: Henry Holt & Co.

Schertle, Alice. 1995. *Advice for a Frog*. New York, NY: Lothrop, Lee & Shepard.

——. 1999. *A Lucky Thing*. San Diego, CA: Harcourt Brace.

Shields, Carol D. 1995. *Lunch Money and Other Poems About School*. New York, NY: Dutton Children's Books.

Soto, Gary. 1995. *Canto Familiar*. San Diego, CA: Harcourt Brace.

Stevenson, James. 1998. *Popcorn*. New York, NY: Greenwillow Books.

Strickland, Michael, ed. 1993. *Poems That Sing to You*. Honesdale, PA: Wordsong/Boyds Mill Press.

——.1997. *My Own Song and Other Poems to Groove*. Honesdale, PA: Wordsong/Boyds Mill Press.

Taberski, Sharon, ed. 1996. *Morning, Noon and Night: Poems to Fill Your Day.* Greenvale, NY: Mondo Publications.

Weil, Zaro. 1992. *Mud, Moon and Me.* Boston, MA: Houghton Mifflin.

Winters, Kay. 1996. *Did You See What I Saw?* New York, NY: Viking.

Series Books for Children

Applegate, K. A. 1998. *Animorphs* books. New York, NY: Scholastic.

Cleary, Beverly. 1955-1999. *Ramona* books. New York, NY: Morrow Junior Books.

Greenburg, Dan. 1996-1997. *The Zack Files* books. New York, NY: Grosset & Dunlap.

King-Smith, Dick. 1989-1995. *Sophie* books. New York, NY: Delacorte Press.

Levy, Elizabeth. 1973-1997. *Something Queer…* books. New York, NY: Delacorte/Hyperion.

Lobel, Arnold. 1972-1999. *Frog and Toad* books. New York, NY: Harper.

Lowry, Lois. 1979-1995. *Anastasia* books. Boston, MA: Houghton Mifflin.

Marshall, James. 1988-1998. *Fox* books. New York, NY: Viking/Puffin.

Martin, Ann. 1991-1999. *Baby-sitters Club Little Sister* books. New York, NY: Scholastic.

Minarik, Else. 1957-1968. *Little Bear* books. New York, NY: Harper.

Osborne, Mary P. 1993-2000. *Magic Tree House* books. New York, NY: Random House.

Parish, Peggy and Herman Parish. 1988-1999. *Amelia Bedelia* books. New York, NY: Harper/Greenwillow.

Park, Barbara. 1992-1999. *Junie B. Jones* books. New York, NY: Random House.

Rey, H. A. 1969-1998. *Curious George* books. Boston, MA: Houghton Mifflin.

Rowling, J. K. 1998-2000. *Harry Potter* books. New York, NY: Arthur. A. Levine.

Sachar, Louis. 1978-1999. *Wayside School* books. New York, NY: Morrow Junior Books.

——. 1992-2000. *Marvin Redpost* books. New York, NY: Random House.

Sharmat, Marjorie Weinman. 1982-1999. *Nate the Great* books. New York, NY: Coward, McCann and Geoghegan.

Smith, Janice L. 1981-1994. *Adam Joshua* books. New York, NY: Harper.

Sobol, Donald. 1963-1999. *Encyclopedia Brown* books. New York, NY: T. Nelson/W. Morrow/Dutton/Delacorte.

Stine, R. L. 1992-1997. *Goosebumps* books. New York, NY: Scholastic.

van Leeuwen, Jean. 1979-1998. *Oliver and Amanda Pig* books. New York, NY: Dial Books for Young Readers.

INDEX